THE NORTHWEST UNDER THREE FLAGS 1635-1796

THE NORTHWEST UNDER THREE FLAGS
1635-1796

BY

CHARLES MOORE

WITH MAPS AND ILLUSTRATIONS

GYAN

Published by

Gyan Publishing House
5, Ansari Road
Daryaganj, New Delhi-110002
Phone: 011-47034999, 9811692060
E-mail: books@gyanbooks.com

Distribution Network
gyanbooks.com
India, USA, Canada, UK, Australia, France

ISBN : 978-81-212-3827-4 (PB)
First Published, 1900

2nd Impression 2020

Printed at: Gyan Press, Delhi.

The Northwest Under Three Flags
Author: Charles Moore

THE NORTHWEST UNDER THREE FLAGS

1635–1796

By

CHARLES MOORE

WITH MAPS AND ILLUSTRATIONS

NEW YORK AND LONDON
HARPER & BROTHERS PUBLISHERS
1900

FATHER MARQUETTE IN ST. IGNACE, 1670

AES + LAURIER PUBLICATIONS

ASIAN EDUCATIONAL SERVICES
31, HAUZ KHAS VILLAGE, NEW DELHI - 110016 (INDIA)

LAURIER BOOKS LTD.
P.O. BOX : 2694, STN, D
OTTAWA, ON. KIP-5W6, CANADA

Canadian Cataloguing in Publication Data

Moore, Charles, 1855-1942
The North West under three flags, 1635-1796
Includes index.
ISBN 1-895959-26-8

1. Northwest, Old-History. 2. Canada--History--17th century. 3. Canada-History--18th century.
I. Title.

FC410.M66 1997 971 C97-900176-5
F483.M66 1997

Library of Congress Catalog Card Number 97-070448

Distributor for the U.S.A. and Canada
Laurier Books Ltd.
P. O. Box 2694, Stn. D
Ottawa, On, K1P-5W6, Canada
Tel. : (613) 738-2163, Fax : (613) 247-0256
E-Mail : educa@travel-net.com.

for ASIAN EDUCATIONAL SERVICES
31, Hauz Khas Village, New Delhi - 110016
Printed at Nice Printing Press, Delhi - 110051

TO

A. W. M. M.

CONTENTS

CHAPTER I

THE FRENCH OCCUPY THE NORTHWEST

Jacques Cartier on the St. Lawrence—Champlain, the Father of New France — Wanderings of Étienne Brulé — Brulé Tells Sagard of Lake Superior and Shows Him a Copper Ingot—Nicolet Discovers Lake Michigan — Green Bay and Its People — Drowning of Nicolet and Birth of Joliet—Raymbault and Jogues at Sault Ste. Marie—The Backbone of the New World—The Relentless Iroquois—Fall of the Huron Missions—Médard Chouart, Sieur des Grosseilliers—Peter Esprit Radisson as a Captive—Grosseilliers and Radisson on Lake Michigan—Near the Mississippi—Ambiguities in Radisson's *Voyages*—Father René Menard on the Great Lake —His Death in the Woods—Radisson Describes the Beauties of Lake Superior—The White-fish—The Grand Sables — Pictured Rocks—The Keweenaw Portage—The Sioux—A Winter Gathering at the Head of Lake Superior—The Ingratitude of Rulers—The Hudson Bay Company—Father Claude Allouez Hears of the Missepi—Marquette Longs to Find the Great River—St. Ignace Founded by Marquette—Sieur Saint Lusson Claims the West for France—Louis Joliet at Sault Ste. Marie—Marquette and Joliet Start for the Mississippi—Their Success and Their Return—Marquette Drawn to the Southern Savages—His Death Voyage—A Strange Funeral Procession—The First Ship on the Upper Lakes —La Salle and the *Griffin*—An Ambitious Explorer—Henry de Tonty—Father Hennepin Longs to See New Countries—Lake Ste. Claire—Pilot Lucas Navigates Fresh Water—The Loss of the *Griffin*—Fort Crèvecœur—A Winter Journey............Page 1

CHAPTER II

CADILLAC FOUNDS DETROIT

France in Control Throughout the Northwest—Inroads of the English—French Forts in the Detroit Country—Fort St. Joseph on the St. Clair—Michilimackinac a Strategic Point for the Fur-trade—Cadillac—Iroquois Broth—Robert Livingston's Plan to Build a Fort on the Detroit—Cadillac at Quebec and Paris—Control of the Indians—Detroit Founded—French Trade Monopolies—Father Carheil, a Devoted Missionary—Cadillac as a Moses—The Sale of Brandy—Beginnings of Family Life in the Northwest—Prosperity of Detroit—The Commandant's Extortions—Dubuisson at Detroit—Attack by the Mascoutins and Ottagamies—Help from the Allies—The Battle at Grosse Pointe—Immigration from France—The Jesuits Engross the Trade—Count Repentigny at Sault Ste. Marie.......................................Page 38

CHAPTER III

THE ENGLISH IN THE OHIO COUNTRY

The French in Possession of the Northwest—The Discoveries of the Cabots the Basis of the English Claims—Sir Walter Raleigh—First English Settlement upon Roanoke Island—Jamestown Founded—Plymouth Company Chartered—Early English Grants—Claims of Virginia, Connecticut, Massachusetts, and New York—The Virginia Corporation Dissolved—Character of the Early Colonists of Virginia—The Washington Family—Lord Fairfax and the Culpeper Grant—George Washington as a Surveyor—Scotch-Irish in the Shenandoah Valley—The Scotch-Irish Undertake to Protect Frontiers if Allowed Liberty of Conscience—The Ohio Company—Céloron on the Ohio—Christopher Gist's Explorations for the Ohio Company—Logstown—Gist and Croghan on the Muskingum—Gist the First Protestant to Hold Religious Services in the Northwest—Treaties with Delawares and Shawanese—The Journey to Piqua—An Ottawa Embassy from Detroit—Gist Returns Home Through Kentucky—Lawrence Washington at the Head of the Ohio Company—Religious Toleration—The Treaty at Logstown in 1752—Gist Removes to Ohio—Céloron at Detroit—Charles Langlade Attacks Piqua—Duquesne Prepares to Occupy the Ohio Country—Governor Dinwiddie Sends George Washington with a Message to the French—Washington at Logstown—The Position of the Indians—Washington at Venango—Captain Joncaire—Washington Delivers His Message—Publication in England of Washington's Journal—Governor Dinwiddie Puts Virginia on the War Footing—Lukewarmness of the Colonies—The Albany Assembly—English Claims to the Ohio—Sir William Johnson—Franklin's Plan for a Union of the Colonies—Franklin Favors Inland Colonies on the Ohio—Fort Necessity—The Braddock Campaign—Washington Becomes a Member of Braddock's Military Family—Braddock's Defeat—Langlade

CONTENTS

Leads the Attack — The English Frontier Rolled Back — The French and Indian War—The Humiliation of England in America and Europe—The Rise of Pitt—General John Forbes Occupies Fort Duquesne—The Fall of Quebec and Montreal—Major Robert Rogers Receives the Surrender of Detroit—Rogers Meets Pontiac—The British Control the Northwest............Page 63

CHAPTER IV

THE PONTIAC WAR

Readjustments after the French and Indian War—Isolation of the Northwest—Captain Donald Campbell's Card-parties—An Indian War Impending—Sir William Johnson Enjoys Detroit Society—Rumors of French and Spanish Conquest—Sir Robert Davers Visits the Upper Lakes—Major Henry Gladwin in Command—Pontiac's Council at the River Ecorses—Reports of Indian Treachery—Carver's Story of Pontiac's Repulse—The Real Informant—Sketch of Henry Gladwin—Murder of the Supposed Traitor—A Fatal Council—The Attack on Detroit—A Restless Corpse—Murder of Sir Robert Davers—The Prospect of Resistance—Council at M. Cuillerier's House—Pontiac Essentially a Savage—Gladwin's Problem—British Disasters at Sandusky, the Miamis, and St. Joseph—Capture of the Bâteaux—The Dark Days—The Massacre at Michilimackinac—Pontiac at Church—Indian Currency—News of the Treaty Between England and France—The French Join the English—Fire-rafts—The Torture of Captain Campbell—Dalyell's Sortie—Robert Rogers Makes a Stand—The Brave Death of Dalyell—Bloody Run—The Attack on the *Gladwin*—Pontiac's Message to the Illinois French—An Unsatisfactory Answer—Gladwin's Opinion of the French—Rum More Potent than Fire-arms—Failure of Pontiac's Conspiracy—Gladwin at Court—Bradstreet at Detroit.................... 106

CHAPTER V

ENGLAND TAKES POSSESSION OF THE NORTHWEST

England's Gains by the Seven Years' War—Franklin Argues for the Retention of Canada—Disunion Among the Colonies—The Barbarity of an Indian Frontier—Pennsylvania's Trade with England—The Governments of Quebec, the Floridas, and Grenada—Restrictions as to Land Grants—Frauds and Abuses in Indian Purchases—The First Charter of the Northwest—The Ohio Company's New Plans—Cresap and Bouquet—Uneasiness in Virginia—Governor Farquier—Bouquet Anticipates a Land Bubble—Character of the Settlers—Indians Alarmed at the Inroads of the

Settlers—The Battle of Bushy Run—The Colonial Militia Laws —Sketch of Colonel Henry Bouquet—Bradstreet's Message—The Bouquet Expedition to the Muskingum—Indian Treaties —The Savages Promise Peace—Sir William Johnson the Peacemaker—Return of the Prisoners—George Croghau on the Ohio —Messages to the French Traders—At the Falls of the Ohio—"Post Vincent"—Father Marest's Letter—François Morgan de Vinsenne—Croghan and His Captors—Pontiac and Croghan at Fort Chartres—The Secret Treaty Between France and Spain—Spain Controls Louisiana—Lieutenant Fraser Rescued by Pontiac—Pontiac at Oswego—Murder of Pontiac—Croghan at Detroit—The Walpole Grant—Sir William Johnson and Benjamin Franklin—Lord Shelburne's Approval, Lord Hillsborough's Opposition —Combination with the Ohio Company—The Treaty of German Flats—The Iroquois Claims—"The Dark and Bloody Ground"—Sketch of Sir William Johnson—The Boundary Moved from the Alleghanies to the Ohio—Franklin's Success; Lord Hillsborough's Resignation—Vandalia—Virginians in the Kentucky Region—Pittsburg a Virginia Town—Lord Dunmore's Perplexities—The Growth of Independence—Dunmore's Land Speculations—The Greathouse Murders—The Dunmore War—The Battle of Point Pleasant—Logan's Message—Jefferson's Injustice to Captain Cresap—The Northwest Pledged to Freedom..........Page 141

CHAPTER VI

THE QUEBEC ACT AND THE REVOLUTION

The British Policy Makes the Northwest a Hunting-ground—The Struggle for New Lands—General James Murray, Governor of Canada—Succeeded by General Guy Carleton—The French Unfitted for English Law—The Quebec Act a Necessity for Canada —The Americans Resent It—The Measure in Parliament—Chatham Opposes It as "Cruel, Odious, and Oppressive"—His Prophecy—Lord North's Defence—The Northwest a Country of "Bears and Beavers"—Church Establishment—Colonel Barré to the Rescue—Charles Fox Objects to Tithes—Edmund Burke Successfully Struggles to Fix New York Boundaries—The Penns Protest—General Carleton Before the Commons—The Canadians Want no Seditious Assemblies Like Those in America—A Governor Doubtful as to the Extent of His Dominions—The Northwest an Asylum for Vagabonds—Indian Independence—Unavailing Protests Against the Quebec Bill—Beginnings of Civil Government in the Northwest—Henry Hamilton, Lieutenant-Governor—Crosses Montreal in Disguise—Reaches Detroit and Likes the Place—The English Crowd Out the French—Trader and Cheat—Indian Debaucheries—Detroit French in Sympathy with the Virginians—Spanish Intrigues—The Declaration of Independence Brought to Detroit—Hamilton's Anger—Daniel Boone a Prisoner at Detroit—Hamilton Tries to Ransom the Pioneer—Boone's Escape—Hamilton Practices the War-dance—Lieutenant-Governor Abbott, of Vincennes—Indians Congratulated on the Number of Scalps Brought in—Carleton to be Succeeded by Haldimand—Savage Diplomacy—M. de Rocheblave's Capture at Kaskaskia Announced to Hamilton—Hamilton Prepares to Drive the Americans from the Illinois—Daniel Boone in Kentucky—The Colony of Transylvania—George Rogers Clark Elected to the Virginia Assembly from Kentucky—He Visits Governor Patrick Henry—Obtains a Supply of Powder—The County of Kentucky—Clark's Bold Plans—The French Alliance with the Colonies Aids Clark—Clark Walks into Kaskaskia—Father Gibault Undertakes a Revolution at Vincennes—Virginia's County of Illinois—American Civil Government Begins in the Northwest—Old Mackinac—Captain Arent Schuyler de Peyster—A Poet-soldier—Langlade Takes the Lake Indians to Montreal—A Boy's Baptism of Fire—A Favorite of the Manitou—Langlade's Exploits at Quebec—He Takes the Oath of Allegiance to the English King—Chevalier St. Luc la Corne and Langlade on Lake Champlain—Burgoyne Charges His Defeat to the Desertion of the Savages—Langlade Incites the Lake Indians to Invade the Illinois Country—Hamilton Supported by the War Ministers—His Difficulties—Lord George Germain Issues Orders to Stir Up the Indians—The Vincennes Expedition—Hamilton Captures Fort Sackville—Francis Vigo—Clark Must Take or Be Taken—A Desperate Chance and a Terrible Journey—Success—Hamilton Makes the Best of a Bad Matter—Mr. Justice Dejean and His Supplies Captured—Jefferson Orders Hamilton in Irons—Clark Plans the Capture of Detroit—The Savages Terrorized—Fort Patrick Henry—Jefferson Plans a Fort on the Mississippi—Land-warrants in Lieu of Bounties—Tobacco Currency—Jefferson's Instructions as to the Indians—Clark's Popularity—Failure of Plans for an Aggressive Campaign in the Northwest .... Page 195

CHAPTER VII

THE WAR IN THE NORTHWEST

Frederick Haldimand—Takes Service with the British—A Successful Administrator—Haldimand Commands the English Forces in America—Gives Way at New York to a Born Briton—He is Transferred to Quebec—Negotiates for a Reunion of Vermont with the Crown—Detroit in Danger—Haldimand's Thrift—The

CONTENTS

Indians Expensive Allies—Captain Richard Beringer Lernoult—Isadore Chene Reports the Capture of Hamilton—Captain Bird Builds Fort Lernoult; Clark's Sarcasm—Bird Leads the Indians to War—The Savages "Always Cooking or Counselling"—Forts McIntosh and Laurens Built and Deserted—Bird in Kentucky—Clark Retaliates—Captain Patt Sinclair at Michilimackinac—He Removes the Fort to the Island—Father Gibault's Mischief—Sinclair Plans an Incursion to the Illinois Country—Attacks the Spanish Town of St. Louis—Spain Plans to Invade the Northwest—The Movable Fort St. Joseph—The Spanish on the Mississippi—A Winter Expedition—St. Joseph Captured—The Effect in Madrid—Spain's Extensive Claims to the Northwest—De Peyster Relieves Lernoult at Detroit—His Kindness to Captives—The Campaign of 1780—Rumors Running Through the Forests—Scalps and Prisoners Sent to Detroit—Butler's Rangers Invade Kentucky—The Removal of the Moravians—De Peyster Summons the Missionaries to Detroit—Captain Pipe—The Moravians Deny Having Aided the Americans—Their Towns in the Muskingum Valley—De Peyster Establishes the Moravians on the Clinton River—Their Wanderings—The Moravian Massacre Excites the Apprehensions of the English—Fort Pitt's Commanders—General Irvine Brings Order Out of Chaos—"One Hundred Lashes, Well Laid On"—The Revolution at an End, but Not in the Northwest—The Crawford Expedition Against the Miami Indians—Washington and Crawford—The Savages Appeal to De Peyster for Aid—Haldimand Exhorts De Peyster to Repel the Raid—Defeat of the Americans by the British and Indians—Retreat—Crawford's Death by Torture—His Fate a Retaliation for the Moravian Massacre—The Attack on Bryan's Station—Clark Ends the Revolution in the Northwest—Border Warfare Must Continue—Liberation of the Captives—The Chamber of Scalps..Page 245

CHAPTER VIII

PEACE THAT PROVES NO PEACE

Lord Chatham's Dying Appeal—France Plans Revenge for the Treaty of 1763—Louis XVI. Forgets and Remembers—Franklin's Unique Position in France—John Adams Made Peace Commissioner—The Demands of Congress—France is Anxious to Curb the Power of the United States—Spain Strives to Win Gibraltar—The Attitude of Prussia and Russia—England's Shifting Policy—Lord Shelburne's Growth in Grace Towards America—Franklin's Paternal Appeals to Louis XVI.—He Begins Separate Negotiations with England—John Adams Negotiates a Treaty with Holland—

John Jay's Failure in Spain—Franklin Summons Him to Paris—Jay Becomes the Leader in the Peace Negotiations—The Fear of American Growth and Power was Natural—Shelburne's Ultimata—Jay Wins Oswald's Confidence—The Northwest Boundary Discussions—Jay's Ingenious Argument to Obtain the Waste Lands—A Choice of Lines Offered to the British—The Treaty Signed—America Congratulated on the Work of the Commissioners—Downfall of the Shelburne Ministry—The North-Fox Coalition Condemns and Adopts the Treaty—Haldimand Warns Townsend to Protect the Fur-trade—Good Reasons for His Apprehensions—Competition the Bane of Trade—The Northwest Company—The Grand Portage—The Spring Flotilla—The Fur-traders in the Northern Wilderness—Dangers of the Bush-ranger's Life—The Opulence of the Trader Barons—Private Vessels Forbidden on the Lakes—Washington Demands the Surrender of the Posts—Baron Steuben's Fruitless Errand—Haldimand's Prudence—Jefferson Argues for the Surrender of the Posts—The British Contention—Haldimand Interested for the Loyalists—Brant Forms a New Indian Confederacy—Brant a Lion in England—A War-whoop at a Masked-ball—The Indian Demands—They Appeal to Heaven for Justification—Message to Congress—Lord Dorchester's Position—The British Anticipate the Failure of the United States—A British Spy in the Northwest—A Critical Situation for the United States—Washington Urges Western Communication—Protecting the Flanks and the Rear—A Group of Farewells.......Page 279

CHAPTER IX

THE NORTHWEST PROVIDED WITH A GOVERNMENT

Silas Deane Advises the Sale of the Western Lands to Raise Funds for the Revolution—Maryland Insists that these Lands Belong to the Nation—Forbids Her Delegates to Ratify the Articles of Confederation—The Basis of Maryland's Complaint—Virginia Establishes a Land-office—Congress Asks the State to Suspend Land Operations in the West—Virginia Protests against Maryland's Course—New York Cedes Her Claims to the Northwest Lands—Congress Takes Action—Connecticut Willing to Cede, with Reservations—Virginia's Offer—Maryland Makes Her Point and Joins the Confederation—The United States Proclaimed at Home and Abroad—Congress Attempts to Overreach Virginia and Connecticut—Loyalty of Virginia—Transfer of Her Claims—Massachusetts' Cessions—Connecticut Secures a Good Bargain—The Moral of the Cessions—Jefferson Plans a Government for the Northwest—The Indian Title of Occupancy—The United States Alone Can Purchase Lands of the Indians—Courts Organized at Vincennes and Kaskaskia—The "Custom of Paris" Still Operative—Freedom the Birthright of the Northwest—Secession Prohibited—Jefferson's Names for the New States—The Government Undertakes to Survey the Western Lands—No "Tomahawk Rights" in the Northwest—The Ordinance of 1783—Struggles of Congress with the Slavery Question—Slave Representation Provided for—Opinions of Webster, Hoar, and Cooley—Freedom of Religion; the Inviolability of Contracts; a Permanent Union; and the Encouragement of Education—The Character of the Western System of Public Education—The Moving Force in Securing the Ordinance—The Ohio Company—Rufus Putnam—Schemes for Settlements in the Northwest—Failure of General Parsons—Manasseh Cutler's Success—Land Laws—The Officers of the Northwest—The State of Ohio Planned in a Boston Tavern—The Settlement of Marietta—Putnam's Discouragements—Arrival at the Mouth of the Muskingum—The Town Named After Marie Antoinette—Pseudo-classicism of the Day—Idealism of the Settlers—Governor St. Clair Arrives—Sketch of the New Governor—His Companions in Office—"The Governor and Judges," a Vicious Form of Government—Patchwork Laws—Setting the Courts in Motion—The Scioto Purchase—A Bit of Lobbying—Colonel William Duer and His Associates—French Immigrants at Gallipolis—Joel Barlow Sells Lands in France—Financial Panic—Comparative Quiet at Marietta—Fort Harmar Built by Major Doughty—The Remnant of an Army....Page 315

CHAPTER X

THE UNITED STATES WIN THE NORTHWEST POSTS

The New Boundaries—President Washington Asserts the Power of the United States—Joseph Brant Betakes Himself to Literary Pursuits—Indians Relinquish Lands in the Northwest—White Settlements Make the Indians Uneasy—Savages Looking Westward—Lord Dorchester's Confidence—Captain Gother Mann Explores the Border—British Preparations to Build New Posts—Perils of the Ohio Passage—The Indians Burn a Prisoner—The Harmar Campaign—A Motley Militia—Jealousy and Demoralization—A Disgraceful Defeat—Rufus Putnam's Advice—Dorchester Writes as to Indian Lands—Washington's Chagrin—St. Clair Selected to Command the Army—The Forces at Cincinnati—Bad Clothing, Bad Pay, Bad Food—Discontent Presages Defeat—The St. Clair Disaster—Bravery of the Regulars—St. Clair's Share in the Blame—After the Battle—Washington's Anger—Mad Anthony Wayne—Drilling the Militia—Former Failures Serve as a Warning—Indian Council at the Mouth of the Detroit—The Indian Ul-

CONTENTS

timatum—British Influence—Secretary Knox Orders the Advance —Fort Recovery—The Indian Respect for a Soldier—Wayne's Successful Campaign—Face to Face with the British—The Treaty of Greenville—John Jay Negotiates a Treaty with England—French and British Spoliations—Jay's Treaty Attacked—New Connecticut—The Surrender of Detroit Demanded and Refused —Lord Dorchester Issues Orders for the Surrender of the Posts —Washington Congratulated on Gaining the Northwest—Fort Miami Given Up to Hamtramck—Captain Moses Porter Receives the Surrender of Detroit—Michilimackinac Evacuated—Compliments to the Retiring British Officers—Fort Niagara Occupied by the Americans—John Francis Hamtramck at Detroit—General Wayne Visits the Posts—His Death at Presque Isle—Condition of Posts—The Advantageous Position of the British—Warnings of Coming War—Retrospect............................Page 345

ILLUSTRATIONS

FATHER MARQUETTE IN ST. IGNACE . . . . *Frontispiece*

JACQUES CARTIER . . . . *Facing p.* 2

THE MISSIONARY . . . . " 4

THE NORTH SHORE, LAKE SUPERIOR . . . . " 8

GRAND ARCH. PICTURED ROCKS, LAKE SUPERIOR . . " 14

JAMES MARQUETTE, S. J. . . . . " 22
[From Trentanove's statue in the Capitol at Washington]

SLEEPING BEAR . . . . " 26

ROBERT CAVELIER, SIEUR DE LA SALLE . . . . . " 30
[From a copper-plate by Van der Gucht (1698). A purely ideal portrait]

NAKED INDIANS IN MONTREAL . . . . " 42

THE LANDING OF CADILLAC . . . . " 46

COUREUR DE BOIS . . . . " 52

INDIAN HUNTER OF 1750 . . . . " 60

SEBASTIAN CABOT . . . . " 64

LAWRENCE WASHINGTON . . . . " 68

WASHINGTON AS A SURVEYOR . . . . " 72

GEORGE WASHINGTON . . . . " 84

BRADDOCK'S HEADQUARTERS AT ALEXANDRIA, VA. . . " 92

GENERAL EDWARD BRADDOCK . . . . " 94

THE BURIAL OF BRADDOCK . . . . " 98

BLOCK-HOUSE OF FORT DUQUESNE . . . . " 100

GENERAL HENRY GLADWIN . . . . " 110

MRS. HENRY GLADWIN . . . . " 116

THE BAFFLED CHIEFS LEAVING THE FORT . . . . . " 118

"ANOTHER PARTY PADDLED SWIFTLY TO THE ISLE AU COCHON" . . . . " 120

ILLUSTRATIONS

THE SIEGE OF THE FORT AT DETROIT	*Facing p.*	124
A LIGHT-INFANTRY SOLDIER OF THE PERIOD	"	132
BENJAMIN FRANKLIN	"	142
A FRENCH TRADER	"	164
DANIEL BOONE	"	184
SIMON KENTON	"	192
EDMUND BURKE	"	202
GRAVE OF DANIEL BOONE	"	210
GEORGE ROGERS CLARK	"	216
PATRICK HENRY	"	218
THOMAS JEFFERSON	"	240
OLD SPANISH TOWER	"	258
ARENT SCHUYLER DE PEYSTER	"	264
JOHN ADAMS	"	282
LORD SHELBURNE	"	284
HENRY LAURENS	"	288
A FUR-TRADER IN THE COUNCIL TEPEE	"	292
THE COUREUR DE BOIS AND THE SAVAGE	"	296
SIR GUY CARLETON	"	302
GEORGE WASHINGTON	"	310
RUFUS PUTNAM GENERAL RUFUS PUTNAM'S LAND-OFFICE	"	330
MANASSEH CUTLER	"	334
GENERAL ARTHUR ST. CLAIR	"	336
SITE OF MARIETTA IN 1788	"	338
FORT HARMAR, BUILT IN 1785 CAMP MARTIUS, THE FIRST HOME OF THE PIONEERS	"	340
PLANTING IN THE NORTHWEST TERRITORY	"	344
ST. CLAIR'S ADVANCE DISCOVERED	"	354
ANTHONY WAYNE	"	358
DRAWING-ROOM, WAYNE HOMESTEAD	"	362
WAYNE HOMESTEAD	"	366
JOHN JAY	"	368
GENERAL WAYNE'S GRAVE	"	380

ILLUSTRATIONS

MAPS

MOLL'S MAP OF THE NORTHWEST IN 1720 . . . . . . *Facing p.* 38

MAP OF THE NORTHWEST AS KNOWN TO THE ENGLISH IN 1755–63 . . . . " 80

FRENCH AND ENGLISH IN NORTH AMERICA, 1755 . . . " 102

EVANS'S MAP OF THE ILLINOIS COUNTRY . . . . . " 168

MAP TO ILLUSTRATE THE HARMAR, ST. CLAIR, AND WAYNE CAMPAIGNS . . . . " 346

INTRODUCTION

FRANCE discovered and occupied the Northwest; but England included that region between the infinite parallels bounding on the north and the south the colonies of Virginia, Massachusetts, and Connecticut. It was not until a full century after France had established her trade from the St. Lawrence to the Mississippi that the English colonies, as their population increased, began to plan the occupation of the valley of the Ohio. Virginia, having crossed the Alleghanies, came into collision with France, and was driven back. England took up the quarrel on behalf of her colonial rights; and at the end of the French and Indian War, New France—the picturesque, romantic, extravagant, squalid New France—disappeared from the map of North America. Next, England undertook to keep her own subjects from settling and civilizing the Northwest; and for the annihilation of the British posts, the occupants of that country entered into the most far-reaching and destructive Indian conspiracy known to this land. No sooner were the savages subdued than the War of the Revolution led to the conquest of the Northwest by Virginia, and during eight years petty warfare was carried on by the Indians and British against the Americans. Maryland conditioned her entrance into the confederation of the

States upon the cession to the general government of the claims of the individual colonies to the Northwestern lands; and the makers of the treaty of 1783 succeeded in drawing the boundary-lines of the new nation through the middle of the Great Lakes and of the Mississippi. Then the Congress of the Confederation gave to this first territorial expansion of the nation a charter of freedom and progress never before equalled among men; and under this Ordinance of 1787, New England men and ideas became the dominating force from the Ohio to Lake Erie. The advent of settlers brought about Indian wars, fought by the United States against savages fed, clothed, and armed by England, that nation having, for the purposes of its fur-trade, made excuse to retain the Northwestern posts. Under the provisions of the treaty of 1795, however, the posts were surrendered, and Great Britain retired across the border, there to nurse grievances that were to find vent in the War of 1812.

We have been accustomed to regard the Northwest as a wilderness that grew into civilization by some vital force within itself. Such, however, was far from being the case. The name of Michilimackinac was a familiar word in the cabinets of European monarchs before it was known to the people dwelling along the Atlantic; the foundation of Detroit was decreed in the councils of France; and the relations of the Jesuit missions in the Northwest were read eagerly even by the polite society of Paris. England, indeed, was comparatively ignorant of the Western country; but Spain was not without ambition to control its waterways.

In our own land, the makers of the Republic were also the makers of the Northwest. In its defence Washington first learned the art of war; Franklin realized its possibilities, and interested himself in its development;

Patrick Henry planned with George Rogers Clark for its conquest; John Jay and Franklin and John Adams drew about it the lines of the United States; Thomas Jefferson bestowed upon it the inestimable boon of freedom; Washington's chief of engineers led its first settlers; and Mad Anthony Wayne subdued its savage inhabitants, and received the surrender of its frontier posts.

Many races united to people and to build up the Northwest; and many interests were in conflict. The story is often one of warfare, of cruelty, and of barbarism; but in writing it care has been taken to attribute no motives that were not clearly indicated. If it shall seem that the traditional hostility to England had been departed from, the excuse must be that during the period under consideration the representatives of that nation acted along the general lines of human nature; and that the British governors and commandants, as a rule, were men of good ability, devoted to the interests of their government; and not infrequently they did all they could to mitigate the barbarities of savage warfare. There were cruelties perpetrated on both sides; but the British government was to blame for ever employing or even countenancing the use of savages in warfare against the whites.

The fact that England was in possession of the Northwest during the greater portion of the period under consideration, makes it necessary to have recourse to the archives and other records of that nation. The Bouquet and Haldimand papers, in so far as they relate to the Western country, have been printed in full in the Michigan Pioneer and Historical Collections, and all these papers have been calendared in the Canadian Archives under the efficient direction of Mr. Douglas

Brymner. The later archives also have been calendared, and important portions of them have been printed.

A year before his death the late Francis Parkman gave me permission to consult his unique collection of manuscripts now in the library of the Massachusetts Historical Society; and through the courtesy of the secretary, Dr. S. A. Greene, I have frequently availed myself of the privilege.

The descendants of General Henry Gladwin—the Reverend Henry Gladwin Jebb, of Firbeck Hall, Rotherham, Yorkshire; R. D. de Uphaugh, Esq., of Hollingbourne House; and the late Captain W. H. G. Gladwin, of Hinchley Wood, Ashbourne, Derbyshire, England—have placed me under obligations by sending manuscript records, letters, and also portraits of General and Mrs. Gladwin. To Senator James McMillan I am indebted for frequent courtesies in obtaining information from official sources both in this country and abroad. It is a pleasure to acknowledge repeated acts of kindness on the part of Mr. David Hutcheson and of Dr. Herbert Friedenwald, of the Library of Congress, in placing at my disposal the rare documents and manuscripts in their respective departments; and also the constant courtesy of Mr. Andrew Hussey Allen and Mr. Stanislaus M. Hamilton, of the Department of State, in facilitating my researches among the Department manuscripts. General F. C. Ainsworth, U. S. A., had made for me copies of documents in the War Department; and I am indebted to him particularly for the diligent search that disclosed how great a destruction of official papers resulted from the burning of the public buildings in Washington by the British during the War of 1812. General A. W. Greeley, U. S. A., also placed at my disposal the valuable collections of rare documents which he is gathering for the library of the War Department. Mr. Clarence M. Burton, of Detroit, whose collection of original documents relating to the Northwest is unrivalled, and Mr. L. G. Stuart, of Grand Rapids, have afforded every assistance in their power.

CHARLES MOORE.

WASHINGTON, D.C., *November* 17, 1899.

THE NORTHWEST UNDER THREE FLAGS

CHAPTER I

THE FRENCH OCCUPY THE NORTHWEST

From the meagre records of the intrepid fur-trader and the incidental allusions of the devoted missionary, one with difficulty pieces together the narrative of discovery along the Great Lakes. Often one catches glimpses of shadowy forms gliding among the whispering pines, or sees afar off a swift darting canoe skimming over the clear waters, only to find that the name of the daring trader who has pushed into unknown regions has disappeared as completely as the print of his snow-shoe or the swirl of his paddle. Thus it happens that the reputed explorers of the Northwest were not always the first who spied out the land; but rather were those who were so fortunate as to leave some record of their adventures, either in the obscure and confused accounts written by the unlettered explorers themselves, or else in the scarcely less uncertain relations of the state of the Church, compiled from letters and stray reports from those distant fields where the triumphs of the cross in the conversion of the heathen seemed of far more moment than the discovery of new countries.

It was in the year 1534 that Jacques Cartier, driving his little fleet through the fogs of Newfoundland, steered up the unknown waters of the broad St. Lawrence. Eighty-one years later—so slow was progress westward—Champlain, the father of New France, was the first white man to look off across the dancing waters of Lake Huron. By his side stood his interpreter Étienne Brulé, dauntless woodsman and pioneer of pioneers, as Parkman calls him.[1] We know that in the three years between the discovery of Lake Huron and 1618, Brulé's wanderings took him down the Susquehanna to the Chesapeake Bay, and that he was the first to make that passage. Perhaps, also, his fleet canoe pushed its way northward even to Lake Superior. Be this as it may, he learned enough of that sea to tell the historian priest Sagard that beyond the Mer Douce (Lake Huron) there was another and a greater lake, which discharges itself into the lower one by rapids nearly two miles broad, called the Falls of Gaston;[2] and that from the Mer Douce to the farther end of the great lake was four hundred leagues.[3] Moreover, Brulé showed to Sagard an ingot of copper, which, he said, came from a deposit of that metal some eighty or one hundred leagues from the country of the Hurons. Brulé did not profess to have found this copper, but said he obtained it from neighbors of the Hurons, when he and his companion Grenolle were on their travels.[4]

Whatever may be Brulé's claims as a discoverer in

[1] *Pioneers of France in the New World*, p. 368, 377–380.

[2] Named for a brother of Louis XIII.

[3] French estimates of distances almost invariably are exaggerated.

[4] Sagard, *Histoire du Canada*, Paris edition, 1865, vol. iii., p. 717. See also *Narrative and Critical History of America*, vol. iv., p. 165; and Winsor's *Cartier to Frontenac*, p. 123.

JAQUES CARTIER

the Northwest, we know that, during the same year (1618) that he returned from his wanderings, there landed at Quebec the son of a Normandy letter-carrier who was destined to traverse western seas where no white man had been before him and where none came after him for a quarter of a century. Jean Nicolet, a native of Cherbourg, was, like Brulé, a protégé of Champlain. Following the custom of the time, the youth was sent to Allumette Island in the Ottawa, there to study Indian languages and thus prepare himself for the work of an interpreter.[1] For sixteen years Nicolet served his apprenticeship among the Jesuit missions in the Huron country; and during the years (1629–32) that Quebec was temporarily in possession of the British, he was sojourning at Lake Nipissing, where his happy disposition, his excellent memory, and his profoundly religious nature all combined to establish for him a wide-spread influence over the Algonquin Indians. He made their ways his ways; he feasted with them in the days of their plenty, and he fasted with them during long weeks when roots and berries were their only food.

It was not strange, therefore, that Champlain, on his return to Quebec in 1633, sent for Nicolet, and bade him prepare to undertake an embassy to the Indians beyond the Mer Douce, in order to induce them to join the Hurons in their annual voyages for traffic at Quebec. Doubtless this expedition was undertaken in the interest of the One Hundred Associates, that powerful monopoly which had been organized in 1627 to control the fur-trade of New France. On the first day of July, 1634, Nicolet started from Quebec, in company with the burly priest

[1] Benj. Sulte, *Mélanges d'Histoire et de Littérature*, Ottawa, 1876. Also *Wisconsin Historical Collections*, 1879.

Bréboeuf,[1] who was bound for the Huron mission. Seated in the canoes of the Indians who were returning from their annual market, voyageur and priest made the hard and tedious journey up the Ottawa and the chain of lakes and streams that in those days formed the wilderness route to the country and the lake of the Hurons. Leaving Bréboeuf at the mission, Nicolet, with seven savages as boatmen, pushed northward, following the curve of the shores until his light bark paused at the foot of the rapids of the strait that discharges the waters of Lake Superior. Returning, he passed through the Straits of Mackinac and was tossed on the billows of Lake Michigan.

During the hazy September days Nicolet and his dusky companions skimmed over the glassy surface of the great lake that he had discovered, and at night camp was made on some jutting point with the thick forest at their backs, by way of security against sudden attack. Before snow fell the little company reached Green Bay, a body of water for many years thereafter known as the Lake of the Stinkards,[2] the name mistakenly applied by the French to the Indians who dwelt near its shores.

Nicolet, well knowing the Indian love of finery,[3] had

[1] Fathers Jean de Bréboeuf and Gabriel Lalemant were burned alive by the Iroquois, at the destruction of St. Ignace in the Huron country, March 16, 1649. For a detailed account of their martyrdom see *Canadian Archives*, 1884, p. lxvii.

[2] "The people of the sea" was the more correct name. The phrase had its origin in the ill-smelling water, supposed by the French to be the salt water of the sea.

[3] Parkman conjectures that Nicolet may have provided himself with a court dress for use in case he should penetrate to regions where Chinese mandarins were domiciled. Later writers have not always been careful to observe Parkman's "perhaps." My statement is less poetic, but certainly is within the bounds of probability. See *La Salle and the Discovery of the Great West*, p. xxiv.

THE MISSIONARY

provided himself with a robe of Chinese silk gayly wrought with flowers and birds of brilliant plumage. Arrayed in this fantastic garment and firing pistols to right and to left of him, the daring explorer seemed to the amazed Indians a veritable Son of Thunder; and they, in their turn, decked themselves in their richest furs to welcome so illustrious an ambassador.[1] The shrewd eyes of the representative of the fur-trade quickly told him that here was a people worthy of cultivation; and he neglected no opportunity to impress upon his attentive hosts the glories of France, the favor that the king was ready to bestow upon his red children, and the allurements of the St. Lawrence markets. In order to establish his hold upon them, he made his way up the Fox River to the land of the brave Mascoutins; and from the reports of the Indians he believed that he was then but three days' journey from the margin of the sea that separated the New World from Cathay, for more than a century the goal of all French adventurers in America. Had he ventured on, he must have reached not the ocean but the Mississippi, that great river the discovery of which was soon to fill the dreams alike of trader and of missionary. Satisfied with his achievements, however, he retraced his way, and in the spring of 1635 he descended the St. Lawrence at the head of a richly laden fleet of canoes. For six years he continued to dwell at the frontier post of Three Rivers. Marrying a god-daughter of Champlain, he relapsed into quiet joys of family life; and his acquaintance with the remote tribes and his unbounded popularity with the Indians were of decided advantage to his employers. In 1639 he went down to Quebec to be present at the marriage of his

[1] Vimont, *Relation of* 1643, p. 3.

friend, the wagon-maker Joliet, whose son was destined to place his name first among French explorers. The same year (1642) that saw the birth of Louis Joliet also witnessed the death of Nicolet, who was drowned in the St. Lawrence while returning from Quebec, whither he went to save an Iroquois prisoner from the torture stake. He died as he had lived, a devoted son of the Church; and a fervent obituary notice in the *Relation* of the succeeding year bears witness to the high esteem in which he was held by the fathers, who as a rule had little cause to speak well of a fur-trader.[1]

We turn now for a moment to a missionary enterprise which, while it was indeed the voice of one crying in the wilderness, nevertheless fixed for all time the name of a place and of a great river. Six years (1641) after the adventurous voyage of Nicolet, the two priests, Charles Raymbault and Isaac Jogues, accepted an invitation to accompany a party of Ojibwas on their return from the feast of the dead, which had been celebrated in the Huron country with all the pomp and circumstance that marked this as the most important of all the ceremonials of that nation.[2] Skirting the northern shores of Lake Huron, the quivering canoes were forced up the broad strait through which Lake Superior finds its outlet. Something of the solemn grandeur of this mighty stream must have impressed itself upon the minds of the priests as they gazed upon the multitude

[1] Vimont, *Relation of* 1643, p. 3. In vol. xi. of these most excellent publications of the Wisconsin Historical Society will be found Henri Jouan's article on Nicolet, translated by Grace Clark. This is followed by a Nicolet bibliography by Consul Willshire Butterfield.

[2] *Relation of* 1642, p. 97. See also Shea's *Catholic Church in Colonial Days*, vol. i., p. 228. For a map and description of the Huron country, by Rev. Arthur E. Jones, S. J., see *The Jesuits' Relations and Allied Documents*, edited by Reuben Gold Thwaites, vol. xxxiv.

of islands whose ragged rocks nature was struggling to hide under an all too scanty covering of green. Now great hills seemed completely to block the way; then, with a sharp bend, the path would open straight before them as the river spread itself out in a shallow lake whose red bottom showed itself plainly through the clear waters.

From the shores the autumn air, laden with the fragrance of spruce, came like wine, bringing an exaltation to the senses. To the minds of the missionaries the rugged hills, pine-clad save here and there where a bald spot showed itself, and the deep, lonesome valleys must have presented a decided contrast to the carefully tended slopes of their native France. Here was indeed the New World. And yet those rounded knobs of rock standing well back from the left bank of the river were to this earth what Adam was to the race. Before ever the waters had parted to let the dry land of the Old World appear, these Laurentian hills had lifted themselves up to form the backbone of what we call the New World. Another bend and the hills melt away; low bluffs of clay easily confine the now quiet river, and the broad terraces are covered with waving grass and pleasing groves. Nature has changed her frown to the brightest of smiles, and far ahead the river breaks into laughter, showing its milk-white teeth in foaming rapids.

Scattered over the sandy plateau beside the rush of waters were the huts of some two thousand Ojibwas and other Algonquins, allured thither by the white-fish that had their homes in pools behind the foam-making rocks. Willingly the curious savages listened to the new docrines of the black-gowns; but when the time for their departure came, they bade no reluctant farewell to the priests. As the ice began to form the missionaries set out on their return journey—Raymbault going to a speedy death at Quebec,[1] and Jogues unwittingly entering the path that five years later led to martyrdom on the banks of the Mohawk.[2] They left behind them only the name St. Mary's, calling the place of their sojourn, as well as the falls and the river, after the Huron mission whence they came.[3]

The warfare that numbered Jogues among its victims was waged by the Iroquois with such stealth, such ferocity, and such far-reaching effects as to change the face of the Indian world. From Quebec to Lake Huron the Indian towns were burned and their inhabitants were driven even to the Mississippi, before they found a rest for the soles of their weary feet. Then, too, pestilence added its ravages to the scourge of the relentless Iroquois. One by one the Jesuit missions in the Huron country succumbed to the onslaughts of the combined foes.[4] St. Joseph, St. Ignace, Ste. Marie, all fell to rise again beyond Lake Huron; and by the middle of the seventeenth century all that great stretch of country from the St. Lawrence to the Straits of Mackinac was debatable territory, traversed alike by white man and red only at the constant risk of ambush and battle.[5] Had the French possessed the numerical strength of the English on the Atlantic coast, they might easily have annihilated the Iroquois; but in the year 1643 the entire population of New France numbered not to exceed three hundred souls; whereas the four colonies of Massachusetts, Plymouth, Connecticut, and New Haven,

[1] Not at Sault Ste. Marie, as Winsor has it. See *Cartier to Frontenac*, p. 160.

[2] Parkman, *Jesuits in North America*, p. 304.

[3] *Relation of* 1642.

[4] Parkman, *The Jesuits in North America*, p. 411, *et seq.*

[5] Radisson's *Voyages*, p. 88.

THE NORTH SHORE, LAKE SUPERIOR

banded together for self-defence, could count a population of 24,000. Thirty-two years later the Indian problem had been settled for New England by the slaughter, in the battle that ended King Philip's War, of as many Indians as the Iroquois ever had on the war-path;[1] but for New France Indian warfare had only fairly begun.

Naturally the rout of the Hurons put a stop for the time being to western exploration; so that it was not until 1657 that the work laid down by Nicolet was taken up by two of his compatriots, who like himself were residents of the trading-post of Three Rivers. In 1641 Médard Chouart,[2] sixteen years old, coming from Brie, in France, had proceeded to the Jesuit missions of Lake Huron, where he became a lay assistant to the fathers. Later he served both as a soldier and as a pilot; and he possessed, or was possessed by, the commercial instinct. A born trader, he so far succeeded that by the time he was twenty-six he owned enough land to assume and to maintain the title by which he is known to fame, that of Sieur des Grosseilliers.[3] The death of

[1] Fiske's *Beginnings of New England*, p. 225.

[2] For a sketch by Grosseilliers, see *The Jesuit Relations and Allied Documents*, vol. xxviii., p. 319.

[3] The narration of the adventures of Des Grosseilliers and Radisson is to be found in "Voyages of Peter Esprit Radisson, being an account of his travels and experiences among the North American Indians from 1652 to 1684. Transcribed from the original manuscripts in the Bodleian Library and the British Museum. With historical illustrations and an introduction by Gideon D. Scull, England. Boston: Published by the Prince Society. 1885." But 250 copies were printed. The manuscript, written by Radisson in semi-English, evidently is made up in part from notes jotted down during his travels and partly from memory. The compilation was made during his voyage to England in 1665, and the fact that it was intended for use at the English court accounts for that language. Radisson had learned English during a visit to London in early youth.

Nicolet in 1642 must have revived in the conversations of the priests, as it did in the *Relation* of their Superior, the story of his exploits; and during his stay in the Huron country Des Grosseilliers must have gained a general knowledge of the St. Mary's River as well as of the upper portions of Lakes Huron and Michigan.

Among the traders at Three Rivers appeared, in May, 1651, Peter Esprit Radisson, from St. Malo; and before the youth had become accustomed to his new surroundings he was captured by the Iroquois, during one of their daring raids on the French outpost.[1] Adopted by an Iroquois chief, Radisson was taken to Fort Orange (Albany) on a peace expedition; and afterwards, escaping from his captors, he returned to the Dutch, who sent him to Holland, whence, in 1654, he made his way back to New France. Three years later he volunteered to go with other Frenchmen to the ill-fated mission at Onondaga, where he remained until that canton was abandoned on March 20, 1658. Returning to Three Rivers, Radisson found there his brother-in-law,[2] Des Grosseilliers, who had but recently returned from an expedition to the Huron country, and who was eager to explore the great lakes, of which he had heard so much from the Indians. No sooner was the project explained to Radisson than he "longed to see himself in a boat." A large party was organized, and in June they started

[1] Radisson was captured while hunting, and during his life among the Iroquois he became much attached to his foster mother, sisters, and brother. His narrative of his capture, his escape, recapture and return to the Iroquois village, and his final successful desertion shows how readily a Frenchman took to savage life.

[2] Des Grosseilliers's first wife was Hélène, a daughter of that Abraham Martin for whom the Plains of Abraham were named. She died in 1651, and three years later Des Grosseilliers married Radisson's sister, Margaret Hayet.

up the Ottawa, only to run into an ambush of Iroquois. The twenty-nine other Frenchmen in the expedition, inexperienced and timid, decided that a path was not worth following when it led through the midst of such wary enemies; and the two brothers-in-law were left to pursue their westward way with Indians alone for companions. Just where the voyage took the adventurous Frenchmen is a matter of great doubt, so confused is Radisson's narrative. He claims that they made the circuit of Lake Huron;[1] but the probability is that they simply coasted along the shores of Georgian Bay, arriving at the Manitoulin Islands.[2] Thence they passed through the Straits of Mackinac, and spent the winter near the southwestern shores of Lake Michigan and in the vicinity of Green Bay. Possibly they reached the western end of Lake Superior; probably they wandered about among the head-waters of the streams that flowed westward into the Mississippi.

"We weare," says Radisson, "4 moneths in our voyage w[th]out doeing any thing but goe from river to river. We mett severall sorts of people. We conversed w[th] them, being long time in alliance w[th] them. By the persuasion of some of them we went into ye great river

[1] *Voyages*, p. 145. Portions of the Third and Fourth Voyages are to be found in vol. xi. of the *Wisconsin Historical Collections*. The full and careful notes are by Mr. Reuben G. Thwaites, whose chronology seems to me in the main satisfactory. I do not think it is probable, however, that Radisson reached Lake Superior on his first voyage northward. Mr. Campbell's article on "Radisson and Grosseilliers," in the *American Historical Review*, January, 1896, gives the various theories advanced, but his conclusion that but one northern voyage was made, which voyage ended in 1660, seems to me improbable.

[2] Had they made the circuit of the lake, mention of River St. Clair and Saginaw Bay would not have been omitted.

that divides itselfe in 2, where the hurrons wth some Ottanake and the wild men (Indians) that had warrs wth them had retired. There is not great difference in their language as we weare told. This nation have warrs against those of forked river. It is so called because it has 2 branches, the one towards the west, the other towards the South, which, we believe, runns towards Mexico, by the tokens they gave us."[1]

Now the *Relation* of 1659–60 says that an Indian, Asatanik by name, set out in the June of 1658 from the Bay des Puants (Green Bay) and wintered on Lake Superior, so called because it is above the Lake of the Hurons, into which it flows by a fall.[2] From Lake Superior the Indian went to Hudson Bay. Returning to Quebec the writer of the *Relation* found two Frenchmen just returned from those upper countries with three hundred canoes laden with peltries; they said they had passed the winter on Lake Superior,[3] among the Hurons of the Tobacco Nation, who had retreated before the Iroquois, "across mountains and over rocks, through the depths of vast unknown forests, and at length had happily arrived at a beautiful river, large, wide, deep, and resembling (the Indians say) our great river St. Lawrence."

The confused and obscure statements in Radisson's narrative, coupled with the passage quoted from the *Relation* of 1660, have been made the basis of the sur-

[1] *Voyages*, pp. 167–68.

[2] *Relation of* 1659, p. 42, *et seq.* For an English translation of this passage and others relating to lake history, see Smith's *History of Wisconsin*, vol. iii. (Madison, 1854).

[3] "Ils ont hiuerne sur les riuages du lac Superior." We know from the Journal of the Jesuits that Grosseilliers returned at this time. But the statement that he *wintered* on Lake Superior is inexact.

mises[1] of some writers and the assertions of others that the two French explorers reached the Mississippi River and were the real discoverers of that stream.[2] On the other hand, it has been maintained with equal positiveness not only that Des Grosseilliers and Radisson never saw the great river, but that they made only a single voyage to the northwest, returning in 1660. The narrative of the first journey is treated as a pure fabrication on Radisson's part.[3] Happily the fewest difficulties attend the theory that in the main Radisson wrote truthfully; and that such errors as are to be found in his accounts are doubtless due to the natural confusion occasioned by trying to supplement meagre field notes by recollections called from an untrained memory. It is possible, also, that in the course of two centuries some parts of the manuscript may have been transposed, thus creating on the printed page of to-day errors not properly chargeable to the writer.[4]

Probably Radisson and his companions reached some of the streams that flow into the Mississippi; and undoubtedly they heard from the Indians vague accounts of the river itself, just as their immediate successors

[1] Winsor, *Cartier to Frontenac*, p. 186.

[2] Reuben G. Thwaites, *Wisconsin Historical Collections*, vol. xi., p. 64, note.

[3] Henry Colin Campbell. "Radisson and Grosseilliers," in *American Historical Review*, January, 1896.

[4] Introduction to Radisson's *Voyages*, p. 13. The Radisson manuscripts covering the period from 1652 to 1664 were presented by Samuel Pepys, of diary fame, who was Secretary of the Admiralty to Charles II. and James II. Mr. Scull conjectures that Pepys received the papers from Sir George Carteret, Treasurer of the Navy. for whom Radisson copied them out in order that they might be brought before Charles II. Pepys's papers were sold to various tradesmen for wrapping-paper, but were found and reclaimed by Richard Rawlinson.

learned of it. Even admitting that they reached the Mississippi, they did not claim the great discovery, nor did their accounts point the way to other explorers.[1] Their thoughts and ambitions were directed northward towards Hudson Bay; and they left to those who came after them the discovery and mapping of the great waterway. To the student of Northwestern history, however, the name of Radisson is of prime importance, because he was the first explorer to describe what he saw on his travels along the boundaries of that region.

Having returned in safety from a highly profitable trip to Lake Michigan, Des Grosseilliers and Radisson were naturally anxious to explore Lake Superior; but they decided to postpone their voyage till the next year. Meanwhile, Father René Menard, feeling upon his conscience the sins of the heathen, embraced an opportunity to return with the Indians who had come down with the two Frenchmen.[2] The tale of Father Menard's perilous journey is one of many relations of self-sacrifice ending in tragic death, that give pathos to

[1] Winsor says that there is no question that Grosseilliers wintered on the shores of Lake Superior in 1658–59, and that he was joined by Radisson on the St. Lawrence during the latter year. Evidently Mr. Winsor prefers to take Sulte's chronology rather than undertake to construct one on the basis of Radisson's statements. I think, however, that any one who will take the pains to make himself familiar with Radisson's writings will come to the conclusion that he was essentially truthful. In his younger days at least he had a tender heart and a real love of wild life. Mr. Gilbert Parker, in his novel *The Trail of the Sword*, uses the name of Radisson in connection with a renegade, manifestly an unjust act towards a man after Mr. Parker's own heart, did he but know it. The detailed statements of Radisson as to the occurrences between his first and second northwestern voyages are not to be ignored.

[2] Winsor falls into the error of supposing that Menard returned with Grosseilliers, whereas the latter did not start back until 1661.

GRAND ARCH, PICTURED ROCKS, LAKE SUPERIOR

the story of New France. On August 27, 1660, he set out to "follow the Algonquins even to the middle of the lake of the maritime nation and of Lake Superior."[1] The trip, tedious enough at best, was made irksome to the last degree by the hard labor at the paddle and on the portage put upon the aged father by Indians made lazy and indolent by the recent debaucheries of the fur-market. Yet in due time the party reached the upper lake, and began the voyage along its southern shores. Almost the first night out a falling tree demolished the canoe assigned to Father Menard and his companion, Jean Guerin; and in this dilemma all but three of their Indian friend deserted them.[2] For days their only food was begged from passing red men; but at length a party of friendly Indians came to their rescue, and thus they were able to reach Keweenaw Bay,[3] where the mission was to be established by building the usual bark chapel. Pathetic indeed is the recital of the good old father, who quickly forgot the pains and perils of the journey in the ecstatic pleasure of celebrating the mass and in bringing the ministrations of the Church to the sick and dying heathen. Had Father Menard's mind turned more to the things of this earth, the long letters he sent back must have contained the first descriptions of the wondrous beauty of the southern shore of Lake Superior; but instead we have the recital of suffering and disappointment borne bravely for the Master's sake. Then the letters come to a sudden end.

[1] *Relation of* 1659–60, p. 147.

[2] Lalemant, *Relations of* 1663 and 1664.

[3] Menard named the waters St. Theresa's Bay, having arrived on her day. Shea places the site of this mission at Old Village Point, on Keweenaw Bay, about seven miles north of the present town of L'Anse (*History of the Catholic Church in Colonial Days*, p. 263).

On the tenth day of August, 1661, after nearly a year of fruitless labors, Father Menard set out for a wilderness journey to the south, and either lost himself and perished from starvation or else was murdered by those he sought to save.[1]

During the same month that Father Menard laid down his life for the heathen, Des Grosseilliers and Radisson, having eluded the vigilance of the governor,[2] who had demanded the right to send two of his servants with them and to share the profits, started on a second northern journey. It is in Radisson's narrative of this trip that we find the first detailed descriptions of any portion of the present State of Michigan. Having reached the mouth of St. Mary's River, they began to ascend that beautiful stream. "We came after to a rapid that makes the separation of the lake of the hurrons, that we calls Superior, or upper, for that ye wildmen hold it to be longer and broader, besides a great many islands, which maks appeare in a bigger extent. This rapid was formerly the dwelling of those with whom wee weare, and consequently we must not aske them if they knew where they have layed. Wee made cottages[3] at our advantages, and found the truth of what those men had often (said), that if once we could come to that place we should make good cheare of a fish that they call *Assickmack*, which signifyeth a white

[1] Shea, following the researches of Rev. Edward Jacker, believes that Menard reached Vieux Desert, the source of the Wisconsin (p. 265). Henry Colin Campbell, in his monograph on Father Menard, published by the Parkman Club of Milwaukee, has traced, with all possible definiteness, the steps of the good priest's journeys.

[2] Baron Dubois d'Avangour was governor at this time. Tracy, Courcelles, and Talon began their reign in 1665.

[3] Radisson uses the phrase "made cottages," as we say "made camp."

fish. The bear, the castors (beavers), and the Oriniack (moose) showed themselves often, but to their cost; indeed it was to us like a terrestrial paradise—after so long fasting, after so great paines yt we had taken (to) finde ourselves so well by chossing our dyet, and resting when we had a mind to it; 'tis here that we must tast with pleasure a sweet bitt. We doe not aske for a good sauce; its better to have it naturally—it is the way to distinguish the sweet from the bitter."[1]

But the season was so far spent that the voyageurs were forced to leave their terrestrial paradise and its whitefish to "the cursed Iroquoits"; yet for very shame they were impelled "to give thanks to the river, to the earth, to the woods and to the rocks that stayes the fish." For days, when sky and water and coast-line imperceptibly melted one into the other in the blue haze, they paddled leisurely along the southern shore of Lake Superior. On the banks of the streams they found pieces of copper, some of which weighed as much as a hundred pounds; and the Indians pointed out a great hill of that metal, but deterred the incredulous explorers from proving the truth of their story by saying that even larger deposits lay beyond.

With mingled wonder and delight they skirted coasts that nature had made pleasant alike "to the eye, the sperit and the belly," until they came to those remarkable plains of shifting sand early named the Grand Sables. "As we went along we saw banckes of sand so high that one of our wildmen went upp for curiositie; being there, did show no more than a crow. That place is most dangerous when there is any storme, being no landing

[1] *Voyages*, p. 187. Had Radisson visited the Sault on his first voyage, as has been held, he would not have been likely to speak of it so minutely in the relation of his second journey.

place so long as the sandy banckes are under water; and when the wind blowes, that sand doth rise by a strange kind of whirlings that are able to choake the passengers. One day you will see 50 small mountains att one side; and the next day, if the wind changes, on the other side. This putts me in mind of the great and vast wilderness of Turkey land, as the Turques makes their pilgrimages."[1]

Pursuing their course they "came to a remarquable place. Its a banke of Rocks that the wild men made a sacrifice to; they calls it *Nanitouckfinagoit*, which signifies the likenesse of the devil. They fling much tobacco and other things in veneration. It is a thing most incredible that the lake should be so boisterous that the waves of it should have the strength to doe what I have to say by this my discours: first, that it's so high and soe deepe yt it's impossible to claime up to the point. There comes many sorte of birds yt makes there nest here, the goilants, which is a white sea-bird of the bignesse of a pigeon, which makes me believe what ye wildmen told me concerning the sea to be neare directly to ye point. It's like a great Portall by reason of the beating of the waves. The lower part of that opening is as big as a tower, and grows bigger in going up. There is, I believe, six acres of land. Above it a ship of 500 tuns could passe by, soe bigg is the arch. I gave it the name of the portall of St. Peter, because my name is so called, and that I was the first Christian that ever saw it.[2] There is in place caves very deepe, caused by

[1] Bela Hubbard, writing of a voyage to Lake Superior that he made in 1840, gives a very graphic description of "the grand and leafless Sables." See *Memorials of Half a Century.*

[2] Radisson did not know of Menard's voyage. With this description compare that of General Cass in Smith's *Life of Lewis Cass.*

the same violence. We must look to ourselves and take time with our small boats. The coast of rocks is 5 or 6 leagues, and there scarce a place to putt a boat in assurance from the waves. When the lake is agitated the waves goeth in these concavities with force and make a most horrible noise, most like the shooting of great guns."

It is strange that in so extended a description of the Pictured Rocks, Radisson has omitted all notice of the one feature that gives to them their present name—the brilliant colors produced on the surface of the rocks by the exuding of mineral paints.

Coming to what are now known as the Huron Islands, Radisson looked upon their beauties and because "there be 3 in triangle," he called them "of ye Trinity." Waiting for fair weather, the Frenchmen sailed across Keweenaw Bay to the mouth of Portage River, and were surprised to find there meadows squared and smooth as a board, the work of the beavers, which industrious animals had cut the trees and flooded many a square mile of territory.[1] The explorers broke through the beaver dams, and at last came to "a trembling ground" over which they dragged their boats. "The ground became trembling by this means: the castors drowning great soyles with dead water, herein grows mosse which is 2 foot thick or there abouts, and when you think to goe safe and dry, if you take not good care you sink downe to your head or to the middle of your body. When you are out of one hole you find yourselfe in another. This I Speake by experience, for I myself have bin catched often. But the wild men warned me, which

[1] Those who are familiar with the outlet of Portage Lake will notice how accurate this description is.

saved me; that is, that when the mosse should break under, I should cast my whole body into the water on sudaine—I must with my hands hold the mosse, and go like a frogg, then to draw my boat after me. There was no danger."

Gloomy Portage Lake passed, they came to the carriage, where is now the government ship-canal. There they found the way "well beaten because of the comers and goers, who by making that passage shortens their passage by 8 days by tourning about the point that goes very farr in that great lake; that is to say, 5 to come to the point and 3 for to come to the landing of that place of carriage." They were told that a league from the end of Keweenaw Point was an island all of copper, and that from this island, when one was "minded to thwart it in a faire and calme weather, beginning from sun rising to sun sett, they come to a great island (Isle Royale) from which they come the next morning to firme lande on the other side."

Pursuing their westward way, the two Frenchmen reached the Chequamegon Bay and wintered among the tribes gathered from the four points of the compass to dwell for a season beside the abundant fisheries of the greatest of lakes. From the east came the nations of the Sault, to regale themselves with "sturgeons of a vast bigness, and Pycts of seaven foot long." From the west the Nadoneseronons (Sioux) appeared, each warrior accompanied by his two wives bearing oats and corn, garments of buffalo fur and "white castor" skins; and following the first embassy came a deputation of young men with "incredible pomp" that reminded Radisson of the entrance of the Polanders into Paris, "save that they had not so many jewells, but instead of them they had so many feathers." From the south came old friends from Green Bay, whom they had met during their first voyage, and who now gave them warm greetings. Best of all, from the north came the Christinos, who filled the willing ears of the Frenchmen with tales of the immense riches in furs of the lands about Hudson Bay.

Returning in 1662 with a rich harvest of peltries, the enterprising brothers-in-law were promptly arrested for presuming to trade without a license; Des Grosseilliers was made a prisoner, and of the £46,000 w· 'th of furs they brought back £24,000 was taken for fines and dues, to show for which they were to have the empty honor of putting their coat of arms above the fort at Three Rivers which was . be built from the proceeds of the confiscated property.[1] So ungrateful was their own government towards these self-sacrificing but exceeding thrifty explorers that they found a way to transfer their allegiance to England and, by the favor of Prince Rupert, to lay the foundations of that vast and wealthy monopoly, the Hudson Bay Company.

While Des Grosseilliers and Radisson were enduring the privations and enjoying the feasts among the Lake Indians, fragments of Menard's letters found their way to Quebec, and the blood of this martyr speedily became the seed of missions at Sault Ste. Marie, at Ashland, and at Green Bay. It fell to the lot of Father Claude Allouez to take up the work of "this great and painful mission." It was early in the September of 1665 that Allouez entered upon the broad expanse of the upper lake, to which he gave the name of his patron, "Mon-

[1] *Voyages*, p. 241. In vol. ii., No 5, of the publications of the Michigan Political Science Association, I have discussed more fully the claims of Radisson and Des Grosseilliers as the discoverers of Lake Superior.

sieur Tracy."[1] Passing the scene of Menard's labors, he came to Chequamegon Bay, where he built a chapel of bark and set up the altar of his church, naming his mission La Pointe d'Esprit. During his frequent missionary journeys he came upon the wandering Sioux, who told him of their home towards the great river "Messepi," of their prairies abounding in game of all kinds, of their fields of tobacco, and of a still more remote tribe beyond whose home the earth is cut off by a great lake whose waters are ill-smelling like the sea.

After two years of wandering and teaching, Allouez returned to Quebec on the third day of August, 1667; yet so great was his zeal that after but forty-eight hours of civilization he plunged again into the wilderness. His importunate appeals for laborers to enter fields white for the harvest called into service Father James Marquette, who in 1668 established himself at Sault Ste. Marie, and there began a permanent mission that became the first white settlement within the present borders of Michigan. When Allouez was called to Green Bay in 1669, Marquette moved on to La Pointe d'Esprit, leaving in his place at the Sault Father Claude Dablon, in whose writings we find the first mention of the Ontonagon copper region, whence a hundred-pound fragment of ore had been brought to him in 1767, and which he himself visited a few years later.[2]

[1] Alexander de Prouville, Marquis de Tracy, lieutenant-general.

[2] The French speak of "mines" of copper, and the word is often transferred into English. It should be translated "deposits." There were copper mines in the Lake Superior region, but they were the work of the Mound-builders, and were not known to the Indians. I have tried to connect the once famous Ontonagon copper bowlder, now in the Smithsonian Institution at Washington, with the work of the "ancient miners." See Smithsonian Institution publications, National Museum report for 1895, pp. 1021–1030.

JAMES MARQUETTE, S. J.

To Marquette at La Pointe came the Illinois Indians from the south, who excited his imagination to as great an extent as the Christinos from the north had excited the imaginations of Grosseilliers and Radisson, and with a correspondingly momentous result. "When the Illinois come to La Pointe," says Marquette, "they pass a great river almost a league in breadth. It flows from north to south, and so far that the Illinois, who know not the use of the canoe, have never so much as heard of the mouth." An Illinois youth who acted as instructor in language to Marquette told the priest that he had seen Indians from the south who were loaded down with glass beads, thus proving that they had trafficked with the whites. That the great river emptied itself in Virginia seemed to Marquette hardly probable; he was inclined to believe that its mouth was in California. At any rate he was determined to secure the company of a white companion, and, with his Indian boy as interpreter, to navigate the river as far as possible, to visit the nations who lived along its banks in order to prepare the way for the fathers of the Church, and to obtain a perfect knowledge of the sea either to the south or to the west.

Before starting on the journey that was to make immortal his name and that of his companion, Marquette all unwittingly must needs prepare the place of his burial. It so happened that in the dispersion of the Hurons by the Iroquois, a remnant of the Tobacco Nation dwelling south of Georgian Bay had taken refuge first on the island of Michilimackinac, celebrated for its fishing. After a stay scarcely longer than that of a modern tourist, the Indians fled from their relentless pursuers first to Green Bay and then to La Pointe, where they dwelt in peace for several years, until by ill chance they incurred the hostility of the Sioux. This most chivalrous nation first returned to Marquette the images he had given to them, and then began a vigorous warfare on the Hurons. In the progress of hostilities the prisoners were burned so freely as to carry consternation to the dispirited Hurons, who quickly abandoned their homes and well-tilled fields and, returning to the Straits of Mackinac, established themselves on the north side of that passage. To his new mission Marquette—for he had followed his fleeing flock—gave the name of St. Ignace, and so the place is known to this day. There the Indians filled his chapel every day,[1] singing praises to God with such devotion as to move even the French *coureurs des bois* who congregated at this gateway of Indian travel; and there the zealous father inspired in his savage converts a degree of affection that all too soon found its last manifestation in the weird journey to discover his body and with wild grief to bring it back to sepulchre beneath the chapel in which he had so patiently instructed them.

While Marquette was still at La Pointe a picturesque if not important ceremony had taken place at Sault Ste. Marie. On the 14th day of June, 1671, Simon François Daumont, Sieur Saint Lusson, as the representative of the ambitious Intendant, Talon, erected on the crest of the hill overlooking the broad expanse of lake and the dashing rapids of the river a cedar cross bearing the arms of France; and in sounding phrase[2] he assumed for his king authority over those unknown lands from

[1] Dablon, *Relations of* 1671 *and* 1672. A full account of Marquette's wanderings is given by Dablon.

[2] Saint Lusson's procès-verbal is given in the *Wisconsin Historical Collections*, vol. xi., p. 26. Bancroft, Parkman, and Winsor all devote considerable attention to this ceremony.

the North Sea to the south and westward to seas the substance of things hoped for. Among the little group of Frenchmen who represented civilization and Louis XIV. before the thousands of Indians whom the indefatigable Perrot had gathered at the Sault was a young man who had left the quiet paths of philosophy and had turned aside from the strait ways of the Church eagerly to pursue the hazardous and exciting life of the fur-trader and explorer. This was not Louis Joliet's first visit to the Lake Superior country. In 1668 he had been sent thither by Talon to discover the copper deposits of which the Jesuit fathers said so much; and failing in the attempt—as those who came after him for two centuries failed—he had returned to the St. Lawrence by the St. Clair and Detroit rivers and by Lake Erie, the discovery of which waterways alone would have given his name a place in history had he left record of his achievement. Joliet was an explorer after Talon's own heart—he could live off the country and pay himself by traffic in peltries, while he was carrying the flag of France into new regions. It is no wonder, then, that to the zeal of the Church, as represented by Marquette, Talon added the enterprise of the state incarnate in Joliet, for the discovery of that western river—forgotten since the days of De Soto—the navigation of which should realize the extravagant claims of Saint Lusson.

Setting out from St. Ignace on May 17, 1673, priest and trader pushed their canoes across the northern end of Lake Michigan to the mission at Green Bay, thence up the Fox, across Lake Winnebago, and by portage to the Wisconsin, down which stream they floated until on June 17th their light canoes were caught and whirled along by the on-rushing Mississippi, thus accomplishing a discovery that, in the words of Bancroft, "changed the destiny of nations." At the mouth of the Arkansas they turned about, being persuaded that the river flowed into the Gulf of Mexico. The return was by way of the Illinois River and Lake Michigan. Marquette rested at his mission of St. Ignace, leaving Joliet to descend to Quebec with the news of the complete success of their enterprise.

Assigned to the Green Bay mission, Marquette felt the conversion of southern Indians so heavily on his conscience that he secured permission to return to them; and in the winter of 1674 he built and furnished a bark chapel in the town of the Kaskaskias. The seeds of disease were in his system, however, and he was seized with a longing to die among his brethren and his devoted flock at St. Ignace. Assisted by two canoemen, he worked his way north to the foot of Lake Michigan and skirted its sandy shores. On the night of May 19, 1675, he made camp near the wild and lonely promontory of the Sleeping Bear; the evening was spent in prayer, and as midnight approached his strength failed. With the music of the lapping waves in his ears and the names of Jesus and Mary on his lips, at the parting of the days, the gentle spirit of the great discoverer journeyed to the undiscovered country. Tenderly his faithful boatmen buried him in the white sands, and two years later a band of Ottawas found his body and bore it to St. Ignace. There, under the chapel he had built, the bones of "the guardian angel of the Ottawa missions" reposed for two full centuries, until a member of his order found them under the ashes of the church and marked their resting-place.[1]

[1] Shea's *History of the Catholic Church in Colonial Days*, p. 319. We are accustomed to think of Marquette as a man well along in years. He was but thirty-eight years old when he died; but he had

SLEEPING BEAR

Meantime, Joliet, after a short stay at Sault Ste. Marie, returned to Quebec to spread the news of the discovery of the Mississippi and to incite the ambitious Talon to fresh enterprises for the spread of the king's domain. The way was now open and the man was at hand.

On a bright August morning, in the year 1679, a well-rigged vessel of some forty-five tons rode easily at anchor under the lee of one of the beautiful islands that dot the green waters at the head of Lake Erie. From the vessel's decks five small guns threatened the peaceful shores; and on the morning breeze that blew lazily over lonely promontory and wooded waste, over Indian lodge and the haunt of wild deer, rose and fell the soft white folds of a flag that bore the lilies of France shining solitary in the wilderness.[1]

René Robert Cavelier, Sieur de la Salle, as he paced the quarter-deck of his little ship that August morning, was at the height of his fortunes. Not only did he bear the royal commission to establish a line of forts along the Great Lakes, whereby to hold for France all that rich fur country, but he had also in his possession letters signed by the powerful King Louis XIV., granting to him large concessions in the matter of the profitable trade in beaver-skins.

On the sharp prow of his vessel La Salle had placed the roughly carved figure of a griffin, a symbol chosen from the armorial bearings of his friend and supporter, Count Frontenac, governor-general of the French pos-

been a priest for twenty-one years. In 1877, Father Jacker discovered Marquette's remains beneath the mission chapel burned in 1705—not in 1700, as Shea has it. Compare Shea, p. 319, with p. 622.

[1] Parkman's *La Salle and the Discovery of the Great West* and Louis Hennepin's *Travels* are the authorities for this voyage.

sessions in the New World; and as he watched his ship take shape on the banks of the Niagara River, he had fondly stroked the head of the monster, swearing to make the griffin fly above the crows. By this oath he meant that in his purposes of trade and exploration he would not allow himself to be thwarted by the Jesuits, who claimed the Indians for their inheritance and who were bent on making the uttermost parts of this new earth their exclusive possession. Such pious purposes, the Jesuits foresaw, must come to nothing, if once the brandy of the fur-traders and the free-and-easy life of the *coureurs de bois* should gain a footing among the savages.

La Salle, on the other hand, looked forward to a chain of forts and trading-posts stretching from Quebec along the Great Lakes and thence down the Mississippi to its mouth. At these posts the rich furs of the north and the valuable buffalo hides of the prairies should be gathered for shipment to France. With the Mississippi an open pathway to Europe, there would be no need of the long voyage across the tempestuous Erie and Ontario, frozen during half the year and guarded perpetually by the blood-thirsty Iroquois, friends of the English and enemies of the French and their allies, the Hurons.

In order to carry out his plans of trade and exploration, La Salle had built the *Griffin* and had gathered a crew of four and thirty men. Behind at Montreal his clamorous creditors, urged on by his commercial rivals, were already in possession of his estate; but before him were untold riches in beaver-skins, and beneath his feet was the stanch vessel whose single voyage should bring him profits sufficient to pay every debt and yet leave him fortune enough to pursue those schemes of exploration which for years had filled his thoughts by day and his dreams by night.[1]

Born of a wealthy and honorable Rouen family, La Salle in his youth had joined the Society of Jesus; but finding himself more inclined to lead than to follow unquestioningly the directions of others, he had left the Jesuits, and at the age of twenty-three had sailed for America, whither his brother, the Abbé Jean Cavelier, had preceded him. His first establishment, nine miles above Montreal, afterwards received in derision the name of La Chine, because of La Salle's failure to find a path to China by way of the Mississippi. In these later days, this name of ridicule has been made good by the passage across La Salle's old possessions of the Canadian Pacific railway, England's new way to China.

La Salle, keenly ambitious, straightforward in all his dealings, and reserved in the expression of his feelings, was one of those men who keep their eyes fixed so steadfastly on the goal that they take no pleasure in the running. For this reason he had little in common with the Recollect priest who made one of the company on board the *Griffin*. In the make-up of Father Louis Hennepin a strong desire to roam the world over constantly warred with an inclination to enjoy in comfort the good things of this life as they came to him. While his fellow monks were doing penance for their sins, Father Hennepin had been accustomed to steal away to some secluded spot, there to spend the rapid hours in poring over the *Relations* sent back to France from the

[1] Sometime during the years 1669–70 La Salle had reached the Ohio from Lake Erie, and had floated down that river to the present site of Louisville. See Parkman's *La Salle and the Discovery of the Great West*, p. 22.

"five hundred convents of Recollects scattered over two and twenty provinces in America."

When such writings failed him, he used often to skulk behind the doors of Dunkirk inns to listen to the talk of seamen. "The smoke of tobacco," he writes, "was disagreeable to me and created pains in my stomach, while I was thus intent upon giving ear to their relations; yet, nevertheless, I was very attentive to the accounts they gave of their encounters by land and sea, the peril they had gone through, and all the accidents which befell them in their long voyages. This occupation was so agreeable to me that I have spent whole days and nights at it without eating."

On the bloody field of Seneff, where Prince Condé and William of Orange heaped the ground with twenty thousand corpses, Father Hennepin was ministering to the dying when he received the long-hoped-for orders to proceed to Rochelle and there take passage for America. On the same vessel with Hennepin were La Salle and his faithful friend Henry de Tonty, the son of the famous financier whose name the word "tontine" preserves for us.

When La Salle came to make up his company, doubtless he was glad to secure the aid of a priest who was not a Jesuit and therefore not an enemy; who, though naturally suspicious, could be brought around by a few words of flattery; who had no ambition save to gratify an insatiable desire to see new places; and who, when an adventure was on foot, could live on boiled corn and sleep in a hole in the snow. Thus it was that while the *Griffin* was building, Father Hennepin's prayers and exhortations were added to Tonty's commands to keep the fickle ship-carpenters at work; and when at last the vessel was ready for her voyage, Hennepin's

ROBERT CAVELIER, SIEUR DE LA SALLE

voice led in the *Te Deum* which celebrated the joyful passage from the rapid waters of Niagara to the broad expanse of Lake Erie.

After a tempestuous voyage across this most fitful of lakes, the *Griffin* awaited but a favorable wind to attempt the passage of the wide river called by the French the strait—Détroit. As the morning breeze came dancing across the glassy waters the pilot quickly got the vessel under way, and the *Griffin*, borne along by her two great square-sails, fairly flew over the white-capped billows. Laying her course between Bois Blanc Island on the right and Sugar Island on the left, the little vessel was soon breasting the rapids between the long, low-lying Grosse Isle and the clay bluffs of the mainland. The swift-running waters eddied and swirled about the struggling vessel, as if to protest against the passage of this sturdy little pioneer of the mighty fleets which in these modern days make that strait the greatest commercial pathway in the world.

Father Hennepin was so moved with the beauty of the scene spread out before him that he would have given over all thoughts of further explorations in order to stay and enjoy the delights of what seemed to him an earthly paradise. He even urged upon La Salle the advantages of a settlement at some point on the strait. The white-fish were excellent, he said; and a post there would keep the Iroquois in check. The pious father further explains that his real reason for wishing to remain was that he might have a chance "to preach the gospel to those ignorant nations"; but La Salle cut short all such ideas by the icy remark to the priest, that considering the great passion he had a few months before for the discovery of a new country, his present proposal was quite unaccountable.

As the *Griffin* rounded the headland that commands the site of Detroit, a canoe, shooting out from the rushes that fringe the shore, glided alongside the ship. An iron hand[1] clutched the low bulwarks and Tonty sprang aboard. He had been sent forward to look after the fifteen men whom La Salle had despatched to the upper lakes to buy furs as a cargo for the vessel; but on being overtaken by the *Griffin*, Tonty joined his leader, and doubtless La Salle was well pleased to have the companionship of the one man whose devotion was as unquestioned as his courage was unlimited, and whose unfailing good humor and ingenuity well fitted him to succeed in daring enterprises.

On the 12th of August the *Griffin*, skirting the marshy shores of the long island that parts the waters of the Detroit River at its head, glided out upon the surface of a small and shallow lake. It was Sainte Claire's day, and Father Hennepin was not slow to suggest that the name of the founder of his order be given to a body of water as beautiful and as even-tempered as Clara d'Assisi is reputed to have been. The twenty miles of lake passed over, Pilot Lucas saw before him vast stretches of rushes, among which the waters from the river above sought the lake through many a serpentine channel. One way after another was sounded, until at last a passage was found and the *Griffin* pursued her course up the island-strewn river. The way into Lake Huron was blocked by a strong northwest wind; and it was not until August 23d, after a voyage of twelve days from Lake Erie, that the vessel, hauled from the shore by a dozen men, and aided by a brisk southerly breeze,

[1] Tonty had lost one hand in the wars, and its place was supplied with an iron hook, hence his name, Tonty of the Iron-hand.

overcame the rapids and was tossed by the waves of the great lake. Then the ship's company sang *Te Deum* "to return thanks to the Almighty for their happy navigation."

On the 24th the *Griffin* ran across Saginaw Bay, then as now the terror of timid ones, by reason of the high winds that sweep across it. Then for two days she lay becalmed among the rocky and pine-clad islands of Thunder Bay. On the fourth day there came a storm. The crew sent down the main-yard and topmast, and then fell on their knees in prayer. Even La Salle gave up hope, and began to prepare for death with the others, excepting only Pilot Lucas, whom, says Hennepin, "we could never force to pray ; and he did nothing all that while but curse and swear against M. la Salle, who, as he said, had brought him thither to make him perish in a nasty lake, and lose the glory he had acquired by his long and happy navigations on the ocean." But fate spared Pilot Lucas for a few months longer. Hennepin had vowed an altar to St. Anthony of Padua, and was prudent enough to promise that it should be set up in the far-distant Louisiana.

The storm died away as quickly as it arose, and the descending sun made a background of glory against which the wooded cliffs of the turtle-shaped island of Michilimackinac stood out in the clear air, a grand sentinel guarding the harbor of St. Ignace. Next day the anchors dropped into the clear waters of the harbor, and lay plainly visible on the white bottom of the lake. Culverin and arquebus boomed a salute, which was taken up and tossed to and fro from island cliff to pine-tipped cape. The booming guns brought crowds of yelping Indians from their bark huts, straggling French traders from their cabins, and two or three black-robed priests from the little mission-house. La Salle, finely dressed, and wearing a scarlet cloak richly trimmed with gold braid, landed with his men, and all sought the rough little chapel in the Ottawa village, to give thanks for a safe voyage. The Ottawas in their canoes accompanied the new-comers back to the ship, surrounding the "big canoe," as they called the *Griffin*, and heaping the vessel's deck with the white-fish and trout so pleasing to the palate of Father Hennepin. The next day, when La Salle visited the palisaded town of the Hurons, these Indians greeted him with a salute of musketry, the Europeans having told them that was the highest form of compliment.

Of the fifteen men whom La Salle had sent before him to buy furs for the return voyage of the *Griffin*, four were found at St. Ignace. They had squandered their goods, and had wasted the proceeds in riotous living. Two others had escaped to Sault Ste. Marie, whither La Salle sent Tonty to fetch them. The leader, however, sailed before his lieutenant returned. Perplexed and annoyed by the hostile feelings that his jealous crew had aroused among the ever-suspicious Indians, he was led to push on, in order to get his cargo before his enemies could tamper with the tribes of the Illinois. Fortune favored him. At Green Bay he found a friend in an old Pottawatomie chief, whose boundless admiration for Count Frontenac he was ready to extend to all who bore the "great chief's" commission. Here, too, he found in waiting a cargo of furs gathered by the few faithful ones of his advance party. Elated at his success, and believing himself now certain to secure the means of continuing his explorations, La Salle placed his pilot in command of the *Griffin* for the return voyage, giving him five picked men for a crew. He himself, with Hennepin and fourteen others, embarked in four canoes and steered southward.

No sooner were the canoes fairly out into the lake, than one of those sudden September storms, so common on Lake Michigan, came down upon them; and it was not until morning that the tempest-tossed voyagers came safe to land. They skirted the Michigan shore as far as the St. Joseph River, where they waited twenty days for Tonty. He brought no tidings of the *Griffin*, and it was several months before La Salle learned for a certainty that the same storm which had so nearly proved his own destruction had sent to the bottom his little vessel and all the high hopes that depended upon it. Whether the loss was due to the pilot's carelessness or to his treachery is not known to this day; for none of the crew was ever again heard of. Thus disastrously ended the only voyage of the first vessel on the Upper Lakes.

La Salle, with Tonty, Hennepin, and his followers, made his slow way south until he came to the banks of the Illinois. Straightway he began to build a new vessel in which to voyage down that river to its junction with the Mississippi. Once more hope fired his soul, and with careful forethought he made his plans. The *Griffin* was to bring the anchors and rigging for the new vessel; but so certain was La Salle that the *Griffin* had been lost that, with a courage that marks him as one of the greatest of the world's explorers, he determined to undertake a winter journey back over the thousand miles that lay between him and Fort Frontenac, in order to obtain the necessary supplies.

Sending the reluctant Hennepin on a voyage of discovery down the Illinois, and leaving Tonty in charge of the pitiful little fort Crèvecœur,[1] La Salle took a few companions and began his perilous March journey through half-frozen swamps and across deep rivers, where his way was constantly endangered by hostile Indians. Reaching his old fort at the mouth of the St. Joseph River, and there learning beyond the shadow of a doubt that the *Griffin* had been wrecked, the little party struck across Michigan. Through dense woods where the thorns tore their clothes into strips and cut their hands and faces till they streamed with blood, for three days they made their slow way. Then their fainting spirits were revived by broad stretches of prairie bordered by groves of oak, the home of deer, bear, and wild turkey. These "oak openings" were at this time the battle-ground for a half-dozen tribes of Indians, no one tribe being able to hold a land so rich in game and with so fertile a soil.

A rapid journey of two days brought them to a series of marshes, through which they waded painfully for three long days, with hostile Indians on their track, so that they dared light no fire at night. Once they took off their water-soaked clothes, and rolling themselves in their blankets, lay down to sleep on a dry knoll. When morning came they were forced to make a fire to thaw out their frozen garments, and the smoke quickly betrayed their presence to a band of Illinois; but when the Indians found that La Salle's party were not Iroquois, they suffered the white men to go in peace.

Ten days out from St. Joseph, they came upon the

[1] La Salle might well have selected the name Crèvecœur (broken-heart) to express the plight into which his expedition had come. But to him the term doubtless had no such meaning. Crèvecœur was the name of a celebrated French fortress, and it was hope, not despair, that led to the selection of the name.

broad Detroit, within a few miles of those islands whence, seven months before, they had looked out with such confidence upon the future. La Salle lost no time in pushing on to Fort Frontenac, where he arrived after a journey in all of sixty-five days. He was able to secure the necessary materials for his vessel, and in time he became master of the Mississippi.[1]

With the narration of the voyage of the *Griffin* the tale of discoveries along the Great Lakes is full. The Lake Superior region—the first of all Northwestern territory to be explored and to boast of settlements — a century and a half after Marquette's day became an unknown and despised wilderness; and statesmen of a nation undreamed of by the founders of New France pronounced these great waterways "beyond the furthest bounds of civilization—if not in the moon."[2] The virgin forests that La Salle was the first white man to tread were not to echo the sound of the settler's axe until the tide of immigration, sweeping through the land of the once-dreaded Iroquois, forced back the Huron remnants as it spread itself over those territories whence the Frenchman, and his English successors as well, confidently expected to draw an annual wealth of furs. The star of empire, that moved so rapidly westward during the second half of the seventeenth century, was to experience more than fifty years of wellnigh total eclipse before it again became the guide of the explorer.

[1] In 1781, La Salle reached the mouth of the Mississippi and named the valley Louisiana. In 1787, while on his way up the great river to Canada, he was murdered.

[2] Henry Clay's speech in 1829 on Senator Norvell's bill to grant lands to build the Sault Ste. Marie canal.

CHAPTER II

CADILLAC FOUNDS DETROIT

THE closing decade of the seventeenth century was a joyous period for New France. The great Frontenac well expressed the feelings of the people whom he governed when, in spite of his seventy years, he sprang into the midst of a circle of Indians gathered at Quebec and danced the war-dance to celebrate his victories. In 1690, simulating a confidence he was far from feeling, he had sent back to New England in disgrace the fleet with which Sir William Phips had confidently expected to capture Quebec; and the land-forces which, under the leadership of Fitz-John Winthrop, were to overrun Canada, never reached the borders of that country. Then, too, the Indian trade, which had been practically cut off by the raids of the Iroquois, began once more to animate the too-long-closed warehouses of Montreal; and France was in a position to assume the aggressive in all her territory from the mouth of the St. Lawrence, through the chain of the Great Lakes, and thence down the Mississippi, a region made hers by right of the discoveries of Marquette and Joliet and of La Salle.

Throughout the region of the upper lakes, however, the English were from time to time sending their scouts, the Iroquois, to open avenues of trade. Unhampered by monopolies or other fetters of feudalism, the English could sell goods a third cheaper than could their ene-

MOLL'S MAP OF THE NORTHWEST IN 1720

(*See page 165*)

mies, and at the same time make a larger profit. Then, again, no conscientious scruples seem to have deterred the English from supplying the Indians with all the rum they had furs to pay for; whereas the French, through their missionaries, had some regard for the morals of the persons they were bent on converting.

To check British advances Du Lhut, sent with fifty soldiers to the Detroit region in 1686, built Fort St. Joseph, at the head of the St. Clair River, near the present site of Port Huron; and the next year Henry de Tonty came across southern Michigan from his station in the Illinois country to the Detroit River,[1] where he met his cousin Du Lhut from the St. Clair, and La Forest and Durantaye from Michilimackinac, all going to assist Frontenac in chastising the Iroquois. On the way down from Michilimackinac, the two Frenchman had the fortune to fall in with and capture thirty Englishmen who had been sent by the indefatigable Governor Dongan, of New York, to capture that post; and a second English party, despatched to reinforce the first, was taken on Lake Erie. For fourteen years Fort St. Joseph was maintained—at least, we have M. de Longueuil's report of two conferences which he held with various tribes of Indians in the Detroit country in 1700, and in these[2] he speaks of "my fort at Detroit" being garrisoned by a small body of French. The object of his negotiations was to induce the Indians to take the war-path against the English on the Ohio, to extirpate "that scum," and to pillage their goods. La Hontan, who passed up the Detroit in the September of 1687, locates Fort St. Joseph on his map of that year. This fort, or earthwork, built

[1] *Louisiana Collections*, p. 69.

[2] *New York Collections Colonial MS.*, vol. ix., p. 704.

by Du Lhut at the foot of Lake Huron, was officially known as the fort at Detroit years before the foundation of the city that now bears the name once given to the entire region between Lakes Erie and Huron. It is probable, however, that instead of being maintained as a permanent post, Fort St. Joseph was simply a summer headquarters for detachments sent out as need was to hold the English in check. This would account for the fact that La Hontan, on his larger map, marks it as an abandoned post; and would also explain the lack of any mention of it in connection with Cadillac's rule over the upper lake territory.[1]

In 1694, Michilimackinac seemed to be the strategic point for the fur-trade; and in order to strengthen that post Frontenac sent thither Antoine de Lamothe Cadillac, a man after the governor-general's own heart. Shea, the great historian of the Catholic Church in colonial times, characterizes Cadillac as "chimerical, grasping, overbearing, regarding religion to be used for the purposes of government or as an element of trade." This is a half-truth. Cadillac was a born soldier, resource-

[1] Briefly the history of Fort St. Joseph is: Built by Du Lhut in 1686; abandoned as a regular post in 1688; occupied as a military station by the English in 1763; Governor Patrick Sinclair builds fortification on the site of St. Clair in 1785; artillery encampment at St. Clair, and skirmish between Americans and British in 1812; in May, 1814, Fort St. Joseph rebuilt and named Fort Gratiot, after Captain Charles Gratiot, U. S. A., the constructing engineer; 1822, post abandoned; 1828, reoccupied; 1832, cholera scourge carries off many soldiers stationed there on their way to the Black Hawk War; 1849, fort repaired; 1858, occupied by caretakers; 1862–5, occupied as recruiting-station; 1879, abandoned and land sold. It was in 1861, while his father was caretaker of Fort Gratiot, that Thomas A. Edison there erected his first electrical battery and began those experiments that have made him famous.—See *Michigan Pioneer Collections*, vol. xi., p. 249.

ful, prompt, and vigorous. He was also a soldier of fortune; and he had come to New France to achieve wealth through government concessions vigorously prosecuted. In those days the soldier was expected to live off the country. He fought the king's enemies indeed, but at the same time he protected his own property, and he regarded the Indian rather as a hunting-machine than as a brand to be plucked from the burning. Hence the Church historian of to-day has no more liking for the memory of La Salle or of Cadillac than the missionaries had for them personally. Indeed, when he reached his new post Cadillac was already under the ban of the Jesuits. During the winter of 1693, he was a member of the military circle that Frontenac had gathered about him at Quebec. The officers, to beguile the long winter evenings, arranged some theatricals, and rumor had it that one of the plays to be presented was Molière's "Tartuffe," in which the falsehood, lust, greed, and ambition of the priesthood are depicted. The storm of anathemas that swept over Canada had a violent centre at Mackinac, and Cadillac on reaching his new station found that the pious Jesuits at that post had prejudiced the officers against their commandant. His prompt action in imprisoning the insubordinate ones, while it established his own authority, resulted on the part of the Jesuits in an even more intense opposition to him and his plans.

In order to put a stop to the Indian intrigues, Cadillac resorted to measures which even the savages were at no loss to understand. The Iroquois had invited the Lake Indians to a council on the banks of the Detroit, and one evening after this meeting had been decided upon the Hurons brought to Michilimackinac seven Iroquois prisoners. As the party landed upon the beach, the

French, acting under orders, stabbed two of the Iroquois. The Hurons promptly defended the others, but finally were prevailed upon to give a chief into the hands of the whites, who at once sent to the Ottawas an invitation to drink the broth of an Iroquois. The victim was first tied to a stake, then tortured by burning with a gun-barrel heated red-hot, and was finally cut in pieces and eaten by the assembled Indians. At another time four Iroquois prisoners, taken in battle by parties sent out by Cadillac, were burned alive, in order to stir up strife between the Lake Indians and the Iroquois; and Cadillac promised that "if they bring any prisoners to me, I can assure you their fate will be no sweeter than that of the others."

In spite of such summary measures, however, Cadillac was unable to keep his Indians from being tampered with while on their way back from Montreal. The Iroquois were mingling with the Detroit Indians, and the only remedy was war. By selling all he possessed and giving his Indians credit, he succeeded in getting the chief Onaske to take the war-path with a strong party of braves. So vigorous was the chase that forty Iroquois, in order to escape their pursuers, jumped into a river and were drowned, thirty scalps and as many prisoners were taken, and four or five hundred beaver-skins, which the Iroquois intended to exchange for English goods, were seized as booty. This success put a stop to Iroquois advances until Cadillac was ready to meet them more than half way.[1]

[1] On the return of this war party Cadillac opened ten kegs of brandy, and, when the missionaries remonstrated, he replied: "If a little hilarity grieve you so much, how will you be able to endure daily exposure of these neophytes to unlimited English rum and heresy?"—See *N. Y. Col. Doc.*, vol. ix., p. 648; also, Parkman's *Half Century of Conflict*, vol. i., chap. 2.

NAKED INDIANS IN MONTREAL

Even to a much duller mind than Cadillac's it would have been clear that the place to check the advances of the Iroquois was not at Michilimackinac, but on the Detroit, through which narrow strait all travel and commerce must pass on their way between the lower and the upper lakes. This was also the key to the Mississippi region; and Robert Livingston had already made up his mind that if England should only seize and hold the Detroit, the French fur-trade would be ruined. Confident that he could easily persuade his superiors of the absolute necessity of occupying the strategic position at the Detroit, and equally sure that he saw a fine opening to make a fortune, Cadillac went to Quebec and there explained his ideas to a distinguished company of traders, headed by Callières, the Governor, and Champigny, the Intendant. A more politic advocate would have satisfied himself with presenting the military and commercial features of his plans, but the impetuous Cadillac laid great stress on the social and moral reformation he proposed to effect by teaching the natives to speak the French language.[1] He was on record as believing that the only fruits of the Jesuit missions consisted in the baptism of infants who died upon reaching the age of reason; and that while the Jesuits were ostensibly employed in the vain labor of saving souls, still they found ample time to enrich their order by traffic in furs. It was no wonder, therefore, that Cadillac met the open and powerful opposition of the Intendant, Champigny, who voiced the sentiment of his friends the Jesuits when he argued that if the savages were to be saved they must be kept as far as possible from the vices of civil-

[1] Cadillac's correspondence in regard to the Detroit settlement is calendared in the Canadian archives for 1887. It is also printed in vol. v. of Margry.

ization. Cadillac did not realize, and indeed it has remained for writers of our own day to point out, that to the savages the virtues of civilization are no less destructive than are its vices. The clothing, ammunition, and other presents provided by the whites begot among the Indians a comparative luxury and ease of living that created a demand for brandy.[1]

Unable to persuade the near-sighted authorities at Quebec, Cadillac carried his case over seas and made his arguments before Count Pontchartrain, the colonial minister of Louis XIV. Into the half-willing ear of the minister the impetuous soldier poured the torrent of his plans for a permanent post, with its garrison, its traders, its schools, and its tribes of friendly Indians, all working together for the advancement of France and the confusion of her enemies, the Iroquois and the English.

When the somewhat sceptical minister inquired how a post at the Detroit would keep the Indians from resorting to the English, the wily Cadillac replied that, although the *will* to go to the English and deal in the cheapest markets would still be present, yet "each savage, one with another, kills per year only fifty or sixty beavers, and, as he is neighbor to the Frenchman, frequently borrows of him, paying in proportion to the returns by the chase. With what little remains to him the Indian is compelled to make purchases for his family. Thus he finds himself unable to go to the English, because his remaining goods are not worth carrying so far. . . . Another reason is that in frequenting the French he receives many caresses; they are too cunning to allow his

[1] Benjamin Kidd in his *Social Evolution*, p. 47, quotes with approval the remark of another that among the causes to which the decay of the New Zealand natives might be attributed are "drink, disease, European clothing, peace, and wealth."

furs to escape, especially when they succeed in making him eat and drink with them."

Cadillac's reasoning seemed good, both to Count Pontchartrain and also to Louis XIV., who at the time was collecting his resources and recruiting his strength to get control of the Spanish succession. The fact that little money from the royal treasury was asked for doubtless made Cadillac's path an easier one; but there can be no doubt that the commander's energy, his uncompromising nature, and his apparent mastery over the conditions of frontier life won for him unusual concessions in the way of trade and land, concessions that were held the more precious in royal eyes because of the very fact that they were so intangible and so distant.[1]

Cadillac was promised protection against his enemies, the Jesuits; enough money and men to carry out his enterprise, and a tract of land fifteen arpents (acres) square, "wherever on the Detroit the new fōrt should be located." Thus equipped he set sail for America; and on June 2, 1701, he left La Chine with fifty soldiers and an equal number of Canadians. Alphonse de Tonty, a brother of La Salle's companion, was Cadillac's captain, and for lieutenants he had M. Dugué and M. Chacornacle. Taking the old route of Indians and traders, in order to avoid the Iroquois, the party paddled up the Ottawa River, made the thirty portages to Lake Nipissing, thence to Georgian Bay and by Lake Huron down to the Detroit. Arriving on the 24th day of July, Cadillac immediately set about making a strong stockade of wooden pickets, with bastions at the four angles.

[1] The documents relating to Cadillac's dealings with Count Pontchartrain are given in Sheldon's *Early History of Michigan;* they are also to be found in part in Margry, vol. v. General Cass furnished the papers to Mrs. Sheldon.

Inside the palisade a few stake-houses were built. To this work the commandant gave the name of Fort Pontchartrain, after the minister to whose interest it was due. The chapel, begun on the feast-day of Saint Ann, July 26, was named in her honor, and this name the successive churches have kept to this day. The little settlement that sprang up about the fort was generally spoken of as Detroit.

The control of the trade with the Indians had been granted to one of those monopolies which at that day were the leading feature of the French economic policy. Among the directors of this Company of the Colony the Jesuits found powerful friends; for the sufficient reason that Cadillac's new enterprise threatened to create a body of independent traders, and so to cut into the profits of the monopoly. Moreover, the success of the settlement at Detroit meant the abandonment by both soldiers and Indians of the post at Michilimackinac, and hence the loss of an old and prominent mission. Accommodating as he was in speech, Cadillac never failed to recognize an enemy, and never lost an opportunity to trample his foes under his feet. To Count Pontchartrain he wrote that the only way to get along with the Jesuits was, "first, to let them do as they please; secondly, to do as they please; and thirdly, to say nothing of what they do." Then with a nice affectation of humility he adds: "If I let the Jesuits do as they please, the savages will not establish themselves at Detroit; if I do as they would desire, it will be necessary to abandon this post; and if I say nothing of what they do, it will only be necessary for me to pursue my present course." Three paragraphs further on in this same letter the old Adam gets the better of the commandant. "Thirty Hurons," he says, "arrived from Michilimackinac on the 28th of

THE LANDING OF CARDILLAC

June (1703). There remained only about twenty-five. Father Carheil, who is missionary there, remains always firm. I hope this Autumn to pluck the last feather out of his wing; and I am persuaded that this obstinate old priest will die in his parish without a single parishioner to bury him." It would be impossible to pay a higher tribute than Cadillac unwittingly pays to the zeal and long-suffering of the old missionary, who saw his flock lured away by the brandy and the vices at the new fort. He labored on until 1705, being sustained by the companionship of Father Aveneau from St. Joseph, whence also the Indians had been lured to Detroit. Then the two, finding themselves without parishioners, burned their chapel, lest it should be profaned, and departed for Quebec.

The eager Cadillac had plans for a copper-mine on Lake Huron; for silk-culture among the mulberry-trees of Lake Erie; for a uniformed Indian militia; for a seminary in which to teach the French language to the savages; and for grants of lands to settlers. In short, he designed to plant at Detroit not simply a trading-post, but a colony. He spoke of himself as one whom "God had raised up to be another Moses to go and deliver the Indians from captivity; or rather, as Caleb, to bring them back to the lands of their fathers. . . . Meanwhile, Montreal (the Jesuits) plays the part of Pharaoh; he cannot see this emigration without trembling, and he arms himself to destroy it."

Cadillac was especially incensed against the Jesuits on account of their opposition to the sale of spirits. So strong was their hostility that Louis XIV. in 1694, referred to the Sorbonne for decision of the question of allowing French brandy to be shipped to Michilimackinac. The decision of the council gave to the Northwest its first prohibitory law; and the commandant was no more willing to enforce the order than his successors have been to carry out similar laws. "A drink of brandy after the repast," he maintained, "seems necessary to cook the bilious meats and the crudities which they leave in the stomach." Again, at Detroit, Cadillac quotes from a sermon by Father Carheil, whose wing he was engaged in plucking. The Jesuit had maintained that there was "no power, either human or divine, which can permit the sale of this drink." "Hence you perceive," argues the crafty commandant, "that this father passes boldly on all matters of state, and will not even submit to the decision of the pope."

The question was indeed a hard one for Cadillac. He understood clearly that unless he had liquor to sell to the savages he might as well abandon the post; for the Indians would go straight to the English at Albany where goods were cheap and rum was unlimited. To give up Detroit never entered into Cadillac's plans. He therefore chose the middle course. Instead of prohibition he would have high license. In the restrictions which he threw about the traffic in liquors he was both honest and earnest; and, as events proved, he was far in advance of his times. In the report of M. d'Aigrement,[1] who inspected Detroit in 1708, it is mentioned as one of the grievances of the savages against Cadillac, that "in order to prevent disturbances which would arise from the excessive use of brandy, he causes it all to be put into the storehouse, and sold at the rate of twenty francs a quart. Those who will have it, French as well as Indians, are obliged to go to the storehouse to drink, and

[1] Mrs. Sheldon gives this report in full, in her *Early History of Michigan.*

each can obtain, at one time, only the twenty-fourth part of a quart. It is certain that the savages cannot become intoxicated on that quantity. The price is high, and as they can get brandy only each in his turn, it sometimes happens that the savages are obliged to return home without a taste of this beverage, and they seem ready to kill themselves with disappointment."

It is refreshing to be able for a time to turn from the petty squabbles between Cadillac and his Jesuit enemies, and to leave the bickerings between the commandant and the traders which fill so many pages of Margry,[1] in order to trace what is to us far more important—the beginnings of family life in the Northwest. In a friendly letter from Père Germain at Quebec to Lamothe Cadillac, at Detroit, dated August 25, 1701, the writer tells of the intense desire of Madame Cadillac to join her husband; and he quotes the reply which that most dutiful wife made to the dames of her native city, when they expostulated with her for proposing to brave the wilderness. "When a woman loves her husband as she ought," responded the plucky wife, "there is nothing more attractive than his society, wherever he may be. All else should be indifferent to her." Suiting the action to the word, she started with Madame Tonty for a companion, and so soon as the ice-bolts had unlocked Detroit in the spring of 1702, the two women arrived safely, and each was installed as the mistress of a stake-house within the palisades of Fort Pontchartrain.

[1] While Lewis Cass was minister to France, he obtained copies of many of the documents relating to the early history of the Northwest; and at his instigation, Margry, the keeper of the records in the Department of the Marine, began to gather those documents which, by the aid of this government, he has published, to the great assistance of historians.

At the time of their marriage Cadillac was less than thirty years old; and already he had seen much of the world. A native of Gascony, the exact place of Cadillac's birth has as yet defied discovery; nor is the year of his birth beyond dispute.[1] It is evident from his writings, however, that he was educated beyond what was common in those days. His pen was ever as ready as his sword; and both were absolutely tireless. He fought his enemies incessantly, both with the rapier of his keen wit and the arquebus of his multitudinous arguments. Yet he was naturally of a kindly disposition, and was the sort of man that a woman would follow to the ends of the earth. Married on the 25th of June, 1687, to Marie Thérèse Guyon, of Quebec, it is probable that the early years of their married life were spent at Port Royal, where Cadillac held a royal grant of land;[2] but a long separation came when he was ordered to Michilimackinac, where ways were rough and food was limited as well in quantity as in variety.[3]

The wives of commandant and captain having led the

[1] *A Sketch of the Life of Antoine de la Mothe Cadillac,* by C. M. Burton (Detroit, 1895), p. 6. Mr. Burton's researches into the early life of Cadillac have been both painstaking and untiring. He has copies of all of Cadillac's manuscripts and of every paper to be found either in France or America that can throw any light on Cadillac. Silas Farmer's *History of Detroit and Michigan* also contains much material gathered at home and abroad. A short sketch of Cadillac is to be found in Parkman's *Half Century of Conflict*, vol. i., p. 17.

[2] Curiously enough, just a century after Cadillac's marriage, his granddaughter, with her husband and three children, became citizens of the United States, and by virtue of an act of the legislature of Massachusetts had restored to them the holdings of Cadillac at a time when he was styled Lord of Donaquec and Mont Desert. Many of the Mount Desert titles are based on this royal grant.

[3] Cadillac writes of the Michilimackinac station: "Neither bread nor meat is eaten there, and no other food is to be had but a little fish and Indian-corn."—*N. Y. Col. Doc.*, ix., p. 586.

way, those of the traders and soldiers were not slow to follow; and gradually there came to be a number of homes at Detroit, with all that the word home then implied. On the oldest of the now extant French parish registers in the west, under the date of February 2, 1704, is recorded the baptism of the seventh of Cadillac's thirteen children,[1] and in the course of the ten years of his sojourn three others were born in Detroit and were duly baptized by the priests of St. Ann's. The same record bears witness to the fact that the wife of one of the habitans at Detroit was the mother of no fewer than thirty children; and that large families were the rule.

If we were to believe implicitly the glowing accounts Cadillac gives to Count Pontchartrain of his success at Detroit, then never was a colony more prosperous. It is true that in 1703 a fire, maliciously started, as Cadillac says, burned the houses of the commandant and of Tonty, together with the church and a portion of the palisades; that Tonty and others conspired to cheat the Company of the Colony by selling the company's goods and retaining the proceeds;[2] that the Indians were ever

[1] Cadillac's eldest son accompanied his father as a cadet. Another son went to Detroit with his mother, two girls being left in school at Quebec. Shea in his *History of the Catholic Church* gives a fac-simile of the record of the baptism. The register itself is in the possession of Mr. R. R. Elliott of Detroit.

[2] Alphonse Tonty, Baron of Paludy, was born in 1659; he became jealous of Cadillac and plotted against him, and out of this plot came the incendiary fire of 1703 that burned a considerable portion of Detroit, including the first St. Ann's Church, the house of the Recollects, and the first parish register. Tonty's daughter Thérèsa was the first child known to have been born in Detroit. Tonty was acting commandant at Detroit from 1704 to 1706, during Cadillac's absence at Quebec to answer charges brought against him; and also from 1720 till his death, November 10, 1727. He was buried at Detroit. His son, Charles Henry Tonty, became governor at Fort St. Louis (Mobile), where Henry Tonty died in 1704.

troublesome; and the Jesuits were persistent in their efforts to ruin the enterprise. But Cadillac was never for a moment discouraged, and the proof that he was correct in his predictions as to the ultimate success and importance of the post is to be found in the fact that Detroit alone, of all the upper lake establishments, has continued to grow in strength and population from the day it was founded down to the present time.

There was much truth, however, in the official report of M. d'Aigrement, who in 1708 spent nineteen July days at Detroit. He found that Cadillac was far from being popular with either the savages or the colonists. Parent, the blacksmith, complained that he had to pay annually six hundred francs and two casks of ale for the privilege of plying his trade; and besides he was compelled to keep all Cadillac's horses shod. To be sure, the commandant had but one horse, yet there was no certainty that he would not have fifty others the next year. Then, too, Pinet,[1] the gunsmith, was required to repair twelve guns each month, besides paying three hundred francs a year. The people also grumbled becaused Cadillac took as grist toll an eighth instead of the customary fourteenth part, although it was admitted that the cost of the mill had been excessive. Of the three hundred and fifty roods of valuable land, Cadillac owned one hundred and fifty-seven, while the French owned but forty-six, and the Hurons held one hundred and fifty; moreover, the commandant required the soldiers and savages to break his land, and make it ready

[1] Joseph Parent, farmer, master-toolmaker, and brewer, came to Detroit in 1606, under a contract for three years of service at his trades. Yves Pinet, gunsmith, came at the same time under a similar contract. The sums mentioned are excessive when compared with the usual rates charged by Cadillac.

COUREUR DE BOIS

for planting. Inside the fort the people owned twenty-nine small log-houses thatched with grass. Of the sixty-three settlers, thirty-four were traders, and the only profitable articles of traffic were ammunition and brandy, the English being able to undersell the French in all other commodities. Cadillac himself bought for four francs a quart the brandy that he sold for twenty francs; he charged two francs and ten sous a front rood for grounds within the palisades, and a double price for corner lots. Besides, each trader paid an annual tax of ten francs for the privilege of dealing with the Indians.

"The soil is poor," continues d'Aigrement, "and is full of water; it is fitted to raise Indian-corn and nothing else; the cider made from native apples is as bitter as gall; and the grasshoppers eat all the garden plants, so that they have to be planted three and four times over." "On the whole," says this pessimistic investigator, "the post was a mistake, and it should be abandoned."

Admitting the truth of all that M. d'Aigrement has alleged, the colony at Detroit experienced only the vicissitudes usual to settlements in New France. The wilderness develops traits not pleasing to contemplate —jealousy, insubordination, and tyranny among them; and the intensity with which these elements of discord operate depends on local circumstances and on race tendencies. Both Louis XIV. and Count Pontchartrain understood the situation; and, within reasonable limits, they were ready to support the zealous Cadillac.

Struggling resolutely to erect at Detroit a marquisate according to the feudal ideas of his day, in 1705 Cadillac wrested from the Company of the Colony the trading privileges at his post, and in addition obtained full authority to make grants of town lots within and of farms without the palisades. The fort itself belonged to him in the same sense that a French castle belonged to its lord; even the church, with its vestments, its bell, and its lock, belonged to the commandant; the brewery, the forge, the grist-mill, the very fruit-trees brought in boxes from Montreal, all were counted among Cadillac's personal possessions. His, too, was that appendage of feudalism, the great dove-cot set high on oak posts; and also the long warehouse with press for baling furs, and the barns for his abundant crops of wheat, his ten cattle, and his horse-of-all-work, known throughout the settlement by the name of Colin.

As Cadillac walked the narrow St. Ann street, his sword clanking at his heels, and his rich military dress proclaiming his importance, every hat was doffed at his approach, and there was none to say him nay, save only Father Cherubin de Deniaux, the Recollect priest of St. Ann. According to their custom the people took their petty disputes to the priest; but justice, such as it was, came from the commandant, who claimed even the power of life and death.

The space within the palisades was of a width of two city blocks and a depth of one. Besides Cadillac's own buildings—ten in number—the holdings of sixty-eight others are known; and thirteen half-acre gardens granted to soldiers have been located. Above the fort thirty-one farms were apportioned to farmers who lived within the wooden defences; and at convenient distances villages of Ottawas, Miamis, Hurons, Loups, and Openagos were located, while even the inquisitive Iroquois were welcomed as visitors, although they were not encouraged to settle. Altogether, the town could boast a population of some six thousand souls or, better, mouths.[1]

The king, however, had other work for the restless and ambitious commandant at Detroit; and in May, 1710, Pontchartrain ordered him to proceed forthwith to Louisiana as the governor of the province that La-Salle and Henry Tonty had founded. With no mind to surrender his property without full compensation, Cadillac so far disregarded his orders as to go down to Montreal and Quebec to settle his affairs, leaving his capable and business-like wife to secure a full and exact inventory of his possessions; and when in June, 1713, he and his family landed in Louisiana, he was conveyed to his new station directly from France, as became his station, in a French frigate. Natchez owes its beginning and Lakes Pontchartrain and Maurepas owe their names to Cadillac; he searched the Mississippi valley for silver and found lead; but there as at Detroit he chafed under the conditions surrounding him, and in 1717 he returned to France to find employment as governor of Castell Sarrazin, where he died on October 18, 1730. In vain he tried to establish his claims at Detroit. The utmost he could obtain was an offer of 4359 livres, made in 1720; but this he rejected, and perhaps his governorship was intended as the gratitude of a monarchy.[2]

Cadillac turned over to his successor, Joseph Guyon Dubuisson, a fairly flourishing establishment, as such

[1] "Cadillac's Village, or Detroit under Cadillac, with a List of Property-owners and a History of the Settlement from 1701 to 1710," by Clarence M. Burton (Detroit, 1896). This pamphlet of thirty-five pages is a nearly complete city directory of Detroit under Cadillac, and is a marvel of antiquarian research in a hitherto unworked field.

[2] For the correspondence relative to Cadillac's claims, see Canadian Archives, 1887, p. cclxxvii.

ventures went in those days. No sooner had Cadillac departed, however, than a thousand and more Mascoutins and Ottagamies from the region west of Green Bay appeared (1712) at Detroit and prepared to establish themselves there. Now the Mascoutins were deadly enemies of the Hurons; but, unfortunately, both the Hurons and Ottawas were away on their winter hunt, and so weak was the garrison that, for the time being, Dubuisson was forced to put up with the lawlessness and insolence of the new-comers. They killed his pigeons, took whatever goods were outside the fort, and began to fortify a camp fixed within hailing distance of Fort Pontchartrain. In his consternation Dubuisson sent messengers to scour the woods for the absent hunters; and he also took the precaution to pull down the church of St. Ann, outside the palisades, lest it should afford a lodgement for the attacking Indians. Under fire he effected the removal of the wheat from the exposed storehouse to the fort: fortunately the cattle had not been sent to pasture.

About the middle of May, as Dubuisson relates in his official report,[1] news came of the approach of the hunting-parties. The two swivels were mounted on logs and provided with slings of iron made by the fort blacksmith; Father Cherubin held himself ready to give a general absolution, and to assist the wounded. Then Dubuisson himself mounted the bastion and watched for the expected help. Soon his straining eyes beheld a movement among the budding trees at the back of the long farms, and from the thick coverts rushed the savages—Illinois, Missouris, Osages, Pottawatomies, Sacs, and

[1] This report is given entire in Smith's *History of Wisconsin*, vol. iii. See also Parkman's *Half Century of Conflict*, vol. i., p. 269.

Menominees—with the Ottawa chief Saguina (Saginaw) at their head. Never before had Detroit seen such a collection of people. Running, yelping, waving their tribal emblems, the red host made for the Huron village, but were turned to the fort by the stay-at-homes, who pointed to the fires in the enemy's camp, crying, "They are burning the women of your village, Saguina, and your wife is among them. Hasten to our father's fort; he has ever had pity on you, and now you should be willing to die for him."

Into the fort swarmed the allies, and on the parade-ground held a council with the commandant, saying: "Father, last year you drew from the fires our flesh, which the Ottagamies were about to roast and eat. Now we bring you our bodies and make you master of them. Care for our women and children, and if we die throw a blade of grass upon our bones to protect them from the flies. And now give us something to eat and tobacco to smoke; we have come from afar and have neither powder nor balls to fight with." These necessaries being forthcoming, the siege of the enemy was begun. For nineteen days the interlopers were kept under fire. Their kindred coming to join them were taken in the woods, and first were made targets of and then were burned for sport; if brave or squaw ventured to the river for water, death was almost certain; if they dug holes to escape the fire of the besiegers, the latter fired down on them from high towers.

One morning the French saw the palisades of their enemies hung with scarlet blankets, while twelve other such sanguinary emblems flew from standards set up within the enclosure. "These," the Mascoutins called to the fort, "are the signals of the English. We have no father but the English king." The Pottawatomie chief, however, answered that the English were the enemies of prayer, so that the Master of Life chastises them; and that their only power was in the liquor which they gave to the Indians to poison them. Then followed unavailing parleys, during which the enemies showed so bold a front that the allies became discouraged and threatened to go away. The enemies, they said, are braver than any other people; it is useless to fight them. The French, too, began to talk of escaping to Michilimackinac; but Dubuisson was able to put heart into them all. Deserters told that in the beleaguered palisade over sixty women and children had died of hunger and thirst, and that their bodies were without burial; and presents and promises were made without stint to the allies. Then, one dark and rainy night, the enemy slipped away to Grosse Pointe, where, after four days of fighting, the end came. Of the three hundred braves behind the improvised defences, not more than one-third escaped. The women and children were spared; but the men were reserved for the sport of their conquerors, who killed three or four each day. So the first siege of Detroit ended in a bloody victory for the garrison, and the annihilation of the Ottagamies and Mascoutins. The price of the victory to the French treasury was about three thousand livres; and one-eighth of this sum was required to pay for the blankets, leggings, and shirts that formed the final equipment of the eight principal Indian allies on their enforced journey to the happy hunting-grounds.

Misfortunes elsewhere aided the upbuilding of the new colony on the Detroit. The collapse of Law's brilliant system of administering the financial and commercial affairs of France in 1721 sent to America many a ruined Frenchman, and not a few found refuge at Detroit.

Among the new-comers were the Chapoton, Goyon, and Lauderoute families, names that in one form or another are still numerous in the Detroit city directory.[1] In 1730 Robert Navarre, in whose veins ran royal blood, established himself as royal notary and sub-delegate of the Intendant of New France, being the first civil magistrate to exercise his office within the present boundaries of the Northwest. Later, in 1755, the banished Acadians, with Gabriel seeking the Beautiful River,[2] left several of their number on the banks of a river not less beautiful than the Ohio.

So uneventful for Detroit was the second quarter of the eighteenth century, that its history is to be read only in the account-books of Father de La Richardie, Superior of the Huron mission at Detroit. In these voluminous records of every-day life at Detroit it is shown that Cadillac was clearly right in saying that the priests, while occupied in saving souls, were most thrifty withal. Under the good father's able direction the garrison was reduced to dependence on the enterprising mission. When a cow was wanted to furnish an Indian barbecue, it was supplied by the mission farmer on Bois Blanc island, who held his well-stocked acres on the condition that he should furnish firewood, chickens, lard, and suet to the good fathers, and also give to the mission half the produce of the farm. The blacksmith also worked on shares; the mission storekeeper supplied the

[1] French proper names are somewhat of a puzzle even after the best of explanations available. The Casse family appeared in Detroit in Cadillac's time. They came from the town of St. Aubin, and for a time were called Casse *dit* St. Aubin; later, "Casse" disappeared, leaving the still persistent family of St. Aubin. Nicknames became family names; and a distinguished female ancestor often furnished the name by which her descendants were known.

[2] The Ohio was called by the French La Belle Rivière.

commandant at the fort with both his canoes and his wines; and the small traders replenished their stocks of wampum-beads, vermilion, knives, powder, and ball at the mission store, where the lay-brother, La Tour, was in charge. Thus Father de la Richardie became the first wholesale merchant at Detroit; and the exactness with which he kept the accounts is evidence that there was profit on other wares besides the masses, which are charged along with the vermilion, the *chemises de femme*, the wheat, and the wampum.[1] Besides his traffic in merchandise, the Superior of the Huron mission dealt in real estate, both within and outside of the palisades; and it was due to him that the Hurons gave up their valuable possessions on the northern borders of the growing town, and removed their long houses to the mission domain of Father de la Richardie, across the river, where the town of Sandwich now stands.

In order to thwart the movements the English were making unceasingly to seduce the Indian nations of the North, Count Repentigny, a native of Canada and an ensign in the French army, was sent about 1751 to Sault Ste. Marie, to make there a palisade fort to stop the Indians on their way to the English posts; and to seize the presents and to intercept the commerce that passed be-

[1] After the departure of Cadillac, opposition being withdrawn, the Jesuits had established themselves at Detroit during the rule of Alphonse de Tonty, who was commandant from 1717 till his death, ten years later. Under the title of *The Jesuit Manuscript*, Mr. Richard R. Elliott published in the Detroit Sunday *News*, during May, 1891, full translations of these account-books. Files are in the Congressional Library and in the Detroit Public Library. From the entries it would appear that the Cuilleriers, husband and wife, were among the principal traders: Charles St. Aubin dealt in furs; Parent was the carpenter; Derruisseau sapped the maples; Carrigan de Cealle and M. Goyon were the millers.

INDIAN HUNTER OF 1750

tween the Upper Lake savages and the rivals of France. The post was to be also a retreat for the French voyageurs trading in the northwestern country; and to that end land was to be cleared, Indian-corn was to be planted, and stock was to be supplied, all at the expense of Repentigny and his partner, Captain Louis De Bonne. In return for such services they received, on October 18, 1750, a grant "in perpetuity by title of feof and seigniory" of six leagues along the portage with a depth of six leagues. During the four years of his stay, the young count reared a small fort, cleared and planted a few acres, built three or four log-huts for his men, and for stock brought thither seven head of cattle and two horses; but the victories of war were more to the taste of Chevalier Repentigny than were the triumphs of peace, and at the battle of Sillery, in 1760, he fought by the side of his partner De Bonne in the vain attempt to recapture Quebec from the English. It was De Bonne's last fight; and when England won the French possessions in the new world, Repentigny, refusing the most pressing offers from the British governor to return to his northern seigniory and cast his lot with the conquerors, left his native country first to fight the Indians in Newfoundland, and finally to become a major-general and the governor of Senegal, in which honorable position death overtook him in 1786. Meantime the Indians, in 1762, burned his fort, and the lands once more became the hunting and fishing grounds of the red men, and so continued for half a century.[1]

[1] In 1824–5 the original brevet of ratification of the De Bonne-Repentigny grant, signed by the King of France, was presented to Mr. Graham, the Commissioner of the General Land Office. During all the intervening years the De Bonne rights had been transferred from person to person; first by De Bonne's son, who sold to James Cald-

Throughout the Northwest, at the numerous portages between the headwaters of the rivers, French traders and woodrangers established themselves, obtaining supplies from Quebec and Montreal, or from the nearer posts of Detroit or Michilimackinac. Little by little the power of the government relaxed, and the individual trader became the controlling force. At Detroit the French inhabitants intermarried scarcely at all with the Indians; and generally family pride held back the thrifty Frenchman from open alliances with Indian maidens; but in the remote settlements there was no such hesitation. There Frenchman and Indian slept in the same hut and ate out of the same dish. It will not be strange if they shall be found shooting with the same gun.

well, of Albany, New York, for £1570⅜. The final possessor was John Rolton, a lieutenant-colonel in the English army. Neither Repentigny nor any of his descendants ever transferred their interests by will or deed; but in 1800 and again in 1846 the Repentigny heirs formally asserted their claims. On April 19, 1860, Congress authorized the two sets of claimants to proceed in the courts; and accordingly the cause was tried, first, in the United States District Court at Detroit, where the claimants were successful; and finally in the Supreme Court, where the decree of the court below was reversed. The case was argued by Jacob M. Howard for the claimants, and by Attorney-General Stanbery and United States District Attorney Alfred Russell for the government. The title of the case is the United States *vs.* Louise Pauline le Gardiur de Repentigny *et al.*, reported in 8 Wall. As to the Repentigny claims, the court held that the count, on refusing to become a British subject and in failing to claim his possessions at Sault Ste. Marie within the time specified in the treaty between France and England, abandoned his rights; the De Bonne claims were rejected on the ground that failure to maintain the fort and settlement caused the lands to revert to the State, and that the United States, by surveying and selling the lands, had worked such reversion.

CHAPTER III

THE ENGLISH IN THE OHIO COUNTRY

THE daring enterprise of the French trader and the devoted heroism of the French missionary in their discovery of the Northwest have been related. Up the rapids of the St. Lawrence, through the chain of the vast inland seas, and down the rushing waters of the Mississippi swept the tide of French discovery. With the exception of a strip of land lying along the Atlantic and extending scarcely a hundred miles back into the wilderness, the continent of North America at the middle of the eighteenth century belonged to his most Christian majesty by the well-recognized right of discovery and occupation. In the court of nations it mattered nothing that the soil was in the actual possession not of Frenchmen but of Indians, and that the foot of white man had never trod more than the smallest fraction of the country over which France claimed dominion. While recognizing the policy of conciliating the Indians, France, nevertheless, claimed the exclusive right to acquire from them, and to dispose of, the land which they occupied, and to make laws for the government of the country.

In the year 1498, more than a third of a century before Jacques Cartier's little vessel ploughed her way up the broad St. Lawrence, the Cabots discovered the continent of North America, and sailed south as far as Virginia.

Acting under their charter[1] to discover countries then unknown to Christian people, and to take possession of them in the name of the King of England, these bold adventurers laid the foundations of the English title to the Atlantic coast.[2] It was not until the beginning of the seventeenth century, however, that France and England followed up their discoveries, and began to perfect their respective titles by actual occupation of the regions discovered by their venturesome navigators.

In the year 1584, Sir Walter Raleigh, "the first man in England who had a right conception of the advantages of settlements abroad," and the only person who at that time had a thorough insight into trade and the proper methods of promoting it, "looked through the work of an age at one glance" and saw how advantageous it might be made to the trade of England to people the new world.[3] Applying to that most enterprising of monarchs, Queen Elizabeth, he secured from his royal patron free liberty and license to discover, search, find out and view remote, heathen, and barbarous lands not actually possessed of any Christian prince, nor inhabited by Christian people.[4]

[1] *The Voyages of the Cabots,* Old South Leaflets, general series, No. 37.

[2] "So early as the year 1496, her (England's) monarch granted a commission to the Cabots, to discover countries then unknown to *Christian people,* and to take possession of them in the name of the King of England. Two years afterwards Cabot proceeded on this voyage, and discovered the continent of North America, along which he sailed as far south as Virginia. To this discovery the English trace their title."—Opinion by Mr. Chief-justice Marshall, Johnson *vs.* McIntosh, 8 Wheaton, p. 571.

[3] *An Account of the European Settlements in America,* vol. ii., p. 218. This work, published anonymously, was written by Edmund Burke.

[4] *Historical Collections,* consisting of State Papers, by Ebenezer Hazard, contains Raleigh's patent, the assignment of it, the first and second charters of Virginia, and other like important documents.

SEBASTIAN CABOT

Raleigh himself was too much engrossed with affairs of state to lead colonists in America; but in 1585 his captain, Sir Richard Grenville, founded upon Roanoke Island, in the present State of North Carolina, the first English settlement established on the continent of North America. The times, however, forbade the success of the undertaking; for the invincible Spanish Armada must be destroyed before colonization could flow unvexed across the seas. Thus it happened that it was not until 1607 that Raleigh's successors planted at Jamestown the first permanent English settlement in America. In 1609, under a new and enlarged charter, the "Treasurer and Company of Merchant Adventurers of the City of London for the First Colony in Virginia" became possessed in absolute property of the lands extending along the sea-coast two hundred miles north and the same distance south from Old Point Comfort, and into the land throughout from sea to sea.[1]

Again, in 1620, a charter was granted to the Duke of Lenox and others, organized under the name of the Plymouth Company, conveying to them all the lands between the fortieth and the forty-eighth degrees of north latitude. In the course of time these special charters were either annulled or surrendered, and the title to the lands revested in the crown, to be disposed of from time to time as his majesty might see fit, in creating colonies along the Atlantic.

These early grants of lands, stretching from the known

[1] It was then believed that the parallel 40° was two hundred miles north of Cape Comfort. The instruments of measurement, however, were clumsy, and the computed length of a degree was not accurate, as Sir Isaac Newton found, nearly a century later. See "The Limits of Virginia," by Hon. Littleton W. Tazewell, in the *Virginia Historical Register*, 1848, p. 17.

Atlantic back through unknown regions to the illusive South Sea dreamed of by adventurers through the ages, comprised within their infinite parallels all the Northwest save only the upper two-thirds of the present States of Michigan and Wisconsin. The lines of Virginia included the lower half of Ohio, Indiana, and Illinois; Connecticut, by virtue of her charter, claimed the upper half of that territory; and Massachusetts likewise obtained the shadow of a title to the southern half of Wisconsin and of the lower peninsula of Michigan. However, it was not until the Treaty of 1763 brought these regions within the actual possession of the British crown that the claims of Connecticut and Massachusetts could be made even upon paper. New York, too, had unsubstantial claims to the Ohio country, based on the conquests of its allies the Iroquois.

In 1624, the Virginia corporation having been dissolved by due process of law, both the powers of government and the title to the lands revested in the crown of England.[1] Thus the colony was changed from a proprietary to a royal government, and the lands within its

[1] By the judgment of the Court of King's Bench on a writ of *quo warranto*, 8 Wheaton, pp. 545, 578.

The phrase "due process of law" must be regarded as a legal fiction. The facts are that King James, acting under Spanish influences, became jealous of the growth and power of the London Company, and determined to put an end to it. When Parliament would have resented such action against the interests of many of its members who were also members of the company, the Speaker read a message from the king, forbidding that body to meddle with the matter; and later, when the case on the *quo warranto* came up before the Court of King's Bench, the Attorney-general gravely argued that the company, under its charter, might depopulate England to people Virginia. Such a catastrophe being too dreadful to contemplate, the Chief-justice declared the charter thenceforth to be null and void. See Fiske's *Old Virginia and Her Neighbors*, vol. i., p. 219.

borders were at the disposal of the king, and so continued until Virginia became a free and independent State. For a century from the dissolution of the Virginia corporation and the establishment of the royal government, the colonists found the lands east of the Alleghanies sufficiently extensive for their uses. They had come to the New World to establish homes for themselves and their posterity; and while an occasional trader penetrated the wilderness of the interior to barter with the Indians, yet there was in Virginia no organized traffic with the savages, such as flourished in Pennsylvania and New York.[1]

The early colonists of Virginia had spread themselves over the country. Towns were few and there was no general trade. Selecting a commanding site on the banks of one of the numerous tidewater streams, the Virginia planter reared his stately mansion of wood, fashioned on the lines of a Greek temple. There, surrounded by his black slaves and white dependents, he lived his solitary life in true patriarchal style. Negroes imported from Africa tilled his broad acres planted with tobacco, a product that, like the flocks of early times, played the double part of the medium and the material of exchange. His one vital connection with the great world was the annual ship that came from England, bringing both the necessities and the luxuries of civilization; and returned laden with tobacco consigned to the

[1] In a letter to the Council of Trade, dated December 15, 1710, Governor Spotswood proposed a plan for carrying the Virginia settlements to the source of the James River, beyond the Blue Ridge, with a view of interposing between the French on the St. Lawrence and those on the Mississippi, and also to establishing trade with the Indians. From this letter it is to be inferred that there were already a few Virginia traders. Spotswood's *Official Letters*, Richmond, 1882, p. 40.

planter's London agent, who not only sold the product, but also made purchases of clothing, furniture, books, and wines for the planter's use. Royalists, aristocrats, firm believers in Church and State, these Virginians kept up all the traditions of England. Often they sent their sons to the mother-country to be educated; the young men served in the British army or navy during the frequent wars waged between England and France; and members of the British nobility, together with naval officers of rank and reputation, were welcome sharers of the abundant hospitality proverbial among the planters.

The Washington family may be taken as a type of tidewater Virginians. Belonging to the party of the king, the brothers John and Andrew Washington had come to America about the middle of the seventeenth century, when so many of the cavaliers found it convenient to escape from the rule of Cromwell. They purchased land between the Potomac and Rappahannock; John married, became a considerable planter, a fighter against the Indians, and a member of the House of Burgesses. As the family persisted from generation to generation, the estate increased; and three-quarters of a century after the coming of the brothers to America, the great-grandson of John had become the head of an established and influential colonial family. In the war that broke out between Spain and France and England in 1740, this Lawrence Washington went to the West Indies as a captain in the colonial regiment raised to aid the king; and during his military service he formed the acquaintance of men of the great world. As his father and grandfathers before him had set themselves to add to their domains, so Lawrence Washington was anxious to increase his holdings of land; and to this end he and his brother Augustine joined others of

LAWRENCE WASHINGTON

(From a portrait by an unknown artist, in possession of Lawrence Washington, Alexandria, Virginia.)

like wealth and influence with themselves to organize a company for the purpose of settling the western country and trading with the Indians.

Lawrence Washington had married a daughter of the Hon. William Fairfax, whose cousin, Lord Fairfax, inherited the rich lands of the Culpeper grant made by Charles II., and comprising, in part, the greater portion of the Shenandoah Valley. Lord Fairfax was a graduate of Oxford; in early life he had been a man of fashion in London; and he had actually contributed one or two papers to the *Spectator*. A disappointment in love had driven him into the wilderness of the New World; and in the midst of the beautiful Shenandoah Valley he had built for himself a home that served as a resting-place between fox-hunts, and a place of business in his dealings with his tenants and the settlers to whom he sold his broad acres. The favorite companion of his lordship was George Washington, a younger brother of Lawrence. Young Washington, then a strapping youth of sixteen, enjoyed to the utmost the sport of riding to hounds; but his occupation was to make the surveys necessary for the sale of the lands to the thousands of immigrants then flocking into the fertile valley.[1]

During the first half of the eighteenth century there

[1] In August, 1716, Governor Spotswood, leading a party of fifteen gentlemen, rangers, pioneers, Indians, and servants into the Shenandoah Valley, had reached the watershed between the rivers flowing into the Atlantic and those emptying into the Ohio. That the party was a merry one may be inferred from the fact that they drank the health of King George the First in Virginia wine both red and white, Irish usquebaugh, brandy, shrub, two kinds of rum, champagne, canary, cherry-punch, and cider. The distance traversed was 219 miles from Williamsburg. Campbell's *Virginia* (Philadelphia, 1860), p. 387.

came into Virginia a numerous immigration, chiefly from Germany and the north of Ireland. Edmund Burke, writing in 1761, places the number of white people in Virginia at between sixty and seventy thousand;[1] and, he says, "they are growing every day more numerous by the migration of the Irish, who, not succeeding so well in Pennsylvania as the more frugal and industrious Germans, sell their lands in that province to the latter, and take up new ground in the more remote counties in Virginia, Maryland, and North Carolina. These are chiefly Presbyterians from the northern part of Ireland, who in America are generally called Scotch-Irish." So early this new force in American affairs found recognition in England.[2]

It is well worth while here to trace the causes that led to results so overmastering in the making of the Northwest. About the time when the English colonists were planting themselves at Jamestown, another immigration, also under the auspices of James I., was going into Ireland, where the Earls of Tyrone and Tyrconnel, leaders in the great Catholic rebellions, were driven from the country and their confiscated estates parcelled among a body of Scotch and English sent across the

[1] *European Settlements in America*, ii., p. 216. (Fifth edition, 1770.)

[2] The population of Pennsylvania increased from 20,000 in 1701 to 250,000 in 1749, largely through the immigration of Scotch-Irish, and Germans from the Palatinate. James Logan, the Scotch-Irish governor of Pennsylvania during this period, was a Quaker, and had small love for Presbyterians. Through his efforts they were forced to the frontiers, where they formed an efficient barrier against the Indians. See *The Puritan in Holland, England, and America*, by Douglass Campbell, ii., p. 484.

Burke's estimate of the population is much too low. In 1715 there were in Virginia 72,500 whites and 23,000 negroes. Only Massachusetts could show a larger population. See *Official Letters* of Alexander Spotswood, p. xi.

border to occupy them. The new-comers made those once barren lands to blossom like the rose; and by the famous defence of Londonderry they saved the throne to William of Orange and the realm to Protestantism. At the beginning of the eighteenth century these stanch Presbyterians fell a victim to test-oaths designed to suppress popery, but used as effectually to check Presbyterianism. Added to the religious persecution were the burdensome restraints on commerce that in Ireland were but the prelude to those later commercial restrictions which were to alienate the American colonies from the mother-country. Then, too, came the extortionate rents and the resulting evictions that in two years drove thirty thousand Scotch-Irish to seek a more abiding home beyond the seas, where, on the frontiers of Maryland and Virginia, Rev. Francis Makemie, in 1683, had founded the first Presbyterian churches in America.[1]

Toleration Acts for a time put a check to this wholesale depopulation of the north of Ireland, but when in 1728 persecution again commenced, Ulster began to send annually twelve thousand persons to "a land where there was no legal robbery, and where those who sowed the seed could reap the harvest." This human stream struck eastern Pennsylvania, then turned southward through Maryland, Virginia, and the Carolinas. In 1738, the Scotch-Irish in large numbers entered the valley beyond the Blue Ridge, and, with the exception of

[1] In Virginia the Presbyterians were the first sect to make headway against the prevailing intolerance. The conflict was carried on by Makemie, for whose followers the Toleration Act of William and Mary brought small share of indulgence. In 1699 there were but three or four Presbyterian meeting-houses in the colony. Three-quarters of a century later two-thirds of the population were dissenters. Lodge's *English Colonies in America*, p. 56.

some German settlements near the lower end, completely possessed it. So strong in numbers were they that in this year the Synod of Philadelphia, at the instance of John Caldwell, the grandfather of John Caldwell Calhoun, sent a commissioner to propose to the governor of Virginia that the Scotch-Irish would protect the colony against the Indians provided only "that they be allowed the liberty of their consciences and of worshipping God in a way agreeable to the principles of their education." To this proposition Governor Gooch made gracious answer; and thus it happened that for a time the free Bible secured the services of the trusty rifle.[1]

During the spring of 1748, George Washington, while making surveys in the Shenandoah Valley, obtained his first experience of border life and border people. Tramping amid beautiful groves of sugar-trees, paddling past lands yielding an abundance of grain, hemp, and tobacco, he ran the lines of Lord Fairfax's possessions with an accuracy that has since become proverbial. At night he rolled himself in a blanket and lay down on a little hay or a bearskin, with man, wife, and children, like dogs and cats; and happy was he who got the berth nearest the fire. At Colonel Cresap's he shared the limited accommodations of the place with a band of thirty Indians coming from war with a single scalp; and for amusement he supplied the liquors necessary to induce a war-dance, which struck the hard-headed young surveyor as highly comical.[2]

[1] The Scotch-Irish of the South. An address at the Scotch-Irish Congress, 1889, by Hon. William Wirt Henry. *Proceedings*, p. 117.

Gooch resigned in 1749. The latter years of his term were embittered by his attempts to suppress heterodox opinions, which attempts had the usual results. See Lodge's *English Colonies in America*, p. 29.

[2] Sparks's *Washington*, vol. ii., contains Washington's letters and journals covering this period of his career.

WASHINGTON AS A SURVEYOR

In this year 1748, while the rich lands of the garden of Virginia were being laid off and populated, the enterprising men of the colony put their heads together to secure the territory beyond the Alleghanies, but still within the chartered limits of the province. The prime mover in the scheme was Thomas Lee, the president of his majesty's Virginia council, and with him were associated, among others, Lawrence and Augustine Washington, half-brothers of George. The London partner was Thomas Hanbury, a merchant of wealth and influence. Taking the name of the Ohio Company, the associates presented to the king a petition for half a million acres of land on the south side of the Ohio River, between the Monongahela and the Kanawha rivers, with the privilege of selecting a portion of the lands on the north side. Two hundred thousand acres were to be taken up at once; one hundred families were to be seated within seven years, and a fort was to be built as a protection against hostile Indians. The king readily assented to a proposition which promised an effective and inexpensive means of occupying the Ohio valley, which was claimed by the French by right of discovery and occupation. These claims France was just then in a mood to make good.

Orders having been sent to the Virginia government to make the grant to the Ohio Company, the projectors of the scheme ordered two cargoes of goods suitable for the Indian trade; they began to construct roads across the mountains, and prepared to send out an explorer both to look over the lands, and also to arrange for an Indian council at which the Virginia authorities should treat with the savages for the Indian title to the lands within the grant.

Before the company's agent could take the field,

France had decided upon her course of action. While the French government, either at home or in Canada, could do little to prevent individual English traders from wandering at will through the forest towns, the formation of the Ohio Company under royal sanction, proposing as it did to carve a half-million acres out of what the French regarded as their domain, was not a matter to be tossed to and fro like a shuttlecock between the Cabinet at Versailles and the Cabinet at St. James. The ministers of his most Christian Majesty now dropped idle discussions as to the whereabouts of "ancient boundaries" mentioned in the Treaty of Utrecht, and put aside their vain attempts to convince the London court that the Treaty of Aix-la-Chapelle was intended to define and not to confuse the limits of empire. The French proceeded to take the only course left open to them. They occupied the Ohio Valley in force.

Preliminary to more active military operations, the Chevalier Céloron de Bienville, with a band of more than two hundred French officers and Canadian soldiers and boatmen, was sent to take formal possession of the Ohio. Up the turbulent St. Lawrence, across placid Lake Ontario, around the far-sounding falls of Niagara, along the shores of fitful Lake Erie the flotilla of twenty-three birch-bark canoes skimmed its rapid way during the verdant June and the hot July of 1749. Striking across country to Lake Chautauqua, the frail barks were again launched on that beautiful sheet of water, and thence a path was found to the headwaters of the Alleghany. Floating down this river and the Ohio, the fleet stopped now to treat with the Indians at one of their numerous villages, and again to bury at the mouth of some tributary a lead plate inscribed with the flower-de-luce and bearing a legend to the effect that thus the French renewed their possession of the river Ohio, and of all those rivers that flow into it, as far as their sources, "the same as was enjoyed, or ought to have been enjoyed by the preceding kings of France, and that they have maintained by their arms and treaties, especially by those of Ryswick, Utrecht, and Aix-la-Chapelle."[1]

From the Ohio the party of occupation made its way up the Miami to Lake Erie, and thence to Quebec. In several of the Indian villages, Céloron had found English traders. These he sent back to the colonies with warnings not to trespass upon French territory; while the Indians who harbored them were warned of the wrath of their father, the French king, in case they continued to receive the English traders—warnings which the savages were not inclined to heed. The fact was that the English traders offered better bargains than did the French, and the Indians were quick to perceive that their interest lay in competition between the white races.

Nothing daunted by the theatrical expedition of Céleron, the Ohio Company, in September, 1750, called from his home on the Yadkin that shrewd and hardy pioneer, Christopher Gist. No better selection could have been made. Gist's father had surveyed the western shore of Maryland, and had aided in laying out the town of Baltimore; and the son had inherited the father's liking for out-door life. The quality of the English blood in his veins is attested by the fact that one son, Richard, was killed in the battle of King's Mountain; another son, Nathaniel, was a colonel in the Virginia line during the Revolution, and was the progenitor of Montgomery

[1] See De Hass's *Western Virginia* for a drawing of the plate found at the mouth of the Kanawha.

Blair, Francis P Blair, and B. Gratz Brown.[1] Gist's instructions directed him "to go out as soon as possible to the westward of the great mountains in order to search out and discover the lands upon the river Ohio (and other adjoining branches of the Mississippi) down as low as the great falls thereof." He was to observe the ways and passes through the mountains; the width and depth of the rivers; what nations of Indians inhabit the lands, whom they trade with, and in what they deal. In particular he was to mark all the good level lands, so that they might easily be found; for it was the purpose of the company to go all the way down to the Mississippi if need were, in order not to take mean, broken land.[2]

On the last day of October, Gist set out from Colonel Cresap's, on the Potomac, in Maryland, and followed an old Indian path up the Juniata. Sleeping in Indian cabins, living on bear and wild turkey, braving rain and snow, throwing off fever by a resort to the Indian custom of going into a sweat-house, Gist was twenty-five days in reaching the Seneca village of Logstown, eighteen miles down the Ohio from the present site of Pittsburg. There he found a parcel of reprobate Indian traders from Pennsylvania, at whose hands he would have fared badly indeed, had he not represented himself as the king's messenger. He inquired for George Croghan, the idol of the Pennsylvania Scotch-Irish; and found that the veteran trader, with Andrew Montour, the interpreter, was a week's journey in advance. At Beaver Creek, Gist fell in with Barney Curran, an Ohio Company's trader, and together they struck across country to the Muskingum, where was an Indian town of a hun-

[1] Lowdermilk's *Cumberland* (Washington, 1878), p. 28.

[2] "Journal of Christopher Gist's Journey," printed in Pownall's *Topographical Description of North America* (London, 1776).

dred families. As Gist's party came in sight of the place, their eyes were rejoiced by the sight of two English flags snapping in the brisk December wind; and on inquiring the cause, he found that George Croghan had raised one flag over the chief's lodge and another over his own, and had sent out runners to call the Indians to council over the capture of some English traders by the French. It transpired that two of Croghan's men had been taken by a band of forty Frenchmen and twenty Indians, and had been hurried to the French post at Presqu' Isle, on Lake Erie. Croghan received Gist with satisfaction.

On Christmas day, Gist proposed to read the prayers appointed by the Church of England. Croghan's followers, however, had no desire to worship after the manner of the king's religion, and had it not been for the good offices of the local blacksmith, Thomas Burney, and the interpreter, Andrew Montour, this pious purpose must have failed. These two white men collected a congregation of Indians; and probably that Christmas of 1750 was the occasion when first the doctrines of salvation, faith, and good works were expounded by a Protestant within the boundaries of the Northwest. The result was embarrassing. The Indians immediately implored Gist to settle among them, baptize their children, and perform their marriage ceremonies. They loved the English, they said, but heretofore had seen little religion among them!

It was not until the middle of January that the Indians assembled in council. Then Croghan acquainted the savages that the great king over the water had sent them a large present of goods in care of the Governor of Virginia, and had invited them to partake of his charity. The Indians replied that they would consider the matter in the great council when spring was come; and with that the envoys, being satisfied, departed. Coming to White Woman's Creek, they found dwelling there with her Indian husband and her half-breed children, Mary Harris, then fifty years old. When but ten years of age she had been captured in New England by allies of the French; and she still remembered that the people used to be very religious in her native country, and wondered that white men could be so wicked as she had found them in the Ohio woods.

On the Scioto Creek they came to a Delaware village, where they were well received; and at the mouth of that stream they found the Shawanese, who also were friendly, for in times gone by the English had saved the Shawanese when attacked by the Six Nations. Both of these tribes promised that they would meet the Virginians at Logstown in the spring. Then Gist, with Croghan, Montour, and Robert Kallendar, turned his face northward, and after a journey of 150 miles came to the Tawightwi town (Piqua), on the Miami, in the present Ohio county of that name. With the English colors at their head, the little band marched into the capital of the powerful western confederacy, the strongest Indian town in that part of the continent. Amid the firing of guns the ambassadors of the colonies were received by the English traders, and by the chief, who raised the English flag above his own lodge. The Tawightwis, or Miamis, were a numerous people, made up of many tribes, each tribe having a chief; and one of these chiefs was selected to rule the entire nation. Formerly they lived on the Wabash, but latterly they had removed to the Miami, in order to deal with the English traders, who offered them much better bargains than did the French. At this time they were on friendly terms with the Six Nations, who were their natural rivals; for the Miamis in the west were quite as powerful a confederacy as were the Six Nations in the east.

Assembled in the long-house of the nation, on Sunday, the 17th of February, 1751, the council was opened by the interpreter Montour, with the usual formalities of presenting wampum belts. Then he gave greeting to the chiefs: "You have made a road for our brothers the English to come and trade among you; but it is now very foul, great logs are fallen across it, and we would have you be strong like men, and have one heart with us to make the road clear, that our brothers, the English, may have free course and recourse between you and us. In the sincerity of our hearts we send you these four strings of wampum." To this the Indians gave their usual grunt of yo-ho, meaning, "We will see." At noon on Wednesday, the chiefs, arrayed in the shirts, blankets, and paint that the Ohio Company's agent had provided, entered the long-house, to smoke the calumet with their visitors; and the next day Croghan on behalf of the Pennsylvania authorities gave presents to the value of £100. The Miamis professed friendship; and their profession was speedily put to the test.

While Croghan and Gist were still at Piqua, four Ottawas from the Detroit appeared in the council-house. They brought with them a French flag, which they raised by the side of the British ensign; and to the usual strings of wampum they added ten pounds of tobacco and two kegs of the milk of the wilderness, also called French brandy. "The French king," said the Ottawa envoys, "had made clean the road to his officers, and he had sent an invitation to the Miamis to visit his posts." To this Gist's friend, the Piankesha chief, replied that foul and bloody was the way to the French, who had made prisoners of some of the English, whom the Miamis regarded as their brothers. Therefore had they cleared the way for the English. So the Ottawas were forced to return unsuccessful.

Gratified by his success, Gist parted from his companions, and returned to the Shawanese town near the mouth of the Scioto, where the Miami alliance was celebrated with feasting and firing. Then he floated down the Ohio nearly to the present site of Louisville. It was now the 18th of March; Gist had been journeying for four months and a half; he had accomplished everything he had set out to do; and with a light heart he turned his face to the south, intending to make his way homeward up the valley of the Cuttawa, or Kentucky, River. Glorious beyond description were the sights that greeted his ravished eyes as from hill-top after hill-top the wild and beautiful scenery of Kentucky in its robes of freshest green lay spread out before him. It was May when he poled his hastily built raft across the Great Kanawha; and it was almost June when, weary and footsore, he reached the banks of the Yadkin, to find as his only welcome a deserted cabin and the unmistakable signs of an Indian massacre. Happily, however, his own family had been spared, and had taken refuge at a Roanoke settlement.

The death of Mr. Lee, soon after the Ohio Company was launched, threw the active management into the hands of Lawrence Washington, who entered into the project zealously. On making overtures to the Pennsylvania Dutch, who had come into the Shenandoah Valley, he found that their one objection to taking up lands on the Ohio was that they would be compelled to support a clergyman of the Established Church, when few understood and none made use of him. He therefore wrote to

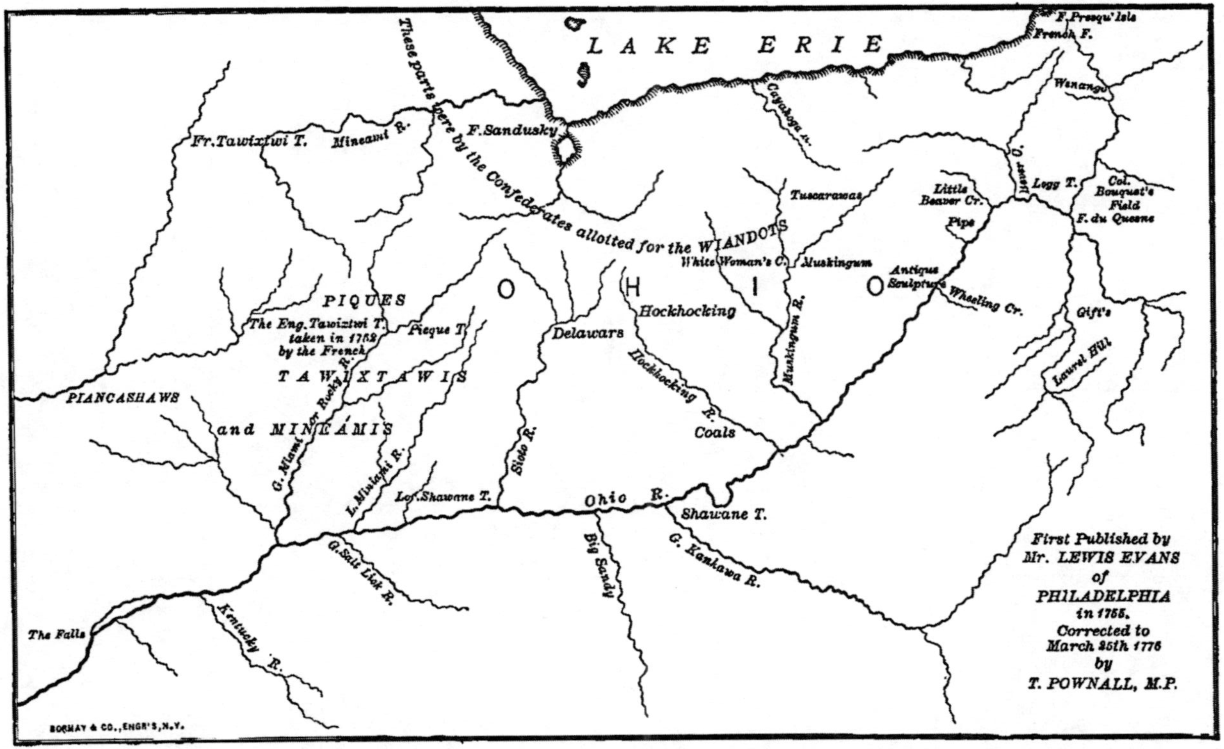

MAP OF THE NORTHWEST AS KNOWN TO THE ENGLISH IN 1755–63

Mr. Hanbury, in the hope that the latter might obtain from the king some sort of a charter to prevent the residents on the Ohio and its branches being subject to parish taxes. "I am well assured," he continues, "that we shall never obtain it by law here. This colony was greatly settled the latter part of Charles the First's time, and during the usurpation, by zealous churchmen; and that spirit, which was then brought in, has ever since continued, so that except a few Quakers we have no dissenters. But what has been the consequence? We have increased by slow degrees, except negroes and convicts, while our neighboring colonies, whose natural advantages are greatly inferior to ours, have become populous." To Governor Dinwiddie, then in London, Lawrence Washington also wrote that the Dutch would take fifty thousand acres of the company's lands, provided they could be assured of religious freedom; but the governor, although he was heartily interested in the project, despaired of obtaining from an over-busy parliament and ministry the attention necessary to procure the requisite exemption. Thus, at the very beginning, arose that question of religious freedom which was to find such ample recognition when the great charter of the Northwest came to be written.

In June, 1752, the Indians met Gist and the Virginian commissioners at Logstown, and in spite of French intrigues, made a treaty whereby the Ohio Company was to be allowed to make settlements south of the Ohio, and to build a fort at the forks of that river. Indeed, the Indians had urged upon Croghan that the Pennsylvanians build such a fort; but the Pennsylvania assembly had neglected their opportunities, and had utterly failed to support Croghan in his dealings with the Indians. Gist surveyed the company's lands; he removed his own habitation from the Yadkin, and began the erection of a fortified trading-post at Shurtees Creek, on the east bank of the Ohio, a little below the present site of Pittsburg. Thus far everything promised well for the Ohio project. The Indians were well disposed to the English; colonial traders overran the entire country from the very gates of Montreal to the Mississippi; and but for the posts on the Great Lakes and their connecting waters, together with Vincennes on the Wabash and Fort Chartres in the Illinois country, the English were at liberty to push their settlements and their trade throughout the regions inhabited by the most powerful tribes, and comprising the richest lands on the continent. Unfortunately for British interests, however, mutual jealousies among the colonies, together with that deliberation in action which is characteristic of popular governments, prevented prompt and harmonious action until France had found a means of compelling the fickle savages to renounce their new friends and to aid their ancient allies.

Meanwhile the French were not altogether idle. Celoron de Bienville, now the commandant at Detroit, was engaged in planting on the fertile banks of the strait the French families that liberal subsidies in farm implements had drawn thither; and at this time the town could boast a population of nearly five hundred whites—the largest French settlement west of Montreal. He was ordered from Quebec to drive the English traders from the Miami villages, and thus to realize his occupation of the Ohio country in 1749. The task, however, required a man of a different stamp. Charles Langlade, a young French trader at Michilimackinac, who had already acquired an ascendency over the Ottawa and Ojibwa tribes of the nortnern portages, was now ready to start on that long and brilliant career of petty warfare that makes his name and fame a part of the history of the Northwest. Early in the June of 1752, Céloron from the block-house bastion of Fort Pontchartrain beheld far up the placid river a fleet of swift darting canoes, hurrying through the shallow passage between the wooded island and the mainland. As the flotilla approached the little town the prows of the canoes were forced up on the sands at the foot of the palisades, and a crowd of a hundred and fifty warriors from Michilimackinac tumbled from the boats and went howling through the narrow streets of the little town. At their head was Charles Langlade, more savage than any Indian in the crowd. What Céloron and his Frenchmen dared not undertake, that Langlade and his followers speedily accomplished. Crossing the corner of Lake Erie, the fleet ascended the Miami of the Lake, and on the 21st of June suddenly attacked the meagre fort at Piqua. Eight English traders and a few Indians were in the town. The surprise was complete. After a short fight fourteen Miamis and one trader were killed. The chief, known as Old Britain, was boiled and eaten; the trading-house was plundered, and five traders were captured and carried to Governor Duquesne, who recommended for Langlade a pension suited to the husband of a squaw![1]

[1] Parkman's *Montcalm and Wolfe* (Boston, 1898), vol. i., p. 89. See also *Minutes of the Provincial Council of Pennsylvania*, vol. iv., p. 599.

The statement that on this occasion the Ottawas were led by Charles de Langlade is made on the authority of Parkman (*Montcalm and Wolfe*, vol. i., p. 89). Tasse in his elaborate sketch of Langlade makes no reference to the episode. The Pennsylvania records also are silent as to the leader of the Indians; and Parkman himself repeatedly speaks of Langlade as married to a squaw at

Meanwhile Duquesne was preparing to cut off the English from the Ohio country. Early in the spring of 1753 a mixed force of king's troops, Canadians, and Indians, numbering not far from fifteen hundred persons, set out from Montreal, and in due time reached that most excellent harbor on Lake Erie then called Presqu' Isle, now known as Erie. There they built a post. Then, advancing, they built another on Le Bœuf creek, and still a third at Venango on the Alleghany. Sickness in the ranks and incompetency among the leaders made them pause; but there the gauntlet was thrown down.

Reports of the French advance having reached Governor Dinwiddie, he conceived it to be his duty to defend the Virginia frontiers against the invaders; and he represented to New York, Pennsylvania, and North Carolina the peril of the situation. The northern colonies held back. Governor Dinwiddie, who had become a member of the Ohio Company, was not slow to see that the plans of the corporation would come to nothing if once the French were allowed to reach the Ohio. He therefore resolved to send a messenger to ascertain the numbers

Green Bay. This is inaccurate. Langlade's eldest child was the son of an Indian woman; but she was never his wife. Langlade's father married an Indian woman, the daughter of an Ottawa chief; but she was hardly to be called a squaw, for at the time of her marriage to Augustin de Langlade she was the widow of a French fur-trader, and the mother of his seven children, all of whom proved to be very respectable people. Charles de Langlade married on August 12, 1754, Charlotte Bourassa, the daughter of a French trader of wealth and position, and it was some time after their marriage that they went to live at Green Bay. Moreover, she was known to be mortally afraid of Indians, and on one occasion nearly suffocated herself by hiding under a lumber-pile, on the approach of a band of Menominees. See Tasse's sketch of Charles de Langlade in *Wisconsin Historical Reports*, 1867.

GEORGE WASHINGTON

(From a portrait painted in 1772 by C. W. Peale, now owned by General George Washington Custis Lee, of Lexington, Virginia.)

and force of the French, and to deliver to their commanding officer the demand of Virginia, that all French troops be withdrawn from the country included within the chartered limits of that colony. The messenger selected for this delicate and arduous task was Major George Washington, then a sedate youth of twenty-one, who had held the position of adjutant-general in the Virginia militia since he was nineteen. The selection was eminently fitting. Major Washington, as the executor of the estate of his brother Lawrence, was now largely interested in the success of the Ohio Company, and he was not likely to repeat the failure of Dinwiddie's first commissioner, Captain William Trent, who went no nearer the French than Logstown.

Armed with proper credentials, Washington started from Mount Vernon, in company with Jacob Vanbraam, a broken-down officer, who had taught the young major the art of fence and had instructed him generally in the duties of a soldier, and who was now to serve as his interpreter. Reaching the Monongahela, Washington secured the services of Christopher Gist, whose success in dealing with the Indians two years before had established his reputation with the company; and the party was completed by four hired servitors, Barnaby Currin and John McQuire, a pair of Scotch-Irish traders, and Henry Stewart and William Jenkins. On reaching Frazier's they learned that the French commander, Marin, had died and that his troops had gone into winter-quarters. Twenty-five days out from Williamsburg the party, reinforced by Shingiss, King of the Delawares, reached Logstown, where they awaited the coming of the Half-king of the Six Nations, from whom they learned the whereabouts of the French. This chief had already been to the invaders with a demand that they withdraw from the Indians' country. "Fathers," he had said to the French, "both you and the English are white; we live in the country between; therefore the land belongs neither to one nor the other. But the Great Being above allowed it to be a place of residence for us; so, fathers, I desire you to withdraw, as I have done our brothers the English; for I will keep you at arm's-length. I lay this down as a trial for both, to see which will have the greatest regard for it, and that side we will stand by, and make equal sharers with us. Our brothers, the English, have heard this, and I now come to tell it to you; for I am not afraid to discharge you off this land."

To this vigorous speech the Frenchman had made contemptuous answer that he was not afraid of flies or mosquitoes, for such the Indians were; that he should go down the Ohio, build upon it, and tread under his feet all opposition. The land, he said, did not belong to the Indians; for the French had taken possession of the Ohio while yet the present tribes were dwelling elsewhere.

As between the French and the English, the Indians might well side with the former; because the French never contemplated the possession and cultivation of the lands, but merely the establishment of trading-stations. The French proposed to trade with the Indians: the English colonists to dispossess them. Eventually the English policy came to be but a continuation of the French, while the policy of the colonists was ever to acquire by purchase or by force, and to bring under cultivation the lands that formed the hunting-grounds of the Indians. It may be admitted that the French policy was the more just to the Indian; but the Scotch-Irish, the Germans, the Swiss, and other peoples of Europe, escaping from the intolerable conditions of the Old World, could not be stopped in their rush to make homes for themselves in the fertile wildernesses of America. Moreover, there was much truth in the reply of the French commander to the half-king. No one of the tribes then in possession of the Ohio country had long held the lands they then occupied; the tribes were at war with one another; and famine and disease added their work to the destruction that ever stalked through the forests and over the prairies of the Northwest. To maintain the richest lands on earth as a game preserve for a few savages when hundreds of thousands of civilized beings were seeking homes and liberty might be theoretical justice, but certainly it was not consistent with the strongest impulses of human nature.

On December 4th, Washington and his party, attended by the half-king, and two other chiefs commissioned to return the French belts, reached Venango, an old Indian town near the junction of French Creek with the Alleghany. There, in a house of which the Englishman John Frazier had been dispossessed, dwelt Captain Joncaire, who received the embassy with effusive courtesy. When wine had loosed the tongues of the French, they swore they meant to take possession of the Ohio, which they claimed by virtue of "a discovery made by one La Salle, sixty years ago." They knew the English could raise double the number of men the French could; but they counted (and with good reason) on the dilatoriness of their enemies to prevent the success of any English undertaking. In Joncaire Washington was called on to deal with an adept. The son of a French officer and a Seneca squaw, he had all the advantages that come from being able to address the savages in their own tongue. He had acted as scout for Céleron's expedition, braving many a danger from Indians favorable to the English; and it was due to his intrigues that the Iroquois were shaken in their allegiance to the British. He now endeavored to win over Washington's red companions, but in this he was unsuccessful; and after many delays the embassy reached Le Bœuf, where Washington presented his letters to the commander, Legardeur de St. Pierre, "an elderly gentleman with much the air of a soldier."

To the qualities of a soldier St. Pierre added the accomplishments of a diplomat. First a translation of Washington's letters was made and duly corrected; then three days were spent in preparing an answer to the effect that the communication of his honor, the Governor of Virginia, had been received and respectfully referred to the Marquis Duquesne, at Quebec, pending whose reply he, St. Pierre, would continue to execute his orders by expelling all Englishmen whom he found within the domains of his most Christian Majesty. While this reply was in preparation the French were using every means to detach the Indian chiefs from the English interest; but here the youthful envoy was more than a match for his elderly rivals. On the 16th of December, Washington turned his face homeward; and after many perils, including a narrow escape from the bullet of a treacherous Indian, he and Gist returned to Virginia.

Washington's journal of his expedition to the Ohio, being sent to the Lords of Trade, and by them published in England, aroused the nation to a sense of the peril in which English territory was placed by the advance of the French. The immediate result was an order from the Lords of Trade addressed to the governors of the colonies, commanding them to meet and consult as to steps for united action against the encroachments of the French, and to renew the covenant with the Six Nations.

Governor Dinwiddie, also, set about putting Virginia on a war footing. The military establishment was increased to six companies under the command of Colonel Joshua Fry, with Washington as lieutenant-colonel; and to stimulate enlistments the governor made a grant of two hundred thousand acres of land on the Ohio, to be divided among the officers and soldiers engaged in the expedition. While Washington was recruiting his force at Alexandria, Captain Trent had raised a company of traders and woodsmen, and had marched to the forks of the Ohio, where they began to build a fort on the site of the present city of Pittsburg. Washington reached Wills Creek on April 20, 1754, and five days later Captain Trent's ensign, Mr. Ward, arrived from the Ohio with the disagreeable news that on the 17th M. Contrecœur, with a thousand men, had appeared before the half-finished fort and demanded its surrender. Captain Trent was at home, and Ensign Ward, taking counsel with Washington's Indian friend the half-king, made terms with Contrecœur and withdrew. With this seizure of the Ohio Company's post by a French armed force began the French and Indian War, which raged for nine years and reached more than half-way round the globe.

The news of this reverse Washington immediately communicated to Governor Hamilton of Pennsylvania, and to the Governor of Maryland, as well as to Governor Dinwiddie. The latter already had sought the aid of New York and South Carolina. In New York and Pennsylvania the assemblies were inclined to the opinion that perhaps France had the best claims to the Ohio. In the latter colony the proprietors absolutely refused to allow their own lands to be taxed for purposes of defence; and in the other colonies either the danger seemed remote, or questions of prerogative between the elective assemblies and the royal governors prevented action.

All unwittingly England now gave the colonies a useful lesson in self-government. In their natural desire to throw on the colonial treasuries the burden of defending the frontiers against the encroachments of the French, the Lords of Trade summoned the various governments to send delegates to an assembly to be convened at Albany in the June of 1754 for the purpose of enlisting the assistance of the Indians and concerting measures for common defence. Albany was selected for the meeting-place because of its proximity to the lands of the Six Nations, always friendly to the English. Indeed, at this time England was disposed to base her title to the Ohio regions not on the voyage of John Howard, who, in 1742, had floated down the Ohio in a buffalo-skin canoe, only to be captured by the French on the Mississippi; nor on the treaty made by the Pennsylvania interpreter, Conrad Weiser, at Logstown, in 1748; nor yet on the prior Lancaster treaty of 1744, recognizing the right of the king to all lands within the colony of Virginia. A much wider, although at the same time a much more indefinite, basis was found in the treaty of Albany, in 1684, when the Six Nations placed all their lands under the protection of England. This treaty was taken to cover the lands conquered by the Six Nations between the Alleghanies and the Great Lakes; and on it New York afterwards, as we shall see, claimed the Ohio country in opposition to the claims of Virginia and Connecticut.

Although the Albany convention failed to accomplish the objects for which it was called, it introduced two men who were destined to have a large share in the history of the western country. The first of these was Colonel William Johnson (afterwards known as Sir William Johnson), whose influence over the Six Nations, acquired by years of honest dealing, familiarity with Indian life and manners, and absolute steadfastness of purpose, exceeded that of any other person who ever had trade relations with that most powerful of all Indian confederacies. It is a significant fact that the convention intrusted to Benjamin Franklin the task of expressing its thanks to Colonel Johnson for his comprehensive plan for dealing with the Six Nations, and for defeating the plans of the French in their encroachments; and it is more than probable that then and afterwards Franklin obtained from Colonel Johnson many of the facts and ideas that he afterwards used to such good purpose in presenting the advantages to be derived from holding the Ohio region.

Franklin's own contribution to the occasion, however, was nothing less than a well-worked-out plan for a definite union of the colonies under a governor to be appointed by the crown—a plan that was adopted by the convention only to be rejected by both the colonies and the crown; by the colonies because it smacked too much of prerogative, and by the ministry because there was in it too much of democracy! There is good reason to believe that had a different fate attended this scheme the war of the Revolution would have been averted, at least for a time.[1]

Returning to Philadelphia, Franklin soon after prepared for Governor Pownall that almost prophetic paper in which he argues that England should take steps to

[1] Sparks's *Franklin*, vol. iii. Sparks gives the Franklin plan of union, together with his paper on the Ohio country.

plant colonies in "the great country back of the Appalachian Mountains, on both sides of the Ohio, and between that river and the lakes," a region "now well known, both to the English and French, to be one of the finest in North America, for the extreme richness and fertility of the land; healthy temperature of the air, the mildness of the climate; the plenty of hunting and fishing and fowling; the facility of trade with the Indians; and the vast convenience of inland navigation or water carriage by the lakes and great rivers, many hundreds of leagues around." His plan included a strong fort at Niagara, with armed vessels on the lakes, and smaller forts on Lake Erie. A second colony was to have its seat on the Scioto, "the finest spot of its bigness in all North America," with the advantage of "sea-coal in plenty (even above ground in two places) for fuel, when the woods shall be destroyed."

Events now hurried England into making a national rather than a colonial issue of the advance of the French into the territories claimed by the British. In May, 1754, Washington in command of the advance force raised by Virginia, and aided by the half-king, fell upon a French detachment, and in a quarter-hour action killed the commander, M. de Jumonville, and nine others, taking twenty-one prisoners. On July 3d, however, Washington was attacked at his half-built Fort Necessity, and was compelled to withdraw, after a spirited contest of nine hours. Evidently the time had come for England to assert her claims to the Northwest.

On the 20th of February, 1755, amid the alternate heats and chills of a Virginia winter, General Edward Braddock appeared on the Potomac as the commander-in-chief of His Majesty's forces in America; and in due time quartered five companies of his little army at Alex-

BRADDOCK'S HEADQUARTERS

andria, disposing the other fifteen companies at the pretentious town of Fredericksburg, at Bladensburg, then a considerable tobacco port, and at five or six other straggling villages in the neighborhood. Meantime the general quartered himself upon Governor Dinwiddie at the brick palace in Williamsburg, whence he sent out his summons for the leading men of America to meet him in council at Alexandria, whither he shortly repaired. Arrogant yet convivial, haughty but condescending, Braddock soon brought into subjection the discordant forces with which he was called upon to deal. He had brought with him from England two regiments of infantry, each five hundred strong, and these he proposed to supplement with an equal number of provincials. Never before had America seen so brave an array. Braddock, himself the son of a major-general, had been trained to arms in the Coldstream Guards, a regiment unsurpassed for valor, the very flower of the British army. In this model regiment he had won promotion by gallantry on the field of battle; and his selection as commander of the American expedition was made by no less a personage than the Duke of Cumberland, who took an intense interest in all that related to the campaign, and who had repeatedly admired Braddock's coolness and intrepidity when under fire.[1]

Washington, in no mood to be humiliated by accepting a command in which he as a provincial would be subordinate to the lowest subaltern holding a king's commission, viewed from a distance the preparations for an expedition in which he burned to share. The astute Braddock avoided the difficulty by making the lover of the whistling-bullet[2] a member of his military family;

[1] Lowdermilk's *Cumberland*, p. 97.

[2] Horace Walpole, in his *Memoirs*, makes merry over a quotation in

and thus he secured the devoted services of the bravest and shrewdest fighter in all America, and this, too, without taking a jot or tittle out of the king's order of precedence.

From his stone castle on the Mohawk came Colonel William Johnson, to be placed in charge of Indian affairs, as a stepping-stone to the baronetcy as dear to his vanity as was a silver medal to a savage. To Johnson was assigned the task of leading a force against Crown Point. From slow-going, peace-loving Philadelphia rode Benjamin Franklin, the shrewd postmaster-general of the colonies, then in his forty-ninth year. At his side trotted two royal governors: Delancy, of New York, and the urbane Shirley, of Massachusetts, who was to lead the attack on Niagara and Fort Frontenac. To Franklin it was given to wring from the close-fisted farmers of Pennsylvania the means of transportation and the supplies necessary for the quartermaster's and commissary's departments; and with a zeal quite contrary to military knowledge he loaded the officers with comforts and luxuries that did much to demoralize the expedition.

To the admiring group gathered about the blazing fire in the Alexandria mansion that still bears his name, Braddock told how he would capture Fort Duquesne and then march on Fort Niagara, driving the French back within their proper territory on the St. Lawrence. The astute Franklin flattered while yet he suggested

some letter of Washington's in which the young soldier confesses that he loves to hear the bullets whistle. Washington would not deny that he wrote some such thing; but excused himself by saying that, if he did, it was when he was young. It is difficult to realize that Washington ever was young in the sense of saying or doing an unpremeditated thing. The incident therefore is valuable in that it tends to humanize his character.

GENERAL EDWARD BRADDOCK

ambuscades; but was silenced, if not convinced, by the lofty reply that the king's regular and disciplined troops were invincible, even in tangled forest and foe-lined defile. With stately balls and convivial suppers the time of preparation was whiled away. Delay after delay ensued. The Virginians were both poor and hard to move, and the resources of the country were meagre beyond the belief of a European commander. Throughout the languid spring the little army watched each westering sun sink behind those low hills and broad stretches of river and plain, where in less than half a century was to be built as the capital of a new nation a city to be named after the energetic youth who was then and there taking those lessons in the art of war that were soon to enable him to cope with the highly trained armies of the old world.

Amid the fierce heats of June and early July, Braddock's army dragged its slow length towards the forks of the Ohio. The Delaware Indians, spying upon the flanks of the English forces, saw that the advance was made in close order, and quickly decided to surround the army, take trees, and shoot down the soldiers like pigeons.[1] On July 9, 1755, James Smith, a captive at Fort Duquesne, while watching the preparations for the encounter, saw the Indians swarm about the ammunition barrels before the gates, in their haste to provide themselves with powder, bullets, and flints. Their wants

[1] *Colonel James Smith's Account of Remarkable Occurrences*, 1755–9 (Philadelphia, 1834), p. 18. Parkman speaks of the exceeding value of this work. Smith, a Pennsylvanian, was captured just before the Braddock defeat; he was made to run the gantlet, and afterwards was adopted in the place of a warrior. For several years he lived the life of an Indian; and his experiences of life among the savages are in the highest degree interesting and valuable.

supplied, they marched off "in rank entire," accompanied by the French Canadians and some regulars, in all about four hundred[1]—a force so small that Smith was in high hopes that he would see them fleeing back before the British troops, and so put an end to his captivity. The Canadians and Lake Indians, who had been summoned by Vaudreuil, were under the command of Cadet Charles de Langlade, whose influence over the fierce savages of the north the governor counted upon to insure a repetition of his former brilliant exploits. It was nine o'clock when the motley crowd of French, Canadians,[2] and Indians, under the command of De Beaujeu, set out from the fort; it was half-past twelve when they came upon the English as the latter were enjoying their mid-day meal, on the south bank of the Monongahela. Unnoticed by the English, each savage and Canadian selected a tree, and prepared for the fray. Seeing the advantage of immediate attack, before the English should take up their arms, Langlade urged De Beaujeu to begin the fight. The Frenchman, made timid by the number of his opponents, refused. Then Langlade called to council the chiefs of the savages, and had them insist upon an order to begin. Again De Beaujeu refused. Thereupon Langlade made a second appeal, and this time won a reluctant consent. Then from the silent forest there broke upon the astonished English a noise of yelling savages and of whirring bullets like the

[1] Tasse puts the number at two hundred and fifty French and six hundred Indians. "Memoir of Charles de Langlade," *Wisconsin Historical Society Reports*, 1876, p. 130.

[2] Among the Canadians were Langlade's brother-in-law, Souligney, his nephew, Gautier de Vierville; Pierre Quéret, La Fortune, Amable de Gere, Philip de Rocheblave, and Louis Hamelin. Beaujeu was killed in the encounter.

breaking loose of pandemonium. The Virginians died while fighting; but the regulars ran like sheep pursued by dogs, nor could their gallant officers rally them. Happily for his fame, Braddock himself found a brave death amid disgraceful defeat; and history is kind to his memory, even while reprobating his fatal mistake of over-confidence. Braddock's disgrace was the beginning of Washington's fame. "I luckily," writes the young soldier to his mother, "escaped without a wound, though I had four bullets through my coat and two horses shot under me." Not only was his personal bravery conspicuous, but the Virginian method of fighting from behind trees proved beyond a doubt that when properly led the provincial was more than a match for the trained European soldier. A commander and the hope of success in any conflict that might come between the Old World and the New were born that July day in the slaughter-pen between the ravines of the Great Meadows.

The defeat of Braddock brought down upon the defenceless settlers the stealthy raids of the relentless savages. With fire and scalping-knife the frontier was rolled back towards the Atlantic, and throughout the Indian towns on the Ohio were distributed the captive wives and children of the murdered backwoodsmen. Meantime, in Pennsylvania the Assembly wrangled with the governor over questions of taxation; New York prudently regarded the matter as one too remote for her concern; and Virginia alone seemed willing to put forth what strength she had to protect her borders and retrieve the disgrace of the late defeat. For two years Washington was charged with the wearying and disheartening work of protecting the frontiers with a poorly equipped, poorly organized, and ill-supported militia.

Thankless as the task then was, those trying and perplexing months were his schooling for like vexations on a larger scale during the eight long years of the Revolution. The insubordination on the part of the troops, and the bickerings in the assemblies, which he learned to bear with patience in 1756 and 1757, were the same problems he was called upon to face twenty years later when he came to lead the armies of the united colonies.[1]

The expeditions of Johnson and Shirley were scarcely more fortunate than was that of Braddock. On September 8, two months after the massacre at Great Meadows, the New York and New England militia, under Colonel Ephraim Williams,[2] were trapped at Lake George, and the Braddock tragedy was repeated; but the rout of the morning was turned into victory later in the day, by reason largely of Johnson's disposition of the reserves and the coolness of Lyman's Connecticut regiment. There again the superiority of the backwoods manner of fighting was made apparent; for no sooner did Dieskau's white-coated French regulars attempt an orderly attack on the provincials than those nimble fighters mowed down the regular formations in the same manner that Braddock's British force was annihilated; and their brave German commander died as gallant a death as did Braddock. For his part in the fray Johnson was made a baronet, and received five thousand pounds; but dissensions among the provin-

[1] Washington's letters, given in the second volume of Sparks, show how perplexing was his work during these years.

[2] Colonel Williams, a few days before his death at Bloody Pond, had made a will under which Williams College was founded; and thus the memory of a brave and modest soldier has been perpetuated in an institution ever noted for a modesty in aim and a thoroughness in execution unsurpassed among the colleges of the country.

THE BURIAL OF BRADDOCK

cials and lukewarmness among the Indians brought the expedition to a sudden end. Governor Shirley, whom the death of Braddock had made commander-in-chief, marched a small army to Oswego; but dared not attempt to capture Niagara lest the French from Fort Frontenac should take Oswego, and could not go against Fort Frontenac because he had no boats fitted to cross Lake Ontario. Consequently in October he returned to Albany. Thus ended for the British the disastrous year of 1755.[1]

Desperate as was the situation for English power in America, in Europe matters were still worse. France had met England on the Weser, and the Duke of Cumberland lived to bear the disgrace from which his protégé Braddock was sheltered by an unknown grave. By the Convention of Closter Seven a brave army of fifteen thousand Englishmen were sent home disbanded and a rabble. Port Mahon, the key to the Mediterranean, hung at the girdle of the Duke of Richelieu. England's ally, Frederick, was hemmed within the narrow borders of Saxony by the wolves gathered from the Seine to the Volga, all snarling to tear Prussia to pieces. Even on the sea the red cross of St. George drooped from the mast-head of Admiral Byng's fleeing flagship; while in remote India the British merchant saw his expulsion decreed by a French adventurer. In parliament corruption walked hand in hand with incompetency.

In that day of wrath and ashes of empire, William Pitt was whirled into power. Making political corruption his slave, with Newcastle for overseer, Pitt infused his own vigor into both parliament and army. Into the military chest of Frederick he poured that stream of

[1] Parkman's *Montcalm and Wolfe* (Boston, 1898), vol. i., p. 339.

gold needed to enable the Prussian emperor to maintain the armies he led with such consummate skill as to make men call him Great. In India "the boy-soldier of Arcot," on June 23, 1757, by the victory of Plassey, laid the foundation of England's East-Indian Empire; and in November, 1759, Admiral Hawke, scorning the shoals and reefs of Quiberon Bay, ruined a French fleet ready to transport a French army gathered to invade England.[1]

It was in America particularly that Pitt determined lastingly to punish England's inveterate foe. From his cabinet the generals of his choice went forth to their work animated by a courage and a zeal such as they had never before known. Amherst and Boscawen opened the campaign in 1758 with the reduction of Louisburg, reputed the strongest fortress in the New World; Abercrombie was repulsed at Ticonderoga, but the next year Amherst, the fortress builder, worked his slow but sure way from the Hudson to the St. Lawrence. The tale of Wolfe's daring victory and heroic death on the Plains of Abraham is still the favorite theme of historian and novelist. A success less brilliant, but not less important; a success scarcely less tragic in its ending, and almost as hardly earned, was the steady march of Forbes through the unbroken forests of Pennsylvania and over the Alleghanies to force the evacuation of Fort Duquesne.

In the July of 1758, General John Forbes gathered his little army at Raystown, now Bedford, on the eastern slope of the Alleghanies. There was Colonel Henry Bouquet, newly arrived from European battle-fields, to lead the Royal American regiment of Pennsylvania

[1] Green's *Short History of the English People,* ¶ 1451.

BLOCK-HOUSE OF FORT DUQUESNE

Germans; and George Washington with the Virginia backwoodsmen, who were ever ready to follow him into battle, no matter how reluctant they might afterwards be to submit to discipline; and twelve hundred of Montgomery's Highlanders, clad in the kilt that the Indian derided as a petticoat; and provincials from Maryland and North Carolina—all determined to avenge the Braddock disgrace.

Exhausted by illness, yet steadfast and determined, the persistent Scotch general played by turns the parts of commander, quartermaster, and commissary. His very delays were made to aid his plans, by detaching from the French their Indian allies; and at his command the governor of Pennsylvania negotiated with the Five Nations and their allies the treaty of Easton, with the result that a joint message of peace was sent to the savages of the Ohio. The hazardous mission of Frederick Post, with these tidings of peace; the cruel slaughter of Major Grant's too precipitate advance; and the dispute between Washington and Bouquet as to whether Braddock's road should be used or a new way cut, are all incidents of the terrible November march of the resolute army. From his swaying litter the pain-tortured general directed the movements of his troops as they made their slow way down the bleak slopes of the mountains and on towards the mingling-place of the Alleghany and the Monongahela, only to find a few harmless Indians prowling amid the ruins of a demolished fort. Some to Venango in the north, some to Fort Chartres in the west, the enemy had dispersed. So without a blow fell Fort Duquesne, and with it fell the power of France on the upper Ohio. About the few remaining houses Forbes drew a line of palisades as a defence against the Indians, and this enclosure he named Pittsburg, for the minister in whose service, before he had reached two score and ten years, he had worn out his life. Leaving to General Stanwix, who came a year later, the task of building Fort Pitt, Forbes was borne back to Philadelphia to die.

It was almost eleven months after the successful Pennsylvania campaign that Quebec capitulated; and it was not until September, 1760, that Vaudreuil, hemmed in by Amherst and Murray and Haviland, yielded up Montreal, and with it the dominion of the Northwest from the St. Lawrence to the Mississippi.[1]

Far away from the scene of hostilities the little colony at Detroit stolidly continued in its accustomed ways, regardless of coming changes. On November 29, 1760, Major Robert Rogers drew up his two companies of rangers and his little detachment of Royal Americans, on a grassy plain under the guns of Fort Pontchartrain, and there awaited with composure the reply of the French commandant, M. Bellestre, to the letter of the Marquis Vaudreil, commanding the surrender of Detroit to the British. Robert Rogers, the leader of the English forces on this delicate mission, was the most famous Indian fighter of his day. Born in the Scotch-Irish settlement of Londonderry, New Hampshire, he began his career as a scout in the Merrimac Valley when he was

[1] Parkman's *Montcalm and Wolfe* treats in a masterly manner of the struggle between France and England. Chapter X. of Green's *Short History of the English People* is devoted to Pitt's work. Macaulay's essay on Lord Chatham treats of this period in retrospect. Thackeray's *Virginians*, in spite of some small inaccuracies, gives the true historical atmosphere of the Braddock expedition. Among the recent successful attempts to deal with the fall of Quebec are Gilbert Parker's *Seats of the Mighty*, and *The Span o' Life*, by William McLennan and J. N. McIlwraith. In *Two Soldiers and a Politician* Clinton Ross shows how the long story of Quebec can be told in a few words.

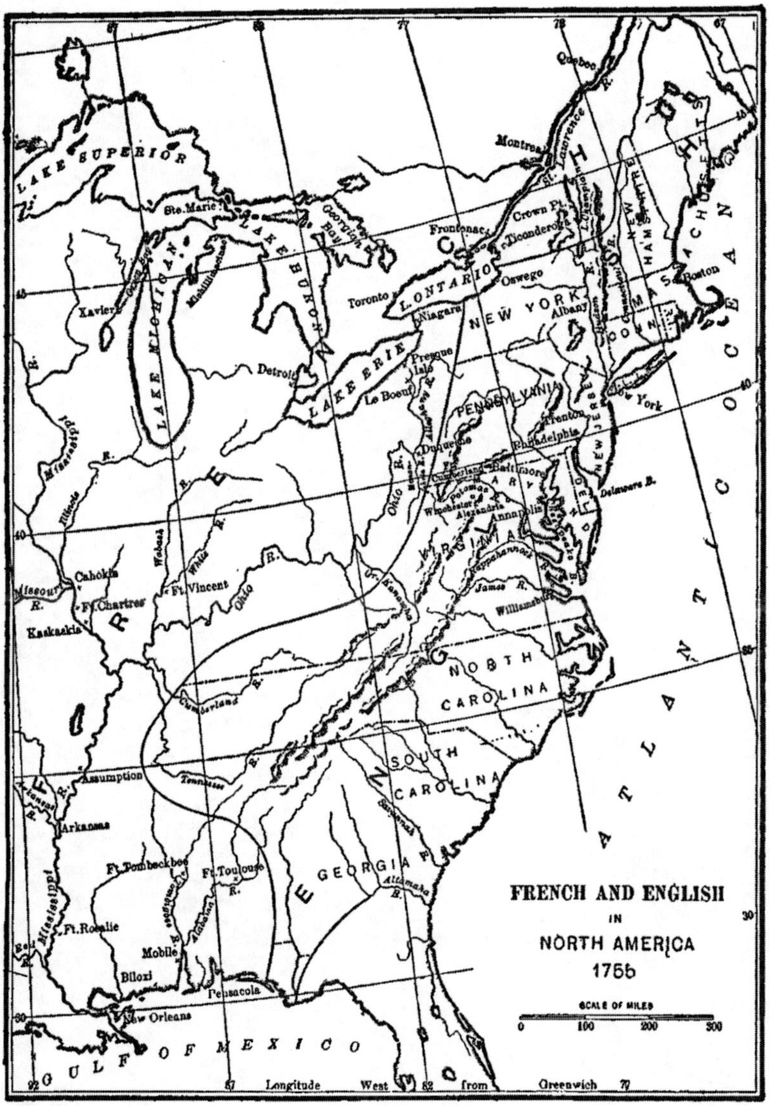

FRENCH AND ENGLISH IN NORTH AMERICA 1755

but nineteen years old, and at this time had been in the king's service fourteen years. Taller by three or four inches than the average of his fellow-townsmen whom he led, like them he wore a close-fitting jacket, a warm cap, coarse woollen small-clothes, leggings, and moccasins. A hatchet was thrust into his belt, a powder-horn hung at his side, a long, keen hunting-knife and a trusty musket completed his armament; and a blanket and a knapsack stuffed with bread and raw salt pork, together with a flask of spirits, made up his outfit. He could speak to the Indian or the Frenchman in a language they could understand; he knew every sign of the forest, every wile of his foes, and repeatedly his bravery and coolness had brought him safely through the most critical situations. He lifted a scalp with as little compunction as did any Indian, and counted it the most successful warfare to creep into an Indian encampment by night, to set fire to the lodges, and to make his escape by the light of the flames, with the screams of the doomed savages rejoicing his ears.[1]

On his way to Detroit Rogers and his party had been stopped at a place near the present site of Cleveland, by an embassy from the Ottawa chief Pontiac, who claimed to be king and lord of the country.[2] When French defeat seemed assured, the prudent Pontiac had gone with the other chiefs from the Detroit to the recently surrendered Fort Pitt[3] to learn how the Indians were likely to fare under British rule. With short-sighted braggadocio, assurance was given him by the British commandant that the rivers would run with

[1] Joseph B. Walker's sketch of Rogers, *New Hampshire Historical and Genealogical Society Publications*, 1885.

[2] *Journals of Major Robert Rogers*, London, 1765.

[3] James Grant's statement, *Gladwin MMS.*

rum, that presents from the great king would be without limit, and that the markets would be the cheapest ever known. These and many other fair promises so reassured Pontiac that he spread the good news far and wide among the Indians, and when Rogers appeared the chief gave him a most hospitable welcome, and even offered to escort him on his journey. Rogers, who was himself a great braggart, confirmed all that had been said at Fort Pitt; and night after night, as ranger and Indian sat by the camp-fire and smoked the pipe of peace, the former told his inquisitive red brother how the English maintained discipline in their forces and handled their armies to the best advantage in battle; also how cloth was made, and iron forged, and what multitudes of white men lived in great cities over seas.

Rogers in all his experience had never before met so noble a son of the forest, and he easily came to understand how great keenness of mind, matched by majesty of appearance, confirmed to Pontiac that ascendency over the various lake tribes which, by right, belonged to him as the chief of the eldest member of their confederacy. Moreover, the shrewd New Englander knew that with Pontiac and the Ottawas on his side, the French commandant must speedily yield. M. Bellestre, however, made his own surrender as humiliating for himself as possible. On hearing of the approach of the English he set on the flag-staff of the fort a wooden effigy of the British leader's head, on which a crow, supposed to represent M. Bellestre, was engaged in scratching at the brains of his foe. But Pontiac's Indians had made known to their friends at the fort the true condition of affairs, and when the French commandant found himself deserted by his Indian allies, he gave the reluctant order to lower the lilies of France, which for more than half a century had floated over Fort Pontchartrain. As the red cross of St. George snapped in the brisk November breeze, above the hoarse cheers of rangers and provincials, came the joyous yelps of the fickle savages, who pelted with jeers their former friends, whom they now took to be cowards.

The entire Northwest had indeed passed into the control of the British; but the inhabitants by no means changed their minds when they changed their flag. In thought, in customs, in speech, whatever of civilization there was in the country was French, and so remained for three-quarters of a century.

CHAPTER IV

THE PONTIAC WAR

THE conquest of Canada by the English brought about several readjustments within the newly acquired territory. The army headquarters were transferred from Quebec to New York, whence General Jeffrey Amherst exercised military control over the posts. Under him Colonel Bouquet at Fort Pitt ranked the commandant at Detroit; but the latter held a general control over the upper lake posts and reported directly to General Amherst. Indian affairs were in charge of Sir William Johnson, whose headquarters, at Johnson Hall in the present State of New York, swarmed with Indian retainers and dependants, as well as with his own half-breed children. Under Sir William was his deputy, George Croghan, who was constantly engaged in going from tribe to tribe in his efforts to keep the peace.

Along the Atlantic coast an American population of English and Dutch descent peopled the country. Nominally colonists, these people formed practically a group of independent states, awaiting only the coming of events already foreshadowed to coalesce into a new nation. From this sturdy civilization the Northwest was completely cut off by the Alleghanies, a barrier not to be crossed by settlers until the close of the Revolution; and for the lake region not until long after that date. As under the French, so under the English, the Northwest continued to be held by garrisons maintained in an Indian country for the protection of the fur trade. The difficulties of the situation arose from the fact that the Indians disputed the right of the French to dispose of the country to the English; while on their part, the English, having no longer to fear the French power, took less and less pains to conciliate the Indians.

Captain Donald Campbell, as he settled down for a long winter at Detroit in 1760, was not ill pleased with his situation. The fort was large and in good repair, with two bastions towards the river and a large, strong bastion towards the Isle au Cochon (Belle Isle); two six-pounders and three mortars made up the battery. Within the high palisades some seventy or eighty houses lined the narrow streets. The fertile country along both banks of the river was cut into narrow farms fronting on the water and extending back into the endless forest. The Indians living in the vicinity of the fort, as well as the settlers, looked to the commandant for both justice[1] and supplies. The soldiers were contented, a fact which the captain ascribed to the absence of rum; and the Indians were seemingly friendly, although the supplies issued to them were meagre in extreme. The social life at Detroit especially pleased the gray-haired bachelor commandant. The women surpassed his expectations; and the men, although very independent, were ever ready for pleasure. The Sunday card-parties

[1] *Gladwin MSS.*, p. 674. Warrant issued by Sir Jeffrey Amherst to Major Henry Gladwin, for the trial and execution of the sentences in the case of two Panis (Pawnee) slaves for the murder of John Clapham. The original warrant was in my possession. The *Gladwin MSS.*, now in possession of the Rev. Henry Gladwin Jebb, of Firbeck Hall, Rotherham, England, are given in the *Michigan Pioneer and Historical Collections*, vol. xxvii.

at the commandant's quarters, attended by both sexes, gave to life at Detroit a zest not known at Fort Pitt; and at a ball, given in honor of the king's birthday, the array of ladies was so fine as to call forth Captain Campbell's hearty commendations, in one of his numerous gossipy letters to Colonel Bouquet.[1] Moreover, both the French and the Indians were as fond of the pleasure-loving captain as their fickle natures would allow.

During the summer, however, emissaries from the Six Nations came to Detroit with large belts, for the purpose of stirring up a general warfare against the English. Matters became so serious that Sir Jeffrey Amherst thought best to send Sir William Johnson to make a treaty at Detroit, and to despatch Major Gladwin with three hundred light infantry to strengthen the western posts. On their arrival in September, Sir William stated his conviction that the conspiracy against the English was universal; but this opinion was not shared by General Amherst. The latter thought the Indians incapable of doing serious harm, but ordered, by way of precaution, that they be kept short of powder.

The visit of Sir William Johnson was the greatest social event that the people of Detroit had ever known. Captain Campbell was in his element. On Sunday evening he gave a ball to which he invited twenty of the French maidens of the settlement. The dance began at eight o'clock in the evening and lasted until five next morning. It was opened by Sir William and Mademoiselle Cuillerier, the daughter of the principal French trader; and her black eyes made such a lasting im-

[1] The correspondence covering this period is to be found in the Bouquet Papers, printed, in so far as they relate to the Northwest, in the *Michigan Pioneer and Historical Collections*, vol. xix. See also Canadian Archives for 1889, and Stone's *Life of Sir William Johnson*.

pression on the gallant Indian agent that the exchange of compliments between them appears in the correspondence for several years, the last mention being found in a letter from James Sterling, who, on behalf of his wife, returns hearty thanks for Sir William's civilities to her four years previous. Before leaving Detroit, Sir William also gave a ball, and on this occasion the dancing continued for eleven hours. There was also a round of dinners and calls, at which wines and cordials were served without stint; presents were showered upon the Indians, and after the final council all the principal inhabitants dined with the diplomat of the forest.

In all these festivities Major Gladwin had no part. Lying in a little house, within hearing of the lively fiddle and the laughter of the dancers, the fever of the country racked his bones and made him long for his Derbyshire home. At evening Sir William would visit him to talk over the events of the day and plan for the future; and it was not until the middle of October that Gladwin was able to leave for Fort William Augustus on his way to England.

In July, 1762, the Indians learned with satisfaction that England was at war with Spain, and soon the report spread far and wide that the French and Spanish were to retake Quebec and all Canada. Here at last was the chance for which the savages had been waiting. With the help of the French they could drive out the English, and once more receive solicitous attention from both nations. At this juncture Major Gladwin again appeared at Detroit, this time with orders to establish posts on Lake Superior and to exercise general supervision over the northwestern establishments. Captain Campbell, although now somewhat wearied by the sameness of garrison pleasures, remained as second in command; and the favor in which he was held by both the French and the Indians was a decided help to the adroit and business-like Gladwin. For company the officers had Sir Robert Davers, an Englishman of education and adventurous disposition, who had been exploring the Lake Superior country [1]

As spring came and the February thaws and March rains loosened the ice bonds that for three long months had locked Detroit from the world, Gladwin at evening must often have stood on the platform within the palisade to look out on the tumultuous river, where the great ice cakes from Lake Ste. Claire, tumbling over each other like marine monsters at play, were hurrying down to the warmer waters of Lake Erie. By day the details of administration kept him busy. The French merchants within the fort grumbled at the increased taxes imposed for the support of a garrison much larger than their own king had maintained; the outlying posts were continually sending for supplies; General Amherst was cautioned against gifts of ammunition and rum to the Indians; and the savages, having bartered their furs for liquor at Niagara, had no means of obtaining the necessaries of life from the traders at Detroit. Some of the French and Indians complained that Gladwin called them dogs, and drove them from his house; and the subsequent career of those persons who made the charges shows that the commandant was an excellent judge of human nature.[2]

[1] All contemporary accounts agree in speaking of "Sir" Robert Davers; but there was no such person in the baronetage of England. Robert Davers, an elder son of Sir Richard Davers, was living at this time, but died before coming into the title. The family has since become extinct.

[2] *Gladwin MSS.*, p. 642. Pierre Barthe claimed that Gladwin's ill-treatment of the French and Indians brought on the war.

GENERAL HENRY GLADWIN

(From a photograph of a painting by John Holland)

Confident of the power of England to hold all she had gained from France, Gladwin had no suspicions that the Indians would foolishly rush to their own destruction by an attack on the British posts. Living behind palisades, and surrounded by a cordon of discontented and intriguing French, Gladwin could have no accurate knowledge of the mischief that for months had been plotted by the Ottawa chief, Pontiac, who had established himself, with his wives, on the narrow Isle a la Peche, rising above the waters of Lake Ste. Claire and concealed from the view of the fort by the thickly wooded Isle au Cochon. There is no reason to believe that Pontiac had impressed himself upon Gladwin as being in any way distinguished above the other chiefs, and doubtless many of the reports—like those of Rogers—of the Ottawa's striking personality are too highly colored. The fact remains, however, that now, at the age of fifty, Pontiac was in the full vigor of his power over the surrounding tribes, and that, during his connection with the whites, his keen intelligence had absorbed valuable military knowledge. According to his own account, he had saved the French at Detroit from massacre in 1746, when the great chief Mickinac (the Turtle) came with his northern bands "to carry off the head of the French commander and eat his heart and drink his blood." Doubtless, too, he had led the Ottawas at Little Meadows in 1755, when Gladwin for the first time heard the Indian war-whoop. At a great council of April, 1763, held on the banks of the River Ecorses, below Detroit, Pontiac had related to the superstitious Indians a dream wherein the Great Spirit sent his message that they were to cast aside the weapons, the manufactures, and the rum of the white men, and, with help from above, drive the dogs in red from every post in their country. The superstitious Indians heard with awe the voice from on high, and left the council prepared to obey the summons.[1]

Detroit being the chief point of attack, Pontiac took upon himself the plan for surprising and massacring that garrison. On May 1st, forty Ottawas danced the calumet dance before Gladwin's house. This visit was for the purpose of spying out the land. Four days later, M. Gouin, a substantial French settler, brought word that his wife, while visiting the Ottawa camp to buy venison, had seen the Indians filing off the ends of their gun-barrels, evidently preparing for some deed of treachery. On the evening of the 6th Gladwin received private information that the next day had been set for the destruction of his garrison. The exact source of this private information is still a matter of some doubt. Lieutenant McDougall, who doubtless knew the secret, gives no hint in his report. It is not impossible that Mademoiselle Cuillerier, whose father and brother unquestionably knew of the conspiracy, put Major Gladwin on his guard, and that James Sterling, who afterwards became her husband, was well rewarded by the British for the timely warning.[2] The reward which Sterling received,

[1] For a full report of this conference, see Parkman's *Conspiracy of Pontiac.* Mr. Parkman has written the history of Pontiac's conspiracy. Those who come after him can but make such corrections in his story as new information requires. Thus he was clearly wrong in spelling the name "Gladwyn"; and he was unfamiliar with Gladwin's antecedents. He wrote from Pontiac's standpoint: as I have attempted to write from Gladwin's.

[2] Mr. C. M. Burton, who propounds this theory, relies on this passage in a letter from Major Henry Basset to Haldimand, dated at Detroit, August 29, 1773, ten years after the siege: "I beg to recommend Mr. James Sterling, who is the first Mercht. at this place & a gentleman, of good character, during the late war, through a Lady, that he then courted, from whom he had the best information, was in

ıowever, might well have been given because he became the leader of the French citizens when they at last determined to support Gladwin. Carver, who visited Detroit five years after the events to be described, and who published three editions of his *Travels through North America* while Gladwin was still living, relates without contemporary contradiction, a story that General Lewis Cass accepted with little hesitation and that Parkman clings to in spite of the doubts thrown upon it by investigations he himself made subsequent to the first edition of his *Conspiracy of Pontiac.*

The evening of May 7th, according to Carver,[1] an Indian girl who had been employed by Major Gladwin to make him a pair of moccasins out of curious elk-skin, brought her work home. The Major was so pleased with the moccasins that, intending them as a present to a friend, he ordered her to take back the remainder of the skin to make a pair for him. Having been paid and dismissed, the woman loitered at the door. Gladwin was quick enough to see that something was amiss. Being urged to tell her trouble, she said, after much hesitation, that as he had always behaved with much goodness to her, she was unwilling to take away the remainder of the skin, because he put so great a value upon it and she should never be able to bring it back. His curiosity being now excited, he insisted that she disclose the secret that seemed to be struggling in her bosom for utterance. At last, on receiving a promise that the intelligence she was about to give him should not turn to her prejudice, and that if it appeared to be

part the means to save this garrison."—*Mich. P. and H. Col.*, vol. xix., p. 311.

[1] Carver is clearly wrong in his date. MacDonald gives May 6th, Friday, as the day of the disclosure.

beneficial she should be rewarded for it, she informed him that at the council to be held with the Indians the following day, Pontiac and his chiefs intended to murder him; and, after having massacred the garrison and inhabitants, to plunder the town. Gladwin then dismissed her with injunctions to secrecy and a promise of reward.

A story at once so romantic and so widely accepted deserves tender treatment; but in the Parkman manuscripts this same tale is found in the mouth of one of Rogers's soldiers, who, as Cass proves, could not have known the facts. The truth probably has been related by the author of the Pontiac Diary. This writer says that an Ottawa Indian called Mahigan, who had entered but reluctantly into the conspiracy, and who felt displeased with the steps his people were taking, came on Friday night, without the knowledge of the other Indians, to the gate of the fort and asked to be admitted to the presence of the commander, saying that he had something of importance to tell him. The gates having been opened, he was conducted to Captain Campbell, second in command, who sent for Gladwin. They wished to call in the interpreter, Labutte, but the Indian objected, saying that he could make himself understood in French. He unfolded the conspiracy of the Indians, and told how they would fall on the English next day. Having obtained a pledge of secrecy, and having refused presents lest the Indians should discover his treachery and kill him, he left the fort secretly. The writer adds that Gladwin made a promise not to disclose the source of his information, and that he kept it.[1]

[1] The Pontiac Diary, written in French, was found in the roof of a Canadian house that was being torn down. Three translations exist: one in manuscript is among the Parkman MSS. in the Library of the Massachusetts Historical Society; another is to be found in School-

The crisis had come in the life of the young commandant of His Majesty's forces at Detroit. Although he could not then have known the extent of the widespread conspiracy which Pontiac had planned, yet he did know that his steadfastness and his knowledge of Indian warfare were about to be put to the test. Gladwin was a soldier by choice and by training, and the seven years he had spent in England's service on the frontiers had not been without its hard lessons. In 1755 he had landed on the banks of the Potomac as a lieutenant in the ill-fated Braddock expedition. He was one of that band of glittering officers whom the provincial soldier, George Washington, had envied as they congregated in the old Braddock House at Alexandria, whose now bare but stately staircase and broad halls seem still to be peopled by the ghosts of fair ladies and dashing soldier gallants of a century and a quarter ago. In the ambush of Little Meadows, Gladwin had learned from the brave yet cautious young Virginian that the military science of the old world was out of place in battling with the denizens of the American forests; and in the campaigns against Ticonderoga and Niagara this new knowledge had stood him in good stead. Scarcely more than a year previous he had given a hostage to fortune by

craft's second volume; and the other in vol. viii. *Michigan Pioneer Collections.* The original has been lost through the carelessness of persons connected with the old Michigan Historical Society; and the loss is a serious one. The authorship of this diary is not known definitely. I believe, however, that it is a portion of the voluminous records of Father de la Richardie, of the Jesuit mission at Sandwich; and that the pages were torn from his books and secreted when the English were endeavoring to obtain evidence of the complicity of the French in the conspiracy. At least the style is his; and the records for 1762 and 1763 are wanting in his manuscripts now in the possession of Mr. Richard R. Elliott, of Detroit.

leading to the altar of the little Wingerwort church in Derbyshire a beautiful girl of nineteen, from whose side military duties in America too quickly recalled him. As the prospective head of an old and honorable county family, yet with little besides his profession of arms to give him support and reputation, Henry Gladwin, at the age of thirty-three, must have realized that the peril which now faced the king's supremacy was for him the door to success or to failure in life, according as he should succeed or fail to hold the post of Detroit against the savages whose hostility and crafty treachery threatened it. And yet, perhaps the warning of danger to come might be without foundation, as so many other warnings had proved to be. Perhaps the prudent, if fickle, Indians were bent merely on extorting more presents and a larger portion of rum. Perhaps the serene river was a pathway of peace and not of war; perhaps the stillness of the trackless forest was not destined to be broken by the warwhoop and the death-cry. Yet if it was to be war he would be found neither unprepared nor wanting in the determination that marks the soldier. In either event, the morrow would tell the story.

About ten o'clock the next morning, as Carver[1] relates, Pontiac and his chiefs arrived, and were conducted to the council chamber, where Gladwin and his principal officers awaited their coming. As the Indians passed on they could not help observing a greater number of troops than usual drawn up on the parade. No sooner had the

[1] Jonathan Carver was born in Connecticut, and when a youth entered the British army, reaching the rank of captain. He was the first to use the name Oregon, and his explorations towards the source of the Mississippi opened that region to the world. For details of his life see Dr. John Coakley's edition of Carver's *Travels*, published in London in 1781, the year after Carver's death. See also Winsor's *Westward Movement* for portrait and maps.

MRS. HENRY GLADWIN

(From a painting attributed to Romney)

Indians entered the council-chamber and seated themselves on the skins prepared for them than Pontiac asked the commandant why his young men, meaning the soldiers, were thus drawn up, and parading the streets. "To keep them perfect in their exercise," was the answer.

Then Pontiac began to protest his friendship and good-will towards the English; and when he came to deliver the belt of wampum, which, according to the warning, was to be the signal for his chiefs to fire, "the governor and all his attendants drew their swords half-way from their scabbards; and the soldiers at the same instant made a clattering with their arms before the doors, which had been purposely left open. Even Pontiac trembled, and instead of giving the belt in the manner proposed, delivered it according to the usual way. His stolid chiefs, who had expected the signal, continued quiet, awaiting the result."

Gladwin, in his turn, made a speech. Instead of thanking Pontiac for the professions of friendship just uttered, he accused him of being a traitor. He said that the English, who knew everything, were convinced of Pontiac's treachery and villanous designs. Then, reaching down to the Indian chief seated nearest him, he drew aside his blanket, discovering the shortened firelock. This entirely disconcerted the Indians. Inasmuch as he had given his word at the time they desired an audience that their persons should be safe, Gladwin said he would hold his promise inviolable, though they so little deserved it. However, he advised them to make the best of their way out of the fort, lest his young men, on being acquainted with their treacherous purposes, should cut every one of them to pieces. Pontiac endeavored to contradict the accusation, and to make excuses for his suspicious conduct; but Gladwin refused to listen, and the Indians sullenly left the fort.

Late that afternoon six warriors returned, bringing with them an old squaw, saying that she had given false information. Gladwin declared that she had never given any kind of advice.[1] When they insisted that he name the author of what he had heard in regard to a plot, he simply replied that it was one of themselves, whose name he promised never to reveal. Whereupon, they went off and carried the old woman with them. When they arrived in camp, Pontiac seized the prisoner and gave her three strokes with a stick on the head, which laid her flat on the ground, and the whole nation assembled around her, and called, "Kill her! kill her!"

The next day was Sunday, and late in the afternoon Pontiac and several of his chiefs paddled across the placid river to smoke the pipe of peace with the officers of the fort. Gladwin, suspicious of so much protestation, refused to go near them; but Captain Campbell, unwilling to lose a chance to pacify the Indians, smoked the peace-pipe with them outside the fort, and took back to Gladwin the message that next day all the nation would come to council, where everything would be settled to the satisfaction of the English, after which the Indians would immediately disperse, so as to remove all suspicion.

At ten o'clock next morning the anxious watchers behind the palisades saw a fleet of canoes coming around the lower point of the long island, and as the swift-darting boats, hurried by paddle and current, covered the three miles of water the soldiers counted fifty-six of these barks, each carrying seven or eight Indians. The

[1] Rogers's *Journal*. Doubtless this is the origin of the romance of the Indian girl.

THE BAFFLED CHIEFS LEAVING THE FORT

bows of the canoes rested lightly on the sand of the sloping bank, and the warriors made their way to the fort only to find the gates fast barred against them. Instead of the cordial welcome they expected, an interpreter met them with the message that not above sixty chiefs might enter. Whereupon Pontiac, enraged at seeing the futility of all his stratagems, and yet confident of ultimate success, in his most peremptory manner bade the interpreter say to Gladwin that if all the Indians had not free access to the fort, none of them would enter it. "Tell him," said the angry chief, "that he may stay in his fort, and that I will keep the country." Then Pontiac strode to his canoe, and paddled for the Ottawa village. His followers, knowing that the fight was on, ran like fiends to the house of an Englishwoman and her two sons, whom they tomahawked and scalped. Another party paddled swiftly to Isle au Cochon, where they first killed twenty-four of King George's bullocks, and then put to death an old English sergeant. Afterwards, the Canadians buried the mutilated corpse; but on returning to the spot, so tradition relates, they were surprised to see an arm protruding from the grave. Thrice the dirt was heaped above the body, and thrice the arm raised itself above the ground, until the mound was sprinkled with holy water; then the perturbed spirit left the body in peace, never since disturbed. Having put to death all the English outside the fort, the Indians sent to Gladwin a Frenchman to report both the killing of the woman and her children, and also the murder of Sir Robert Davers, Captain Robertson, and a boat's crew of six persons,[1] who had been sent to the St. Clair flats to discover a passage for

[1] See Clairmont's testimony, *Gladwin MSS.*, p. 663.

one of the schooners bound to Michilimackinac. This information removed all lingering doubts that the Indians were determined to wipe out the English at Detroit.

On his return to the Ottawa village, Pontiac ordered the squaws to change the camp to the western bank, above the fort. As the night mists gathered upon the tireless river, dropping a curtain between the great chief and his enemies, Pontiac himself, hideous in war paint, leaped into the centre of the ring of braves, and flourishing his tomahawk, began to chant the record of his valorous deeds. One by one the listening braves, catching the contagion from their mighty chief, were drawn into the ring, until at last every savage was wildly dancing the war-dance. There was no sleep for the garrison that night. Gladwin, as he paced the wide street that encircled the buildings of the fort just within the pickets, took counsel with himself as to how he might withstand his crafty enemies. Burning arrows, silent messengers of destruction, might easily set fire to the fourscore or more wooden buildings within the enclosure; and the church, standing near the palisades, was particularly exposed, unless, indeed, the superstitious Indians should hearken to their only less superstitious French allies, who had threatened the savages with the vengeance of the Great Spirit if they should attempt to destroy the house of God. The two six-pounders, the three-pounder, and the mortars composing the battery of the fort were of little avail against an enemy that fought singly and from behind trees or whatever protection the opportunities might afford; but, on the other hand, an English head above the pickets or an English body at a port-hole was the sure lodgement for an Indian bullet. The garrison was made up of one

"ANOTHER PARTY PADDLED SWIFTLY TO THE ISLE AU COCHONS"

hundred and twenty-two soldiers and eight officers, together with about forty fur-traders and their assistants. These traders would fight to save their lives, but were inclined to the French rather than to the English. Between this little garrison and the thousand savages was a single row of palisades made by planting logs close together so that they would stand twenty-five feet above ground. Block-houses at the angles and at the gates afforded additional protection; and, best of all, the brimming river, whose little waves lapped the sandy shore near the south line of palisades, gave an abundant water-supply. A schooner and a sloop,[1] both armed, might be relied on to keep open the line of communication with Niagara, whence Major Walters would send supplies. Promotion would be the reward of success; the torture-stake the penalty of failure.

The chill that comes before dawn was in the air when Gladwin joined the anxious watchers in the block-house. The placid river seemed a great mirror reflecting the brighter stars. Gradually the black outlines of low farm-houses and encircling woods melted into gray; and then beyond the wooded island a disk of molten gold, pushing itself higher and higher, made of the deep waters a broad pathway of shimmering light. On the low bluff far up the river, Gladwin's anxious eye discovered the lodges of Pontiac's Ottawas, who, under the cover of the night, had paddled around the head of the island and noiselessly established themselves above the line of French farm-houses. This meant a siege; and as the commandant was still gazing at the preparations for

[1] These vessels were built in 1761 on an island in the Niagara. The schooner when loaded drew seven feet of water; she carried six guns, and the sloop carried ten. The schooner was named *The Gladwin*, and survived until about 1778. She was lost for want of ballast.

war, a pattering of bullets against the block-house announced the beginning of hostilities.

During the morning a party of Wyandottes, summoned by Pontiac to a council, stopped at the fort on their way. Fortified by English rum, they went off to the meeting-place under promise to Gladwin that they would do all they could to appease the Ottawas and dissuade them from further hostilities. Next came a number of the French settlers, bringing with them chiefs of the Ottawas, Wyandottes, Chippewas, and Pottawatomies, who told Gladwin that almost all the French had gathered at the house of the trader M. Cuillerier,[1] where the Indians were to hold their council. They assured Gladwin that if he would allow Captain Campbell and another officer to go to the council, it would not be hard to persuade the Indians to make peace. At any rate, it could do no harm to try; for both the French and the Indians promised to see that the popular old captain and his companion returned in safety that very night. Gladwin, having little hope of turning Pontiac from his purposes, was reluctant to intrust Captain Campbell to their hands; but the captain, relying on the friendship that had existed between him and the savages, no less than on the promises of the French, urged to be allowed to go to the council. The deciding influence which brought Gladwin to consent was the absolute necessity of getting into the fort a supply of corn, flour, and bear's grease; for

[1] The Cuillerier family disappeared through the marriage of John Cuillerier to Mary Trotier de Beaubien. Her children by her first marriage called themselves Cuillerier *dit* Beaubien, and finally the Cuillerier was dropped, leaving the still well-known name of Beaubien. Mary Beaubien married for her second husband François Picote de Belestre (or Belêtre), which may account for Pontiac's choice of M. Cuillerier as commandant *ad interim*. See Burton's *Cadillac's Village*, p. 42.

the garrison had in store not more than enough for three weeks. So, while Captain Campbell and Lieutenant McDougall went off with high hopes, the prudent commandant, under cover of the darkness, set about gathering provisions from the French settlers across the river.

Scarcely had the embassy of peace crossed the cleared space about the fort than they were met by M. Gouin, who first urged and then begged them not to trust their lives in the keeping of the now excited Indians. The appeal was vain. Yet even while the party were making their way along the bank of the river, they were set upon by a crowd of Indians, at whose hands they would have fared ill indeed had not Pontiac himself come to the rescue. On reaching the appointed place of meeting, they found the largest room filled with French and Indians. In the centre of the group sat M. Cuillerier, arrayed in a hat and coat adorned with gold lace.[1] He kept his seat when the two officers entered and remained covered during the conference. When bread was passed, he ate one piece to show the Indians, as he said, that it was not poisoned. Pontiac, addressing himself to M. Cuillerier, craftily said that he looked upon the Frenchman as his father come to life, and as the commandant at Detroit until the arrival of M. Belêtre, the former French commandant. Then Pontiac, turning to the British officers, told them plainly that to secure peace, the English must leave the country under escort and without arms or baggage. Thereupon M. Cuillerier warmly shook Lieutenant McDougall's hand, saying, "My friend, this is my work; rejoice that I have obtained such good terms for you. I thought Pontiac would be much harder." Hoping against hope for the garrison,

[1] *Gladwin MSS.* Testimony of Mr. Rutherford, p. 638 *et seq.*

but apprehensive of no present danger to himself and his brother officer, Captain Campbell made a short but earnest plea for peace. Then he and Lieutenant McDougall waited anxiously for the usual grunt of approval. The moments dragged, and still the Indians sat impassive. For the space of an hour there was unbroken silence. Then Captain Campbell, dejected by evident failure, arose to retrace his steps to the fort. "My father," said Pontiac, quietly, "will sleep to-night in the lodges of his red children."

The unusual intelligence that had raised Pontiac above every other Indian chief, had led the English to rely on his sense of honor, a quality rare indeed among savages. What civilized races call treachery is to the Indian legitimate warfare. It never occurs to a savage to expose himself to harm in order to accomplish an end that he can attain safely by deception. In spite of all promises, therefore, the two Englishmen were sent under strong guard to the house of M. Meloche. That they were not immediately put to death was due solely to the fact that Gladwin held several Pottawatomie prisoners, and Pontiac shrewdly enough feared that if the commandant should retaliate on his hostages, that tribe would vanish into the forest, leaving him without the support he so much needed.

Captain Campbell and Lieutenant McDougall trusted to the promises of the French more than to those of the Indians. It has been assumed that the French at Detroit were the victims of the Pontiac conspiracy only to a less degree than were the English. It is true that there were a few prudent French farmers who gave to Gladwin what assistance they could give without drawing down on themselves the enmity of the Indians; but it was generally believed among the French

THE SIEGE OF THE FORT AT DETROIT

that the English would soon be driven out of New France, and that the French king would again be their monarch. For two centuries the warfare between French and English over the fur-trade had been as barbarous as war was in Europe during the same time; human life on either side of the Atlantic was not considered worth a king's serious consideration; and the soldier of that day in every nation was a freebooter. It is not surprising that the French traders and wood-rangers at Detroit should have seized upon Pontiac's war to despoil their ancient enemies and their conquerors of less than three years' standing. The only cause for surprise is that the French did not from the start openly make common cause with Pontiac. That they secretly gave aid and encouragement to the Indians was repeatedly charged by Gladwin. The convincing proof of his assertions is to be found in the official reports of inquiries he caused to be held at Detroit during the siege, reports which after more than a century and a quarter of oblivion, have been found and made available by one of Gladwin's descendants.[1] The problem for Gladwin was to hold out at Detroit until both the French and Indians could be convinced that the French Government would not assist them and that the peace with England was definite and lasting.

The terms proposed to Captain Campbell were offered next day to Gladwin, and the French urged him to escape while he might; but the young Englishman abso-

[1] *Gladwin MSS.*, Jadoc's testimony, p. 656. It appears that the heads of the French families were unwilling to place their wives, children, and possessions in jeopardy; but were ready enough to sacrifice the three hundred young men "who had neither parents, nor much property to lose." "The villany of the settlement in general, to write it, would fill a volume."

lutely refused to make any terms with savages. His soldiers caught his spirit, so that he was able to write confidently to General Amherst, that he would hold out until succor should come. The schooner *Gladwin*, which bore the despatch, eluded Pontiac's canoes; and when the chief reported his failure to M. Cuillerier, the Frenchman jeered at him because five canoes withdrew at the death of a single Pottawatomie.[1]

Now began a long series of disasters to the English. One by one the results of Pontiac's plotting transpired. Everything seemed to be giving way before the exulting savages. On May 22d news came of the capture of Fort Sandusky.[2] At the inquiry Ensign Paully related that on May 16th his sentry called him to speak with some Indians at the gate. Finding several of his own Indians in the party, he allowed seven to enter the fort and gave them tobacco. Soon one of the seven raised his head as a signal, whereupon the two sitting next the officer seized and bound him and hurried him from the room. He passed his sentry dead in the gateway, and saw lying about the corpses of his little garrison. His sergeant was killed in the garden where he had been planting; the merchants were dead and their stores were plundered. The Indians spared Paully and took him to their camp at Detroit, where he was adopted as the husband of a widowed squaw, from whose toils he finally escaped to his friends in the fort.

On May 18th, Ensign Holmes, who commanded the garrison at Fort Miami, on the Maumee, was told by a Frenchman that Detroit had been attacked, whereupon the ensign called in his men and set them at work making cartridges. Three days later Holmes's Indian ser-

[1] *Gladwin MSS.*, p. 641.

[2] *Ibid.*, p. 636.

vant besought him to bleed one of her friends who lay ill in a cabin outside the stockade. On his errand of mercy he was shot dead. The terrified garrison of nine were only too glad to surrender at the command of two Frenchmen, Pontiac's messengers, who were on their way to the Illinois to get a commandant for Detroit.[1] On May 25th, at Fort St. Joseph, seventeen Pottawatomies came into Ensign Schlosser's room on the pretence of holding a council. A Frenchman who had heard that treachery was planned, rushed in to give the alarm, whereupon Ensign Schlosser was seized, ten of the garrison were killed, and the other three with the commandant were made prisoners. They were afterwards brought to Detroit and exchanged.[2]

On the 29th the long expected bateaux from Niagara were seen coming up the river. With joyful hearts the garrison looked forward to the end of their tedious siege. But as the boats came nearer, the English saw with dismay that Indians were the masters of the craft. When the foremost bateaux came opposite the schooner, two soldiers in her, made the motion to change rowing places. Quickly they seized the Indians and threw them overboard. One Indian carried his assailant with him and in the struggle both found death. Another soldier struck the remaining Indian over the head with an oar and killed him. Under the fire of sixty savages on the shore the three plucky Englishmen escaped to the vessel with their prize, which contained eight barrels of most acceptable pork and flour. Of the ten bateaux that had set out from Niagara under Lieutenant Cuyler, eight had been captured and the force had been completely

[1] *Gladwin MSS.*, Testimony of James Beems, p. 637. The Frenchmen were Godfroy and Chene.

[2] *Ibid.*, Testimony of Ensign Schlosser, p. 636.

routed by an Indian surprise and night attack at the mouth of the Detroit.[1]

Following the capture of the bateaux came the darkest days of the siege. Often during a whole day the Indians, drunken on the rum from the captured stores, did not fire a shot, but in their fiendish glee they gave notice of their presence by sending the scalped and mangled bodies of English captives to float past the palisades in sight of the sentries.

To add to these tales of disaster came Father La Jaunay, missionary at Michilimackinac,[2] to tell the bloodiest story of all. On June 2d, the Chippewas living near the fort assembled for their usual game of ball. They played from morning till noon, and Captain George Etherington and Lieutenant Leslie stood by to watch the sport. Suddenly the ball was struck over the palisades. A dozen Indians rushed through the gate to get it. Before the dazed sentry could recover, the captain and lieutenant were seized and hurried off; the Indians within the fort had received from the squaws stationed there hatchets hidden under their blankets; in an instant Lieutenant Jamet, fifteen soldiers, and a trader named Tracy were put to death, five others were reserved for a like fate, and the remainder of the garrison were made prisoners. Had it not been for the powerful

[1] *Bouquet Papers*, *Canadian Archives*, 1889, p. 227. Cuyler himself escaped to Presque Isle, Surgeon Cope and fifteen men were killed. On June 20th, as he was returning to Detroit from Niagara, Cuyler witnessed the destruction of Presque Isle, but being ten miles out in the lake could give no assistance. See *Gladwin MSS.*, pp. 637, 638.

[2] In 1712, Father Marest built a church on the south side of the Straits of Mackinac near the present site of Mackinac City, and two years later Louvigny built a fort there. Thereafter the name Michilimackinac, which had been applied to the region, was confined to the settlement and the island.

influence of Charles Langlade[1] and his friends the Ottawas, all the English must have perished; as it was, Captain Etherington and Lieutenant Leslie, with fourteen men, were held until July 18th, and were then taken to Montreal by the Ottawas.[2]

On Sunday, the 26th of June, Pontiac, for mingled purposes of religion and business, paddled across the Detroit river to attend mass in the little French chapel. When the services were over, the chief selected three of the chairs in which the thrifty French had been carried to church, and making the owners his chairmen, he and his guard set off on a search for provisions. He imitated the credit certificates issued by Gladwin and gave in payment for cattle billets signed by his mark, the picture of a coon. The provisions were transported to Pontiac's camp near Parent's Creek, and in due time the billets were redeemed. The next day Pontiac sent another summons to surrender, saying that nine hundred Indians were on their way from Michilimackinac, and if Gladwin waited till those Indians arrived he would not be answerable for the consequences. Gladwin replied that until Captain Campbell and Lieutenant

[1] *Gladwin MSS.* Etherington to Gladwin, p. 631. Mrs. Catherwood's story, *The White Islander*, relates the experience of Alexander Henry, who was one of the survivors of the massacre. Henry's own published narrative forms the basis for the story and for Parkman's chapter.

[2] Etherington had warned the little garrison at La Bay (Green Bay); Lieutenant Gorrell and his men were brought as prisoners to Michilimackinac, and were sent to Montreal with Etherington and Leslie. The garrison at Ouatanon (Lafayette), on the Wabash, was to have been massacred on June 1st; but the French persuaded the Indians to make prisoners of Lieutenant Jenkins and his men and to send them to the Illinois. See *Gladwin MSS.*, Letters from Etherington and Jenkins to Gladwin, pp. 633, 639. Le Bœuf, Venango, Carlisle, and Bedford were cut off on June 18th.

McDougall were returned, Pontiac might save himself the trouble of sending messages to the fort. To this the wily Pontiac made answer that he had too much regard for his distinguished captives to send them back; because the kettle was on the fire for the entire garrison, and in case they were returned he should have to boil them with the rest.

On the 30th of June, the *Gladwin*, returning from Niagara, ploughed her way up the white-capped river and landed a force of fifty men, together with provisions and some much needed ammunition. For two months Gladwin had guarded Detroit against surprise and had sustained a siege conducted by Pontiac in person, while fort after fort had fallen before the savages. As the Indians returned from their successes elsewhere they were more and more eager for the overthrow of the one fort that hitherto had baffled all their efforts. In his extremity Pontiac now turned on the French and threatened to force them to take up arms against the English. During the siege, however, copies of the definitive treaty between France and England had reached Detroit; and, on July 4th, Gladwin assembled the French, read to them the articles of peace, and sent a copy across the river to the priest. Thereupon forty Frenchmen, choosing James Sterling as their leader, took service under Gladwin. On this same day a party from the fort made a sortie for the purpose of bringing in some powder and lead from the house of M. Baby, who had taken refuge in the fort. Lieutenant Hay, an old Indian-fighter, commanded the force, and in his exultation over driving off an attacking party, he tore the scalp from the head of a wounded Indian and shook his trophy in the face of his enemies. It happened that the one of the savages killed was the son of a Chippewa chief; and as soon as the tribe heard of their disaster they went to Pontiac to reproach him for being the cause of their ills, saying that he was very brave in taking a loaf of bread or a beef from a Frenchman who made no resistance, but it was the Chippewas who had all the men killed and wounded every day. Therefore, they said, they intended to take from him what he had been saving. Lieutenant McDougall had already made his escape to the fort; but they went to Meloche's house, where the brave old Captain Campbell was still confined. They stripped him, carried him to their camp, killed him, took out his heart and ate it, cut off his head, and divided his body into small pieces. Such was the end a brave soldier, esteemed, loved, and sincerely mourned in the army, from General Amherst and Colonel Bouquet down to the privates who served under him.

At midnight on July 10th the sentries in the fort saw floating down the black river a great mass of fire. The flames, feeding on fagots and birch-bark, leaped high in the air, lighting up the forest-covered island in the background and bringing into high relief the whitewashed cottages that lined the shore. Hurried by the swift current, a great fire-raft, built by the French[1] and Indians, made for the two vessels anchored in the stream; but the alert crews had anticipated their danger and were prepared for it. The vessels were anchored by two cables, and as the flaming pile approached, they slipped one cable and easily swung out of the way of the enemy.

The hot days succeeded one another all too slowly. On the 29th of July the guards heard firing down the river, and half an hour later the surprised sentries saw

[1] *Gladwin MSS.*, p. 647.

the broad surface of the river dotted with bateaux, the regular dip of whose oars was borne a long way on the still morning air. A detachment of two hundred and sixty men under the command of Captain Dalyell, one of General Amherst's aides-de-camp, had come to put an end to the siege. Captain Dalyell was an officer of undoubted bravery, and the tales of slaughter he had heard at Presque Isle and Sandusky on his way to Detroit made him anxious to crush Pontiac by one bold stroke. Gladwin, whom months of close acquaintance with the wary Indian chief had taught discretion, gave consent to Dalyell's plan of a night attack, only on the threat of the latter to leave Detroit unless such a blow should be struck.[1] The treacherous French, learning the details of the plan, immediately put Pontiac on his guard.[2] In the earliest hours of the 31st of July, Dalyell marched a force of two hundred and fifty men along the sandy bank of the swift-flowing river, passed the well-enclosed cottages of the French and on towards Parent's creek, a little stream that fell into the river about a mile and a half above the fort.

The twenty-five men in advance had just stepped on the rude bridge across the run, when from the ridges

[1] Gladwin and McDonald agree that the night attack was strenuously opposed by the former. There is a tradition (Fred. Carlisle relates it as a fact, in his report to the Wayne County Historical Society for 1890) that Dalyell and Gladwin both sought the hand of Madeleine de Tonnancour, and that when she favored the aide-de-camp, Gladwin willingly sent him to his death. Inasmuch as Gladwin was happily married during the previous year, this story is simply another illustration of the fables that have gained currency in connection with the Pontiac conspiracy.

[2] Bart, the gunsmith, went through the Ottawa village shouting "Down with your huts! Down with your huts! Send your squaws and children to the woods!"—*Gladwin MSS.*, p. 646.

A LIGHT-INFANTRY SOLDIER OF THE PERIOD

that formed the farther side of the gully came a volley of musketry that hurled the little band in confusion back on the main body. In the pitchy darkness, cheered on by Dalyell's steady words of command, the British swept the ridges only to find themselves chasing those deadly will-o'-the-wisps, the flashes of an enemy's guns. To fall back was absolutely necessary; but here again the soldiers were met by the rapid firing of the Indians who had occupied the houses and orchards between the English and the fort. Every charge of the soldiers only enveloped the pursuers in a maze of buildings, trees, and fences, while the Indians beat a nimble retreat, firing from behind any shelter they could find. From an open cellar the concealed savages poured a deadly fire into the British ranks; but still Dalyell was undismayed. Where commands were of no effect, he beat the men with the flat of his sword. Captain Robert Rogers,[1]

[1] After receiving the surrender of Detroit, Rogers had been with Colonel Grant in South Carolina, fighting the Cherokees. He now had twenty Rangers in his party. Two years before he had married the daughter of Rev. Arthur Brown, rector of St. John's Church, Portsmouth, New Hampshire, and after leaving Detroit he received a grant of land in Rumford, now Concord, New Hampshire, where the Rogers House was still standing in 1885. He was in London in 1765, and there published his *Journals* and his *Concise Account of North America;* possibly, too, he was the author of *Ponteach; or the Savages of America;* a tragedy printed in 1766 by Rogers's publisher, J. Millan, of London. In 1766 General Gage sent Rogers to Michilimackinac, where he plotted to turn the post over to the French, out of revenge for the steps taken by government to curb his extravagance and stop his illicit trade. In 1770 he appeared again in London, was presented at court, had his accounts settled, but failed to obtain the baronetcy he demanded. He tried to obtain a command in the American army, but Washington would have nothing to do with him. On October 21, 1776, as lieutenant-colonel of a British regiment, he was defeated by the Americans at Mamaroneck, New York. His wife secured a divorce by act of the New Hampshire Legislature, in 1778, and he

trained in frontier warfare, burst open the door of a cottage filled with Indians, and with his Rangers put the ambushed savages to flight. Captain Gray fell mortally wounded in a charge. Dalyell himself, twice wounded, went to the succor of a helpless sergeant, when he too fell dead, and the Indians smeared their faces with his heart's blood. Major Rogers, who succeeded to the command, took possession of the well-built Campau house, where his soldiers, fortified without by solid logs and bales of furs, and strengthened within by copious draughts from a keg of whiskey, held the enemy at bay until communication could be had with the fort. Two bateaux armed with swivels soon came to the rescue of Rogers, who had been besieged by about two hundred Indians. The remainder of the force under Captain Grant beat an orderly retreat. Of the two hundred and fifty who went out, one hundred and fifty-nine were killed or wounded, while the Indian loss did not exceed twenty.

This victory of Bloody Run, as Parent's Creek was ever afterwards called, restored the waning fortunes of Pontiac, and every day brought accessions to his forces. Yet never since the siege began was Major Gladwin more hopeful of ultimate success. So the heats of August passed with an occasional skirmish, and September began. The Indians, powerless against the palisades, again turned their attention to the vessels that kept open the food communication with the settlers across the river and made occasional trips to Fort Niagara for supplies and ammunition. From one of these latter voyages the schooner *Gladwin* was returning on the

died in obscurity in London, about 1800. Dr. F. B. Hough's edition of Rogers's *Journals* (Albany, 1883), and J. B. Walker's sketch, before adverted to, are the best authorities.

night of September 4th, when, the wind failing, she anchored nine miles below the fort, having on board her commander, Horst, her mate, Jacobs, and a crew of ten men. Six Iroquois, supposed to be friendly to the English, had been landed that morning, and to their brethren was probably due the night attack made by a large force of Indians, whose light canoes dropped so silently down the dark river that a single cannon-shot and one volley of musketry were all the welcome that could be given them. Horst fell in the first onslaught, and Jacobs, seeing that all hope was gone, gave the command to blow up the vessel. At the word some Wyandottes, who knew the meaning of the command, gave warning to their companions, and all made a dash overboard, swimming for dear life to be clear of the dreaded destruction. Jacobs, no less astonished than gratified at the effect of his words, had no further trouble that night, and the next morning he sailed away to the fort. Six of the sailors escaped unhurt to wear the medals presented to them for bravery.

From the beginning of the siege Pontiac[1] had relied on help from the French in the Illinois country, to whom he had sent an appeal for aid. " Since our father, Mr. Belêtre, departed," he said, "the Indians had no news, nor did any letters come to the French, but the English alone received letters. The English say incessantly that

[1] There is evidence that Le Duc St. Corne Le Duc and other French agitators spread abroad the report that the French were in the St. Lawrence ready to drive out the English, and that Pontiac, in common with the Indians and French traders, relied on these reports.—See *Gladwin MSS.*, p. 652, testimony of John Seger. The Delawares and Shawanese also did their utmost to stir up strife. In fact, there was no Indian trouble in the Northwest for more than half a century in which the Shawanese were not the instigators.—See *Gladwin MSS.*, pp. 644, 671.

since the French and Spaniards have been overthrown, they own all the country. When our father, Mr. Belêtre, was going off from hence, he told us, 'My children, the English to-day overthrow your father; as long as they have the upper hand ye will not have what ye stand in need of; but this will not last.' We pray our father at the Illinois to take pity on us and say, 'These poor children are willing to raise me up.' Why do we that which we are doing to-day? It is because we are unwilling that the English should possess these lands; this is what causeth thy children to rise up and strike everywhere."

This message was indorsed by the Chippewas and by the French inhabitants at Detroit, the latter complaining that they were obliged to submit to Indian exactions. M. Neyeon, the French commandant at Fort Chartres, in the Illinois country, acting under pressure from General Amherst (who had learned from Gladwin how essential to Pontiac's success was the expected help from the French), replied to the appeal that "the great day had come at last wherein it had pleased the Master of Life to command the Great King of France and him of England to make peace between them, sorry to see the blood of men spilled so long." So these kings had ordered all their chiefs and warriors to bury the hatchet. He promised that when this was done the Indians would see the road free, the lakes and rivers unstopped, and ammunition and merchandise would abound in their villages; their women and children would be cloaked; they would go to dances and festivals, not cumbered with heavy clothes, but with skirts, blankets, and ribbons. "Forget then, my dear children," he commanded,[1]

[1] *Gladwin MSS.*, Letters from Peter Joseph Neyeon de Villiere, pp. 363, 364, 365.

"all evil talks. Leave off from spilling the blood of your brethren, the English. Our hearts are now but one; you cannot, at present, strike the one without having the other for an enemy also."

This message had the desired effect. Dated on September 27th, its contents so dashed Pontiac's hopes that on October 12th he sued most submissively for peace. Gladwin, being in need of flour, granted a truce, but made no promises, saying that General Amherst alone had power to grant pardon. To Amherst the commandant wrote that it would be good policy to leave matters open until the spring, when the Indians would be so reduced for want of powder there would be no danger that they would break out again, "provided some examples are made of our good friends, the French, who set them on." Gladwin then adds, "No advantage can be gained by prosecuting the war, owing to the difficulty of catching them [the Indians]. Add to this the expense of such a war, which, if continued, the ruin of our entire peltry trade must follow, and the loss of a prodigious consumption of our merchandise. It will be the means of their retiring, which will reinforce other nations on the Mississippi, whom they will push against us, and make them our enemies forever. Consequently it will render it extremely difficult to pass that country, and especially as the French have promised to supply them with everything they want."

Then follows the passage,[1] often quoted to show Gladwin's cynical brutality: "They have lost between eighty and ninety of their best warriors; but if your Excellency still intends to punish them for their barbarities, it may be easier done, without any expense to

[1] *Gladwin MSS.*, p. 675. This letter is in Gladwin's own handwriting, and is doubtless his original draft.

the crown, by permitting a free sale of rum, which will destroy them more effectually than fire and sword." Parkman closes the quotation at this point; but a very different turn is given to the matter in the next sentence, taken from the draft of the letter in Gladwin's own handwriting, as follows: "But on the contrary, if you intend to accommodate matters in spring, which I hope you will for the above reasons, it may be necessary to send up Sir William Johnson." This is the letter of a warrior, who was also somewhat of a statesman.

Pontiac's conspiracy ended in failure. For five months the little garrison at Detroit had been surrounded by a thousand or more savages; and nothing but the untiring watchfulness and the intrepid coolness of the resourceful commandant saved the post from annihilation and prevented the Indian occupation of the Lake country. General Amherst was so well pleased with Gladwin's course during the first four months of the siege that on September 17th he wrote to the Secretary at War, Ellis: "As there have been two deputy adjutant-generals serving here, I have taken the liberty to show a mark of my entire satisfaction of Major Gladwin's good conduct and commendable behavior in appointing him a deputy adjutant-general; but to remain with the troops at Detroit in the same manner as has been ordered.[1] This is no more than a name, but should it be your gracious pleasure to approve it, and honor Major Gladwin with the rank of lieutenant-colonel, I am firmly of the opinion that the promotion of so deserving an officer must at any time be a benefit to his Majesty's service, and this is the sole view I have in mentioning it to you."

[1] *Gladwin MSS.*, p. 675.

It fell to the lot of Colonel Bradstreet, the hero of Fort Frontenac, to lead the great force which was to confirm the British power in the Lake country. The vainglory of that officer led him to make with the Indians a peace which General Gage, who had succeeded Amherst, was compelled to repudiate. Bradstreet's expedition got no farther than Sandusky, but a detachment reached Detroit late in the August of 1764, and on the last day of that month Colonel Gladwin departed from Niagara on his way to New York. He was heartily tired of fighting Indians, and preferred to resign rather than to undertake another campaign of that kind. Returning to England, we find him in 1774 living a contented life with his wife and children, but ready again to take up arms for his king. On a visit to London he was presented to George III., who asked him how long he had been in town. "Three weeks," replied the soldier, to the consternation of George Wert, who whispered to him to say that he had just arrived. "But," says Gladwin, in a letter to General Gage, "as I went to court only on that occasion, I thought there could be no harm in speaking the truth."

Gladwin saw no further military service.[1] From time to time he was promoted until he reached the grade of major-general; and for a quarter of a century he enjoyed a well-earned rest. He died on the 22d of June, 1791, and a tablet in the Wingerworth church, in Derbyshire, still bears record that "early trained to arms and martial deeds, he sought for fame amidst the toils of hostile war with that ardour which animates the breast of a brave soldier. On the plains of North

[1] For a full record of the facts relating to Gladwin, see *Gladwin MSS.*, pp. 606–611.

America he reaped the laurels at the battles of Niagara and Ticonderoga, in which he was wounded. His courage was conspicuous, and his memorable defence of Fort Detroit against the attacks of the Indians will long be recorded in the annals of a grateful country."

CHAPTER V

ENGLAND TAKES POSSESSION OF THE NORTHWEST

WHEN England came to sum up her gains in the Seven Years' War, she found to her credit an embarrassment of riches. From France she had wrested both Canada and Guadaloupe, besides quieting forever French pretensions in India. Spain, taking up the cudgels for France after the fall of Quebec, when the ultimate triumph of England was assured, had lost Cuba by the fall of Havana in 1762. Happy had it been for civilization had Spain's grip on the "gem of the Antilles" been released forever; but in the readjustments that followed she received back Cuba from England in exchange for the Floridas, and from France by secret treaty she secured Louisiana, from the Mississippi to the Pacific. If Pitt had remained in power to make the treaty that his genius and energy had compelled, the choice might not have been between restoring to France either the fur-producing Canada or Guadaloupe, rich in sugar. His ability would have sufficed to confirm to England what her armies and her fleets had won.

To Benjamin Franklin is due the credit, if not for the retention of Canada, at least for making the people of England appreciate the wisdom of the choice. William Burke, the brother, and at this time the thought-sharer, of the great Edmund, ingeniously argued for the sugar plantations, and caught the ear of English prejudice, both commercial and political, with the proposition that it would be good policy to keep an enemy at the back of the lusty and arrogant young colonies, whose ideas of independence already had begun to alarm the mother-country. At this time (1760) Franklin was in London as the agent of the Pennsylvania Assembly. Controversy being the breath of his nostrils, he brought to the discussion such a wealth of knowledge, such a keenness of sarcasm, and such an intimate acquaintance with the conditions in America, that Burke gave him the credit of having "said everything, and everything in the best manner, that the cause could bear."[1]

The apprehensions of American independence he brushed aside with the statement that already there were fourteen separate governments on the Atlantic; and if the settlements should be extended, probably as many more would spring up on the inland side. Not only were these colonies under different governors, but they had different forms of government, different laws, different interests, and some of them different religious persuasions and different manners. So great was their jealousy of one another that however necessary a union of the colonies had long been for their common defence and security against their enemies, yet they had never agreed either themselves to form such a union, or to ask the mother-county to establish it. Nothing but the immediate command of the crown had been able to produce even the imperfect union, but lately seen there, of the forces of some colonies. "If they could not agree to unite for their defence against the French and Indians, who were perpetually harassing their settlements,

[1] Sparks's *Franklin*, vol. iv., p. 2.

BENJAMIN FRANKLIN

burning their villages, and murdering their people, could it reasonably be supposed there was danger of their uniting against their own nation, which protects and encourages them, with which they have so many connections and ties of blood, interest, and affection, and which, it is well known, they all love much more than they love one another!"

So much for the special pleader. Franklin, however, seems already to have noted a fall in the barometer. "When I say," he continues, "that such a union is impossible, I mean without the most grievous tyranny and oppression. . . . While the government is mild and just, while important civil and religious rights are secure, such subjects will be dutiful and obedient. *The waves do not rise but when the winds blow.*"

He set forth, too, the barbarity of maintaining on the frontier of the colonies a nation that, even in times of peace between the two crowns, instigated the ravages of savages "that delight in war, and take pride in murder"; and, on the contrary, he showed the advantage of providing in the easily accessible lands of the interior such an outlet for the increasing population as should keep the people to agriculture and thus prevent competition with the British manufacturer. The fur regions of America were more accessible to London than those of Siberia; American iron and hemp journeyed to market not so far as the Russian; and already the single province of Pennsylvania was taking annually English manufactures to the extent of more than a quarter of a million pounds sterling. Such reasoning prevailed; Canada became a part of the realm of England.

The "vast empire on the frozen shores of Ontario," added to Great Britain by the energy of the elder Pitt, was divided by royal proclamation into four distinct and separate governments: Quebec, East Florida, West Florida, and Grenada.[1] The government of Quebec had for its western boundary a line drawn from Lake Nepissing to the foot of Lake Champlain. East and West Florida included the lands within the present State of Florida; and Grenada comprehended the island of that name, together with the Grenadines, Dominico, St. Vincent, and Tobago.

Within their respective colonies, governors and councils might dispose of the crown lands to settlers; but no governor or commander-in-chief should presume, upon any pretence whatever, to grant warrants of survey or pass patents for lands beyond the bounds of their respective governments; and, until the king's pleasure should be further known, the lands beyond the heads or sources of any of the rivers which fall into the Atlantic were especially reserved to the Indian tribes for hunting-grounds. The valley of the Ohio and the country about the Great Lakes was not open to settlement or to purchase without special leave and license, and all persons who had either wilfully or inadvertently seated themselves upon any lands within the prohibited zone between the Alleghanies and the southern limits of the Hudson Bay Company's territory were warned to remove themselves from such settlements.

[1] For the text of the proclamation October 7, 1763, see Debates of the House of Commons, in the year 1774, on the bill for making more effectual provision for the government of the province of Quebec, drawn up from the notes of the Right Honorable Sir Henry Cavendish, Bart., member for Lostwithiel: London, 1839. The speeches were taken in short-hand by Cavendish and were printed forty-eight years later when the subject of Canadian government was again up in Parliament. The report also contains Dr. John Mitchell's map of the North American provinces prepared in 1755 for the Board of Trade and Plantations. The *Canadian Archives for* 1889 also contain the proclamation, in so far as it relates to Indian lands.

In order to put a stop to the "great frauds and abuses that had been committed in purchasing lands from the Indians, to the great prejudice of our interests and to the great dissatisfaction of the Indians, and to convince the Indians of the justice and determined resolution to remove all reasonable cause of discontent," no private purchases of Indian lands within the colonies were to be allowed; but all such Indian lands must first be purchased by the representatives of the crown from the Indians in open assembly. Trade with the Indians was to be free and open to all British subjects; but every trader was to be required to take out a license and to give security to observe such regulations as might be made for the regulation of such trade. Fugitives from justice found within the Indian lands were to be seized and returned to the settlements for trial.

Such was the first charter of the Northwest, if charter is the correct word to apply to an instrument that created a forest preserve, and provided merely for the apprehension and deportation of rogues and trespassers. To the new provinces was held out the hope that in time they might grow into the stature of colonies, each with a popular assembly instead of an appointive council; and within their borders English law was to prevail; but the Northwest was treated simply as the roaming place of savages.

While the partition of North America was engaging the attention of the three great nations of Europe, the people of the colonies were eager to occupy the new regions won by their valor. The members of the Ohio Company, whose enterprise had been rudely checked by the French occupation of the lands patented to them, at once set about establishing their rights. To this end, Colonel Thomas Cresap most diplomatically made overtures to Bouquet, the British commandant at Fort Pitt; for on the protection of that garrison all attempts at settlement must depend for success. Inasmuch, also, as it was the purpose of the company to settle on the lands immigrants from Germany and Switzerland, the name and fame of the Swiss general, Henry Bouquet, would make it quite worth while to enlist the active co-operation of this hero of three armies, by admitting him to an equal share in their undertaking.[1]

From Presque Isle, whither he had gone to restore the fort burned by the retreating French, and to establish a base of supplies on Lake Erie,[2] Bouquet sent an evasive reply to Colonel Cresap. While leaving open the subject of joining the Ohio Company, and admitting his ability to procure German and Swiss settlers on proper conditions, Bouquet pointed out the fact that by the late treaty at Easton, approved and confirmed by the ministry at home, the British engaged not to settle the lands beyond the Alleghany; and although the governments of Virginia and Maryland did not accede to that treaty, still they were equally bound by it, and

[1] The correspondence is to be found in the *Canadian Archives for* 1889. Bouquet had served in the Dutch and Sardinian armies; in 1754 he and Frederick Haldimand were selected to raise men for the "Royal Americans," afterwards known as the Sixtieth Rifles, the officers of which were either American or foreign Protestants. He died at Pensacola, Florida, about September 4, 1765. His papers are calendared in the *Canadian Archives*, and many of them have been printed in the *Michigan Pioneer and Historical Collections*.

[2] *Canadian Archives*, 1889, Bouquet Correspondence, p. 45 *et seq.* Bouquet left Fort Pitt July 7, 1760, with a detachment, and reached Presque Isle on the 17th, the distance being eighty-one and a half miles to Venango, then forty-six to Le Bœuf, then fifteen to Presque Isle, a total of one hundred and forty-two and a half miles. By the orders of General Amherst, Major Henry Gladwin was exploring Lake Erie. Monckton was in command at Fort Pitt.

no settlement would be permitted on the Ohio until the consent of the Indians should be procured.

It is not unlikely that Bouquet and Franklin had talked over plans for the settlement of the country beyond the mountains; for, in the letter to Colonel Cresap, Bouquet asserts that the lands are too remote to be dependent upon any one of the provinces, thus making it necessary first to fix the form of government for this new colony. This idea, as will appear, was fully developed in Franklin's correspondence and argument on the Walpole grant. The members of the company, several of whom were of his Majesty's council in Virginia, treated Bouquet's letter as an acceptance of their proposition; and Lieutenant-colonel Mercer, in a statement of the financial condition of the enterprise, set forth that there were twenty shares on each of which £500 had been paid, and the cash on hand together with the outstanding debts due to the company made the assets upward of £2000.

Bouquet's answer was a proclamation, dated at Fort Pitt, October 30, 1761, in which, after referring to the fact that the treaty of Easton preserved as an Indian hunting-ground the country to the west of the Alleghanies, he forbade either settlements or hunting in the western country, unless by special permission of the commander-in-chief or of the governor of one of the provinces.[1] As might have been expected, this proclamation gave rise to uneasiness in Virginia, as it seemed to obstruct the resettling of lands which had been taken

[1] *Canadian Archives*, 1889, p. 73. The treaty of Easton having been negotiated under the direction of General Forbes, Bouquet seemed to regard it as especially sacred. Indeed, he never was inclined to favor the Virginians, or to consider that they had any rights beyond the mountains. His sympathies were wholly with the Pennsylvanians.

up by patent under his Majesty, and from which the settlers had been driven by the war. Lieutenant-governor Farquier stated that there were such Virginia settlements on the Monongahela, the Greenbrier, and the New River to the westward of the Alleghanies, and on the waters of the Ohio; and he objected to the returning settlers being subjected to court-martial proceedings when they should attempt to secure their homes.[1]

Governor Farquier admitted that he, in common with the other governors of provinces, had received, through the Lords of Trade and Plantations, orders to make no grants of land on the Ohio until his Majesty's further pleasure be known; but Bouquet's proclamation appears to have been issued entirely on his own motion, as the result of his extensive knowledge of the conditions in the western country. Certainly he received no orders from General Amherst, whose first information in regard to Bouquet's action came in a letter from Governor Farquier inclosing a copy of the proclamation. Amherst saw nothing in the document beyond protection to those persons who had a just title, and the exclusion of those who had not. At the same time he good-naturedly cautioned Bouquet to "avoid doing anything that could give the colonies the least room to complain of the military power."

[1] Before 1749 there were no settlers in western Virginia. In that year a demented man wandered from Frederick County into the wilderness of Greenbrier County, and on his return told his neighbors that he had found streams running northwest. Lured by his reports, Jacob Martin and Stephen Sewell built a cabin on Greenbrier River. In 1762 a few families established themselves on Muddy Creek and the Big Levels. Those families which did not remove as commanded were cut off by the Indians in 1763–64, and from that time until 1769 there was not a single white settler in Greenbrier County. —De Hass's *Indian Wars of Western Virginia*, p. 42.

Before receiving General Amherst's letter, Bouquet had explained to the Virginia authorities that for the past two years the western lands had been overrun by "vagabonds," who under a pretence of hunting were making settlements, of which the Indians made grievous and repeated complaints as being contrary to the treaty of Easton. In consequence General Monckton had ordered the new-comers to be driven off, and when the complaints continued Bouquet issued the proclamation to prevent such encroachments. Yet notwithstanding what he had done, representatives of the Six Nations had complained that they had discovered ten new huts in the woods, and many fields cleared for corn. All such persons Bouquet determined to remove; and, inasmuch as there was no civil judicature in that country, he proposed to try them by court-martial, a proceeding which could in no manner affect any settlement to be made thereafter in a part of the country within the known limits of one of the provinces. Furthermore, the governor was told that it would be necessary to obtain orders from the commander-in-chief before any patents could be surveyed on the Ohio.

Governor Farquier professed himself entirely satisfied with the answer, and looked forward to an adjustment of land matters by an absolute prohibition of all future settlements on lands not regularly ceded to the king's subjects by the Indians, which cessions would be by treaty and not by private purchase. The action of the Virginia governor in appealing to Amherst, however, rankled in the breast of the Swiss soldier, who wrote to his commanding officer that he considered the governor's complaints too trivial to be referred to headquarters. He said further that he had succeeded in breaking up the practice of the "outlaws" in making settlements contrary to law; and he added, what he had purposely kept from Governor Farquier, the fact that one reason for his action was the importunities of Colonel Cresap for him to join in the scheme of the Ohio Company to settle Maryland and Virginia families on the Ohio. "I foresaw," he says, "that these poor people would be ruined by that bubble." He then suggests that the real reason for the governor's complaint was to be found in the fact that he had dared to differ from some persons of Virginia about roads and provisions in the campaign of 1758, and that he was still obnoxious to them. The person from whom he differed was George Washington.[1]

"Vagabonds" and "outlaws" Bouquet called those settlers who in defiance of Indian treaty and the threat of court-martial had planted their cabins and cleared their fields beyond the Alleghanies; and so in the eyes of the law they were. Yet they were but the pioneers of a mighty immigration that soon was to control the valley of the Ohio and to conquer the Northwest. Nay, more; they were part and parcel of that tide of humanity which, overwhelming the conservative forces along the seaboard, was soon to force, both in assembly and in the field, the independence of the United States of America. Taking their lives in their hands, they were ready to fight with the Indians for the possession

[1] Washington strongly advised that Forbes's army march to Fort Duquesne by the Braddock road, which needed few repairs. Bouquet however, decided to cut a new road through Pennsylvania, a tedious and wasteful operation for the army, but an excellent thing for the Pennsylvanians. See Washington to Farquier, Sparks's *Washington*, vol. ii., p. 308 (note). The Bouquet-Washington correspondence is calendared in the *Canadian Archives*, 1889. Bouquet always showed a high respect for Washington's opinions, although on this occasion he did not take the young colonel's advice.

of the new lands which their valor had helped to conquer for England; and neither the rights of chartered company nor yet a king's proclamation could stop them. At the same time, the treaty of Easton had been negotiated at the instance of Bouquet's superior, General Forbes, with the express purpose of quieting the Ohio Indians by confirming to them the right to occupy their lands north of that river; and Bouquet was justified in using all means in his power to compel the observance of the compact. The task, however, was beyond the abilities of any commander.

With Washington the settlers beyond the Blue Ridge had defended Fort Necessity, and their steadiness saved from destruction the remnant of Braddock's army.[1] "A pernicious and pugnatious people," the Quakers called them, and so they were.[2] It has been well said of them that "they kept the commandments of God and everything else they could lay their hands on."[3] They were now ready to possess the rich lands on the Ohio in spite of the treaty of Easton[4] and Colonel Bouquet's proclamation.

Meanwhile the Indians throughout the Northwest had become aroused at the encroachments of the whites, and were preparing to defend their country against the invaders. On July 3, 1763, Bouquet, who was moving through Pennsylvania with a force of regulars and provincials to garrison the posts on the head-waters of the Ohio, received news that Presque Isle, Le Bœuf, and Ve-

[1] *Proceedings of the Scotch-Irish Congress*, 1889, Henry's address, p. 118.

[2] *Ibid.*, Colonel A. K. McClure's address, 1889, p. 184.

[3] *Ibid.*, Dr. McIntosh's address, 1889, p. 118.

[4] George Croghan's journal of the proceedings at the treaty of Easton is to be found in the *Colonial History of New York*, vol. vii., p. 280 *et seq.*

nango had been captured by the Indians, and that Fort Pitt was invested by savages. In vain he sought substantial aid from Pennsylvania. The people of that province were too much engrossed with their quarrels with the proprietors to provide efficient protection to the frontiers. About noon on the 5th of July, when the little army of Highlanders and Rangers was within twenty-six miles of Fort Pitt, the savages suddenly attacked the advance-guard, but were driven from their ambush and up the heights. While the action in front was in progress another band of savages attacked the convoy in the rear, and at nightfall Bouquet found himself completely hemmed in by the enemy, with a loss of sixty killed or wounded. In the midst of his dead and dying, the gallant leader that night reported to General Amherst his "admiration of the cool and steady behavior of the troops, who did not fire a shot without orders, and drove the enemy from their posts with fixed bayonets." In the morning the savages surrounded the camp, and with shouts and yelps made several bold efforts to penetrate the breastworks hastily constructed of bags of flour. Tired by a morning march of seventeen miles and an afternoon of battle, suffering from thirst more intolerable than the enemy's fire, even the gallant Highlanders and stubborn Rangers were disheartened when their enemy retreated only to come back the stronger when they had lured the soldiers from their defences. In his perplexity, Bouquet hit upon the daring expedient of ordering two companies within the circle of flour bags, and filling the space by opening the files on right and left, as if to cover a retreat. The deceived savages with daring intrepidity rushed headlong on; but at the very moment when they thought themselves masters of the camp, the companies under Major Campbell struck their right flank; and although the savages resolutely returned the fire, they could not stand the irresistible shock of the English. As they turned to run, the soldiers concealed behind the breastworks poured in a galling fire; and this so overawed the left of the Indian line that they too joined in the run. So bravely did the troops behave that, as Bouquet reports, "to attempt their eulogium would but detract from their merit."[1]

Colonel Bouquet's signal victory over the savages at Bushy Run made him the hero of the frontiers, and when it was known that he was to lead an expedition to the Ohio towns, volunteers flocked to his standard. Colonel Cresap promised to bring a party of Virginia woodsmen; Sir William Johnson offered to send a band of friendly Indians; and Pennsylvania undertook to raise a thousand men. This change in the temper of the colonists was most agreeable to Colonel Bouquet, who in times past had chafed at the colonial peace proclivities, and also at the extreme reluctance of the border settlers to protect their own homes and families. Even now he was hampered by the militia laws of the colonies, that forbade payment for services rendered beyond their own boundaries; for while Virginia was ever ready to claim the territories embraced in the original charter, when it came to paying for militia to conquer those territories, the authorities at this time construed the militia law as limited in its operation to the banks of the Ohio. To overcome this obstacle, Bouquet suggested that a reward for scalps would make the expedition profitable to volunteers; and he was not in the least hard-hearted or blood-thirsty in so doing, for such

[1] Bouquet's reports to Amherst are given in the *Canadian Archives*, 1889, pp. 59–71.

bounties were so usual among the colonies that we find Washington advising the payment of a bounty for the scalp of M. Donville, a French officer, "the same as if he had been an Indian."[1]

Born near the shores of the beautiful Lake Geneva, in the year 1719, Henry Bouquet was seventeen years old when he began his military career as a cadet in the regiment of Constant, in service of the States-General of Holland. Later he served the King of Sardinia as an adjutant; and at the battle of Cony he obeyed orders by occupying the brink of a precipice and then beguiling his men so that they should not become apprehensive of the danger of their position. His record of service against France and Spain led the Prince of Orange to make him a lieutenant-colonel in the regiment of Swiss Guards formed at the Hague in 1748; and in this capacity he was one of the three officers who received the towns in the Low Countries evacuated by the French, arranging also for the exchange of prisoners after the treaty of Aix-la-Chapelle. Then came a tour of France and Italy with Lord Middleton; and afterwards study of military art and a few years spent in the highly intellectual society at the Hague. Sir Joseph Yorke, having been acquainted with Bouquet and his friend Frederick Haldimand, persuaded them to take

[1] "Monsieur Donville, commander of the party, was killed and scalped, and his instructions found about him. . . . Mr. Paris sent the scalp by Jenkins; and I hope, though it is not an Indian's, they will meet with adequate reward."—Washington to Dinwiddie, Sparks's *Washington*, vol. ii., p. 136.

There was no scalp bounty in Virginia at this time; but shortly afterwards the bounty was £10 for every Indian captured or killed. In Maryland the reward was as high as £50. In Massachusetts and New Hampshire the bounty varied at different times from £8 to £100. —Sparks's *Washington*, vol. ii., p. 136 (note).

service as colonels in the Royal Americans, a regiment recruiting among the German settlers of Pennsylvania and Maryland, and officered in the main by men who had seen hard service in the army of the Dutch Republic. Attractive in person, a vastly entertaining correspondent with his fellow-officers, Bouquet was yet so thoroughly a soldier as to present only a rough edge to civilians. He found in his profession that support for his pride which a lack of family and fortune had denied. Without kith or kin, he sought in vain the love of a woman averse to his profession; and during his American campaigns he carried on with her a correspondence that reveals a depth of feeling one would little suspect in a man who seemed entirely self-sufficient. His soldiers believed in him; the colonial governments highly appreciated his services, and men of learning found him most congenial. To a rare degree he combined the qualities of a resourceful soldier and a careful administrator.[1]

[1] A sketch of Brigadier-general Henry Bouquet, by George Harrison Fisher, together with a portrait engraved from a painting in the possession of Mrs. J. Francis Fisher, is given in the *Pennsylvania Magazine of History and Biography*, vol. iii., No. 2, 1879. The Philadelphia edition (1765) of *Bouquet's Expedition*, by Dr. William Smith, is rare; there was a London (1766) and an Amsterdam edition (1769) in French. In 1868, Robert Clarke & Co., Cincinnati, reprinted the work, with a preface by Francis Parkman and a translation of Dumas's biographical sketch from the Amsterdam edition. HARPER'S MAGAZINE for October, 1861, has a popular account of the expedition, based on the Philadelphia edition. Mr. Fisher's article contains Bouquet's letters to Miss Anne Willing, the last of which is dated at Fort Pitt, January 15, 1761. Early in 1762 Miss Willing married a Mr. Frances, but recently come from England, and a man of family and wealth. In spite of the plain intimations in her letters that she would not choose a soldier for a husband, Bouquet seems to have been ill prepared for the news of her approaching marriage; and so deeply was he interested that two of his fellow-officers entered into a friend-

On August 14, 1764, Bouquet received Bradstreet's message from Presque Isle, saying that he had concluded a peace with the Delawares and Shawanese. Inasmuch as murders and depredations by these two nations continued as before, Bouquet kept up his preparations, nor was he to be dissuaded from his purpose by the Indians who came to assure him that his force was insufficient to withstand the power of the numerous nations through whose country he was to pass. On October 3d the long march began. First went a corps of volunteers raised in Virginia but paid by Pennsylvania to complete its complement. These expert woodsmen acted as skirmishers, protecting both flanks of the army. Then came the axe-men supported by light infantry; these were followed by the regulars of the Forty-third and the Sixtieth regiments, marching in three columns; and after them as rear-guard and flankers came two platoons of Pennsylvania militia, the reserve corps of grenadiers, light-horsemen, and Virginia and Pennsylvania volunteers. In silence the men marched, and a halt was the signal for the whole body to face outward ready for an attack.

The start was made on Wednesday. On Friday the army passed through Logstown, seventeen and a half miles from Fort Pitt, a place once noted for the thriving trade carried on there between the French and English traders and the Shawanese and Delawares, but since

ly conspiracy first to break the news gently to him, and afterwards to soften the blow that evidently had seriously affected his peace of mind. His friendship with the Willing family was not interrupted, however, and in his will of 1763 Thomas Willing was named as executor. Subsequently, however, in the will made just before his death in 1765, he appointed his friend and companion, Frederick Haldimand, his executor and heir, a trust Haldimand had on his mind so late as 1786, as his diary shows.—See *Canadian Archives*, 1889, p. xxvii. and 137.

1750 a deserted village. The next day the army filed down the steep banks near the mouth of the Beaver, and below the present town of New Brighton found a ford stony and pretty deep. On the fertile bottom-lands where the town of Beaver now stands they passed through an old French trading-post with its houses of hewn logs and chimneys of stone. Thus far the march had been like an excursion. On the left was the broad river, island strewn, with here a rush of narrowed waters and there a spreading of clear water over a bed of shale, seen plainly far out into the shallows. Beyond the placid river were stretches of verdure, bordered by hills glorified in the haze of autumn. As they marched, the beauties of frost-touched leaf delighted the eye, and the pungent smells of forest fires were as incense to the nostrils. From their triumphant advance the Indians either fled or else hid themselves to watch its progress and carry a swift report of the invincible character of the expedition.

Turning to the west, Bouquet's little army, now cut off from its base of supplies at Fort Pitt, entered the Indian country, a region of trackless forests filled with unknown numbers of the subtlest savages east of the Mississippi. Yet so strict was the discipline of the regulars, and so vigilant were the volunteers, that not a hostile shot was fired on the entire march to the Muskingum. On the 16th, after a wilderness journey of two weeks, Colonel Bouquet was met by six Indians who came as an embassy to say that eight miles farther on the savages were assembled to sue for peace; and on the 17th the meeting began with the usual formalities of peace-pipe and wampum-belts. The Senecas, Delawares, and Shawanese, represented by their chiefs, made the usual excuses and the usual promises. On Bouquet's part the ceremonial delay after receiving a message of such importance was prolonged by autumn rains, so that it was the 20th before he made answer.

Brushing aside as frivolous the Indian excuses that they were driven to war by the Western nations, Bouquet charged them with plundering and killing or capturing the traders who had been sent among them at their own request; with attacking Fort Pitt, which had been built with their express consent; with murdering four men who had been sent to them with a public message, thereby violating customs sacred even among barbarous nations; with attacking the king's troops at Bushy Run, and, when defeated, ravaging the frontiers; with violating the promises they had made General Bradstreet that they would deliver their prisoners to him and recall their war-parties.

"I have brought with me," said Bouquet, "the relations of the people you have massacred or taken as prisoners. They are impatient for revenge; and it is with great difficulty that I can protect you against their just resentment, which is only restrained by the assurances given them that no peace shall ever be concluded until you have given us full satisfaction. Your former allies—the Ottawas, Chippewas, and Wyandots—have made their peace with us; and the Six Nations have joined us against you. We now surround you, having possession of all the waters of the Ohio, the Mississippi, the Miamis, and the lakes. All the French living in those parts are now subjects of Great Britain, and dare no longer assist you. It is therefore in our power totally to extirpate you. But the English are a merciful and generous nation, averse to shed the blood even of their most cruel enemies, and if you convince us that you repent your past perfidy and that we can depend on your good behavior in the future, you may yet hope for mercy and peace."

Thoroughly frightened by Bouquet's threats, and yet encouraged by his promises of peace, the savages prepared to give up their prisoners. A strange scene was enacted on the 9th of November, the day fixed for the surrender of the two hundred and six captives, more than half of whom were women and children.[1] Attended by his principal officers, Colonel Bouquet moved to a bower hastily built to answer the purposes of a council-chamber. Ranged in ranks opposite to him were the Indian ambassadors, a motley array, clad some in skins of wild animals, some in shirts of linen or of dressed skin, with breech-clouts, and leggings reaching half-way up the thigh from their moccasin-covered feet. Their heads were shaved, save for a small tuft of hair on top; and their elongated ears and their noses were adorned with heavy rings of gold and silver, while their faces were streaked with paint of various colors. A rifle, shot-pouch, powder-horn, tomahawk, and a scalping-knife hanging about the neck, completed the equipment of each warrior.

Kiyashuta, chief of the Senecas, backed by fifteen warriors, was the first to speak. "With this string of wampum," he said, "we wipe the tears from your eyes. We deliver these prisoners, the last of your flesh and blood remaining among us. We gather together and bury with this belt all the bones of the people that have been killed during this unhappy war, which the evil spirit has caused. We cover the bones which have been buried, that they may never more be remembered.

[1] Of the Virginians there were thirty-two males and fifty-eight women and children; of the Pennsylvanians forty-nine males and sixty-seven women and children.

Again we cover their place with leaves that it may no more be seen. We have been long astray. The path between you and us has been stopped. We give this belt that it may be cleared again. While you hold it fast by one end and we by the other, we shall always be able to discover anything that might disturb our friendship."

Bouquet expressed his readiness to join in covering the bones of the slain, so that their place might no more be known. The king, his master and their father, had appointed him to make war. To Sir William Johnson belonged the duty of making peace. To him they must go; but first they must give hostages that they would commit no further violence against his Majesty's subjects until peace should be concluded, and furthermore they must agree to abide by the treaty they were to make. The next day, the Turkey, the Turtle, and the Castalogas tribes of the Delawares made their peace and rendered up six hostages and also five deputies to treat with Sir William Johnson; and on the 12th the haughty Shawanese, conscious of ill-doing, put forth Red Hawk to clean the ears of the English of the evil stories they had heard; to take the tomahawk from their hands and throw it up to the Great Spirit to dispose of it as he might see fit; and to grasp with their white brothers the chain of friendship, so that the old men, the women and the children, should know an end of war. They promised to yield their remaining prisoners when the others of their nation should return from the hunt; and they asked that the peace treaty made with Pennsylvania in 1701 might be renewed.

Peace being now assured, the prisoners were brought forth. Then husbands clasped in fond embrace wives who had been torn from them months and years ago;

mothers recognized in bronzed and naked children the babes from whom they had been separated by the fortunes of border warfare; brothers with difficulty talked with sisters who had forgotten their own language and now understood only the jargon of the forest. Saddest sight of all were the men who, hoping against hope, had made the long march only to find at the end no trace of their lost ones.

Nor was all joy in the restoration. The Indians, so stoical in defeat and torture, now were melted even to tears, so reluctant were they to part from captives whom they had treated with all the consideration of which their savage nature was capable. On the other hand, many a woman had found an Indian husband from whose embraces she had to be torn; and many a youth bitterly fought against a return to even such light restraints as border-life imposed. Offerings of corn and horses and skins the Indians brought to ease the journey of the returning captives; and one young Mingo warrior, regardless of the danger he ran from revengeful relatives, was not to be restrained from following the object of his affections even to the gates of Fort Pitt.

Without adventure the expedition returned, and for a time peace reigned along the Ohio. Bouquet, belonging to that class of soldiers who look upon war only as a means of securing peace, had in mind a plan whereby all grants of land westward of the Alleghany Mountains, including the charter of the Ohio Company, should be annulled, also the proprietors of Pennsylvania should be brought to surrender that portion of their charter which related to lands beyond the mountains, and Virginia should have her boundaries curtailed by the arbitrary action of the king. Then a new military government might be formed to the westward of the Alleghanies, thus covering Pennsylvania from Indian attacks, and enhancing the value of the remaining lands.[1] The very suggestion of such a plan to the people struggling to force their way into the fertile Ohio country would have aroused overpowering opposition; and it is fortunate for Bouquet's reputation that, as a reward for his successful Muskingum expedition, he received well-merited promotion, and an assignment to Pensacola. He had no sooner become settled in his new post, however, than he succumbed to disease, and after nearly eight years of arduous service in America he died at the height of his fame and usefulness.[2]

To follow up the peace conquered by Bouquet, Sir William Johnson sent his deputy, George Croghan, on a voyage of discovery to the Illinois country. The middle of May, 1765, the party set out from Fort Pitt in two bateaux, and were soon joined by deputies of the Senecas, Shawanese, and Delawares. Aided by the swift current, the light boats made rapid progress down the island-strewn river. After a brief stop at the ruins of the Shawanese village of Logstown, the party re-embarked and before nightfall passed the old stone chimneys marking the site of the town the French built for the Delawares a mile below Beaver Creek; passed also the mouth of the Little Beaver, and reached a camping spot near Yellow Creek—a journey of fifty-four miles. The next day brought them into the midst of the Seneca villages; on the fourth day they passed the mouth of the Muskingum and the Little Kanawha rivers, and

[1] *Canadian Archives*, 1889, Bouquet to Gage, p. 65.

[2] Bouquet arrived in Philadelphia in April, 1757, and until 1759 was employed in South Carolina, with headquarters at Charleston. He died at Pensacola some time before September, 1765.

came into a country of rich bottom-lands, where roamed buffaloes, deer, bears, and turkeys. So plentiful was the game that a good hunter, without much fatigue to himself, could supply meat for a hundred men.

From camp on the Hockhocking, Croghan sent a runner to summon the French traders in the Illinois country to meet him on the banks of the Scioto, and there swear allegiance to his Britannic Majesty, whose subjects they had become and whose license to trade they must obtain. Should the French refuse to obey the summons the Shawanese were warned to compel them to come. On the 23d they passed the mouth of the Scioto and came to the spot where formerly stood the Shawanese Lower Town that was washed away by a "fresh," during which, as Croghan relates from personal experience, the waters rose until they covered the plateau forty feet above the river and stood nine feet deep, compelling the inhabitants to take to canoes. Afterwards the Shawanese built their town on the south side of the Ohio, but during the late war they had retired to a safer situation on the plains of the Scioto.[1]

From the 24th to the 27th was spent with the French traders, and on the last day of May Croghan came to the great salt-lick, celebrated as the place where the "elephants' bones are found." On the way to the lick, which was four miles back from the south bank of the Ohio, the party passed along "a large road which the

[1] The record of Croghan's journey must be pieced together from his official journal transmitted to Sir William Johnson (*New York Colonial Documents*, vol. vii., p. 779); his topographical journal, which appeared in the *Monthly American Journal of Geology and Natural Science*, December, 1831, and is reprinted in Butler's *History of Kentucky;* and from a third journal printed in S. P. Hildreth's *Pioneer History*. For a discussion as to these journals, see *Narrative and Critical History of America*, vol. vi., p. 704.

buffaloes have beaten, spacious enough for two wagons to go abreast." On the bank at the edge of the lick they found two tusks about six feet in length; one of these they took away with them. On the same day they passed the mouth of the River Kentucky, or Holsten's River; and on the 1st of June they reached the Falls of the Ohio, the present site of Louisville. Six days later they arrived at the mouth of the Wabash, a river that "runs through one of the finest countries in the world, the lands being extremely rich and well watered." Making camp, Croghan despatched messages to "Lord Frazer," an English officer who had been sent from Fort Pitt, and to M. St. Ange, the French commandant at Fort Chartres.[1] To the Illinois Indians he sent belts announcing the peace made with the Delawares, the Shawanese, and the Six Nations, and summoning them to conclude matters after the same manner.

At daybreak on the 8th, an outbreak of hideous yells mingled with the crack of muskets awoke the camp; and Croghan jumped to his feet to receive a shot from the concealed enemy. Two of his men and three Indians were killed, and but two whites and one Indian escaped unhurt. The attacking party was made up of eighty Kickapoos and Mascoutens. A wounded Shawanese, angry and contemptuous, threatened the Kickapoos with the vengeance of the combined nations of the

[1] Lieutenant Alexander Fraser had been sent with a small force to Kaskaskia to prepare the way for Croghan. The latter had been delayed by the plunder of his goods by a party of masked men near Fort Louden, the country people being fearful lest the traders for their own profit would supply the Indians with guns and ammunition with which to ravage the frontiers.—See *Canadian Archives*, 1889, pp. 278 and 279; also Col. James Smith's *Account of Remarkable Occurrences*.

A FRENCH TRADER

north; but the only effect of the speech was to hasten the division of the spoils and to hurry the march of the prisoners up the Wabash to "Post Vincent." A week's march through thin woodland interspersed with broad savannas, brought the party to the post, which at that time consisted of some fourscore French families settled on the east side of the river in the midst of a country rich in wheat and tobacco. The French, secretly pleased at the misfortunes of the English, speedily began to barter for the plunder, and Croghan, himself a veteran trader, must have been chagrined indeed to see how the price of a pound of vermilion rose to ten half-johannes specie, and was eagerly purchased by the Indians with the gold and silver stolen from his considerable hoard.[1] In spite of his misfortune, Croghan noted the excellent situation for trade at Vincennes, the village being in a fine hunting country, and the distance to the Illinois or any other post being too great for the sedentary Indians to journey elsewhere for their necessaries.

Years before either the French or the English knew of the Ohio by that name, they laid down on their maps the Onabash or St. Jerome, rising south of the foot of Lake Erie and flowing westward into the Mississippi.[2] Father Marest, writing from Kaskaskia, in 1712, speaks of the "Onabache" as a river of three branches, one ex-

[1] The johannes of Portugal of 18 dwt. 17 grs. were valued at £4 16*s.*; then there were current the moydore, the caroline of Germany, the guinea, the louis d'or, the Spanish or French pistole, the Seville, Mexico, or pillar dollar, the French crown or six-livre piece, the British shilling, and the pistereen. The dollar was reckoned at eight shillings.—See *Mich. P. & H. Col.*, vol. x., p. 214.

[2] I have before me a map of North America, "according to the most exact observations," dedicated to John, Lord Sommers, president of the Privy Council, by Herman Moll, Geographer, 1719, in which the Ohio appears as the "Onabash now R. St. Jerome."

tending as far as the Iroquois, another running into Virginia and Carolina, and a third heading among the Miamis. In his letter, Father Marest mentions the fort lately established by the French on the Wabash, which came to be known as "*the* Post." Some time about the year 1732, François Morgan de Vinsenne, who had seen considerable service in New France, was sent to the post on the Wabash. There he quickly acquired land, and by his marriage to the daughter of M. Philip Longprie, of Kaskaskia, he obtained for father-in-law the wealthiest citizen of that place. Madame Vinsenne was unable to write her own name; but she brought to her husband a *dot* of 100 pistoles, and, at her father's death in 1735, 408 pounds of pork was a part of her inheritance by will. It is possible that M. de Vinsenne was killed in 1736 during an expedition against the Chickasaws, but not before he had given his own name to the fort at which he was the only commandant of note under the French rule. Indeed, the only other name connected with the place before Croghan's advent is that of the first missionary, Father Mirmet, who had been sent for the spiritual edification of the ancestors of Croghan's captors, the Mascoutins, formerly occupants of the region.[1]

Dividing booty and scalps with the French, whose protection they sought, the Kickapoos hurried their captives northward through a region where no wood was to be seen, the country appearing like an ocean, with waving billows of wild hemp. After a journey of two hundred and ten miles from Vincennes they reached Fort Ouiatanon,[2] on the headwaters of the Wabash,

[1] *Colonial History of Vincennes*, by Judge John Law (Vincennes, 1858), p. 15 *et seq.*

[2] Fort Ouiatanon, now Lafayette, Indiana, was built about 1721.

where some fourteen French families were found dwelling within the palisades, and enjoying a large and profitable traffic in furs. The Indians from whom the post took its name were greatly concerned when they learned of the folly of the Kickapoos, in so yielding to the wiles of the French as to strike a British embassy; and when Croghan received from St. Ange a message inviting him to visit Fort Chartres, his well-scared captors were only too glad to allow their prisoners to depart in peace. On his way he was met by no less a personage than the Ottawa chief Pontiac, who had come to make peace with the envoy of the English.

As Pontiac and Croghan,[1] subtlest savage and most

Shea mentions the fact that Father John de Saint Pé went in 1721 from St. Joseph to the new Fort Ouiatanon.

[1] George Croghan, born in Ireland and schooled in Dublin, had his home on the beautiful banks of the wide Susquehanna, near the place where the traveller of to-day is shunted back and forth from track to track before crossing to the city of Harrisburg. As early as 1746 he was a trader on Lake Erie, between the old Indian town of Sandusky and the site of the present city of Cleveland. His success in dealing with savages led Pennsylvania to appoint him Indian agent. The French and Indian War plunged him into bankruptcy. It appears from a letter addressed by Colonel John Carlyle to Washington, on June 17, 1754 (Hamilton's *Letters to Washington*, vol. i., p. 5), that Croghan had agreed to furnish the army with 50,000 lbs. of flour that was in store, when he had but a small fraction of the amount, and was, according to Carlyle, "not a man of the truth." Under Braddock he was a captain; he built a fort at Aughwick, in Huntington County; and when Pennsylvania treated him ill he became Sir William Johnson's deputy. In fact, he became a second, though a much smaller, Sir William, so essentially similar were these two sons of Erin. Shrewd, fair in their dealings with the Indians, inflexible in purpose and untiring in action, they served well their country, while at the same time they made very handsome profits for themselves. Croghan had met Pontiac in 1760, and had formed one of the circle about the camp-fire when Robert Rogers was instructing the Ottawa chief in the art of war, as they journeyed to receive the

stalwart trader, made their way through the swarms of now awed and submissive savages, on their return to the tumble-down Fort Ouiatanon, the old order passed away, giving place to the new. For nearly a century the country between the foot of Lake Michigan and the mouth of the Ohio had been the pathway of the French adventurer on his way to the lower Mississippi, and also the favorite field of labor of the devoted servants of the Cross. There the intrepid La Salle, the faithful Tonty, and the romantic and romancing Hennepin had built the monument of their failure in the pitiful Fort Crevecœur; and there the zealous explorer-priest, Marquette, counting it more gain to have saved a perishing soul than to have discovered the Mississippi, had contracted the disease that cut short his young life.

Fort Chartres, the seat of government for the Illinois country, was a dependency of New Orleans, the major-commandant at the upper post being connected with the governor of the province often by ties of relationship, and always by partnership in trade. Thus was realized La Salle's plan of opening a Mississippi channel for the fur-trade of the prairies. The legitimate profits of the trade were swelled by the system of Indian

surrender of Detroit. In 1763 Croghan was wrecked on the French coast, while on his way to England to give information to the Lords of Trade and Plantations respecting the Indian boundary. In 1766 he settled on the Alleghany, and two years later he acquired 118,000 acres of land in New York State; in 1770 he entertained Washington on his way to the Kanawha; he sided with Virginia in the dispute as to the boundary between that State and Pennsylvania; and in 1775 he took a leading part in the beginnings of the Revolution. He seems to have been suspected, however, for Congress made Colonel Morgan Indian agent in his place, and he was required to prove his loyalty. This he was able to do; at least he kept possession of his property. He died at Passaynak, Pennsylvania, in August, 1782. The Croghan who became famous in the War of 1812 was his nephew.

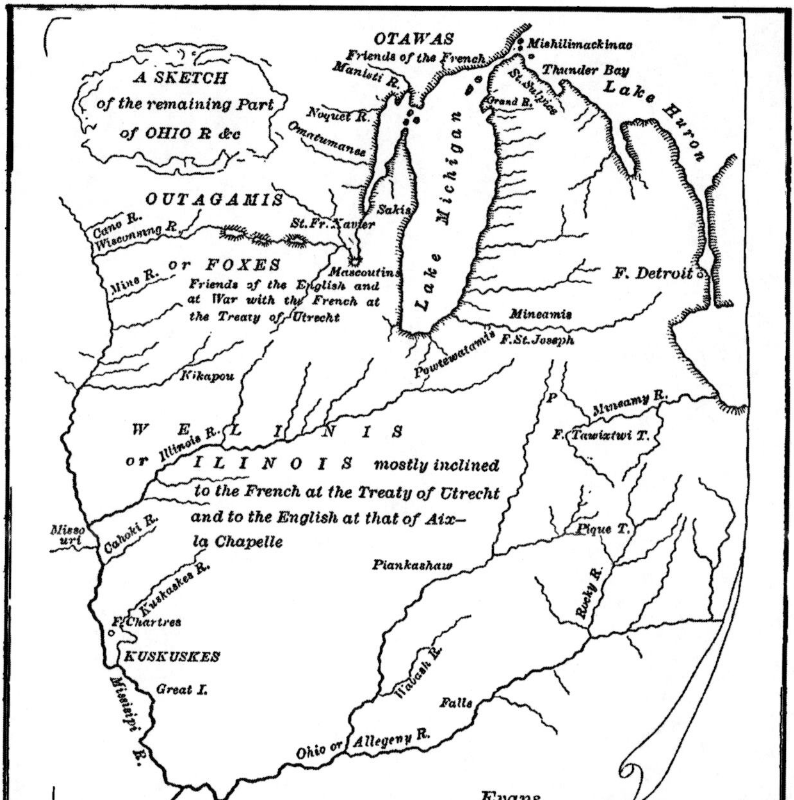

EVANS'S MAP OF THE ILLINOIS COUNTRY

presents, and by license fees required of the traders. Presents to the Indians came from the king; but presents from the Indians in return were absorbed by the commandant and his partner, the governor; and if any trader presumed to traffic without a license from Fort Chartres he held his goods at the peril alike of white man and of red. To be sure, the Illinois Indians were "poor, debauched, and dastardly," and could count not more than three hundred and fifty warriors; but the traffic reached to surrounding tribes on the north and west, and was both easy of access and of considerable volume.

Lest this lucrative trade should fall into the hands of the English, Kerlerec, the governor at New Orleans, had sent forth Pierre Laclede Liguest, armed with extensive rights of trade on the Missouri; and in the April of 1764 his lieutenant, Chouteau, with thirty others, laid the foundations of St. Louis, whither the French of the Illinois flocked in order to escape the necessity of changing their flag. Farther down the river the hamlet of St. Genevieve, covering the approach to the lead-mines that supplied the country with shot, also built itself up at the expense of the Illinois towns. Indeed, the exodus of the French threatened to depopulate the Illinois country. At Cahokia, opposite St. Louis, the town was deserted, excepting only the fine mission-farm of St. Sulpice, which, with its thirty slaves, its herd of cattle, and its mill for grinding corn and sawing planks, had been sold to a thrifty Frenchman not averse to becoming an English subject. The fathers returned to France. The settlement could boast of no more than forty-five houses, the poorest of which was called the fort; and so badly selected was the site that the spring freshets tumbled through the broken palisades and overflowed the town. At St. Philip, between Cahokia and Fort Chartres, the sixteen houses and the church were deserted by all but the captain of militia, who remained with his mill, his cattle, and his twenty slaves. The more industrious and prosperous inhabitants of Prairie du Rocher, however, stayed by their wide cornfields, exhibiting the proverbial stability of those who build their house upon a rock.

By far the most important settlement in the Illinois country was Kaskaskia, where there was at this time a small fort destined to be destroyed by fire during the ensuing year (1766) and to be replaced in 1772 by Fort Gage, the successor of Fort Chartres. The sixty-five families dwelt in houses of stone; and so convenient was the natural wharfage that heavy bateaux lay with their sides to the bank, ready for loading. The establishment that gave to the town prosperity and name—Notre Dame de Cascasquias—was the well-tilled Jesuit farm of two hundred and forty arpents; but when the command went forth for the suppression of the Jesuits, this entire property was sold, ostensibly for the benefit of the crown, to M. Beauvais, the richest man in the Illinois country. Eighty slaves were employed either in the well-built mill that ground the corn and wheat and sawed the planks, or in the wealth-producing brewery; and in one season the opulent proprietor sold the king eighty-six thousand pounds of flour without parting with more than a portion of his harvest.

Fort Chartres itself had the reputation of being "the most commodious and best built fort in North America"; commodious possibly because four dungeons were included within its subterranean depths; well-built, either because its walls of but two feet and two inches in thickness were plastered over to present a smooth surface, or else because the entrance to the fortress led through a handsome rustic gate — a touch of the incongruous truly French. An irregular quadrilateral, with a length of four hundred and ninety feet, the fort was partly surrounded by a half-finished ditch; and its bastions were supplied with more port-holes than cannon. The town at its foot had once boasted as many as forty families, who gathered on Sundays and saints' days at the Church of St. Ann, where a Franciscan father shepherded the flock; but during the nine years since the rebuilding of the fort in 1756, a more relentless enemy than either red-skin or red-coat had threatened both town and fortress. The capricious river, then as now laughing at the works of man, had eaten away so much of the half mile of land between fort and water that scarcely more than eighty paces remained; and the French families, except three or four of the poorest ones, had crossed to the other shore. Seven years after Croghan's visit the British were forced to abandon the fort, whose dungeons were occupied, probably for the first time, by the waters of the Mississippi. Having accomplished this work of destruction the Father of Rivers withdrew himself, and the ruins of Fort Chartres are now a mile inland.[1]

While many of the well-established French remained to await the coming of the English, and numbers of the less prosperous transported their belongings to St. Louis or St. Genevieve, still others embarked with De Villiere to swell the population of New Orleans, already a city of some six or seven thousand people. Following them had gone messengers from Pontiac to stir up the

[1] Captain Philip Pittman's *Present State of European Settlements on the Mississippi* (London, 1770), and Winsor's *Westward Movement*, p. 26.

river Indians to oppose the English, and so effective were these exhortations that the expedition of Major Loftus was turned back in the spring of 1764, and that of Captain Pittman, a few months later, met no better success in its efforts to reach the Illinois country. Rejoiced by these triumphs of his allies, and unwilling to yield so long as a single spark of hope remained, Pontiac despatched an embassy to New Orleans imploring and demanding that the French unite with their ancient friends the Indians to drive "the red dogs" from the land. Death spared D'Abbadie the dire necessity of telling the Indians that from their fathers, the French, also the broad lands of the Western continent had been taken away by the powers over-seas; and that even the unknown lands beyond the Mississippi had passed into the possession of Spain. From Aubry, the successor of D'Abbadie, the embassy received the message that, on being delivered to Pontiac during the March of 1765, broke the spirit of the persistent Ottawa chieftain, and at last forced him to the resolution of making peace with dignity.

The genuineness of Pontiac's resolve had been tested even before Croghan's arrival. Eager to forestall any change of sentiment on the part of the Illinois people, General Gage had sent ahead Lieutenant Fraser with letters to St. Ange de Bellerive, the commandant at Fort Chartres. Fraser was received with favor by the much perturbed Frenchman, who joyfully looked forward to a relief from an intolerable situation, where he was beset on one side by the Indians and the French traders eager to make war on the English, while on the other hand he had positive orders to keep the peace until a British force should come to occupy the post. The traders, however, roughly used the young lieutenant, and in the drunken commotion that occurred he narrowly escaped with his life. The next day, however, Pontiac having recovered the use of his reason, took Fraser under his own protection.[1] Croghan's mission to the Illinois having paved the way for the peaceful occupation of the British, Captain Sterling and a hundred Highlanders descended the Ohio; and, five years after the surrender of Detroit, on October 10, 1765, St. Ange had the mournful honor and the secret relief of hauling down the last French flag in the Northwest.

The great chief Pontiac might indeed make way for Croghan; but his own dignity demanded that his submission be made to a higher power. Accordingly we find him at Oswego in the June of 1766, professing to Sir William Johnson that he had taken Colonel Croghan by the hand and had never let go his hold, because he saw that the Great Spirit would have him a friend of the English. Returning to his wives and children, Pontiac settled down to the regular life of the Indian on the banks of the Maumee. In April, 1769, he appeared at St. Louis, apparently on a visit of friendship to St. Ange. One day he crossed to Cahokia to join in an Indian celebration; and on his return from the carousal he was tomahawked by an Illinois Indian, who had been bribed to do the deed by an English trader, Wilkinson by name, the payment being a barrel of rum.[2] St. Ange, ready to do justice to the memory of the greatest among Indians, gave his body, clad in the full

[1] *Michigan Pioneer and Historical Collections*, vol. x., p. 216.

[2] After carefully examining the various conflicting accounts of Pontiac's death, preserved among the Parkman MSS., I have followed Mr. Parkman's account, in spite of Winsor's doubts. Parkman had the details from Lyman C. Draper, who obtained them from Col. L. V. Bogy, of St. Louis, to whom Chouteau related them. See also *Pennsylvania Gazette*, August 17, 1769.

uniform of a French officer—a gift from Montcalm himself—a military burial near the Council-house at St. Louis; and there the forest warrior found peace.

Returning now to George Croghan, whom we left at Fort Ouiatanon, we find him ready to push northward to carry to his principal the tidings of his success. Crossing to the Eel River, he came to the village of the Twightwees, on the river St. Joseph, near its junction with the Miami. The hundred Indian cabins were supplemented by nine or ten huts that housed a runaway colony from Detroit, Frenchmen who, having been concerned in Pontiac's war, had retired to this place to escape the just punishment of evil-doing. Then dropping down the Miami through Ottawa and Wyandotte villages, Croghan came to Lake Erie, and on August 16th, after a journey of three months, he reached Detroit, where he passed a month or more in holding satisfactory conferences with the Indians. Then, having traversed a very considerable portion of the new possessions of the English, he set out for Niagara.

Great issues were depending on George Croghan's voyage down the Ohio. We have seen that Colonel Bouquet was convinced that the Ohio country should be organized as a separate colony. This obvious conclusion was also reached by others conversant with the situation; notably by Sir William Johnson, who had taken a keen interest in Bouquet's expedition and who had despatched Croghan to make peace with the remote tribes of the Illinois. Thus it happened that while the deputy Indian agent was making his explorations, a strong company was organizing to obtain the control of the territory lying between the Alleghanies and the Ohio, with the purpose of beginning there a new government. On this side of the Atlantic the leading spirits in the scheme were Sir William Johnson and Governor Franklin, of New Jersey. The head of the company, however, was Thomas Walpole, a London banker; and its most active promoter was Benjamin Franklin, who had returned to London as the agent of Pennsylvania. When the matter was mentioned to Franklin he wrote home to his son, the governor: "I like the project of a colony in the Illinois country, and will forward it to my utmost here."

Two things were necessary to the success of the enterprise: first, a grant must be obtained from the crown; and, secondly, the Indians must be prevailed upon to relinquish their title as occupants of the lands. The plan for the new colony was drawn by Sir William Johnson, and Franklin placed it before the king in council. In order to strengthen the position, a few persons of influence were taken into the company. Franklin won a reluctant approval from Lord Shelburne, but found a strenuous opponent in Lord Hillsborough, who was then at the head of the Board of Trade and Plantations. The latter was very much afraid that if the Ohio lands should be opened to settlement, all Ireland would resort thither—a very reasonable apprehension, considering the fact that the Scotch-Irish already peopled the frontiers. Then, too, colonies remote from the sea-coast would force the people into manufactures, to the detriment of English trade. Moreover, distant posts meant enormous crown expenses; and Indian superintendency had already become so expensive that a return to the colonial management of Indian affairs was seriously contemplated as a means of relieving the nation of so vast an outlay.[1]

[1] "I was again at Lord Shelburne's a few davs since, and said a good

Besides all else, a new colony beyond the mountains might prove too independent of the home government, and so foment independence in the other colonies.

Croghan's journal and Sir William's letters were used with good effect; and to obtain still greater weight for the plan, General Lyman, who was urging the renewal of the grant to the old Ohio Company, was induced to unite his forces with those championing the Walpole grant. In case the superintendencies should be abolished, Sir William was to be provided for by making him governor of the new colony. Then, too, in order to clear away the Indian title, Franklin had instructions sent to Sir William to enter into a treaty with the savages. To accomplish this much required two years.[1]

Sir William Johnson was eager enough to conclude the Indian boundary. Indeed, either he or his friends had urged Franklin to procure orders for the settlement of this vexed question; for, without orders, Sir William could not charge up to the crown the goods and provisions with which this thrifty trader supplied the Indians in council. It is not necessary to seek private motives for Sir William's haste; the Indian situation

deal to him on the affair of the Illinois settlement. He was pleased to say he really approved of it; but intimated that every new proposed expense for America would meet with great difficulty here, the treasury being alarmed and astonished at the growing charges there, and the heavy accounts and drafts continually brought in from thence. That Major Farmer, for instance, had lately drawn for no less than £30,000 extraordinary charges, on his going to take possession of the Illinois; and that the superintendents, particularly the southern one, began also to draw very largely. He spoke, however, very handsomely of Sir William on many accounts."—Franklin to his son, Sparks's *Franklin*, vol. iv., p. 236.

[1] Franklin's correspondence with his son, in regard to the Walpole grant, begins in March, 1766, and ends in March, 1768.

made the settlement of boundaries imperative. At the Congress held at the German Flats in 1765 the Six Nations had offered to part with their title to all their lands east of the Ohio; but this offer had been neglected. The Indians resented the delay, and especially resented the lack of presents and supplies. A great gathering of Delawares and Senecas was held in the Shawanese country on the Scioto in March of that year; and English traders on the Ohio had their bateaux stopped and the ammunition, scalping-knives, and tomahawks stolen. Pennsylvania, taking alarm at these unmistakable signs of an Indian uprising, voted £2500 to be used by Sir William in gifts to those savages who had lost relatives in border warfare. The astute superintendent accepted the appropriation, with the remark that "good laws vigorously enforced are the best guarantee against Indian resentment." [1]

During the winter of 1767–68 the newspapers had been full of reports of the fertility of the Ohio valley; and from the frontiersmen the Indians quickly learned about the projects to form new settlements in that region. The Six Nations complained that when they went to hunt in their own land it wearied them to climb the fences of the white men; and that there were neither deer to shoot nor trees to furnish bark for their huts. In February, 1768, however, Sir William received his belated orders to perfect the boundary; and as a preliminary thereto he accommodated the troubles between the Cherokees and the Six Nations, using Pennsylvania's appropriation for the purpose. At this time the Six Nations claimed the lands between the Ohio and the Alleghanies, by virtue of their conquests over the tribes resorting to

[1] Stone's *Life of Sir William Johnson*, vol. ii., p. 296.

those regions. Indeed, the claims of the Iroquois Confederacy included the whole territory westward from New York to the Mississippi; but whatever may have been their conquests in the past, it is certain that at this time the Western Confederacy was scarcely less strong than the Eastern; and that the tribes occupying the lands northwest of the Ohio admitted no control whatever on the part of their ancient conquerors, the Iroquois, although they met with them in council. As to the lands south of the Ohio, the case was different. That region was in the possession of no one tribe, but was the hunting-grounds of many tribes—"the dark and bloody ground" where savage fought with savage after the manner of their kind.

It was fitting that the treaty for the transfer of title to this region should take place in the country of the Iroquois, the traditional friends and allies of the English, and that it should be conducted by Sir William Johnson. At Fort Orange, on July 21, 1661, a little band of Dutch immigrants led by Arendt Van Curler, a cousin of the absentee Patroon Van Rensselaer, purchased from the Mohawk chiefs the site of an old Indian village. Early the next spring they settled on this site, and for a time the place was known as Corlaer; but after the English conquest the old Indian name of Schenectady was adopted. Freed from the trammels of feudalism, these settlers held their lands in fee-simple; and, after a prolonged struggle against both the colony and the manor restrictive policy, they established for themselves, in 1727, freedom to trade with the Indians. Through the open door of Schenectady poured a flood of German immigration from the Rhine valley — a vigorous, liberty-loving people, who proved extremely troublesome to the church-and-state powers that were in control in the colony.

In the year 1738, William Johnson, a young Irishman from County Meath, made his way to the banks of the Mohawk as the agent of his uncle, Captain Peter Warren, R. N., who was the possessor of some fifteen thousand acres of wilderness. Young Johnson speedily placed settlers on the lands, opened a country store, began to clear his own farm, and married the daughter of a German settler. He never lied to, cheated, or deceived an Indian; and he never granted to a savage what he had once refused. This rule, early adopted, gave him an ever-increasing influence with the Indians, and enabled him to build up a trade that took his agents to the remote tribes from the St. Lawrence wellnigh to the Mississippi, and gave him commercial connections in London and the West Indies as well as in the Atlantic seaboard cities. The policy of Van Curler and Peter Schuyler in dealing with the Iroquois was adopted by Johnson; he talked with them in their own language, and in no punctilio of savage etiquette was he wanting. The ready words inspired by the Blarney-stone with him took the form of trope and metaphor drawn from those powers of nature so dear to the Indian mind. On the death of his wife he took for his companion a sister of that Joseph Brant whose name became a terror to American patriots of the Revolution; and by the Indian alliance as well as by his adoption into the Mohawk tribe he confirmed his power over the savages.

At the Albany conference of 1746, Johnson, hideous in the war-paint and feathers of his tribe, led the Mohawk band; in the old French War he had command of the frontier, with the rank of colonel; in 1750 he took his seat in the governor's council, and with that representative of royalty made a stand for prerogative as against the growing power of the assembly. At the celebrated

Albany Congress in 1754, the forerunner of the Revolutionary Congress, Johnson took the lead in those dealings of the nine colonies with the Iroquois which attached the Six Nations to the cause of the English in the struggle for the Ohio valley; and thus he paved the way for his appointment by Braddock as superintendent of Indian affairs. In the Seven Years' War Johnson by his military successes, particularly at Niagara, had increased his prestige with the home government; and in all Indian matters he was easily the first man in America.

By September, 1768, all was prepared for the council that was to move the boundary westward from the Alleghanies to the Ohio. Fort Stanwix, on the present site of Rome, New York, was the gathering-place, and thither repaired Sir William, attended by his three deputies, George Croghan, Daniel Claus, and Guy Johnson. Governor Franklin of New Jersey, Lieutenant-Governor Penn, and commissioners from Pennsylvania and Virginia also were in attendance. The Indians were slow in arriving, the Senecas having been detained by the death of a sachem, and the Delawares and Shawanese having dallied with belts and promises from the French and Spanish of the Mississippi. On September 24th, Sir William's deputies reported thirty-two hundred Indians in attendance, and the council began with the usual ceremonies. For six days the Indians pondered the proposition to buy their lands, and on the seventh day they assented, but not without many promises and presents to the influential sachems. For six thousand dollars in money and goods the Indian title to Kentucky, West Virginia, and the western portion of Pennsylvania was acquired by the crown. Thus was the way opened for a new colony beyond the Alleghanies.

In his treaty Sir William had exceeded his instructions. Lord Hillsborough had sent to him a map of the boundaries he proposed. These stopped at the mouth of the Great Kanawha instead of the Tennessee; but Sir William preferred to offend Lord Hillsborough in England rather than to incur the anger of the ever-present Six Nations, who insisted on parting with the larger territory in order to show their authority over lands claimed also by the Cherokees. Had the more restricted boundary been adopted, mortal offence would have been given to the northern Indians, who claimed to have conquered all the lands to the Mississippi. In vain Lord Hillsborough referred the matter back for adjustment in accordance with his ideas. Sir William professed himself earnest to cede back to the Indians a portion of the grant. They would not have it so.

For two years more the Illinois project lay dormant; but on May 25, 1770, the council sent Walpole's petition to the Board of Trade. The Lords Commissioners, after two more years of delay, reported against the proposition. The report, drawn by Lord Hillsborough, after reciting that portions of the proposed grant were in the colony of Virginia, and other portions were Indian hunting-grounds, reminded the Lords of the Treasury "of that principle which was adopted by this Board, and approved and confirmed by his Majesty, immediately after the treaty of Paris—viz., the confining the western extent of settlements to such a distance from the sea-coast as that those settlements should lie within reach of the trade and commerce of this kingdom, upon which the strength and riches of it depend, and also of the exercise of that authority and jurisdiction which was conceived to be necessary for the preservation of the colonies in a due subordination to, and dependence upon, the mother-country."[1]

Franklin toyed with Lord Hillsborough's adverse report in much the same manner that a cat plays with a mouse. He corrected its geography and its history; he controverted its arguments; and he proved to the satisfaction of the king in council that the royal heart had never been so cold and selfish as the Lords Commissioners for Trade and Plantations would have his Majesty believe it was in 1763, when, it was alleged, he would have confined his loving subjects in America to the lands east of the Alleghanies. The grant to the Ohio Company proved that settlements to the westward were contemplated, and the restrictions of 1763 were but temporary, until the lands should be purchased from the Indians. This purchase had been made by the treaty of Fort Stanwix; and Pennsylvania, by virtue of that treaty, had already erected Bedford County from territory beyond the mountains, and was exercising civil government therein.[2]

Franklin's argument was unanswerable. The offer of the company was to repay to the crown the £10,460 7*s.* 3*d.*, which was all the money the whole country (of which the Walpole grant was only a part) cost the government; in addition quit-rents, to begin twenty years after the survey of each lot or plantation, were to be paid to the king's agent. The expenses of civil government were to be borne by the proprietors. This offer was accepted, and on August 14, 1772, the Walpole grant was approved. Lord Hillsborough, cha-

[1] Sparks's *Franklin*, vol. iv., p. 305.

[2] Sparks gives the report of the Board of Trade, Franklin's reply, and the proclamation of 1763. See *Franklin's Works*, vol. iv., pp. 302–380.

grined and humiliated at Franklin's triumph, offered his resignation, as perhaps his colleagues expected he would do; and, much to his surprise, he promptly found himself out of office. He was succeeded by Lord Dartmouth, reputed to be a friend of the colonies.

Rumors of the proposed new colony of Vandalia were rife in Virginia, and George Washington was ill pleased with a scheme which seemed likely to prevent him from locating the twenty-five thousand acres that were due to him for services rendered in the French war; nor was he satisfied with the coalition made by the agent of the Ohio Company and the promoters of the Walpole grant.[1] As it happened, however, an especial reservation was made in that grant in favor of the bounty lands provided for in the proclamation of 1763, so that Washington's individual claims were interfered with in nowise.

Bouquet, and after him Gage, saw the military advantage of interposing a strong government between the seaboard colonies and the Indians. Sir William Johnson, the Franklins (father and son), the restless, enterprising, and well-informed Pownall, who had carried back to England a wide knowledge of America, and such influential merchants as Walpole, all recognized the commercial advantages of a proprietary province on the Ohio; but the day for new royal colonies in America had passed. The Walpole grant, like the Ohio Company's concession, was doomed to failure. Nor was there the slightest hope of success, either in the king's

[1] The basis of combination was that the members of the Ohio Company were to receive two shares, or one thirty-sixth, of the stock of Walpole's, or the Grand Company, as it was called. These terms were never approved by the Ohio Company; and, as a matter of fact, neither the Ohio nor the Walpole grant was ever completed.

cabinet or in America, for the Mississippi Company[1] or any other of the numerous associations formed for the purpose of acquiring lands from the Indians and planting thereon settlers subject to quit-rents, religious establishments, and governments privately supported.

That numerous, hardy, independent, and often lawless population which had occupied the frontiers of Virginia was now ready to push westward, and, in the wilderness south of the Ohio, to make homes for their children. They went first as hunters, then as prospectors, and finally as settlers. They purchased lands with bullets, and surveyed claims with tomahawks. As Virginians they built their cabins within the original boundaries of their own colony, and to their colony they looked for protection. Singly or in groups these adventurous backwoodsmen hunted big game, set up "tomahawk claims," cleared fields, built cabins, and began to people the wilderness. Even Washington, with land claims purchased by his valor, was unable to make headway against this swarming of new people into new lands.

In the autumn of 1770, when Washington, piloted by George Croghan and accompanied by his surveyor Crawford, descended the Ohio to the Kanawha, the lonely banks of the beautiful river gave no indications that soon a mighty human stream would flow down

[1] A copy of the articles of association of the Mississippi Company was recently discovered among the manuscripts in the Library of Congress, by Mr. Herbert Friedenwald. It covers three large pages closely written by George Washington, and is dated June 3, 1763. The first name is that of Francis Lightfoot Lee, the next is John Augustine Washington, and among the nineteen are the names of Richard Henry Lee, Henry Fitzhugh, and Thomas Bullitt, the latter being one of the earliest settlers of Kentucky. Washington's name stands at the end. The company was organized to send an agent to England to obtain a grant of lands on the Mississippi and its waters.

DANIEL BOONE

(From a painting by Chester Harding, owned by W. H. King, Chicago. Photographed by C. L. Moore, Springfield, Mass.)

that winding course. Yet in the previous year Daniel and Squire Boone, with a party of hunters, had started to explore the Kentucky wilderness; and during the year 1773 the blue-grass conntry was crossed by many a bold home-seeker like Simon Kenton and the three brothers McAfee, who had taken life in hand while venturing into the favorite hunting-grounds of savages eager for scalps. In September, 1773, Daniel Boone led his own family, with five other families and forty frontiersmen, from the Yadkin over the mountains, with the intention of settling in Kentucky. Attacked by Indians, they made a resting-place on the Clinch River. In April, 1744, Floyd, with a party of surveyors, began to survey military lands on the Kanawha for Patrick Henry and Washington. While voyaging down the Ohio on their way to Kentucky, they were overtaken by a messenger sent from Fort Pitt to warn them that they were in danger of being cut off by an Indian war.[1]

Besides the Kentucky explorers, who had crossed the mountains, a considerable number of Virginians had settled along the Ohio below Fort Pitt, thereby encroaching on the lands of the Delawares and Shawanese. At this time Pittsburg was a Virginia town, although Pennsylvania claimed the territory. The royal governor of Virginia, Lord Dunmore, now found himself in a perplexing situation. The Walpole grant threatened to carve a new province out of the colony of

[1] In 1747 Dr. Walker, of Virginia, led an exploring party through northeastern Kentucky, and named the Cumberland River for "the Bloody Duke"; and in 1767 John Finley, of North Carolina, made a visit to the same region. Finley was one of Boone's party of 1769. For the details of Boone's trip, see Filson's *Boone* and Mann Butler's *Kentucky*. There are no more fascinating chapters in Roosevelt's *Winning of the West* than those in the first volume which relate to the settlement of Kentucky.

which he was governor; the Pennsylvania traders and the adherents of Lord Dunmore's representative, Dr. Conolly, had almost come to blows over the possession of the forks of the Ohio; and the Virginia settlers in the western country were clamoring for aid against Indian attacks.[1]

Besides the threatened encroachments on the territory of Virginia, Lord Dunmore, in common with his fellow royal governors, was called upon to face the steady, persistent, determined opposition of the responsible men of his colony to the peculiar measures by which Great Britain was undertaking to bring America into subjection. Nine years had passed since that May day in 1765 when Patrick Henry dared to set up the two-sided shield of treason and independence. The stamp act had been passed and repealed; non-intercourse resolutions, offered by the conservative Washington, had been adopted; and already, by the effective methods of the committees of correspondence, colonists were being transformed into Americans. Boston, no longer a far-off town of mere traders, had become to Virginians a martyr to the cause of liberty, and her citizens were indeed brothers in adversity. The suave Lord Bote-

[1] The Indians slew the Virginians because they came as settlers, but spared the Pennsylvania traders. The tale of Indian robberies and massacres is far too long to tell. Lyman C. Draper, certainly a good authority, estimates that during the ten years of so-called peace that followed Bouquet's expedition, more lives were sacrificed along the western frontiers than during the whole outbreak of 1774, including the battle of Point Pleasant.—Brantz Mayer's *Tah-Gah-Jute; or, Logan and Cresap* (Albany, 1867), p. 67.

Lord Dunmore, before he could possibly have known of the Greathouse murders, had issued (April 25, 1774) a proclamation referring to the Pittsburg territorial troubles, and calling out the militia to repel any assault whatever, thus showing that he proposed to sustain Dr. Conolly no less than to chastise the savages.

tourt had indeed kept the fire from breaking through the roof, but his successor in office, the impulsive Earl of Dunmore, found that the grave and courtly Virginians, while punctiliously courteous to himself and his attractive family, fasted and prayed to be delivered from the tyranny whose agent and exemplar he was.[1]

Add to all these troubles the circumstance that Lord Dunmore was anxious to obtain for himself a share in the rich domain that was awaiting the settler's axe, and one has a sufficient number of reasons why the chief magistrate of Virginia might well feel that it would be a capital stroke to use Pittsburg as the headquarters for a Virginia military expedition which should confirm the title of his colony not only to that important post, but also to the entire Ohio country, while at the same time attention might be diverted from English troubles, a patriotic sentiment on behalf of the border settlers might be aroused, and an opportunity provided to obtain from the Indians extensive lands in the Illinois country.[2]

[1] Washington went from a meeting at the Raleigh Tavern, where the Boston bill was denounced, to dine with Lord Dunmore; next day the two rode together, and in the evening Washington attended her ladyship's ball; but on the day of fasting, humiliation, and prayer, he fasted and attended the appointed services. See Lodge's *Washington*, vol. i., p. 119.

[2] It appears from Chief-justice Marshall's decision in Johnson *v.* McIntosh (8 *Wheaton*), that on July 5, 1773, a large portion of the Illinois country lying on the Mississippi was purchased at an Indian council held at Kaskaskia, by a company of London, Pennsylvania, and Illinois people; and on October 18, 1775, the principal persons in the first purchase were associated with Lord Dunmore and Honorable John Murray, his son, in two grants on the Wabash near Vincennes. The title ran to the purchasers, or to the King of England for their benefit, and the lands were described as being within the chartered limits of Virginia. After the Revolution the assigns of the original grantees undertook to establish claim to the lands in question; but

The particular occasion for the Indian war of 1774 was an attack made by some thieving Cherokees, one April night, on three of trader Butler's men. Dr. Conolly, as the representative of Virginia, immediately called on the frontiersmen to hold themselves ready to repel an attack of hostile Shawanese. Among those who jumped to the call was Michael Cresap (a son of Washington's frontier friend and partner in the Ohio Company's venture), who was then at the head of a band of explorers pausing at Wheeling until they could make certain whether there was to be an Indian uprising. Cresap's party made a bad matter worse by ambushing and killing two Shawanese employed by Butler to recover his plundered goods; and the passion for blood, which was so often to manifest itself in the vicinity of Pittsburg, having got hold upon them, they determined to hasten to the mouth of the Big Beaver and there attack the camp of Logan, an Iroquois of commanding influence among Indians and also much trusted by the settlers. Calmer judgment, however, led them to turn back; but before April closed ten Indians, including a number of Logan's relatives, all of whom had crossed the Ohio to get liquor, were massacred while drunk, and it was generally believed that Cresap had done this base deed. As a matter of fact, the murders were committed by one Greathouse and a party of twenty men. On the wings of the forest-telegraph news of the foul murder reached Croghan and Sir William Johnson, by whom it was reported to London as an act certain to bring on an Indian war.[1]

the court held that individuals had no rights of purchase from Indians. It is not strange that Lord Dunmore should have succumbed to the then prevailing disease of land speculation.

[1] Colonel Cresap the elder came to Maryland from Yorkshire when

The frontier was now in an uproar. From village to village throughout the Northwest coursed the fleet runners calling to the war-path. At the instigation of the Pennsylvania traders that colony held itself neutral, putting upon Virginia the onerous task of meeting the hostility of the savages. Leaving the rebellious house of burgesses to what he considered their treasonable devices, Lord Dunmore placed himself at the head of the popular backwoods movement to chastise the savages who were now devastating the frontier, Logan himself taking frequent and terrible revenge for the treacherous murder of his relatives.[1]

Lord Dunmore's plan of campaign was for the army to gather in two divisions: he himself, commanding the right wing, was to proceed by the way of Pittsburg to

fifteen years old. After many financial vicissitudes and much hard fighting he became a comparatively wealthy man with a large property on the Potomac. At the age of seventy he visited England; at eighty he married for the last time; at ninety he planned to explore the country to the Pacific, but was forced by failing powers to give up the undertaking, and he died at the ripe age of one hundred and six years. His son, Captain Michael Cresap, had been brought up to fight Indians; he had thrown away the advantages of education, and, after financial troubles, entered the Ohio country early in 1774. At this time he was working about fifteen miles above the Kanawha, and was called upon to lead the frontiersmen whom Dr. Conolly's summons had aroused. It appears that he advised against the attack on Logan's camp, and that while not differing from his companions in his general hostility to Indians, he was above the treachery of murdering drunken savages.

[1] On July 21, 1774, Logan addressed to Captain Cresap a letter asking why the latter had slain Logan's people on the Yellow Creek, and boasting that he had been three times to war since. This letter, written in gunpowder ink by a captive, was dictated by Logan; it was attached to a war-club and left at the house of the murdered Roberts family, whence it was taken to Colonel Preston, whose granddaughter married Hon. Thomas H. Benton.—Brantz Mayer's *Logan and Cresap*, p. 111.

the banks of the Kanawha, there to join the left wing under General Andrew Lewis. On the great levels of the Greenbrier General Lewis gathered his army of stalwart and experienced Indian fighters—men from the back counties of Virginia and from the Watauga commonwealth, then perforce an independent state under the leadership of Sevier and Robertson. On October 10th, while this army of about eleven hundred men was in camp at Point Pleasant, with the Kanawha at the rear and the Ohio on the left, it was suddenly attacked by a large force of Indians led by the Shawanese chief Cornstalk; and in the desperate all-day battle that ensued one-fifth of the whites were either killed or wounded, while the Indians withdrew with a loss of about forty killed. Both in discipline and in valor the Indians were at least the equals of the whites; in numbers the two forces were about the same; but there is always a point where the Indians will give up the hope of ultimate success rather than suffer the loss of their comrades, and so it was that in the battle of Point Pleasant the savages withdrew, although they had suffered the smaller loss.[1]

Eager to follow up his dearly bought victory, Lewis crossed the Ohio and marched his army to the Pickaway Plains, whither he had been summoned by Lord Dunmore. As the two armies approached, General Lewis was ordered into camp to await the conclusion of a peace that the reluctant Cornstalk was forced to make when his burning exhortations to battle fell upon the ears of his disheartened braves like sparks upon the water. The great chief Logan refused to enter the

[1] For an account of the battle, see *American Archives*, fourth series, vol. i., p. 1016 *et seq.* The best account of the Dunmore expedition is to be found in Whittlesey's *Fugitive Essays* (Hudson, Ohio, 1852).

council; and when Lord Dunmore summoned him he sent this reply, which has taken a place in our literature as the greatest of Indian prose elegies:

"I appeal to any white man to say if ever he entered Logan's cabin hungry and he gave him not meat, if ever he came cold and naked and he clothed him not. During the course of the last long and bloody war, Logan remained idle in his cabin, an advocate for peace. Such was my love for the whites that my countrymen pointed as they passed and said, 'Logan is the friend of white men.' I had even thought to have lived with you, but for the injuries of one man. Colonel Cresap, last spring, in cold blood and unprovoked, murdered all the relations of Logan, not even sparing my women and children. There runs not a drop of my blood in the veins of any living creature. This called on me for revenge. I have sought it. I have killed many. I have fully glutted my vengeance. For my country I rejoice at the beams of peace; but do not harbor a thought that mine is the joy of fear. Logan never felt fear. He will not turn on his heel to save his life. Who is there to mourn for Logan? Not one!"[1]

[1] There are many versions of this message. The one above is taken from Jefferson's *Notes on the State of Virginia* (London, 1787), p. 105. Jefferson says of it: "I may challenge the whole orations of Demosthenes and Cicero, and of any more eminent orator, if Europe has furnished more eminent, to produce a single passage superior to the messages of Logan, a Mingo chief, to Lord Dunmore." He also speaks of "Colonel Cresap, a man infamous for the many murders committed on those much-injured people." Jefferson never wholly retracted this slander on Captain Cresap, although he had full opportunity of knowing that Cresap was not within fifty miles of the place of the murder at the time when it was committed. The soldiers of Dunmore's army knew that Cresap was unjustly charged with the murder, and, when the message was read to them at the treaty, George Rogers Clark, who was in Cresap's party at Wheeling, joked him about being so impor-

Cornstalk and Logan assented to the peace determined upon, according to the Indian custom, by a majority of the council; and Lord Dunmore marched back to Virginia to receive the applause and honor never withheld from a conqueror. If General Lewis and his brave officers suspected that Lord Dunmore had left them to their fate at Point Pleasant, that he was over-eager to make peace when chastisement would have produced better results, and was anxious to claim credit for success achieved only through their vic-

tant an Indian fighter as to be credited with all the attacks on the savages. Not only was Cresap innocent of the murder, but, as a matter of fact, Logan had a number of relatives (he had no children by his wife) remaining after the massacre. Moreover, the language on which the message—it was not a speech—depends for its rhetorical effect was not Logan's, but Colonel John Gibson's, and he in turn in part paraphrased the Bible and in part adopted the biblical style. Gibson, as it appears, received Logan's message from Simon Girty, who had been sent to find Logan. Girty translated it into English, and Gibson put it into its present shape. It is idle, therefore, to regard the production as a specimen of Indian eloquence; but the message as given to Lord Dunmore made a decided impression at the time, and Jefferson fixed it among classics. Both Logan and Jefferson spoke of "Colonel" Cresap. Colonel Cresap was the father; the son was a captain then and until his death.—See Whittlesey's *Fugitive Essays*, p. 143, and Butterfield's *History of the Girtys*, p. 29.

Logan was a son of the chief Skikellamy, who lived at Shamokin, on the Susquehanna. Perhaps the father was a Frenchman who had been transformed into an Indian. Logan was named for his father's friend, James Logan, at one time Secretary of the colony of Pennsylvania. Although not technically a chief, he was not without followers; his father was of the Iroquois, but Logan married a Shawanese. During the Revolution he was actively employed by the British until about 1780, when he was killed in self-defence by a relative. Having become a victim of the Englishman's rum, he struck his wife while at Detroit, and escaped into the forest lest he should be killed by her people. Meeting one of his relatives while in a crazy condition, Logan attacked him and was shot.—See Brantz Mayer's *Logan and Cresap*.

SIMON KENTON

(From a painting by Robert Clarke, Cincinnati, Ohio)

tory, nevertheless they joined with the army in thanking Lord Dunmore for his leadership in the expedition. Perhaps, however, the vote of thanks passed by the assembly of officers, held when they reached Fort Gower, at the mouth of the Hocking, was intended to take the personal sting out of the remaining resolutions, wherein the backwoods Virginians proclaimed that, although bearing faithful allegiance to George III., they were resolved to exert every power within them "for the defence of American liberty, and for the support of her just rights and privileges, not in any precipitous, riotous, or tumultuous manner, but when regularly called forth by the unanimous voice of our countrymen." Thus at the very beginning of the struggle for independence the men of the frontiers, gathered on the soil of the Northwest, pledged the new lands to freedom.[1]

During the following year Captain Cresap raised a company of backwoodsmen and marched with them over the Alleghanies to join Washington at Cambridge. His own strength, however, was insufficient for the great struggle, and after a brief stay with the army he turned his face westward only to die when he had reached New York. He was buried with military honors in Trinity church-yard.

Not alone through the eight long and bitter years of the Revolution, but through the forty years that were to come before England finally relinquished her grasp on the territory between the Ohio and the Great Lakes, the pledge made on the banks of the Hocking was held good by the pioneers of Kentucky and their descendants. Boone and Kenton, Clark and Shelby,

[1] The resolutions are given in full in Whittlesey's *Fugitive Essays*, p. 152.

Lewis and Gibson—these are the names borne by makers and preservers of the Northwest. The Dunmore war, so far from being a mere episode of the border, conquered the peace that opened Kentucky to settlement; and Kentucky in its turn not only made an impassable frontier barrier to protect the rear of the colonies during the Revolution, but also furnished the men and the leaders who subdued the savages of the Northwest, and finally broke the power of the British at the battle of the Thames in the War of 1812.

CHAPTER VI

THE QUEBEC ACT AND THE REVOLUTION

THE British policy of maintaining the Northwest as an Indian hunting-ground was a failure. To the colonies the fertile lands along the Ohio were a temptation to be disposed of only by yielding to it; and the Indians had no power to protect their possessions when once the settlers had learned to fight after the fashion of the savages. Indeed, both in woodcraft and in ambush, the whites became more expert than the Indians themselves; in endurance the backwoodsman was not excelled, and he was vastly superior to his red enemy in self-control and persistency of purpose. Moreover, even such law-abiding subjects as Washington never took seriously the proclamation of 1763, as prohibiting settlements beyond the mountains;[1] but steadfastly maintained that the Ohio country was within the chartered limits of Virginia. Also the impossibility of controlling the Northwest by means of scattered military posts and without laws or courts soon became apparent.[2] Added to this was the signal failure of the proclamation of 1763 as a means of dealing with the many and perplexing questions that arose in the province of Quebec.

[1] *Secret Journals of Congress* (Boston, 1821), vol. iii., p. 153 *et seq.*

[2] Virginia held courts beyond the Alleghanies in 1773; but there was no regular government southwest of Fort Pitt; and Conolly's courts were scarcely to be classed as such (see *Secret Journals of Congress*, vol. iii., p. 187).

The ebbing tide of war left in control at Quebec General James Murray, who was styled in his commission "captain-general and governor-in-chief" of the province.[1] The most extensive powers were conferred upon him and his council; but no assembly was provided for, though a promise of self-government at some future time was made in the proclamation of 1763. The cardinal difficulty experienced in government arose from the attempt to give English laws to a people unacquainted with trial by jury or the *habeas corpus*. General Murray, although a distinguished soldier at the siege of Quebec, was not a successful administrator; and after two years of weary life in the new government he gave place to one of his fellow-generals, Guy Carleton, on whom was conferred the larger title of governor of Canada.[2]

In a letter to Lord Hillsborough, written in 1770, Carleton called attention to the fact that the Protestants who had settled, or rather sojourned, in Quebec since the conquest, were traders, disbanded soldiers, and officers below the rank of captain. Of those who would naturally be called on to administer justice, the ones who were successful in business had no time to act as judges; while those whose ill success resulted in bankruptcy naturally sought to repair their broken fortunes at the expense of the people. Hence arose a variety of schemes to increase their business, and consequently their fees; bailiffs of their own creation—mostly French soldiers, either disbanded or deserters—were dispersed through the parishes with blank citations, to catch at every little

[1] Murray's commission is given in full in *American Archives*, 4th series, vol. i., p. 175.

[2] Murray was the fifth son of the fourth Lord Elibank, and, after leaving Canada, was made governor of Minorca. He died in 1794.

feud among the people and force them to litigate quarrels which, had the people been left to themselves, might easily have been accommodated. In order to put a stop to such abuses, Carleton reduced the power of the justices of the peace, in part revived the old laws of Canada, and arranged to have matters relating to property decided by king's judges paid by the crown.[1]

This action was taken after a careful examination of the entire question by a committee of five, headed by Chief-justice Hey and Lieutenant-governor Cramahé. The committee reported that the authority and powers of the justices of the peace in matters of property, as contained in the ordinance of 1764, were very injudicious. Even in England, where the justices of the peace were, for the most part, men of large fortunes, who had a considerable interest in common with the people over whom their authority was exercised, the justices had no such extensive powers as in Canada; and yet in Canada the justices had even usurped authority not given to them in their commissions; so that titles to land had been determined and possessions disturbed in a way unknown to the laws of England. Moreover, in the absence of any manner of ascertaining how their judgments were to be enforced, the magistrates had assumed authority in such a way as to fill the jails with numbers of unhappy subjects whose families were reduced to beggary and ruin. It had become a common practice to take lands in execution and sell them to satisfy even a small debt. The very powers originally calculated for the ease of the suitor and to facilitate the courts of justice had become the very instrument of his

[1] "Carleton to Hillsborough," and also "Letter from an ex-Captain of Militia," *Canadian Archives*, 1890, pp. 1–5.

oppression and ruin. In one instance the expense of suing for a debt of eleven livres amounted to eighty-four livres. The ordinance prepared to make the changes indicated above was approved by the king, who, wrote Lord Hillsborough, "wishes that every just ground of discontent should be removed, and every real grievance remedied as far as may be."

As was to be expected, the justices rebelled against this diminution of their authority; but Carleton warned them that they were acting against their own interests. In this ordinance is to be found, in part, the basis for the Quebec act in 1774.

The Quebec act was so obnoxious to the American colonists that it was cited in the Declaration of Independence as "abolishing the free system of English laws in a neighboring province, establishing therein an arbitrary government, and enlarging its boundaries so as to render it at once an example and fit instrument for introducing the same arbitrary rule into these colonies." Taken as one of the many measures by which the ministers of George III. sought to curb and repress the colonies, the Quebec act was unwise and impolitic. Viewed from the stand-point of a quiet administration of England's new territories, it was so successful that during the Revolution the Americans failed in all their efforts to detach the Canadians generally from their allegiance to the British. In Parliament, however, the bill met with vigorous but ineffectual opposition, both from the friends of the colonists and also from the British merchants doing business in Canada.

The bill, brought up in the House of Lords by the Earl of Dartmouth, on May 2, 1774, passed without opposition fifteen days later. On June 18 it was returned to the House of Lords with amendments introduced by the House of Commons. At this stage it was opposed by the Earl of Chatham, who threw into his opposition all the energy which his seriously enfeebled condition allowed him to give to a measure that seemed to him a "cruel, oppressive, and odious" means of governing a realm that under his rule had been conquered by British arms and dedicated to the widest freedom then known to mankind. In prophetic words he described the bill as "destructive of that liberty which ought to be the groundwork of every constitution," and as "calculated to shake the affections and confidence of his Majesty's subjects in England and Ireland, and finally lose him the hearts of all Americans."[1]

In the House of Commons the ministry defended and explained the bill as one calculated to do only simple justice to a people conquered indeed, but still alien to the laws, the language, and the customs of their conquerors; a people as yet too ignorant to appreciate and to take advantage of the freedom that was to an Englishman as the very air he breathed. They explained that the bill was drawn by the Earl of Dartmouth, secretary of state for the colonies,[2] with the advice of the then governor of Quebec, Sir Guy Carleton, and of the chief-justice of that colony, William Hey, both of whom must be credited with unusual ability, with a wide practical experience in the affairs of Canada, and with a sincere desire to promote the well-being of the vast majority of the people of that country.

The bill provided for a governor and council; the criminal laws of England were continued in force throughout the colony of Quebec, but all civil causes were to be determined according to the custom of

[1] Cavendish's *Report*, p. 4.

[2] Cavendish's *Report*. Speech of Lord North, p. 8.

Paris; the Roman Catholic religion was established by continuing the stipends of bishops and clergy; and the boundaries of the colony were enlarged by including the Labrador coast and the country north of the Ohio.

In defending the bill, Lord North, then the leader of the ministry, explained that the value of the Labrador fisheries, but recently discovered, made it absolutely necessary, for the preservation of those fisheries, to detach the country from New York and to attach it to Quebec. The scattered posts in the Northwest were annexed to Canada because the traders demanded some government for them, and a single government was preferable to several separate governments. If the bill did extend the ancient limits of Canada, as had been charged, "the country to which it is extended is the habitation of bears and beavers; and all these regulations, which only pretend to protect the trader, as far as they can protect him, undoubtedly cannot be considered oppressive to any of the inhabitants in that part of the world, who are very few, except about the coast, and at present in a very disorderly and ungovernable condition." An assembly, Lord North argued, could not be granted, because, the bulk of inhabitants being Roman Catholics, an assembly of Roman Catholics would be a hardship to the few British subjects, while, on the other hand, an assembly confined to the English would prove oppressive to the Roman Catholics. Before the conquest France had ruled the country by means of a governor and council; now the English proposed to do the same. The English civil law might be better than the French, but property in Canada had become established under French law, and it was but fair that, inasmuch as the treaty of 1763 established the Canadians in their possessions, they should be maintained in those possessions by the law under which they were created, subject to such changes as the governor and council might find necessary. As for the establishment of the Roman Catholic religion, the Act of Supremacy expressly guarded against papal authority; and the free exercise of their religion was guaranteed to the Canadians by the treaty of 1763.[1]

The brave Colonel Barré, who had shed his blood on the Plains of Abraham, resented the sneers of Lord North. The Northwestern country, he said, so far from being given up to bears and beavers, already contained the houses of many thousands of English subjects who had crossed the Alleghanies, as they had a right to do, to make settlements.[2] By making the St. Lawrence and the Great Lakes the boundary of Canada, as it was made in the peace negotiations with France in 1763, the scattered posts in the neighborhood of Detroit and Lake Michigan could be included, and thus the Ohio be left open to settlement. The youthful orator, Charles Fox,[3] who had ceased to be a Lord of the Treasury but fourteen days previous to the debate, opposed the right of the Roman Catholic clergy to receive tithes as to his mind a fatal objection to the bill.

[1] Cavendish's *Report*, p. 12. The treaty provided "that every Canadian should have the full enjoyment of all his property, particularly the religious orders of the Canadians, and that the free exercise of the Roman Catholic religion should be continued."—Speech of Edward Thurlow, Attorney-general, Cavendish's *Report*, p. 28.

[2] Colonel Isaac Barré, member for Wycombe, is represented in West's picture of the death of Wolfe as one of the group of officers standing near the dying general. He was severely wounded in the engagement on the Plains of Abraham.

[3] At this time Fox was just twenty-five years old, and had already been a member of the House for six years.

Edmund Burke[1] opposed the bill on the ground that the boundaries came within those of the colony of New York, and also because the House was without sufficient information as to the condition of affairs in Canada; and he succeeded in having the bill amended so as to secure to the colony of New York substantially the same western boundaries that the State now enjoys.

Thomas Penn, the son, and John Penn, the grandson, of William Penn, by petition protested that their rights as proprietors were affected adversely by the boundaries; and the British merchants trading in Canada objected to the provisions doing away with trial by jury in civil cases, and subjecting their property to Canadian laws contained in some thirty volumes and administered by judges ignorant of those laws.

At this juncture General Carleton, having been called before the House, testified, as to the result of four years of experience in the governorship,[2] that the Canadians objected to the expense of trial by jury and to the fact that trials were conducted in a language they did not understand. They thought it "very strange that the English residing in Canada should prefer to have matters of law decided by tailors and shoemakers, mixed up with respectable gentlemen in trade and commerce; that they should prefer their decision to that of a judge."[3] In 1770, he said, there were in Canada

[1] Burke was a member for Wendover, and also agent for the colony of New York in England.

[2] Carleton had been in office four years when, in 1770, he was called to London to assist in drafting the Quebec Bill. During the four years of his absence the government was administered by H. T. Cramahé, Lieutenant-governor. See *Canadian Archives*, 1890, p. 12.

[3] Cavendish's *Report*, p. 102. Carleton's testimony in an abridged form is found in the *Parliamentary Debates* for 1774, and in *American Archives*, 4th series, vol. i., p. 190.

EDMUND BURKE

about 360 men who claimed to be Protestants; whereas the number of Roman Catholics was about 150,000 souls. The clergy had continued to receive their tithes and parochial dues as under the French; but from motives of policy such tithes and dues had not been enforced against the few English land-owners.

When asked by Lord North whether the Canadians desired assemblies, Governor Carleton promptly answered: "Certainly not. I put the question to several of the Canadians. They told me assemblies had drawn upon other colonies so much distress, had occasioned such riots and confusion, that they wished never to have one of any kind whatever." This answer, which was entirely consistent with the Canadian temperament, also throws a strong light on the determination of the ministry not to raise up in Canada another seditious colony by granting an assembly. When it came to the question of wider boundaries, General Carleton spoke with reluctance born of ignorance. The Ohio country, he said, was not included within the government of Quebec; Detroit was not under the government, but Michigan was; he thought that the Illinois country was a part of Old Canada, and that New Orleans was under the government of Quebec, but precisely where the district ended he really did not know, nor did he know how far the Illinois was from Quebec. The difficulties with the narrow boundaries of Quebec named in the proclamation of 1763 were practical ones. Both the Canadian and the English traders complained that they were obliged to send their property to posts where there were no courts of justice, and even their grants of land were without the protection of law; as a result the Upper Country was the asylum for vagabonds. He admitted that the Indians might object to the new boundaries; for he said, "there are a great many tribes of Indians who think that neither we, nor France, nor any European power, have any title to the country; nor do they acknowledge themselves to be our subjects;" but the Indians look upon their hunting-grounds as free.

On June 22, 1774, four days after the Quebec bill passed the House of Commons, the Lord Mayor of London, together with several aldermen and upwards of one hundred and fifty of the common council, appeared at St. James Palace with an address and petition to the king, supplicating his Majesty to refuse his assent to the bill. The king replied through the lord chamberlain that the bill was not yet before him; and thereupon proceeded to Westminster to prorogue Parliament, going first to the House of Lords, where he gave his assent to the bill, saying that it was "founded on the clearest principles of justice and humanity, and would, he doubted not, have the best effect in quieting the minds and promoting the happiness of his Canadian subjects."[1]

Governor Carleton returned to Quebec, September 18, 1774, to find the Canadians well disposed towards the new act;[2] but the British subjects were indignant at being deprived of "the franchises which they inherited from their forefathers," at their loss of the protection of English laws, "so universally admired for their wisdom and lenity," and at the introduction of the laws of Canada, to which they were total strangers.[3] But in spite of petitions and motions to repeal the act, it went into operation and continued in force until 1791, when a new government was given to Quebec, and Canada was divided into Upper and Lower Canada.

[1] Cavendish's *Report*, p. 4. [2] *Canadian Archives*, 1890, p. 14.

[3] Petition of the English settlers. See Cavendish's *Report*, p. 14.

From the Quebec act dates the beginning of civil government in the Northwest.[1] Under the provisions of the act Detroit was made the capital of the territory northwest of the Ohio, and civil officers were selected according to the spoils system, then at its height in England.

Henry Hamilton, by the grace of King George the Third and the favor of the Earl of Dartmouth, lieutenant-governor and superintendent at Detroit, reached his new station on the 9th of November, 1775. His journey was not without the spice of adventure. At Cambridge Washington was in command of the American army, and General Montgomery's little force patrolled the waters and the paths leading to the island-city of Montreal, that was soon (November 13th) to yield a temporary conquest. Through these ineffectual lines Hamilton passed in the disguise of a Canadian. The Americans, having come to Canada not so much to conquer the province as to make an offer of freedom to the Canadians, had yet to learn that the dwellers along the St. Lawrence were well satisfied to endure the ills they had, rather than ally themselves with a heretic people turbulent for liberty.[2] After four days of travel

[1] The Quebec act is given in full in *American Archives*, 4th series, vol. i., p. 216 *et seq.*

[2] On April 2, 1776, Franklin, Samuel Chase, and Charles Carroll, of Carrollton, commissioners, accompanied by Rev. John Carroll, S. J. (afterwards the first Roman Catholic Archbishop of the United States), left Albany "to promote or to form a union between the colonies and the people of Canada." The complete failure of their mission is to be attributed mainly to the fact that under the Quebec act the Canadians had been left free in the exercise of the Roman Catholic religion, and to a large degree that religion "was established"; whereas Congress, in their address to the people of Great Britain (October 21, 1774), could not "suppress astonishment that a British Parliament should ever consent to establish in that country (Canada)

in a wooden canoe, and "unprovided with everything," he reached a point of safety, and thereafter travelled in a manner more befitting an officer of the king. Once in Detroit, however, all perils were forgotten in contemplating the charms of the place. The kindly fruits of the earth abounded; the woods were full of blossoming shrubs, wild flowers, and aromatic herbs; and no other climate he had ever known was so agreeable. The shingled houses of the settlers, each backed by a bounteous orchard and flanked by barns and stables making a continuous row, smiled a welcome to the traveller as he sailed up the brimming river. From the clear depths of the stream a few hours of amusement with the line would draw enough fish to furnish several families; and so fertile was the land that even the careless and very ignorant French farmers raised great crops of wheat, corn, barley, and buckwheat. The whites numbered about 1500;[1] and among them the law of the survival of the fittest was already at work. The English settlers, more industrious and more enterprising than

a religion that has deluged your island in blood, and dispersed impiety, bigotry, persecution, and rebellion through every part of the world." Such an attack on the religion of a people could not be glossed over by the mild statement in the address of Congress to the inhabitants of Quebec, that "we are too well acquainted with the liberality of sentiment distinguishing your nation, to imagine that difference of religion will prejudice you against a hearty amity with us." See *American Archives*, vol. v., p. 66; *Journal of Charles Carroll of Carrollton*, with memoir by Brantz Mayer, *Maryland Historical Society Publications*, 1845; and Emily Mason's *Charles Carroll of Carrollton.*

[1] A survey of the settlement of Detroit in March, 1779, shows 1011 men, 265 women, 253 "lodgers hired or young men," 484 boys, 402 girls, 60 male slaves, and 78 female slaves; there were 413 oxen, 779 cows, 619 steers, 1076 hogs, 664 horses, 313 sheep, and 141,000 pounds of flour, besides wheat, Indian-corn, pease and oats in good quantity.—*Michigan Pioneer and Historical Collections*, 1886, p. 327.

the French, were rapidly absorbing the traffic, were building vessels to navigate the lakes, and were stocking the farms with cattle, horses, and sheep.[1]

Yet all was not joy. The country was overrun by traders who made it their business to cheat the Indians by false weights and measures, by debasing the silver trinkets with copper, and by a thousand other artifices so persistently resorted to as to make the words trader and cheat synonymous, and thus to lead to disputes, quarrels, and murders. The Indians themselves were as the leaves blown by the autumn winds for number; and their thirst was as that of the ground parched by the August heats; and although usually they did not steal from one another, yet they thought it no wrong to take from the whites what provisions they could lay their hands on. On arriving at Detroit an Indian hunting party would trade perhaps a third of their peltries for fine clothes, ammunition, paint, tobacco, and like articles. Then a keg of brandy would be purchased, and a council held to decide who was to get drunk and who to keep sober. All arms and clubs were taken away and hidden, and the orgy would begin, all the Indians in the neighborhood being called in. It was the task of those who kept sober to prevent the drunken ones from killing one another, a task always hazardous and frequently unsuccessful, sometimes as many as five being killed in a night. When the keg was empty, brandy was brought by the kettleful and ladled out with large wooden spoons; and this was kept up until the last skin had been disposed of. Then, dejected, wounded, lamed, with their fine new shirts torn, their blankets burned, and with nothing but

[1] Hamilton to the Earl of Dartmouth.—*Michigan Pioneer and Historical Collections*, 1886, p. 265.

their ammunition and tobacco saved, they would start off down the river to hunt in the Ohio country, and begin again the same round of alternating toil and debauchery.[1]

Hamilton found the fort in a tolerable state of defence against either the savages or an enemy unprovided with cannon; the new stockade of cedar, twelve hundred paces in extent and fifteen feet high, was fortified by eleven block-houses and batteries, and on two sides of the citadel was a protected ditch. Echoes from the conflict in the east came from time to time, in the shape of rumors that the Virginians were tampering with the savages; but for a time at least Hamilton was able to carry matters with a high hand, promising to protect the whole Indian country from the inroads of the colonists. Not a few of the French were in sympathy with the Virginians, and some were secretly in communication with Fort Pitt.[2] Moreover, the Spanish across the Mississippi were losing no opportunity to prejudice the Indians against the English; for by so doing they hoped to divert the fur-trade to their own posts.[3]

Such were the conditions when, one day in the latter part of August, 1776, an Englishman, a Delaware chief

[1] Colonel James Smith's *Narrative*, p. 83.

[2] "Jean Baptiste Chapoton (who had been captain of militia at Detroit), Bosseron the younger, and M. Le Gras are on the best possible footing with the rebels at Vincennes."—Hamilton to Cramahé, *Michigan Pioneer and Historical Collections*, 1883, p. 289.

[3] De Peyster to Carleton, June 17, 1777, *Michigan Pioneer and Historical Collections*, vol. x., p. 278; Hamilton to Carleton, March, 1778, *Michigan Pioneer and Historical Collections*, vol. ix., p. 432. At the Detroit council, on June 29, 1778, the Illinois Indians present begged Hamilton to believe that they were all as one man for the English. "Don't imagine," they said, "that although we go for rum to the Spaniards, they have our hearts!"

known as Captain White Eyes, and an Indian educated in Virginia and called Moutons, had the insolence to appear at Detroit with a letter, a string, and a belt from the agent of the Virginian Congress, soliciting the confederacy of Western Indians to go to a conference at Pittsburg. Hamilton, angered by their audacity, tore their letter, cut their belts in the presence of the assembled savages, and sent them out of the settlement. The messengers, however, had brought with them a copy of the *Pennsylvania Gazette* of July 24, 1776, containing the declaration of the colonies by which they entirely threw off all dependence on the mother-country.[1] In such fashion was the birth of the new nation announced at the capital of the Northwest!

On April 5, 1778, Charles Beaubien and young Lorimer reached Detroit with a fine string of captives. Starting from the Miamis early in February, they easily prevailed upon fourscore Shawanese to accompany them on a raid up the Kentucky River, where they were so fortunate as to find Daniel Boone and twenty-six of his men making salt at the salt-lick near their fort. The Indians so completely surprised the settlers that, without the loss of a single man, they brought the party off; but no inducement could lead the cautious savages to attempt the fort. To Hamilton, Boone told a pitiful story: because of the Indians the settlers had been unable to sow grain, and by June there would be not a morsel of food in Kentucky; clothing was not to be had; nor was relief to be expected from Congress.

[1] Hamilton to Lord Dartmouth, *Michigan Pioneer and Historical Collections*, 1886, p. 269. Hamilton made the mistake of one day in the date of the *Gazette*. There was no paper published on the 25th, Hamilton's date; but the regular weekly issue appeared on the 24th.

"Their dilemma," says Hamilton, "will probably induce them to trust to the savages, who have shown so much humanity to their prisoners, and come to this place before winter."[1]

Boone was about forty-four years old, had passed his life in the forest, and his bravery and knowledge of woodcraft endeared him to the Indians no less than to the pioneers, whose leader he was. Hamilton would have paid heavily for Boone's ransom, but the Indian family that had adopted him refused to give him up.[2] For five months he endured captivity; but on learning that a large force was about to attack Boonsborough, he eluded his captors, and in five days travelled one hundred and sixty miles, having eaten but one meal during his entire journey. Happily his escape diverted the Indians from their purpose.

In June, 1778, a grand council of Indians assembled on the banks of the broad Detroit. There were Chippewas from Saginaw Bay, Hurons from Sandusky, and Pottawatomies from St. Joseph; there were Mohawks, Del-

[1] Hamilton to Carleton, April, 1778, *Michigan Pioneer and Historical Collections*, vol. ix., p. 435.

[2] "On the 10th day of March following, I and ten of my men were conducted by forty Indians to Detroit, where we arrived on the 30th day, and were treated by Governor Hamilton, the British commander of that post, with great humanity. During our travels, the Indians entertained me well; and their affection for me was so great that they utterly refused to leave me there with the others, although the governor offered them £100 sterling for me, on purpose to give me a parole to go home. Several English gentlemen there, being sensible of my adverse fortune, and touched with human sympathy, generously offered me a friendly supply for my wants, which I refused, with many thanks for their kindness, adding that I never expected it would be in my power to recompense such unmerited generosity."—"Filson's Adventures of Colonel Daniel Boon," in Imlay's *Topographical Description of the Western Territory* (London, 1797), p. 347.

GRAVE OF DANIEL BOONE

awares, and Senecas, eager for rum and presents; and there were the Ottawas and the Hurons from the villages across the river. To meet and greet them were Lieutenant-Governor Hamilton, who by this time had learned to dance the war-dance, to chant the war-song, and to handle the wampum-belts; also Lieutenant-Governor Edward Abbott from Vincennes, who, regarding discretion the better part of valor, had slipped away to Detroit, so that the Indians should not find him without a supply of presents when they returned from their winter hunt; and the Indian agents Hay and McKee; and Captain Lernoult and Lieutenant Caldwell, of the king's regiment stationed at Detroit; and eight interpreters, among whom was Simon Girty. Lately escaped from Fort Pitt, Girty and McKee were now just beginning their notorious career as partisans.[1]

During the period of more than a quarter of a century from the outbreak of the Revolution, the brothers Simon, James, and George Girty, together with Alexander McKee, played a part in the history of the Northwest far more important than did any British commander. In the estimation of the Americans, Simon Girty was the arch-fiend of the realms of savagery. There were many redeeming traits about McKee, with whom the somewhat fastidious De Peyster associated on terms of intimacy; but the instances in which Simon Girty showed humanity served only by contrast to blacken an ingeniously diabolical career. The responsibility of the English commandants for border cruelties lies not so much in their personal acts as in their employment of such agents to do their work.

[1] The minutes of the council are given in the *Michigan Pioneer and Historical Collections*, vol. ix., p. 442 *et seq.*

The Girtys were sons of that Simon Girty who, coming from Ireland at some date before 1737, made his home on the banks of the Susquehanna, and engaged in Indian trade. Marrying Mary Newton at Fort Duquesne, his second son, Simon, was born in 1741, James was born two years later, and George in 1745. In 1751 the elder Girty was killed in a drunken revel by an Indian known as The Fish, who in turn was slain by John Turner, and as a reward the latter received the hand of the widow. In 1756, when the entire family were taken prisoners by the Indians and the French under Neyon de Villiere, Turner, as the slayer of The Fish, was put to death by torture, in the presence of his family. After repeatedly witnessing the most revolting cruelties practised on prisoners, the family was separated, Simon being adopted by the Senecas, James by the Shawanese, and George by the Delawares; but in 1759 they were reunited at the surrender of prisoners after the treaty of Easton. As opportunity offered, the Girty boys put to use their understanding of Indian dialects, acting as interpreters, traders, or hunters, their headquarters being at Pittsburg. Simon, finding Dr. Conolly a congenial spirit, espoused Virginia's side of the boundary dispute, and was arrested on some charge, at the instance of Arthur St. Clair, the leader of the Pennsylvanians. When Lord Dunmore reached Pittsburg he made Simon Girty one of his scouts, and Girty it was who received from Logan the celebrated message, as has been told.

After the Dunmore war, Girty was a second lieutenant in Conolly's militia, until the outbreak of the Revolution drove both Dunmore and Conolly from the scene, restoring to Fort Pitt the name which the ambitious governor had attempted to exchange for his own. Congress having created an Indian department, Girty was employed as an interpreter by the agent, George Morgan, and in that capacity was doubtless present at the conference held at Fort Pitt, on July 6, 1775, when the Virginian commandant, Captain Neville, secured the promise of Mingoes, Delawares, and Shawanese that they would remain neutral, provided their rights, both to the sovereignty and to the lands of their country, were not invaded by either the Americans or the British.[1]

For ill-behavior Girty lost his place as interpreter; but the Continental general, Edward Hand, on taking possession of Fort Pitt, early in 1777, commissioned him a second lieutenant and employed him actively among the Indians. Girty's loyalty was suspected, although his work was efficient; and in 1778 he fell under the influence of Alexander McKee, who had been Sir William Johnson's deputy during the two years prior to the superintendent's death in 1774. McKee was a native of Pennsylvania, a trader of wealth and position; but possibly because of his position as crown deputy, suspicion attached to him, and he had been placed on parole by General Hand. Joined with McKee was

[1] *Pennsylvania Gazette*, August 7, 1776. At this conference were present Kiashuta, a Mingo chief just returned from Niagara with belts from the Six Nations commanding neutrality; Captain Pipe, a Delaware chief, whose career we shall follow; The Shade, a Shawanese chief, and She-ge-na-ba, a son of Pontiac. The latter received from Morgan a fine gun, as a reward for having saved the life of a young man named Field, the son of Colonel John Field who was killed at Point Pleasant. Pontiac's son alone of those present remained neutral, and refused to obey Hamilton's summons to the warpath. His home was at Fallen Timbers, the site of Wayne's victory. See letter from Lyman C. Draper in Parkman MSS., volume entitled *French Documents*.

another Pennsylvania trader, Matthew Elliott, an Irishman by birth, who was on such friendly terms with the Shawanese that they made him their messenger to Lord Dunmore when they sued for peace after their defeat at Point Pleasant. On the 28th of March, 1778, just as General Hand was about to send a force to arrest McKee, that worthy, together with Elliott, Girty, and a few others, escaped to Detroit. Doubtless they knew that a warm welcome would await them, for during the previous March Elliott had been captured and brought to Hamilton, who sent him to Quebec, whence he returned to Pittsburg on parole. Yet, however important these three men might consider themselves, even they could not have apprehended the consternation their desertion caused throughout the frontier regions, from the headwaters of the Alleghany even to the Mississippi; it would have been impossible for the British to have selected three more effective tools for the purposes of border warfare.[1]

The council having been opened with prayer,[2] Lieutenant-Governor Hamilton congratulated the assembled Indians on their almost uniform success in their raids, on the number of their prisoners, and *the far greater number of scalps.* He reminded them that they had driven the rebels to a great distance from the Indian hunting-grounds, and had forced them to the coast, where they had fallen into the hands of the king's troops; he an-

[1] Butterfield's *History of the Girtys* (Cincinnati, 1890). This most painstaking work corrects innumerable errors in regard to the renegades of the Ohio; and with conscientiousness Mr. Butterfield has not hesitated to contradict his own statements made in previous publications.

[2] "Having returned thanks to the Great Spirit, I must thank you all for having attended my call," began Hamilton

nounced the recall of Carleton and the appointment of Haldimand, "well known through that country as the chief warrior at New York, a brave officer, a wise man, esteemed by all who know him;" he took from the Indians the silvered medals given to them by the French, and hung about their necks those furnished by the English; and in the name of the king he put the axe into the hands of his Indian children, "in order to drive the rebels from their land, while his ships-of-war and armies cleared them from the sea."

To these exhortations the Indians made answer after their own fashion: they boasted their fortitude in withstanding the seductions of Virginians and Spanish; and with a diplomacy that is still current among nations, they promised on their return to refer the whole matter to their war-chiefs, "who know how to act in war." Forced to be satisfied with these equivocal answers, Hamilton covered the council-fire, and the council adjourned to partake of one of those riotous feasts whose expense so wrung the heart of the economical Haldimand.

The last canoe of the returning Indians had not disappeared behind Montreal Point before an express arrived from the Illinois country, saying that a party of rebels, in number about three hundred, having taken prisoner M. de Rocheblave, the commander at Fort Gage, had laid him in irons and had exacted from the inhabitants an oath of allegiance to the Congress. Also the express announced that a detachment had been sent to Cahokia; and even as the messenger was leaving Kaskaskia "one Gibault, a French priest, had his horse ready saddled to go to St. Vincennes to receive the submission of the inhabitants in the name of the rebels." [1]

[1] Hamilton to Carleton, August 8, 1778.

This was too much for Governor Hamilton's warlike spirit. He had been forced to yield to the tamer councils of his superiors in opposition to his plan to reduce Fort Pitt;[1] but here was an insult that he could not brook. To have a band of rebels invade his own territory, lay one of his commandants in irons and confine him in a pig-pen was too much for British blood.

Leaving Detroit in the hurry and bustle of preparation for an expedition to the Illinois country, we now turn our attention to the events leading up to Clark's capture of the posts on the Mississippi and the Wabash.

The peace effected by Lord Dunmore, in 1774, once more had opened Kentucky to settlers, who began to flock to that region and to take up lands purchased from the Cherokees by Colonel Richard Henderson.[2] The company set up courts, gave laws, organized a militia—in short, erected the proprietary government of the colony of Transylvania. The commander of the militia was George Rogers Clark, a bold and adventurous surveyor of twenty-two, who was born in Albemarle County, Virginia, two years before Braddock's defeat, and who had seen military service with the Dunmore expedition. The Kentuckians had outgrown the idea of quit-rents; the lands they cleared, cultivated, and defended were their lands in fee-simple; and when the company showed its power by attempting to raise rentals, the people elected Clark and Gabriel John Jones members of the Assembly of Virginia. That body had adjourned before the new representatives completed their hazardous journey through the mountains; but Clark had a message for the new governor,

[1] "Haldimand to Hamilton," August 6, 1778.

[2] By the treaty of Watauga, March, 1775.

GEORGE ROGERS CLARK

(Photographed by L. Bergman, Louisville, Kentucky)

"a certain Patrick Henry, of Hanover County," as Lord Dunmore contemptuously styled his successor.[1] In one thing, at least, the two men agreed; both the last governor of the king and the first governor of the people were bent on extending the authority of Virginia throughout the lands included within her ancient boundaries.

Henry being ill at his home, thither Clark bent his steps. Picture the scene: the ardent youth, with tall, well-knit frame and flashing eye, pacing up and down the sick-chamber of the no less ardent governor, and pouring forth a torrent of ambition, hope, and pathos—of ambition that his native commonwealth should win the glory and the gain of conquering the Northwest for Virginia; of hope that the Virginians of the tide-water would not leave their brothers beyond the mountains to be cut off by prowling savages led by renegade whites; and of pathos almost beyond words in the grim story of ambushed paths, of red demons lurking behind garden-bush or even behind fort-gate, ready with the brutal tomahawk to deal the swift blow, and disappear into the dark forest! The warm-hearted governor quickly espoused the cause of the Kentuckians, and the two men wrung from the reluctant council a large gift of powder for the protection of the frontiers. When the assembly convened, Clark and Jones were admitted, and before the session ended they succeeded in having created the county of Kentucky, thus putting an end to the Colony of Transylvania. This accomplished, they set off, by way of Fort Pitt, for the dark and bloody ground they had come to call home.[2]

[1] Moses Coit Tyler's *Life of Patrick Henry*, p. 189.

[2] Mann Butler's *Kentucky*, p. 39 *et seq.* Clark and Jones wore not allowed to vote. They accomplished the inclusion of the Kentucky

On his return, Clark found that the natural hostility of the Indians had been increased both in intensity and in sagacity by the leadership of paid agents of England, and by the British presents that sent the savages to war and welcomed their return, scalp laden. He saw what was apparent to all his fellows: that so long as the British held Detroit, Kaskaskia, Vincennes, and the connecting forts, so long would England be able to keep up an effective warfare along the rear of the colonies. He did what no one else thought of doing: he sent Moore and Dunn into the Illinois country as spies. Armed with their report he again presented himself before Governor Henry, and on December 10, 1777, he laid before him a plan of conquest that should balance in the south the great northern victory of Saratoga, over which the whole country was rejoicing. Into their councils Governor Henry called George Wythe, George Mason, and Thomas Jefferson; and by their influential aid Clark, without trouble, obtained two sets of orders—one public, ordering him to defend Kentucky; the other secret, ordering an attack on the British post of Kaskaskia. Clothed with all the authority he could wish, with £1200 in depreciated paper, and an order on the commandant at Fort Pitt for ammunition and boats, Clark set forth to raise west of the mountains a force with which to conquer the Northwest.

As fortune would have it, Clark, on his way down the Ohio, learned of the alliance between France and the colonies; and this information was worth as much to him as a heavy reinforcement. From John Duff and a party of hunters whom he met near the mouth of the

country notwithstanding the opposition of the president of the Transylvania Company, Colonel Henderson.

PATRICK HENRY

Tennessee, Clark learned that M. Rocheblave had no apprehensions of an attack. Indeed, it was in the highest degree improbable that from the meagre settlements, separated as they were by three or four hundred miles from the nearest post of their friends at Fort Pitt, and by six hundred miles from the seat of government in Virginia, a force should issue against the strong British posts of the Illinois, placed in the midst of powerful Indian tribes hostile to the Americans. The very audacity of the plan secured success. Approaching Kaskaskia on the evening of July 4, 1778, Clark sent a portion of his command across the river to the town, while he himself, at the head of a handful of troops, walked quietly in at the open postern gate of Fort Gage. Acting on those theatrical impulses which were a large part of his stock in trade, he completely terrified the inhabitants; and then, having led them to expect another expulsion like that of the Acadians, he assured them that Americans "disdained to make war on helpless innocence"; and that it was simply to protect their own wives and children that they had "penetrated to this stronghold of British and Indian barbarity." When the people of Kaskaskia learned that neither their lives nor their property were at stake they joyfully set the church-bells ringing, and then even offered to go with Major Bowman to inform their relatives and friends at Cahokia of the good tidings. There, too, the terror inspired by the unexpected coming of the terrible "Big Knives" was speedily turned into huzzas for freedom and for the Americans; and thus, without the shedding of a drop of blood, the Illinois country was conquered for Virginia.

Vincennes now remained to be dealt with; and here Clark was puzzled. His force was not sufficient to hold the towns he had taken, even with the help of his Spanish friends across the Mississippi; and at any moment the Indians, led by the English, might cut him off from his base. At this juncture, Father Gibault, a priest whose parish extended from Lake Superior to the Ohio, offered to undertake to convert tne people of the Wabash post to the American cause, a proposition readily accepted by Clark and faithfully carried out by this member of the church militant. Electing a commandant, the people of O. Post (as Vincennes was commonly called) ran up over the fort the strange flag of the Virginians, much to the surprise of the Indians, to whom explanation was made that their old father, the King of France, was come to life again, and that if they did not wish their land to run red with blood they must make peace with the Americans. Successful beyond his most sanguine expectations, Clark formed a French militia company at Kaskaskia; placed Captain Williams in command of the fort; continued Captain Bowman at Cahokia; sent Colonel William Linn to build at the Falls of the Ohio the fort that has developed into the city of Louisville; and announced his conquest to Virginia, accompanying his message with the vituperative captive Rocheblave, as an evidence of good faith. In October, 1778, Virginia acknowledged her responsibility in the matter by establishing the County of Illinois, embracing all the chartered limits of the colony west of the Ohio River. Colonel John Todd was made lieutenant-colonel of the county, and American civil government began in that region.[1]

[1] William Hayden English's *Conquest of the Country Northwest of the River Ohio.* Governor English's volumes are a perfect storehouse of information concerning Clark and his associates. It is necessary, however, to verify his statements, because of the great discrepancy in the accounts. A suggestive article is Carl E. Boyd's "County of Illinois," *American Historical Review*, July, 1899.

We now turn northward to the Straits of Mackinac, the meeting-place of lakes Huron and Michigan, waters first traversed by Nicolet, and afterwards the scene of Marquette's labors in shepherding his Iroquois-driven flock. From the last resting-place of the great explorer one looks across waters burnished by the summer sun, or in winter gazes along the pathway of the ice-breaking steamer, to the ever-shifting sands of Old Mackinaw, the scene of the massacre of 1763. There within a rude stockade were gathered the cabins of the most important fur-trading post possessed by the British at the outbreak of the Revolution.

Thither Captain Arent Schuyler de Peyster of the Eighth, or King's regiment of foot, set out from Quebec in the May of 1774, with a commission not only to take command of the post, but also to enter upon the much more difficult task of superintending the Lake Indians, comprising sixteen or more tribes roaming forest and prairie on both sides of the Mississippi, from the Ohio even to the unknown regions north of Lake Superior. Born in the City of New York, on June 27, 1736, De Peyster's baptism was attended by his two uncles, Philip Van Cortlandt and Peter Schuyler and by his aunt, Eve Bayard, who there assumed those official responsibilities required to give a fitting start in the world to the scion of a family that traced its lineage far back of that Johannes de Peyster who came to New Amsterdam in 1633. As a second son, the youth was destined for the army, and was sent to England for his preliminary training. Entering the service in the year of Braddock's defeat, in 1768 he came with his regiment to Canada. Of commanding stature and soldier-like appearance, he possessed an affability of manner that endeared him to his fellow-officers, and also gave him an unusual control over the savages. Without being conspicuously great, he never failed to fill with real credit every position to which he was assigned.

On his journey to the ends of civilization the young captain was accompanied by his wife, a daughter of Prevost Blair, of Dumfries, Scotland; and their voyage forms the theme of one of those poems of his, in which the entire absence of the poetic quality is atoned for by the abundance of interesting facts. Making the slow passage up the St. Lawrence in an open bateau, they crossed the Ontario in the ship-of-war named for the lake, and at Fort Erie they embarked on the sloop-of-war *Dunmore*, which carried them to their destination. For six years this devoted couple were the first English-speaking people to exemplify in the northern wilderness the blessings of a Christian home.

On June 27, 1776, the Indians about Michilimackinac received through the medium of Father Matavit, the priest of the Two Mountains, strings of wampum from St. Lawrence River savages, who announced that Montreal was in possession of the Americans and asked aid, lest the Indians be driven quite out of Canada. On carrying the news to the commandant, they were told to look after their hunting until they heard from Sir Guy Carleton. A few days later an express came from the Six Nations, calling the Lake Indians to a council at Connesedaga; and when De Peyster found traders bearing passes signed by General Worcester and Benjamin Franklin, stipulating that they should furnish no supplies to the garrison, he set himself to the task of sending reinforcements to Montreal.

On the day that the independence of the colonies was proclaimed at Philadelphia, De Peyster placed Charles de Langlade in charge of a force of savages and Canadian volunteers, with orders to report to the commander of the king's troops in the neighborhood of Montreal; to annoy the rebels wherever he might meet them, and in everything to conduct himself with his usual prudence and moderation.[1] Montreal having been recovered, and the Indians not having gone prepared to spend the winter, Carleton gave them presents, and promptly sent them home, with orders to return in the spring if wanted. Langlade, however, remained below during the early winter, and returned north in February with an order to bring back two hundred chosen Indians for the Burgoyne expedition. The difficulty was not so much to obtain the necessary force as "to prevent the whole country from going down"; for the presents, the medals, the gorgets, and especially the rum furnished by the British were to the eager Indians but a foretaste of the plunder in store for them when once they should take the war-path. Moreover, he was indeed a faint-hearted Indian who would not follow where Langlade led.

For length and variety of service, and for successful leadership of Indians in war, America has never known the equal of Charles de Langlade. Langlade's great-grandfather, Pierre Mouet, landlord of Maras, and first known as Mouet de Maras, was born of a family located in Castel Sarraisin, in Basse Guyenne, France; and in 1668 he came to settle at Three Rivers, then a most influential trading-post. His eldest son, Pierre, like his

[1] The correspondence between Carleton and Captain de Peyster is to be found partly in the "Haldimand Papers," printed in vol. x. of the *Michigan Pioneer and Historical Collections* (1876); and partly in the appendix to *Miscellanies by an Officer* (Colonel Arent Schuyler de Peyster), by General J. Watts de Peyster (New York, 1888). I am indebted to General de Peyster for his courtesy in furnishing to me many documents and pictures not otherwise available.

father, was an ensign in the army; and also like his father, he had seven children. Of this family the sixth, Augustin, born in 1703, was the first to bear the name of Sieur de Langlade. Entering the fur-trade, he made headquarters at Michilimackinac, where he married the widow of Daniel Villeneuve, who was also the sister of the principal chief of the Ottawas, a great warrior known as The Fork. In May, 1729, Charles Michel de Langlade was born and duly baptized. From the energetic and faithful missionary priest, Father Du Jaunay, young Langlade obtained the beginnings of an education in letters; and at an age before boys usually leave the nursery he took his first lessons in Indian warfare. In 1734, when the French were seeking the aid of the Upper Lake savages in their war against the English traders north of the Ohio, The Fork, moved by a superstition not unknown even in these days, refused to take up the hatchet unless he were allowed to carry with him his five years old grandson, in the capacity of what now would be known as a mascot; and the father, on being entreated, sent his son upon the war-path with the injunction never to dishonor a brave name. Never was paternal blessing better deserved or more carefully heeded; and the scalps brought back to adorn the wigwams of Michilimackinac testified abundantly to the success of the expedition. The superstitious Indians came to look upon young Langlade as one on whom a great manitou smiled; and from that day his influence over the savages exceeded that of any of his fellows.[1]

[1] *Memoir of Charles de Langlade*, by Joseph Tasse, of Ottawa, Canada; translated from the French by Mrs. Sarah Fairchild Dean; *Wisconsin Historical Society Reports*, vol. vii., 1876. This sketch is based on Lyman C. Draper's report of the narrative of Captain Grigon, also published in the very valuable *Wisconsin Reports*.

Langlade's exploits at Piqua and at Braddock's defeat have already been recorded. In 1757 Langlade had joined Montcalm, and, with his Lake Indians, was at the taking of Fort George, where his services were rewarded by Vaudreuil by the position of second officer at Michilimackinac, under a brother of that Beaujeu who was killed at Fort Duquesne. In June, 1759, at the head of a numerous band of Indians, Langlade set out for Quebec, where his skill and craft suggested a plan of cutting off Wolfe. Had M. de Levis been quick enough to act upon the Canadian's suggestions, important results might have followed; but in those days fortune everywhere favored the English. With desperate valor Langlade fought through the battle on the Plains of Abraham, calmly smoking his pipe during the pauses in the combat. Saddened by the death of two of his brothers, and mortified by what he called the cowardly surrender of Quebec, Langlade once more set his face northward; but the next April he was again on hand (this time with the king's commission as a lieutenant) to fight, with the Chevalier de Levis, the last fight for French supremacy in America. It was a short-lived triumph, for English reinforcements put an end to the struggle; and on the 9th of September Langlade received from Vaudreuil the announcement of the surrender of Montreal, coupled with the hope of a meeting in France. Langlade's interests, however, bade him stay in America; and before George Etherington, who came to Michilimackinac in 1761, as the first English commander, both Augustin and Charles de Langlade took the oath of allegiance. The Englishman, quick to appreciate the advantages of the powerful support of the Langlades, made Charles the Indian superintendent for Green Bay, and also commander of the militia—a trust that was never dishonored. The massacre at Michilimackinac, in 1763, might have been averted had his warnings been heeded, but when they were not, he did all he could to save those who were not butchered in the first onslaught.

The outbreak of the Revolution found Langlade as ready to serve England as he had been ready to serve France twenty-two years previous. Hence it happened that when De Peyster was called upon for a band of Lake Indians to accompany the Burgoyne expedition, he ordered the ox for the barbecue, opened the rum casks, and served out ammunition to the bloody Sioux, the Iroquois of the Northwest; to the Chippewas of Sault Ste. Marie, to the Sacs and Foxes of the Illinois; to the Winnebagoes and Menominees of Wisconsin; and to the Ottawas of Lower Michigan. As soon as the ice left the Straits of Mackinac in the spring of 1776, the flotilla started for Georgian Bay, with Langlade leading the way. Down the rapids of the Ottawa shot the fleet canoes; thence to the St. Lawrence, and to the present town of Whitehall. There the motley troop joined themselves to the St. Lawrence Indians under the command of Langlade's old friend, the Chevalier St. Luc la Corne, who had won fame in Abercrombie's disastrous fight at Ticonderoga, and had been spared in the battles about Quebec for that later service he was destined to render the Canadians in his capacity as legislative councillor. Burgoyne, ignominiously beaten at Saratoga, October 14, 1777, was disposed to charge his failure to the lack of support given by the Canadians and Indians; and in a measure he was correct. The Canadians of the St. Lawrence, who had no heart in the struggle against the colonists, much preferred to stay quietly at home, and let England attend to her own quarrel. As for the Indians, Burgoyne gave them to understand that he would allow neither scalps nor plunder; and in so doing he took away from the savages all incentive to fight. Le Duc summed up the matter in the sentence: "General Burgoyne is a brave man; but he is as heavy as a German."

In 1778 for the last time Langlade took up arms. Word had come to De Peyster that Hamilton was preparing for an expedition to recapture Vincennes, and reinforcements were needed. The Indians, summoned to a council at l'Arbre Croche, sulked in their wigwams at Milwaukee, in spite of Pierre Queret's belts and De Vierville's entreaties; and the powerful influence of the veteran leader himself was needed. Going from village to village, he built in each a lodge with an opening at either end. Then calling the Indians to a dog-feast, and tearing the quivering hearts from the animals, he affixed one to a stake set at each doorway. Passing around the lodge, at each door he tasted the dog-heart, chanting the war-song meanwhile. This appeal was too much even for the stolidity of the Indians; they sprang to the dance, and next day took their way to l'Arbre Croche.

We left the Lieutenant-Governor at Detroit busy with preparations for the expedition he had undertaken for the recovery of the Illinois country. There has been a disposition to blame Hamilton personally for acting without authority in his government of Detroit, in undertaking an important expedition without the express orders from his immediate superiors, and for barbarity in warfare. A sufficient answer to these accusations is to be found in the fact that he undertook to carry out the plans and desires of those in power in London, and that everything he did met with their approval. Had he been endowed with more ability, or had he been pitted against American leaders of ordinary capacity, he would have been justified amply by success. He was the legitimate product of the then English system of favoritism, and he was employed in supporting a cause bad in itself and entirely out of harmony with the natural trend of events, so that he simply suffered the common lot of British commanders in America. Nominally in absolute control at Detroit, Hamilton was hampered in the administration of justice by the fact that the salaries allowed for judges were too small to command the services of worthy men, and so he himself was forced to administer the law.[1] Moreover, the naval control of the Upper Lakes was committed to Colonel Bolton at Niagara, and the troops at Detroit were under the command of the senior military officer; so that Hamilton, although bred in the army, was forced to ask rather than to command the support of the naval and military forces. Again, although Sir Guy Carleton was nominally in control of the entire region from Quebec to the Ohio, Lord George Germain issued directly from Whitehall the orders under which Lieutenant-Colonel Barry St. Leger dealt with the Six Nations, and by virtue of which also Hamilton called the Indian councils at Detroit, sent out parties of the savages against the frontiers of Virginia and Pennsylvania, and issued a proclamation inviting "loyal subjects" to join the king's forces, with an offer of pay and land bounties for so doing—a proclamation

[1] On September 7, 1778, Hamilton and Philip Dejean were indicted at Montreal for "divers unjust and illegal, Terranical and felonious acts and things contrary to good Government and the safety of His Majesty's Liege subjects." Haldimand sent the presentments to Lord Germain with the explanation that Hamilton's usurpation of authority was due to his difficult situation. Lord Germain was entirely satisfied. This correspondence and that relative to the naval command is to be found in the *Haldimand Papers*.

that, when found upon the dead bodies of partisans, naturally embittered the Americans against the signer.[1]

Early in the October of 1778, all being in readiness for the start, Hamilton assembled his force of regulars, volunteers, and Indians, on the common at Detroit, not far from the Campus Martius, which was the centre of Detroit's stirring military life during the war of the Rebellion. From the mission across the river came Père Potier, and the articles of war having been read and the oath of allegiance having been renewed, the venerable priest gave his blessing to the Catholics present, conditioned on their strict adherence to their oath. "The subsequent behavior of these people," significantly says Hamilton, "has occasioned my recalling this circumstance."

The dreamy haze of Indian summer, blending low-reaching sky with autumn-tinted shore and opalescent water; the click of the oars in the thole-pins, borne far on the still air; the triangular flocks of ducks flying from one bed of wild-rice to another, preparatory to their winter migration; the steady current of the island-strewn river, ready to speed the journey, all combined to make a propitious beginning. Before the flotilla had covered the eighteen miles of river, however, the wind, suddenly shifting to the north, brought down upon them a flurry of snow and fringed the reedy shores with thin ice. Rain and darkness were their portion as they made the traverse of Lake Erie to the Miami (now the Maumee), and landed on an oozy beach, where they spent

[1] See Lord George Germain's letter of instructions, March 26, 1777, in *Michigan Pioneer and Historical Collections*, vol. ix., p. 347. Copies of Hamilton's proclamation and the letter from the Detroit loyalists accompany Captain White Eyes' letter to Colonel Morgan, of March 14, 1778.—*State Department MSS.*

the night without tent or fire. With no more than the ordinary difficulty, the force of one hundred and fourteen whites and about sixty Indians pursued their journey to the headwaters of the Wabash, down which stream they floated amid the running ice. Seventy-one days out from Detroit, as they were approaching Vincennes, Hamilton sent Major Hay in advance, and to him, on December 17th, Captain Helm surrendered his wretched fort, with its two iron three-pounders and a very limited stock of ammunition, its lockless gate, and its miserable barracks without even a well of water. The second surrender was like unto the first—not war, but a game of chess.[1]

Having won so easy a victory, Hamilton now considered whether he should not go on to complete his work by the conquest of Kaskaskia and Cahokia; but the more he thought over the matter, the more convinced his moderate-sized mind became that his present situation was best. Animated by the spirit of a post-commander, he repaired the fort, called the fickle French to repentance, and sent off war-parties to waylay and murder the Virginians on the Ohio. Hamilton's force had been increased by accessions of Indians to five hundred persons, and he had not then the supplies requisite for a more extended campaign. Indeed, he was forced to send away some of his Indians to hunt. Again, the spring freshets were at hand, and by them Vincennes would be cut off from the Illinois posts by miles of overflowed lands; and this should also prove a defence. Under ordinary circumstances, events would have justified this reasoning; but unfortunately for him Hamilton

[1] Hamilton's account of his expedition from the time of leaving Detroit to his arrival in England is given in the *Michigan Pioneer and Historical Collections*, vol. ix., p. 489 *et seq.*

had now to deal with two men of most uncommon spirit and resolution.

Of Clark's character we have already had a foretaste. Of Francis Vigo we have now to learn. Born a Sardinian, he early enlisted as a private in a Spanish regiment, and was sent to New Orleans. Procuring an honorable discharge, he engaged in the fur-trade on the Arkansas, and after St. Louis was founded he removed to that post and became a prosperous trader on the Missouri. With a love of liberty that Spanish service could not efface, he went to Clark at Kaskaskia and made offer of his means and his influence to advance the cause of liberty. Clark gladly accepted, and quickly made use of Vigo's services, by sending him to Vincennes with supplies for Captain Helm. Accompanied by a single servant Vigo set out with a pack of goods, but on reaching the river Embarrass he was seized by Indians, his goods were stolen, and, a prisoner, he was taken before Hamilton.[1] As a Spanish non-combatant Vigo was not subject to capture; and Hamilton, having some suspicions of his errand, was glad to part with him after exacting a promise that he would do nothing injurious

[1] During his years of affluence Vigo never claimed payment for his losses and never sought to collect a draft drawn by Clark on Oliver Pollock, agent for Virginia; but about 1802 Vigo was taken ill, and his affairs went badly. He then sought from the United States payment for the last draft, amounting to about $8000. Much interesting history in regard to Vigo and the Illinois campaign is to be found in House of Representatives Report, No. 122, Twenty-third Congress, second session, and No. 513, Twenty-sixth Congress, first session. The former of these reports contains most complimentary letters on Vigo and his services, by George Rogers Clark, William Henry Harrison, Judge J. Burnett, General Anthony Wayne, and Secretary of War Knox. Vigo was a trader during Wayne's campaign of 1795, and performed services for that general akin to those performed for Clark.

to British interests on his way to St. Louis. This promise Vigo kept to the letter. Departing down the Wabash, the same pirogue that took him to St. Louis returned with him to Kaskaskia, where he laid before Clark the information that led to his great campaign.[1]

Colonel Vigo's report having confirmed Clark in his belief that either he must capture Hamilton or else Hamilton would take him, he decided upon one of those desperate chances that in war almost invariably succeed. First equipping a flatboat with supplies, he sent it around to the Wabash, with forty-six men under the command of his cousin, Lieutenant John Rogers. Then he gathered a force of French militia to eke out his own scanty numbers; and with a miniature army of four or five companies, embracing altogether one hundred and seventy men, he set out, on the 5th of February, to capture a British commander ensconced, as the Virginia commander had every reason to suppose, in a rebuilt fort armed with cannon and well supplied for a siege, and with a garrison equal to half the number of the besiegers. Striking north to reach the well-defined

[1] Law's *Colonial History of Vincennes* (Vincennes, 1858), p. 28. Law says that it was through the influence of Father Gibault that Vigo was released. At Gibault's instance the people refused to supply the garrison with food unless Vigo was set free. Probably this was one of the various causes that led Hamilton to compliment Gibault by calling him "an active agent of the rebels, and whose vicious and immoral conduct was sufficient to do infinite mischief in a country where ignorance and bigotry give full scope to the depravity of a licentious ecclesiastic. This wretch it was who absolved the French inhabitants from their allegiance to the King of Great Britain. To enumerate the vices of the inhabitants would be to give a long catalogue, but to assert that they are not in possession of a single virtue, is not more than truth and justice require; still the most eminently vicious and scandalous was the Reverend Mousr. Gibault."—*Hamilton's Report.*

St. Louis trail, by day Clark's men made slow marches, with the rain pelting their faces and soaking their clothes, and the mud often knee-deep. At night Clark cheered their drooping spirits by feasts of buffalo-meat and other game shot during the day, and by songs and war-dances after the Indian fashion. Twelve days out they came to the Embarrass River only to find the country all under water, save only a small hillock where they passed the night without food or fire.

Next day they heard with joy Hamilton's morning gun. Men were sent off to find boats; but after spending a day and a night in the water they returned to report not a foot of dry land to be discovered. For two days they were without food of any kind, but on the third day a deer was killed; two more days followed without so much as a bite of provision; the sea of waters seemed unending; and nothing but the unfailing good-nature and tact of the leader kept the French from turning back and the Virginians from being discouraged. The morning and evening guns at Fort Sackville came over the waters with their tantalizing boom; and still the rains descended and the floods increased. On the 21st of February things had come to the most serious pass. The water ahead was neck-high, and Clark's looks showed how serious was the situation. Realizing from the wave of dejection that passed over his men when they saw his troubled face, that all depended absolutely on his own courage and fortitude, he immediately took a handful of powder and, wetting it, smeared his face after the manner of the savages. It was the signal for the onslaught, and when he plunged into the flood the others followed as if rushing on the foe. Then he struck up a backwoods ditty, and that too was taken up; and before the song was suffered to die out all had reached Sugar Camp and a half acre of dry land. Next morning at sunrise they again dashed into the waters; but this time instead of a song there was a stern command to Major Bowman to shoot the first who turned back. The water was waist-high; and when Clark found himself sensibly failing he began to fear for the weak ones. So he ordered the canoes to ply back and forth, supporting the men, till all had come safely to land. Smiling fortune now came in the guise of a canoeful of squaws with a quarter of buffalo, corn, tallow, and kettles. While the stronger ones walked their weaker brothers up and down the shore in order to restore circulation, broth was made and the hungry were nourished. Then, too, the sun, long hidden, came out to dry the soaked clothing, and put heart into the men. Its beams lit up the wide and level plain, and in plain sight stood Fort Sackville, the goal of their march indeed, but still to be conquered.

At this juncture Clark was so fortunate as to capture some duck-hunters, from whom he learned that Hamilton had no thought of attack, and that the French and Indians in the town were well disposed towards the Virginians. With a fine knowledge of French character, Clark sent to the people of Vincennes a message saying that he proposed to take the town that night, warning the friendly ones to keep in their houses, and advising the adherents of the British to seek the fort and, joining the hair-buyer general, to fight like men. It is needless to say that the people stayed at home. Not an intimation of Clark's coming was given to Hamilton, and the first patter of bullets against the palisades was thought to be the usual friendly salute from a party of savages returning from the hunt. Having stolen up to good positions behind houses, ditches, and the banks of the river, Clark's men, tired and hungry as they were, kept up an intermittent fire throughout the night of the 23d, wounding six of the garrison. Meantime the besieged sent cannon-balls over the heads of the Virginians, doing no damage to life and not much to property. When daylight came, the frontier riflemen picked off the gunners as they served the cannon; and about nine in the morning Clark sent a peremptory demand for the surrender of the fort. "If I am obliged to storm," says Clark, "you may depend on such treatment as is justly due a murderer." These are strong words, but they expressed mildly the feelings of the Virginians towards those who had employed Indians to murder settlers. Virginians, moved by revenge, at times might commit atrocious massacres of savages, but they did not employ Indians against the British; and Clark even refused the request of The Tobacco's Son and his warriors to take part in the assault of Fort Sackville.

Hamilton, finding his men determined "to stick by him as the shirt to his back," replied that he and his garrison were "not disposed to be awed into any action unworthy of British subjects"; but in the afternoon the two commanders arranged a meeting at the little log church near the fort, the scene of Gibault's absolution of the people from the oath of allegiance and also the place where the same people had kissed the crucifix in token of abject submission to the King of England. Hamilton was willing to retire with his garrison to Pensacola; Clark insisted on unconditional surrender, saying that his men were eager to avenge the murder of their relatives and friends, and that nothing less than immediate surrender would satisfy them. As for himself, Clark said that he knew that the greater part of the Indian partisans from Detroit were in the fort, and he wanted an excuse either to put them to death or otherwise treat them as he saw fit. The choice, therefore, was between massacre and surrender at discretion. Even while the parley was in progress, Clark's men had taken some fifteen or sixteen Indians within sight of the fort, and there had made them sing their death-song and had tomahawked them one by one, by way of warning. On consultation with his officers, Clark was led to modify his demands; and late in the evening articles of capitulation were signed.

At ten o'clock on the morning of February 25th, the garrison marched out with fixed bayonets. The colors not having been hoisted that morning, Hamilton was spared the humiliation of hauling them down, a fact soothing to his much-wounded pride. There is no doubt that Hamilton made the best of a bad situation. The French at Vincennes were favorable to the Americans because France was in alliance with the Colonies; and there was some prospect that the French rule might be re-established; and because in his slender garrison the only persons on whom he could rely were the few regulars whom he had brought with him. The Indians, fickle by nature, were on the side of the winners.

Having taken possession of the fort, Clark ordered a salute of thirteen guns in honor of the Colonies. To add to the hilarity, Captain Helm brought in Mr. Justice Dejean, with a party from Detroit, and an abundance of stores and clothing. Now poverty was turned to affluence, and in the joy of success the pains and hunger of the long march were forgotten. On March 8th, the prisoners, twenty-seven in number, began their journey to Williamsburg, a distance of twelve hundred miles. It was not a comfortable trip even to a backwoodsman; but to the humiliated Hamilton, used to all the comforts of life, the crowded boat, the lack of shelter from the rain, the long day at the oars, the scanty allowance of bear's flesh and Indian-meal, and the long march to the James River, all gave him nearly three months of keenest misery. On June 15th, he was met at Chesterfield with an order from Governor Thomas Jefferson, by virtue of which he was taken in irons to Williamsburg. Weary, hungry, thirsty, in wet clothes, the British lieutenant-governor at Detroit stood at the door of the executive palace while the mob gathered to escort him to jail. There he found Justice Dejean also in fetters, and the two were thrust into a narrow cell already occupied by five drunken criminals. On the last day of August Major Hay and the other prisoners arrived, and the officers were made to share Hamilton's "dungeon." For nineteen months Hamilton endured his confinement; on October 10, 1780, he was suffered to go to New York on parole, and in the following March he returned to England.[1]

Gratified, but not elated, by his success at Vincennes, Clark now sat down to count the cost of continuing his

[1] There is no question that the treatment accorded to Hamilton by the Virginia authorities was severe beyond the rules of warfare, and when the matter was reported to Washington he succeeded in bringing about a modification of it. Had Hamilton been willing to give the usual parole he would have fared better. At the same time, it should be remembered that Virginia held a court of inquiry, in which it was shown, at least to the satisfaction of those who were called on to decide the question, that Hamilton had been guilty of buying scalps of Virginians from the Indians—a crime that stirred every drop of resentful blood in the veins of the countrymen of the victims. Hamilton's kindness to Boone, and his repeated warnings to the Indians to bring prisoners instead of scalps, were overlooked, and not unnaturally.

expedition to Detroit, where, as he learned, there were but eighty men in the garrison, and the people were well disposed towards the Americans. At this juncture the flat-boat *Willing* appeared, coming up the Wabash with the reinforcements and supplies from Kaskaskia. On board was Morris, a messenger from Governor Thomas Jefferson, who sent assurances that more troops would be forthcoming from Virginia. This decided Clark to appoint a rendezvous at Vincennes in July, preparatory to a dash for the capital of the Northwest. In anticipation of this new venture he first terrorized the Detroit militia, then he gave them boats, arms, and provisions. He told them that he was anxious to restore them to the families from whom they had been torn, and afterwards he sent them home to spread the news of the kindly disposition of the Virginians. Next he gave the Indians to understand that he was not very particular whether they sided with him or not. If they were disposed to keep the peace, they would fare the better for so doing; if they did not behave themselves they would suffer for their misconduct. This method of procedure had the best possible effect; for while it did not keep the Indians from mischief—nothing could do that—it caused Clark to be feared from New Orleans to Lake Superior.

Making Lieutenant Brashear commandant of the fort, renamed Fort Patrick Henry, and placing Captain Helm in charge of civil affairs, Clark embarked on the *Willing* and dropped down the Wabash, bound for Kaskaskia. On his arrival he found that Captain Robert George and his company of twoscore men had come from New Orleans, and in May Colonel Todd came to establish courts at Kaskaskia, Cahokia, and Vincennes. In July Clark returned to Vincennes to find but a handful of Kentucky troops, and none from Virginia. Then he knew that, for the present, at least, all thoughts of capturing Detroit must be given up, and afterwards the propitious time never came.

The conquest of the Illinois country, brilliant as the exploit was in itself, was to be made of permanent value by the statesmen who afterwards used it as the basis of claims and negotiations in the making of treaties. Governor Thomas Jefferson, thoroughly appreciating the advantages of Clark's work, now turned his attention to making it effective not only against England, our enemy, but also against France and Spain, our momentary friends. In pursuance of this policy, he sent Clark to select a location for a fort on the Mississippi below the mouth of the Ohio, the object being to establish the American claim to the navigation of the great river. In order to make sure of his ground, Jefferson sent the surveyors Walker and Smith to take observations of the latitudes; and he gave instructions to Major Martin, Virginia's Cherokee agent, to purchase from that tribe the "little tract of country between the Mississippi, Ohio, Tanissee, and Carolina line," in which the fort was to be located. Clark was to build the fort "as near the mouth of the Ohio as can be found fit for fortification and within our own lines," and Jefferson charged him to have a care as to the wood of which he made stockades, "that it be of the most lasting kind." Such was the origin of Fort Jefferson; and the foresight of Virginia's governor at this time gives him strong claims to the title of the original expansionist.[1]

Jefferson's instructions to Clark show vividly the

[1] For the diplomatic importance of this step, see *Kitchen's History of the United States*, vol. ii., p. 512 *et seq.*

financial distress of Virginia at a time when these plans for western expansion were being carried out, and give the reason why more extensive campaigns could not be undertaken.[1] Instead of bounty money, Jefferson sent three hundred land-warrants of 560 acres each, "which at forty pounds the hundred, being the Treasury price, amounts to the bounty allowed by law"; also he sent twenty-four blank commissions for the eight companies of the battalion Clark was authorized to raise. The drafts for the Illinois expedition were coming in, and, as the paper currency was badly depreciated, Jefferson was perplexed as to the amount that ought to be paid on them. "The difficulty of answering demands of hard money," writes Jefferson, "makes it necessary for us to contract no debts where our paper is not current. It throws on us the tedious and perplexing question of investing paper money in tobacco, finding transportation for the tobacco to France—repeating this as often as the dangers of capture render necessary to insure the safe arrival of some part—and negotiating bills, besides the expensive train of agents to do all this, and the delay it occasions to the creditor. We must, therefore, recommend you to purchase nothing beyond the Ohio which you can do without, or which may be obtained from the east side, where our paper is current." Clark is warned that supplies of clothing will be precarious, and that as far as possible he should rely on skins. "In short," says the governor, "I must confide in you to take such care of the men under you as an economical householder would of his own family, doing everything within himself as far as he can, and calling for as few sup-

[1] Jefferson to Clark, January 29, 1780, *Peter Force MMS.* in Library of Congress.

THOMAS JEFFERSON

plies as possible." Jefferson further advised the withdrawal of a portion of the troops from west of the Ohio, leaving only so many as might be necessary for keeping the Illinois settlements in spirits and for their real protection; he questioned the expediency of building a fort at Kaskaskia; he approved the mild measures taken towards the French; because "we wish them to consider us as brothers and participate with us in the benefit of our laws."

Jefferson instructed Clark to cultivate peace and cordial friendship with all Indians but the Shawanese. "Endeavor that those who are in friendship with us live in peace also with one another. Against those who are our enemies let loose the friendly tribes. The Kikapous should be encouraged against the hostile tribes of Chickasaws and Choctaws, and the others against the Shawanese. With the latter be cautious of the terms of peace you admit. An evacuation of their country and removal utterly out of interference with us would be the most satisfactory."

"As to the English," says Jefferson, in a spirit of magnanimity that shines out brightly amid the exasperations of barbarous warfare, "notwithstanding their base example, we wish not to expose them to the inhumanity of a savage enemy. Let this reproach remain on them. But for ourselves, we would not have our national character tarnished with such a practice. If, indeed, they strike the Indians, these will have a natural right to punish the aggressors, and with none to hinder them. It will then be no act of ours. But to invite them to a participation of the war is what we would avoid by all possible means. If the English would admit them to trade, and by that means get those wants supplied which we cannot supply, I should think it right, provided they require from them no terms of departing from their neutrality. If they will not permit this, I think the Indians might be urged to break off all correspondence with them, to forbid their emissaries from coming among them, and to send them to you if they disregard the prohibition. It would be well to communicate honestly to them our present want of those articles necessary for them, and our inability to get them; to encourage them to struggle with the difficulties as we do till peace, when they may be confidently assured we will spare nothing to put their trade on a comfortable and just footing. In the mean time we must endeavor to furnish them with ammunition to provide skins to clothe themselves. With a disposition to do them every friendly office and to gain their love we would yet wish to avoid their visits."

That Jefferson was thoroughly alive to the importance of a Detroit expedition as a means of punishing the Indians is made plain by his letters to Washington. In the spring of 1780, when the commander-in-chief was contemplating an expedition from Fort Pitt, to be commanded by Colonel Brodhead, Jefferson wrote to suggest that Clark also was planning such an attack, that two expeditions were unnecessary, and that a joint expedition was impossible, because the two officers could not act together. Again, in September, Jefferson[1] called Washington's attention to the fact that Virginia at great expense was maintaining from five to eight hundred men for the defence of her frontiers against the British-paid Indians; he suggested that the reduction of Detroit would "cover all the States to the southeast of it," and said that nothing but the cost (which had been figured at two million pounds of

[1] Jefferson to Washington, February 10 and September 26, 1780.

the current money) prevented the colony from undertaking the task. As it was, Virginia stood ready to furnish the men, provisions, and every necessary except powder, provided her money burdens in other quarters could be lightened. "When I speak of furnishing the men," writes the governor, "I mean they should be militia, such being the popularity of Colonel Clarke and the confidence of the Western people in him that he could raise the requisite number at any time." Jefferson suggested that Washington consider whether he would not be justified in authorizing the expedition at the general expense, particularly "as the ratification of the confederation has been rested on our cession of a part of our western claim, a cession which (speaking my private opinion) I verily believe will be agreed to if the quantity demanded is not unreasonably great."

By December matters had reached such a pass that Jefferson regarded as imperative an advance on Detroit. A formidable movement of British and Indians was organizing for the purpose of spreading destruction and dismay through the whole frontier; and in order to prevent this the Western enemy must be employed in his own country. Virginia, in her own defence, was prepared to commit this work to Clark, leaving it to Congress to decide afterwards as to whether the expense should be State or Continental. At this time the only thing asked was the loan of artillery, ammunition, and tools from Fort Pitt; and this favor Jefferson did not hesitate to ask, because Virginia had furnished to that fort supplies which had been loaned freely to both the Northern and the Southern army.[1]

Clark also appealed to Washington, and the com-

[1] Jefferson to Washington, December 13, 1780.

mander-in-chief was glad enough to order Colonel Brodhead at Fort Pitt to supply the Virginia leader with the necessary stores. None could appreciate better than Washington himself the advantages of offensive measures against Detroit; and possibly even at this time he was turning over in his mind the idea he afterwards expressed—that if the Americans should be defeated along the sea-coast, he would gather the remnants of the armies, and beyond the Alleghanies would found a new State on the fertile banks of the Ohio. Unfortunately for Clark's plan to reduce Detroit, however, every attempt to collect men for so long an expedition failed; and during the remainder of the war the country between the Ohio and the Great Lakes was one vast neutral ground, over which now prowled a band of savages and rangers from Detroit, on their murderous way to the Kentucky forts; and again dashed pursuing Kentucky backwoodsmen, frantic to revenge the murders of neighbors and relatives.

CHAPTER VII

THE WAR IN THE NORTHWEST

FREDERICK HALDIMAND, whose fortune it was to govern the Northwest during the latter part of the Revolution, had attained the rank of lieutenant-colonel in the Swiss Guards, a regiment in the service of the States-General of Holland, when the Seven Years' War led England to organize the Royal American Regiment for service in this country. Through the urgency of the British minister at the Hague, Major-General Sir Joseph Yorke, Haldimand and his intimate friend Henry Bouquet had accepted commissions to serve under John, Earl of Loudoun, the colonel of the battalion, the understanding being that the two Swiss officers should be placed immediately as colonels commanding, in order to remove their natural objections to taking service under an officer inferior to them in rank in Europe. In 1756 Haldimand began his service in America as commandant at Philadelphia; next he went to Albany as colonel of the Royal Americans, whence he returned to Pennsylvania to command the troops charged with the protection of the frontiers. In 1758 he was in the terrible repulse of Abercrombie by Montcalm at Fort Edward, and he served in the Ticonderoga campaign. During the next year he had the satisfaction of rebuilding Sir William Johnson's fort at Oswego, and repelling the attack of that noted partisan leader, St. Luc la Corne, and his Indians. When the French surrendered Montreal, in 1760, Haldimand took command, and two years later was transferred to Three Rivers, once noted as a fur market and then prospectively the seat of the manufacture of iron at the St. Maurice forges.

While at this post, Haldimand took advantage of the law allowing officers who had served two years in the Royal Americans to become British citizens. In 1767 he was promoted to the rank of brigadier-general and ordered to Pensacola as commander of his Majesty's troops in all the southern colonies, the position that was held by Bouquet at the time of his death in the autumn of 1765. Having exercised his energy to put that post in a sanitary condition, Haldimand received his reward in the shape of a transfer to New York.[1] There the tea troubles found him; and when he was importuned to call out the troops to suppress rioting, he wrote to General Amherst that he should "remain a quiet spectator of their (the peoples') follies until the civil, having made use of all its power, demand the assistance of the military, which I shall grant them with all the precautions required by the constitution"; and he refused absolutely to use the militia without a civil magistrate at their head. The people of New York, being in no mood to make fine distinctions, took the occasion of his visit to Gage at Boston to break into his house, demolish the furniture, and loot his stables.

But for England's desire to have the chief command

[1] Pensacola consisted of a stockade fort, a few straggling houses, a governor's house, and miserable bark huts, without floors, for the officers and men. Haldimand widened the streets so as to give a free circulation of air, and made other sanitary improvements, by which he reduced sickness and banished death during the ensuing summer, though the mercury stood at 114°.—Pittman's *Present State of English Settlements on the Mississippi*.

in America devolve upon a Briton born, Haldimand might have been continued in New York; as it was, he was made a major-general and sent to inspect the West Indian forces, from which position he was called to succeed Carleton at Quebec. Reaching his new post on June 30, 1778, Haldimand immediately set himself to administer his government with conscientious thoroughness. With Ethan Allen and his fellows Haldimand carried on negotiations for a reunion of Vermont with the crown of England; and he was active in seating the loyalists, or Tories, on the crown-lands of Canada. Just and considerate towards the officers under him, yet inflexible in doing his duty, and prudent in his expenditures, he never failed to recognize merit or to call offenders to account. It was fortunate for the United States and for the people of the frontiers that the commanding officer at Qecbec contented himself with administering his government in an unexceptionable manner. A more ambitious officer, or an Englishman of vigor and initiative, might have driven the Americans from the Wabash and the Illinois, and thus forced the national boundary back to the Ohio.[1] He was quite satisfied to let the border war drag on, without urging his subordinates to more activity than they displayed, his greatest concern being that the expenses of feeding and clothing the Indians were so enormously out of proportion to the results attained.[2]

[1] The death of Sir William Johnson, on July 4, 1774, and of Bouquet in 1765, together with the return of Amherst in 1764, and the supplanting of Carleton with Burgoyne for the New York campaign, were circumstances favorable to the Americans—how favorable has been the subject of much speculation.

[2] See Brymner's Introduction to the *Canadian Archives*, 1887, and Smith's *Bouquet's Expedition* for details of Haldimand's life. After a perusal of the Haldimand correspondence one can scarcely fail to

Clark's capture of Vincennes and the Illinois posts paralyzed the English efforts to carry on an offensive campaign on the frontiers of the United States, and confined their efforts to petty warfare in the shape of Indian raids against the Ohio River and the Kentucky settlements. Haldimand even despaired of being able to prevent the Western Indians from deserting the British cause, so active were the American emissaries, and such was the effect on the fickle savages of the capture of Hamilton. The Six Nations, however, were loyal, notwithstanding the fact that the Americans had destroyed many of their villages and had forced their women and children to take refuge at Niagara. But Haldimand foresaw that, should the indifference of the Western tribes continue, Detroit must share the fate of Vincennes, in case Clark were to advance with a considerable force. The only successes Haldimand could report to Lord George Germain during the summer of 1779 were the savage massacres on the Susquehanna and Mohawk rivers, where the settlements had been broken up, the stock destroyed, and the inhabitants driven back into the interior. To offset this the Americans had destroyed the fort at Oswego.

Two difficulties beset Haldimand—lack of troops and lack of provisions. To his eminently practical mind it seemed little short of a crime that the fertile lands about the posts of Detroit and Niagara had not been put under cultivation to supply the wants of the garrisons, thus to save the enormous expense of transporting provisions all the way from England to the Upper Lakes, an expense increased by the way American privateers

appreciate the integrity and the justice of this officer; and a reading of his diary, written after his return to England, will reveal a very engaging personality.

had adopted of lying in wait for the "victuallers" appearing at the mouth of the St. Lawrence. In addition to the support of the regular garrisons, the British had Indian mouths to feed—the Six Nations at Niagara, and at Detroit the nations as far south as the Ohio, in all between three and five thousand persons, at an expense of nearly $90,000.[1] And this "notwithstanding the numbers of war-parties continually kept abroad to lessen the consumption." The merchants of the country took every advantage of war-times to get a great profit on their wares, especially on rum, paint, and other Indian necessaries; so that Haldimand was impelled to take measures to break up the "corners" and "trusts" that these enterprising traders devised.[2]

Richard Beringer Lernoult, a captain in the King's regiment with thirty-three years of service to his credit, was left in charge of both civil and military affairs at Detroit when Hamilton started on his ill-fated expedition to the Wabash. The captain did not feel himself capable, either physically or mentally, of bearing the burdens of so onerous a command; but nevertheless he

[1] "It evidently appears that the Indians in general wish to protract the war, and are most happy when most frequently fitted out; it is impossible they can draw resources from the Rebels, and they absolutely depend upon us for every blanket they are covered with."—Haldimand to De Peyster, August 10, 1780. "I observe with great concern the astonishing cousumption of Rum at Detroit, amounting to 17,520 gallons per year."—Haldimand to Lernoult, July 23, 1779.

There were also troubles of like character in England. A Mr. Stuart cleared £70,000 by contracting for a supply of beads, tomahawks, and scalping knives for the Indians; and a Mr. Atkinson took a rum contract at exactly double the price which it cost him. These facts were notorious; but Lord North stifled tbe investigation.—Fitzmaurice's *Life of Shelburne*, vol. iii., p. 70.

[2] Haldimand's letters to Lord George Germain, 1779–80, in *Michigan Pioneer Collections*, vol. x.

acquitted himself so acceptably that, on being ordered to Niagara after two years of service at Detroit, he was promoted to a majority. From the interpreter Isadore Chene, the only white man in the expedition to escape capture, Lernoult learned of Hamilton's misfortune a full month after Vincennes was captured. "This most unlucky shake," as the captain called it, "with the approach of so large a party of Virginians advancing towards St. Duskie, has greatly damped the spirits of the Indians." The situation at Detroit called for something more than a simple tall fence of pickets; for it was expected the Americans would bring cannon with them, and in that case the town would be at their mercy. Therefore Captain Lernoult set about building a fort on the rise of ground back of the town, the site being that now occupied in part by the federal building. Captain Bird, an assistant engineer of the Eighth, having been intrusted with the new construction, traced a square on the hill and added half-bastions—not a satisfactory piece of work from an engineer's stand-point, as he himself admitted;[1] but the best that could be done in the hurry of the occasion. From the November of 1778 to the following February, Bird pressed on the work; but when the ice began to leave the river his military soul longed for more active service. Turning over to Lieutenant Du Vernett the task of completing Fort Lernoult, Captain Bird joined himself to a band of Indians going on the war-path. Possibly his martial ardor had been stirred by Clark's message that he was glad to hear that the British were making new works at Detroit, "as it saves the Americans some expenses in building."

Having collected at Upper Sandusky a force of about

[1] Bird to Brigadier-general Powell, August 13, 1782.—*Haldmiand Papers.*

two hundred savages, chiefly Shawanese, Bird was anxious to start; but, just at the hour for departure, a runner appeared, bringing news that the Kentuckians[1] had attacked the Shawanese towns, had burned houses, carried off horses, and wounded five or six Indians.[2] In an instant all was confusion. The savages were in a panic. "There was much counselling and no resolves." Bird was forced to sacrifice four of his cattle for the feasts; the "unsteady rogues" put him out of all patience; they were "always cooking or counselling!" And thus the expedition came to an end. This action on the part of the Shawanese, the bravest and most revengeful of all the Western Indians was characteristic. Again and again they importuned the commandant at Detroit for help against the Americans; but although they were fed and clothed at British expense, a rumor running through the forest, or the report of an ambush planned by the whites, threw them into such consternation that months of feasting and idleness were necessary to work them up to the fighting pitch.

Captain Bird, however, was not to be disappointed. During the spring of 1778 a small force of regulars from Fort Pitt had built Fort McIntosh on the site now occupied by the quiet old town of Beaver; and that autumn General Lachlin McIntosh had advanced to the banks of the Upper Muskingum, called the Tuscarawas, where he had built, near the present site of Bolivar, Fort Laurens, named for the President of Congress. During the winter the garrison had little trouble; but one day in the spring the Indians stole the fort

[1] Bird to Lernoult, June 9, 1779.—*Haldimand Papers.*

[2] This was the raid of John Bowman, Logan, Harrod, and others, against Chillicothe. In the end the Kentuckians were defeated. See Roosevelt's *Winning of the West*, vol. ii., p. 97.

horses, took off their bells, and jangled them along a wood-path. Of the sixteen men who went out to bring in the horses, fourteen were killed on the spot and the other two were captured. That evening the anxious garrison counted eight hundred and forty-seven savages in war-paint and feathers marching across the prairie exultingly celebrating their victory.[1] Then they disappeared; and Colonel Gibson, thinking the occasion opportune for sending the invalids to Fort Pitt, started a dozen sick men under an escort of fifteen soldiers. Of this party only four escaped an ambush laid within two miles of the fort. A few days later, as General McIntosh was coming up with a relief of seven hundred men, the pack-horses took fright at the welcoming salute from the fort and carried the provisions off into the wood, so that they were not recovered. That autumn the well-nigh starved garrison retreated, and the story of Fort Laurens was told.[2]

Bird was present at some of the attacks on Fort Laurens, and in May he led a party of one hundred and fifty whites and a thousand Indians to Kentucky, where he captured two small stockades on the Licking, and then retreated rapidly to Detroit, probably because the Indians were, as usual, satisfied with a small success secured by surprise, and had no inclination to give battle to an enemy on the alert. Nor did they escape too soon; for the Kentuckians, enraged at so defiant an on-

[1] Simon Girty reported the number of Indians as between seven hundred and eight hundred — Six Nations, Delawares, and Shawanese. Lernoult wrote to Colonel Bolton at Niagara that he had done everything in his power to encourage the Indians, having sent them large supplies of ammunition, clothing, and presents for the chief warriors.

[2] Doddridge's *Settlement and Indian Wars of Virginia and Pennsylvania* (Albany, 1867), p. 244 *et seq.*

set, making Clark their leader, hurried up the Ohio and struck across to Pickaway, where they battered the palisades with a three-pounder and scattered the Indians, driving them into the forests.[1] After this thrust and counter-thrust, quiet came for a season.

The broad waters of Lake Huron were darkening under the sharp October winds when, in 1779, the bustling, garrulous, impecunious old soldier, Patt Sinclair, as he signed himself, landed on the sandy stretches of Michilimackinac to succeed De Peyster, ordered to Detroit.[2] Sinclair had been sent to America by Lord George Germain to join Lord Howe at Philadelphia. Evidently he was not wanted in Philadelphia; whereupon he was sent to the hyperborean regions of Mackinac as Lieutenant-Governor and Superintendent of Indian Affairs, his commission being the same as the one Hamilton had carried to Detroit. By purchase, and twenty-five years of service, Sinclair had attained a rank in the army that he was not disposed to relinquish; and he insisted that Lord George Germain had intended him to enjoy both the military and the civil command, and especially the emoluments thereof. He even threatened to return to England if his desires on this point should not be satisfied; but Haldimand, knowing the man, requested him to repair to his post with all convenient despatch.

Before reaching his new station, Sinclair had landed on the turtle-shaped island of Michilimackinac, the fa-

[1] Theodore Roosevelt, in vol. ii. of his *Winning of the West*, gives a graphic account of this inroad, basing his narrative on the Durrett, Bradford, and McAffee manuscripts.

[2] On October 4th Sinclair arrived at "Old Machinaw," or Michilimackinac. De Peyster sailed on his Majesty's sloop *Welcome*, on October 15th, arriving at Detroit on October 20th, after a voyage of four days and fifteen hours.—Kelton's *Annals of Fort Mackinac* (Jacker edition, 1891), p. 132.

bled home of the fairies and the favorite abode of the manitous of the Indians. Decked out in the gorgeous hues of autumn, the stately island, with wooded cliffs rising high above the clear waters of the lake, seemed to Sinclair a natural site for fort and trading-post. With him to see was to decide, and to decide was to act. Without waiting for the governor's sanction, he built a block-house to command Haldimand Bay, as he ingratiatingly named the harbor; and Quebec, entirely willing to have the change made, spared no pains to furnish the requisite carpenters and supplies. All through the winter of 1779–80 work was pushed on wharf and stockade; four acres were cleared for the fort, and all the preparations were made for burning the abundant limestone. Haldimand expressed his desire that the post continue to bear the name of Michilimackinac, and that the fort be styled Fort Mackinac. "I have never known any advantage result," he says, "from changing the names of places long inhabited by the same people." [1]

Fort building did not occupy Captain Sinclair to the exclusion of his war duties. Before he had been a month in his command he had heard of Father Gibault, who had been at Michilimackinac on a mission, Sinclair says, from General Carleton and the Bishop of Quebec; but against whom, even though he was "an Individual of the Sacred and respectable Clergy," the doughty captain proposed to direct the severity of the Indians. Nor was his ardor cooled during the winter; on the contrary, he sought two mandates against the "vagabond

[1] The Sinclair-Haldimand correspondence is given in vols. ix. and x. of the *Michigan Pioneer and Historical Collections*.

Work on the new post was begun on November 6th, the title to the island having been secured by De Peyster from the Chippewa chief Kitchienago.—Kelton's *Annals*, p. 133.

who styles himself vicar-general of the Illinois," in order to "blast any remains of reputation which the wretch may have been able to preserve among scoundrels almost as worthless as himself"; and these he proposed to serve on Gibault by means of the band of Indians he was planning to send down the Mississippi to act against the Spanish settlements, in conjunction with General Campbell's proposed attack on New Orleans and the lower towns. Nor was he to be duped into forgetting the near-by post of St. Joseph. That "nest of tares," as Sinclair called it, "he proposed to sweep clean" for the reception of the American general—a mixture of metaphors more expressive than accurate.[1]

When, at the coming of Captain Sterling, in October, 1765, St. Ange de Bellerive had hauled down the French flag at Fort Chartres, to hoist it again temporarily on the territory yielded by his nation to Spain by the secret treaty of November 3, 1762, he was virtually at the head of an independent government composed of himself as commandant, M. Lefebre as judge, and Joseph Labusciere as notary, all of whom had come from the Illinois country. The French on the English side of the Mississippi were so well satisfied with this impromptu St. Louis government that when Captain Sterling died, in the December following his advent, the people at Fort Chartres appealed to St. Ange to settle their disputes until a new commandant should arrive. Thus it happened that a French-Canadian was ruler over both English and Spanish territory. So well did the old man fulfil his trust

[1] From 1768 to 1775 Father Gibault, as vicar-general of the Illinois country, extended his ministrations to Michilimackinac; his Jesuit predecessor, Father M. L. Lefranc, having been the last settled priest at that post. From 1761 till 1830 no priest was stationed at the post. See list of priests in Kelton's *Annals*, p. 45 *et seq.*

that in 1767, when the Spanish captain, Rios, and twenty-five men came to St. Louis, they built their fort, St. Charles, fourteen miles up the river. It was not until May 20, 1770, that St. Ange delivered possession of Upper Louisiana to Captain Piernas, and soon afterwards the omnipresent Gibault celebrated at St. Louis the first baptism under the Spanish flag. Placed upon the half-pay of a Spanish captain, the paternal old St. Ange passed the uneventful years until his death on December 27, 1774. Under the mild rule of genial Spanish commanders, the French town of St. Louis continued steadily to grow, notwithstanding the death, on June 20, 1778, of its founder, Pierre Laclede Liguest. He was succeeded in business by his chief clerk, Auguste Choteau, who became the great trader of the Missouri.[1]

Much to the captain's chagrin, Haldimand professed small faith in Sinclair's expedition; and, indeed, it amounted to little. In May, 1780, a band of seven hundred and fifty traders, servants, and Indians started off down the Mississippi to attack the Spanish settlements and the Illinois posts. Assembling at Prairie du Chien, they intercepted river craft and captured boats loaded with provisions; and from the lead-mines they brought away seventeen Spanish and American prisoners. Twenty of the Canadian volunteers from Michilimackinac and a few of the traders attacked the defenceless town of St. Louis, but early in the fight, so soon as the Spaniards began to defend themselves, the Sacs and Foxes under M. Calvé fell back, thereby making the Indians suspicious of treachery; and M. Ducharme

[1] F. L. Billon's *Annals of St. Louis under the French and Spanish Dominations* (St. Louis, 1886).

and other traders interested in the lead-mines proved equally perfidious. The attack failed, but not until seven or more whites had been killed and eighteen prisoners taken and sent north to work on Sinclair's new island fort. A chief and three or four Winnebagos were the only Indian losses.[1]

The attack on St. Louis and on Cahokia, across the river, would not deserve attention were it not for a return attack on St. Joseph, which was in itself even less important than the St. Louis expedition, but which, as seen through the magnifying-glass of Spanish pretensions, was made a matter of importance in the courts of Europe. A mile or so west of the present city of Niles, Michigan, on the south bank of the river St. Joseph, the peripatetic post of St. Joseph was resting at the time of the Revolution. The name originated with La Salle, who paused at the mouth of the river, in 1679, and while waiting for Tonty, employed his men in building a fort. From its situation on the line of travel to the Mississippi, St. Joseph was too important to be abandoned altogether, while at the same time it was not of enough moment for extensive fortifications. Consequently, when one set of pickets fell into decay another stockade was built at a different place on the river, until the site near Niles was hit upon. After the peace of 1763, England had placed a small garrison at the post, but when the tornado of the Pontiac war passed over the place, it was not re-established, although it continued to be occupied as a trading-post among the Pottawatomies, the leading trader, Louis Chevallier, being the

[1] Sinclair places the number of whites killed at sixty-eight; Elihu H. Shepard, in his *Early History of St. Louis*, says that forty were killed. Billon says seven, and gives the names. A few others may have been killed at Cahokia.

king's man in the district.[1] In October, 1777, Thomas Brady, Clark's commandant at Cahokia, had headed a raid on the place and captured some merchandise; but on his retreat he and his party were captured. Brady professed his entire willingness to join the English cause; but ultimately made his escape and returned to Cahokia. In time he became sheriff of St. Clair County. In 1780 St. Joseph contained eight houses and seven shanties, and the entire population consisted of forty-five French persons and four Pawnee slaves.[2]

Sinclair's attack on St. Louis, as has been said, was a part of a larger plan to recover the Mississippi valley for England. When Spain declared war against England in 1779, she made good her declaration by seizing the English posts of Natchez, Baton Rouge, and Mobile; and these stations, together with St. Louis, gave her practically the control of the Mississippi valley. If now she could establish herself in the Northwest, she would then be in a position either to secure the Lake country, or at least would have something to trade with England for Gibraltar, the British possession of which stronghold was a thorn in the side of his most Catholic Majesty.[3] Accordingly, in the January of 1781, Don Francisco Cruzat, commander and lieutenant-governor of the western parts and districts of Illinois, sent forth from his stone palace the militia officers Don Eugenio Pourré, Don Carlos Tayon, and the interpreter Don Luis Cheval-

[1] Petition of Chevallier, October 9, 1780.—*Haldimand Papers.*

[2] Census of St. Joseph, in the letter of C. Anisé, dated St. Joseph, June 30, 1780.—*Haldimand Papers.*

[3] Edward G. Mason, in the *Magazine of American History*, for May, 1886, has discussed, with a wealth of detail, "The March of the Spaniards across Illinois." The *Haldimand Papers* correct some of the details, but Mr. Mason has worked out his problem with great fulness of knowledge.

OLD SPANISH TOWER

lier,[1] accompanied by a band of Indians to make a winter journey of four hundred miles to capture the deserted post of St. Joseph! The fatigues of that march, the cold of the winter, the weight of their food-burdens, all were set forth in strongest phrase in the report made by the intrepid Spaniards. As they toiled northward they gathered Indian adherents as a snowball gathers snow—for their cry was booty. With considerate lack of details, they reported that they made prisoners of the few English they found at the post, the fact being that there were at the place certainly no English and probably no French, save perhaps a few trappers. "Don Eugenio Purre took possession, in the name of the king, of that place and its dependencies, and of the river of the Illinois; in consequence whereof," says the Spanish report,[2] "the standard of his Majesty was there displayed during the whole time. He took the English one and delivered it on his arrival at St. Louis to Don Francisco

[1] Mr. Mason conjectures that this was the Louis Chevallier who was king's man at St. Joseph; but such could not have been the case. Chevallier of St. Joseph settled at that post about 1745; at the outbreak of the Revolution he acted under the orders of Hamilton and De Peyster in fitting out the Indians against Vincennes, and clothing them when they returned naked. In June, 1780, a detachment of Canadians and Indians appeared at St. Joseph to remove the white people to Michilimackinac. Chevallier, then sixty-eight years old, together with his wife (aged seventy years), abandoning lands and houses, orchards and gardens, furniture, cattle, and debts, left the banks of the St. Joseph for the upper country, where he was ill-treated by Sinclair. He petitioned Haldimand for payment of his advances, and he could scarcely have acted against St. Joseph during the time he was pressing for a settlement. Sinclair's objection to auditing his accounts was that Chevallier had no right to trade on his own account, being a member of the General Company of the Merchants of Mackinac, with whom the commandant dealt exclusively.

[2] Wharton's *Revolutionary Diplomatic Correspondence of the United States*, vol. v., p. 363.

Cruzat, the commandant of that post." The report of this expedition, forwarded through military channels, either reached Madrid more than a year after it occurred, or else it was purposely held back. At any rate, it appeared in the Madrid *Gazette* of March 12, 1782, at the exact time it was needed to disturb the discussions of France, Spain, England, and America as to the questions of boundaries, and gave a color of justice to Spain's demand that the line of demarcation be drawn so as to give her the territory now included within the States of Mississippi, Alabama, a part of Georgia, Tennessee, Kentucky, a large part of Ohio, and all of Michigan, Indiana, Illinois, and Wisconsin. Happily, however, the American commissioners ever contended for, and ultimately obtained, the Mississippi as our western boundary.

In October, 1779, De Peyster, having turned the post at Michilimackinac over to Patrick Sinclair, relieved Lernoult at Detroit. De Peyster was nothing if not energetic, and in his first report to Haldimand he was able to announce the surprise and capture of Colonel Rogers's party, on their way from the falls of the Ohio to Fort Pitt, by the Girtys and Elliott with their Shawanese band—"a stroke that must greatly disconcert the rebels at Pittsburg."[1] To Captain McKee,[2] at the Shawanese towns, De Peyster wrote begging the discovery and return of a woman named Peggy West and her young daughter Nancy, both of whom had been taken a year before, near Fort Pitt, when the father was

[1] De Peyster to Haldimand, November 1, 1779.

[2] McKee was called captain, but he had no rank. He had been in the Indian service for twenty-two years, and Lord Dunmore had offered him a commission in one of the provincial battalions to be raised near Pittsburg; but the commissions were intercepted by the Americans.—De Peyster to Haldimand, March 10, 1780.

killed, and the mother and two daughters were divided. "If, sir, it be possible to find the mother and the other sister," writes the commandant, "I will not spare expense; please therefore to employ some active people to go in search of them, assuring the Indians of a good price, and my grateful acknowledgment." One of the girls had been brought to Detroit, where she had found a friend and protector in Mrs. de Peyster; and the heart of this motherly Scotchwoman had been touched by the child's woes.

The plan of campaign for 1780 was for a Detroit party of soldiers to join the Indians in clearing the valley of the Miami to the Ohio, while Sinclair's Upper Lake Indians joined their brothers on the Wabash in "amusing Mr. Clark at the falls." M. Chevallier, at St. Joseph, reported that the Pottawatomies in that region had awakened from their lethargy and were ready to take the war-path. Unfortunately for all these fine plans, there spread from St. Louis throughout all the Indian country the report that Ireland had revolted; that Jamaica had been taken by Count D'Estaing, who had beaten Admiral Biron; that New York was blockaded by the French and Americans; that the "Prince of Monfacon" was in the St. Lawrence for the siege of Quebec; that Natchez, Mobile, and Pensacola had been taken by M. Galvez, governor of New Orleans; that the United States had sent Colonel Clark to establish a considerable stone fort at the entrance of the Ohio River and another at Cahokia; and, to cap the climax, that the Empress of Russia appeared to be surprised that England should suppose that she would mix herself in any of Britain's troubles,[1] while the inhabitants of Artois had furnished

[1] Mr. Papin, trader at St. Louis, to Mr. Reilhe, his comrade at Mi-

the King of France a vessel of the line of six guns, with promise of a large reward to all the crew, from captain to the lowest sailor, if they should take another vessel with even one man and one gun more. All this and much more of like tenor the Pottawatomies heard on their way to Vincennes, and thereupon the greater part turned back;[1] and those who did go on found, to their chagrin, that but twenty-three Virginians occupied the post. The Delawares and Shawanese, however, daily sent into Detroit scalps and prisoners. They had a great field to act upon; for a thousand families, in order to shun the oppression of Congress, report said, had gone to Kentucky, where they threatened to become formidable to both the Indians and the posts.

In the September of 1781 the Indian agent Alexander McKee, in company with a detachment of Butler's Rangers and Brant's Mingo band, made a descent into Kentucky; but when the Indians learned that Clark was unlikely to disturb their towns that year, they refused to advance to the falls of the Ohio,[2] and contented themselves with petty warfare. On his return to the Upper Shawanese villages McKee found his helper Elliott, who told how his party, having discovered that the Moravian Indians were secretly sending intelligence to Fort Pitt and endeavoring to bring the Americans down upon them, had fallen upon these peace-loving folk and forced them to find new homes at Upper Sandusky. Six of their teachers went with them, the principal one of whom

chilimackinac, March 23, 1780. In this letter "the United States" is first mentioned in Northwestern correspondence.

[1] Chevallier to ——, April 30, 1780. De Peyster to Haldimand, May 17, 1780.

[2] *Haldimand Papers*, Captain Thompson to De Peyster, September 26, 1781.

appeared to McKee to be "a Jesuitical old man, and, if I am not mistaken, employed by the enemy, though he denies it."[1] McKee thought it not likely that the Moravian Indians would be friends to the English so long as their white teachers remained with them.[2]

De Peyster called the Moravian teachers before him at Detroit. They were accompanied by Captain Pipe, a Delaware, who not only spoke a good word for the prisoners, but added emphasis to his remarks by depositing fourteen scalps as a token of his sincerity, also calling attention to the "fresh-meat" (prisoners) he had sent to prepare his way. After replying to Captain Pipe that the universal complaint of the warriors was that the Moravian teachers had always kept the Americans informed as to the British and Indian movements, De Peyster closely questioned the teachers, who denied having given any information.[3]

The Moravians were not strictly truthful in their professions of innocence. On March 14, 1778, their leader, Zeisberger, had sent to Colonel Morgan at Fort Pitt a message from that Captain White Eyes, who had announced to Detroit the independence of the United States; and in his letter he gave to the Americans information that the Wyandots were on the war-path, together with such like intelligence as had come to him. He also enclosed copies of Hamilton's proclamations—the one inviting loyal subjects of Great Britain to repair to

[1] *Haldimand Papers*, McKee to De Peyster, September 26, 1781.

[2] Haldimand was deeply chagrined over the failure of this expedition, for he had hoped to destroy Clark's activity. He bitterly reproaches the Indians, though he admits that they acted as was their custom; and he laments the useless expense of clothing and feeding such thankless allies.—Haldimand to ——, November 1, 1781.

[3] *Haldimand Papers*, Minutes of Council of November 9, 1781

Detroit, and the other promising safe escort to such as might desire to "change the hardships experienced under their present masters for security and freedom under their lawful sovereign." The proclamations were accompanied by a manifesto signed by eight refugees who, with their families, had sought shelter at Detroit. White Eyes reported that he had just returned from Detroit, whither Colonel Morgan had sent him, and that nothing was to be apprehended from that quarter. "I observed," says this shrewd Indian, "that the governor wants to restore peace by making war, but I don't see that he is strong enough to do that." Unquestionably the Moravians did all they dared to do in warning the Americans; they were settled in war's pathway, and they were made to suffer from both sides.[1]

Had they accepted the invitation of Colonel Brodhead, who, in 1781, urged them to return to Fort Pitt, two frontier tragedies would have been spared. When the followers of John Huss were driven from Bohemia and Moravia, early in the eighteenth century, they had found a friend in the pious Count von Zinzendorf, the young son of a Saxon minister of state. On his estates the Moravian brotherhood was organized; and in 1741 Zinzendorf, having been banished from Saxony, came to America and founded the Moravian Church at Bethlehem, Pennsylvania. Successful far beyond other missions, the Moravian churches pushed into the wilderness their banner of peace and good-will; and in 1768 they founded in the Tuscarawas and Muskingum valleys Schonbrunn (the shining spring), Lichtenau (the pasture of light), Salem (peace), and Gnadenhütten (the

[1] The originals of this correspondence are to be found in the State Department MSS.

ARENT SCHUYLER DE PEYSTER

Major and Lieut. Colonel 8th or King's Regiment of Foot, 1777–1793
Colonel in the British Army, 1793
Colonel 1st Regiment Dumfries Volunteers, 1796

tents of grace), surrounding their huts and rude chapels with smiling fields of corn. Opposed to war, these Christian Indians were objects of suspicion by both the English and the Americans.

Part of this story David Zeisberger told to De Peyster. The little old missionary, his face seamed by the cares of frontier life, but still smiling and cheerful by reason of inward content, stood before his accuser and made answer for himself and his companions, Sensemann and Edwards. The more rugged and defiant Heckewelder pleaded his own cause. The missionaries made a favorable impression not only on De Peyster, but also on the townspeople generally. Although he could not speak their language, Father Peter Simple, the priest, offered them the hospitalities of the place; McKee and Elliott paid them a visit; Protestant merchants brought children to be baptized, and some there were who sought them for the marriage ceremony. Returning to Sandusky they spent a bitter winter with their little flock; but in March, 1782, the teachers and their families were ordered to Detroit, and were established on Chippewa lands along the banks of the Clinton River, near the southwest corner of the present city of Mt. Clemens. There they pitched anew their "tents of grace" and founded another Gnadenhütten. Supported through the long spring by an ample supply of provisions from the king's stores, the little band of nineteen persons was increased to half a hundred, all dwelling in well-built houses. With the end of the Revolution and the death of the generous Chippewa chief who had offered them hospitality, the meek Moravian converts were driven from their retreat by the heathen nations; and on April 20, 1786, they gathered for the last time to sing songs of praise and thanksgiving before taking to the boats that were to bear them down the tortuous river and on to the Cuyahoga, whence, as a remnant, they returned to dwell on the banks of the Thames, not far from the spot where Tecumseh met his fate in the War of 1812.[1]

Scarcely had the Moravians reached their Michigan home than they learned of the terrible massacre of their brothers on the Muskingum.[2] Starvation having threatened the Sandusky settlement, a band of the Moravian exiles returned to the towns of Salem and Gnadenhütten to gather the corn that had been left in the fields during the winter of 1781–82. In the March of the latter year a band of some eighty or ninety Americans under Colonel David Williamson surrounded the harmless and unsuspecting corn-gatherers, captured them, voted to put them to death, and in cold blood massacred ninety-six young men, old men, women, and children belonging to a people who had actually embraced the religion professed by their butchers.

In reporting the massacre of the Moravian Indians, De Peyster would not pretend to say how it would operate when the Indians had overcome the consternation this unparalleled cruelty had thrown them in; "they

[1] Captain Henry A. Ford spent much time and labor in tracing the history of the old Moravian mission at Mt. Clemens. See his article in *Michigan Pioneer and Historical Collections*, vol. x., p. 107. Zeisberger died at Goshen in the Tuscarawas valley, in 1801, at the age of 88. Heckewelder died at Bethlehem, in 1823, at the age of 80. Of all the colony at Gnadenhütten, Richard Connor remained behind. Born in Ireland, he came to Maryland, married a white girl who had been a Shawanese prisoner; in 1774 the two had gone to the Moravian towns in search of their captive son, and there they became attached to these peaceful people and went with them to Clinton, or Huron, as the river was then called. The family has continued in Mt. Clemens to this day.

[2] *Haldimand Papers*, De Peyster to Haldimand, May 13, 1782.

daily bring me provisions and beg of me to observe they give aid to their enemies, who acknowledge to have received kind treatment; and I am bold to say that, except in cases where prisoners have been too weak to march, few people have suffered, and we have had many instances of the Indians having carried the sick for several days."

Next to the capture of Hamilton, the massacre of the Moravian Indians proved to be the most important event in the Northwest during the Revolution; for that slaughter of innocents found its consequences in the Crawford campaign. From the English at Detroit and Michilimackinac, we turn now to the Americans at Fort Pitt.

The abortive campaign of General McIntosh in 1778–79, followed by the abandonment of Fort Laurens—the first strictly American work within the present State of Ohio—and then of Fort McIntosh on the Beaver, naturally caused great uneasiness along the frontiers. At the outbreak of the Revolution Fort Pitt was occupied by John Neville, with a small force of Virginia militia; but in 1778 Neville was succeeded by Brigadier-general Edward Hand, and the post came into the possession of the United States. After Hand came McIntosh, who in turn was succeeded by Colonel Brodhead, under whom, in April, 1781, the Delaware villages on the Muskingum were laid waste. Brodhead had been ordered to aid Clark in his western enterprises, and in the August of 1781 a Pennsylvania force of one hundred and seven mounted men under Colonel Archibald Lochry, on its way to join the Virginia leader, had been ambushed at the mouth of the Great Miami, and all had been either killed or captured. The old territorial quarrels over the site of Fort Pitt now broke out afresh, and a dispute between Colonel Brodhead and his successor, Colonel Gibson, added fuel to the flame; so that the post was in a state of anarchy when, in October, 1781, the Scotch-Irish general, William Irvine, of Carlisle, with the veteran Second Brigade of the Pennsylvania line, appeared on the scene to bring order out of chaos.[1]

General Irvine, a post commander of the most approved type, set about building a substantial fort, providing for the small post at Wheeling, and drilling his men. Those were the days of flogging in the army, and "one hundred lashes well laid on" was a daily occurrence as the punishment of desertion or other flagrant infraction of army regulations. The fact seems to be that Pittsburg, in those days, was the centre of turbulence and disorder; and that the Scotch-Irish living thereabouts were much better at gouging each other's eyes out in their fights, or at massacring Indians, than they were at regular, systematic warfare under proper officers. As a result, there were more Indian forays into the neighborhood of Fort Pitt, and more disastrous expeditions from that post, than happened on the Kentucky frontier. The Indians had respect for Clark, but up to this time they had no reason to fear the commandants at Fort Pitt, whose only successes had consisted in burning deserted Indian towns.

It required no remarkable foresight on General Ir-

[1] Irvine was born near Enniskillen, Ireland, November 3, 1741. His grandfather was at the battle of the Boyne, and he was a College of Dublin man, and a cornet of dragoons, before he came to Pennsylvania with his brothers, Andrew and Matthew, in 1764. He was a colonel in the Quebec expedition of 1776, and was captured. On his belated exchange, in May, 1776, he was promoted to the rank of brigadier-general. For particulars of his life, see C. W. Butterfield's *Crawford's Campaign* (Cincinnati, 1873).

vine's part to reach the same conclusion that Clark had reached four years before—that the best way to defend the frontier is to carry the war into the enemy's country. An attack on Detroit, therefore, was planned, and General Irvine went to Philadelphia to lay the matter before Congress and Washington. He left in command that Colonel John Gibson who put into English Logan's message to Lord Dunmore.[1]

On General Irvine's return in the March of 1782 the Revolution was virtually at an end; but Indian raids continued unabated, and among the restless frontiersmen at Fort Pitt there was talk, and something more, of an irruption into Ohio and the formation of an independent state.

To put a stop to both of these disturbances an expedition against Sandusky[2] made rendezvous near the present site of Steubenville, in May, 1782, and on the twenty-fifth began its march of one hundred and fifty miles, with a force of four hundred and eighty men, organized

[1] Butterfield's *Crawford's Campaign*, p. 33. Gibson was born at Lancaster, Pennsylvania, May 23, 1740; he was an excellent classical scholar for his day; at eighteen he was in Forbes's expedition for the recovery of Fort Pitt; after the French and Indian War he was a trader of that post; he was captured by the Indians, was adopted by a squaw, and was made acquainted with Indian manners, customs, and language; he escaped in time to enter the Dunmore expedition of 1774, during which the Mingo chief made his lament in language that Gibson translated into classical English; he served in the New York and New Jersey campaigns as commander of a Virginia regiment; he was a member of the Pennsylvania Constitutional Convention in 1790; was secretary of the Indiana from 1800 till that territory became a state; and on April 10, 1822, he died at his daughter's home, on Braddock's Field.

[2] Mr. Butterfield takes pains to prove that the Crawford expedition was against Sandusky, and not against the Moravian remnant, as Heckewelder, Hildreth, and others have asserted. See his *Crawford's Campaign*, p. 78.

into eighteen companies under officers selected by the men. For commander the soldiers elected the Virginian, William Crawford, by five majority over General Williamson, the leader of the ninety men who, during the previous March, had put to death the Moravian Indians under circumstances of such cold-blooded cruelty as to induce Benjamin Franklin to believe in a hereafter of punishments and rewards. In youth Crawford and Washington had been playmates; in early manhood they fought together at Braddock's defeat, and marched together with Forbes's army of reoccupation; when war was over for a time it was Crawford who surveyed Washington's lands on the Ohio, and who, in 1770, acted as the latter's host and guide in the journey down the mouth of the Great Kanawha; and in the Revolution the two friends were together on Long Island, in crossing the Delaware, and at Trenton and Princeton.

No sooner had the Americans crossed the Ohio than the Indian scouts learned from a deserter that a force of a thousand men were advancing on the Sandusky towns. Immediately the chiefs despatched a runner to demand both ammunition and a detachment of men from Detroit. De Peyster was not slow to comply. On May 15th, he called together the chiefs of the Wyandots, Pottawatomies, Chippewas, and Ottawas, and, on presenting the war-belts from the Six Nations and the Shawanese, Delawares, and Mingoes, he urged them to join their brothers of the South in repelling the advance of the white men, "for it is your villages the Indians are coming against." De Peyster apologized for the fact that the strings were dry, explaining that such had been the desire of their brethren, who feared that if rum were given the savages they would "continue drunk in the streets," and not go to war. "Father!" reproachfully cried a Huron chief, "I arise to tell you that I want 'water' to sharpen your axe, and I shall sing the war-song although one-half of my people are already killed by the enemy."

Although Haldimand was not alarmed for the safety of Detroit, and also was opposed to yielding to the demands of the Six Nations and Delawares for an expedition to reduce Fort Pitt, yet he gave cordial sanction to the Sandusky expedition. "I hope," he writes to De Peyster, "that the melancholy event at Muskingum will rouse the Indians to a firm and vigorous opposition and resentment at Sandusky, or wherever they shall meet the enemy. . . . I depend upon your exerting your utmost efforts and abilities as well to convince the Indians of the indispensable necessity there is for their resisting this shock with unanimity and firmness, their future existence as a people depending on it, as in taking every possible precaution for the security of your post, in which I am persuaded I shall not be disappointed."[1] Mounting a body of Rangers under the command of Captain Caldwell, De Peyster sent them, together with McKee and a number of Canadians, to support the savages.

Marching along Wilkinson's trail, Crawford's force, on June 4th, reached a deserted town of the Wyandots, and proceeded to Upper Sandusky, where, in his perplexity, the leader called a council of war, at which it was decided to continue the advance during that afternoon. If the Indians were not encountered the army was to return. Meanwhile the scouts found an Indian trace, but did not discover the impassable swamp that

[1] *Haldimand Papers.* De Peyster's letter of May 14, 1782, and correspondence following.

flanked it. Pursuing their way, the scouts met the Indians running towards the advancing force, and immediately fell back slowly before the on-coming savages, sending a mounted messenger to warn the general. Highly elated at the prospect of battle, the men ran forward. From a grove in which the little band of Delawares endeavored to make a stand, Crawford dislodged them; and when they attempted to gain the right of the army, Major Leet gallantly prevented. At this juncture the Wyandots appeared, and the Delawares slipped around to attack the Americans in the rear. At nightfall the still hopeful Crawford saw the Indians withdraw; and all night through the Americans and the savages lay on their arms behind great fires built to guard against a night attack. With returning daylight the battle was renewed, the Americans maintaining their position in the island-grove, while all about them the Indians were concealed in the tall prairie-grass, the Delawares on the south and the Wyandots on the north. Although many of his men were overcome by heat and the scanty and bad water, and although many were wounded, Crawford was preparing for an attack in force, when suddenly the squadron of Rangers from Detroit appeared on the field. Attack now was changed to defence; and while the officers were deliberating a band of two hundred Shawanese swept up from the south. Retreat became imperative. The dead were buried and fires kindled over their graves; the wounded were placed on horses, and at dark the force moved. The savages, uncertain whether the movement was an advance or a retreat, did not attack promptly; and although in the confusion some of the Americans rode into the swamp, yet at daybreak the little army, now three hundred in number, had regained Upper Sandusky. Then it was discovered that Colonel Crawford was missing. The command having devolved on Williamson, that officer succeeded in organizing the retreat. On the 6th a stand was made in the present Whitestone township of Crawford County, and in the midst of a pelting rainstorm an attack of the savages was repelled; and on the site of the present town of Cresline the Indians ceased the pursuit. On the 17th of June the force reached the Mingo Bottom on the Ohio, whence they had set out with such high hopes twenty-three days before.

At the beginning of the retreat, Colonel Crawford having missed his son John, his son-in-law Major Harrison, and his nephews Major Rose and William Crawford, halted to wait until they should come up. The army having passed without them, his wearied horse was unequal to the task of overtaking the fugitives, and in company with Dr. Knight and others he pushed on. The next day they met Captain Josh Biggs and Lieutenant Ashley, with whom they made camp; but on the 11th of June Crawford and Knight were captured by a band of Delawares, Biggs and Ashley making their escape only to be killed the next day. Taken to the near-by camp of the savages, they found there nine prisoners. The two officers were handed over to the Delaware chiefs, Captain Pipe and Wingenund. Knight was reserved for the torture-fire of a neighboring town, but made an almost miraculous escape. For Crawford a stake fifteen feet high was driven into the ground, and about it a fire of hickory wood was laid in a circle some six yards from the post. By way of preparation the remaining prisoners were sent off to be tomahawked by the squaws and small boys.

Then Colonel Crawford was stripped naked, and the savages beat him with sticks. Next his tormentors fastened him to the stake by a short rope, and began to fire powder into his bruised body. From the cordon of flames squaws snatched coals and hot ashes to throw at him, until, in his agony, he walked round and round the stake on a pathway of fire.

Among the spectators stood Simon Girty, who had often been a guest at Crawford's hospitable table on the Ohio. Crawford begged him to shoot and end the terrible agony; but the renegade made taunting answer, "I have no gun." For three hours the torture continued. Then the brave man, the friend and companion of the commander-in-chief of the American armies, fell on his face; an Indian quickly rushed in and scalped him, and a squaw threw burning coals on his mutilated head. Stung into life again, he once more arose and started around the deadly post. But his end was at hand. The exhausted body dropped into the flames.

De Peyster lamented that the murder of the Moravians, coming at a time when the Indians were almost weaned from cruelties, "had awakened their old custom of putting prisoners to the most severe tortures;" yet he looked upon the torture of Crawford and the massacre of prisoners as retaliation on nearly the same body of troops that perpetrated the slaughter of the Christian Indians, and that had similar intentions upon Sandusky.[1] Haldimand, deeply shocked by the report De Peyster sent of the torture of Crawford, had "not a doubt that every possible argument was used to prevent that unhappy event, and that it alone proceeded from

[1] *Haldimand Papers.* De Peyster to Haldimand, June 23 and August 18, 1782.

the massacre of the Moravian Indians, a circumstance that will not extenuate the guilt in the eyes of Congress. When you see a fit occasion, express in the proper terms the concern I feel at their having followed so base an example, and the abhorrence I have had throughout the war at acts of cruelty, which, until this instance, they have so humanely avoided." The correspondence between Haldimand and De Peyster shows that these officers of the king were sincerely impressed by the twin horrors that marked the last year of the Revolution in the Northwest; and they took pains to put their ideas into orders directed to the Indians.

Before the middle of June news came to Detroit that peace was likely to follow the cessation of arms which had taken place. On August 15th De Peyster despatched an express to Captain Caldwell and to Brant and McKee, operating on the Ohio, ordering them to cease from offensive work, although news had come that another expedition was fitting out at Fort McIntosh and at Wheeling, "under the command of the blood-thirsty Colonel Williamson, who so much distinguished himself in the massacre of the Christian Indians." The messenger, however, was too late to reach Captain Caldwell. On August 15th that officer, with thirty picked Rangers and about two hundred Lake Indians, besides some Delawares and Shawanese, made an unsuccessful attack on Bryan's station, in Kentucky, ending in the battle of Blue Licks, at which ill-advised encounter Clark's county lieutenant of the Illinois, Colonel John Todd, and seventy of his command were killed, with a loss to their enemy of a single Ranger and six Indians!

The terrible slaughter of Blue Licks (occasioned by

Major Hugh McGarry usurping leadership in spite of Boone's advice to await reinforcements), brought Clark once more to the command; and on November 10th his mounted riflemen, a thousand and fifty strong, struck the Miami towns, burning crops, capturing prisoners, recapturing whites, and destroying the establishments of the British traders. With this attack the war of the Revolution ended in the Northwest.[1]

[1] *Haldimand Papers.* De Peyster to McKee, August 6, 1782. De Peyster to Brigadier-general Powell, August 27th.

For an account of the battle of Blue Licks, see Roosevelt's *Winning of the West*, vol. ii., p. 207. Mr. Roosevelt there gives McKee's and Caldwell's reports, and corrects several errors in accepted accounts.

In a suggestive paper prepared for the Wisconsin Historical Society, and printed in the *Michigan Pioneer and Historical Reports*, vol. iii., the late Judge Charles I. Walker, of Detroit, was the first one to call the attention of historians to the valuable documents at Quebec, as sources of Northwestern history during the Revolutionary period; he made as careful study of these documents as circumstances would permit, and this led to the publication of considerable portions of the Bouquet and Haldimand Papers by the Michigan Pioneer and Historical Society. Judge Walker made a valuable collection of publications relating to the Northwest, and when failing eyesight forced him to give up his own studies, he generously placed his collection in the Detroit public library. Dr. W. J. Poole's chapter on "The West" from 1763 to 1783, in volume vi. of the *Narrative and Critical History of America*, and Andrew McFarland Davis's chapter on "The Indians and the Border Warfare of the Revolution" in the same volume, are valuable not alone in themselves, but also for their references to other writings.

Of all writers on Western history, the most untiring searcher for truth amid the multitude of legends and traditions was Mr. Consul Willshire Butterfield, who was born in Oswego County, New York, in 1824, and who for fifty years pursued his inquiries into the history of the Ohio valley. He died in South Omaha, Nebraska, in October, 1899. His biography of George Rogers Clark is yet to appear.

The war between England and America was indeed ended; but for the Northwest the peace that had come to the Atlantic coast was long years in the future. The Revolution had but rolled up the curtain on the tragedy that was to end only with the treaty of Ghent, then more than a quarter of a century distant. De Peyster, looking the situation squarely in the face, wrote to Haldimand: "I have a very difficult card to play at this post and its dependencies, which differs widely from the situation of affairs at Michilimackinac, Niagara, and others in the upper district of Canada. It is evident that the back settlers will continue to make war upon the Shawanese, Delawares, and Wyandots, even after a truce shall be agreed to betwixt Great Britain and her revolted colonies. In which case, while we continue to support the Indians with troops (which they are calling aloud for), or only with arms, ammunition, and necessaries, we shall incur the odium of encouraging incursions into the back settlements—for it is evident that when the Indians are on foot, occasioned by the constant alarms they receive from the enemies entering their country, they will occasionally enter the settlements, and bring off prisoners and scalps—so that while in alliance with a people we are bound to support, a defensive war will, in spite of human prudence, almost always terminate in an offensive one."

The war was over. Peace meant liberation for the captives. At Detroit the doors of "Yankee Hall," the Libby Prison of the Northwest, were opened, and as speedily as possible De Peyster sent the captives to the lower country. Not all of them wished to leave. There were Germans who had taken the oath of allegiance to the king, and who were settled with their families near

Detroit or on the present Belle Isle; there were also women whose children were with the Indians—Rachels still to be comforted; and there were orphans who knew not their parents. The women and children De Peyster "fixed in decent houses, where they will be taken care of without being of the least expense to government,"[1] and he did all that lay in his power to accommodate all matters.

But there was one door that could not be opened. In the cellar of the council-house was a room set apart for the deposit[2] of the scalps brought to Detroit by the Indians when they came to claim provisions and clothing, guns and knives, powder and lead, and, above all, rum. For the moment the forests had echoed the shrieks of the victims — women rushing to death in defence of their children, men struck down at the very gates of their log forts, or shot in the fields while at work, innocent children playing about the doorstep of the cabin builded in the wilderness that they might have a home. Their bones whitened in the forest; their scalps rotted in the council-house; their only memorial was the grandfather's tale told about the fireside long years afterwards, when the frontier had been pushed far north of the Ohio and the log-cabin had given place to the secure farm-house set amid smiling fields. Let it be said in honor to the Americans that, whatever cruelties they may have perpetrated on the Indians, their souls revolted from employing savages to make war on white people.

[1] *Haldimand Papers.* De Peyster to Powell, August 27, 1782.

[2] See also the chapter on the Revolutionary War in Silas Farmer's *History of Detroit and Michigan*, a veritable storehouse of facts gathered during years of diligent research.

CHAPTER VIII

PEACE THAT PROVES NO PEACE

"My lords," piteously cried Lord Chatham, tottering on the very brink of the grave—"my lords, his Majesty succeeded to an empire as great in extent as its reputation was unsullied. Shall we tarnish the lustre of this nation by an ignominious surrender of its rights and fairest possessions?" With his latest breath the great statesman uttered his almost incoherent lamentation over what he believed to be the impending doom of England—the independence of those very colonies he himself had taught how to fight, and had encouraged to revolt by his own ringing words of freedom. Chatham had been in his grave three years and a half before the surrender of Cornwallis at Yorktown made England understand that the inevitable day of separation was at hand; but for a year longer still she fought in the cabinet to postpone that acknowledgment of independence which successive defeats in the field had forced upon her.[1]

The treaty of 1763, so humiliating to France, had prepared that nation for the alliance with the colonies on which the success of the Revolution depended; and the hope of ousting England from her possession of

[1] Chatham's last speech in the House of Lords was delivered April 7, 1778; he died four days later. Yorktown was surrendered October 19, 1781, and the preliminary articles of peace were signed November 30, 1782.

Gibraltar was the one thing that brought Spain into the contest. From the very day that New France disappeared from the map of America the French minister Choiseul had pursued the policy of encouraging the colonies to revolt and to form an independent nation, by which means he hoped and expected to curb and restrain England's overmastering power on the seas. Louis XVI., coming to the throne at the very time when the port of Boston was closed by British orders, chose to forget that the American colonists were revolting at the divine right of kings, and in his eagerness to punish the hereditary enemy of France and to curb the commercial supremacy of England, he was ready to furnish the fleets, the soldiers, and the money needed to insure the success of the new nation. When it came to the peace negotiations, however, the conflicting interests of England and France and Spain all had to be considered before the United States could take a position among the nations of the world.[1]

Throughout the Revolution, Franklin, as the representative of the United States, had occupied a position of first importance at Paris, where he had acted not only as diplomatic agent, but had also negotiated loans to the amount of 51,000,000 francs, had disbursed the funds so obtained, and had directed the little navy operating in European waters. After the evacuation of Bos-

[1] For a discussion of motives see the introduction to Wharton's *Revolutionary Diplomatic Correspondence of the United States*. Dr. Wharton's introduction is especially valuable for the light it throws on the various actors in the diplomacy of the Revolution. John Jay's article on the peace negotiations, in vol. vii. of the *Narrative and Critical History of America*, shows the various twistings and turnings involved in the prolonged discussions, and especially illustrates the reluctance with which England came to the acknowledgment of independence.

ton and the surrender of Burgoyne at Saratoga in 1778 had proved the ability of the colonists to cope with England, an open alliance with France, also negotiated by Franklin, gave to this country a national existence, at least so far as that nation was concerned. Early in 1779, when the hope of peace seemed not unreasonable, Congress made John Adams a commissioner to negotiate a peace; and afterwards, at the instance of France, associated with him others, of whom Franklin and Jay bore an active part in the actual negotiations. It is not necessary here to go into the intricate and delicate subject of the prolonged negotiations that led up to the treaty of 1783; but for present purposes it is sufficient to outline the general attitude of the four nations in interest.

Congress naturally took a large view of the rights and the boundaries which should accrue to the United States by virtue of having prosecuted a successful war against England. After the recognition of the independence of the United States, which was always of first consideration, Congress stipulated for a participation in the Newfoundland fisheries, for the free navigation of the Mississippi, and for the enlarged boundaries of the Great Lakes on the north and the Mississippi on the west. These demands were afterwards modified both in terms, and especially by the instruction that the American commissioners were not to take action without consulting France, a restriction always embarrassing and well calculated to defeat all efforts at successful negotiation had the commissioners adhered to it.

France, willing to humiliate England, was quite unwilling to give to the new nation the room and the opportunity to grow; and in pursuit of this policy the French minister Vergennes set on foot an intrigue with

England to keep the United States out of the fisheries and to confine the boundaries to the Ohio, if not to the Alleghanies, leaving to England all of Canada as enlarged under the Quebec act of 1774. It was Vergennes's object to prolong negotiations until the purposes of Spain had been accomplished; for he had agreed, as the price of Spain's help against England, first to make no peace that did not involve the surrender of Gibraltar; and, secondly, to have Spain free to exact from the United States a renunciation of the navigation of the Mississippi, and of the entire Northwest from the St. Lawrence to the Alleghanies.

Spain, in order to protect her interests in the Philippines and in the hope of recovering the key to the Mediterranean, gave to France for the use of the United States a million francs, by way of encouraging the colonies in their struggle against England; but when the colonies coalesced into a nation, Spain immediately began to consider the danger to her own North American possessions that would result from building up a strong government east of the Mississippi. Then, having been drawn into the war by France, Spain determined to seize the opportunity to recover the ground she had lost in the Seven Years' War and again to become a nation of the first class. Grudgingly she gave ineffective aid to the United States, expecting at the end to profit at their expense.

In Prussia Frederick the Great was willing to aid America up to the point of getting into a war with England; in Russia Catharine II. welcomed the war as an opportunity for her to build up a neutral commerce, but she had no sympathy with the object of the Americans to form a new nation; and the same state of affairs that existed in Russia prevailed also in the Netherlands.

JOHN ADAMS

The surrender at Yorktown having proved to England the futility of continuing the struggle with the United States, the House of Commons, on March 4, 1782, voted to consider as enemies to the king and country those who should attempt the further prosecution of the war with America; and within a fortnight thereafter Lord North gave way to Rockingham, whose cabinet was made up largely of the friends of America, including Fox and Burke. The peace negotiations, however, were conducted mainly by Lord Shelburne, first as the colonial secretary and afterwards as the leader of the ministry. Without attempting too close an analysis of the complex character of Shelburne, it is enough to say that after long dodging the humiliating question of acknowledging the independence of the United States as the preliminary step to a treaty, he was slowly but surely educated into a condition of high esteem for the character and abilities of the American commissioners; and in the end he was persuaded that it was for the best interests of England herself to give to the new nation such rights and boundaries as would insure the development of a prosperous nation with which Great Britain might trade on fair terms. He was led to these conclusions not only by the straightforward dealings of Jay and Adams and Franklin, but also by the duplicity of Vergennes.

Of the three American peace commissioners, Franklin was seventy years old when, in 1776, he was elected commissioner to France, and he was then moved to speak of himself as a remnant—a fag-end. Yet by his profound knowledge, his wide experience at court, and his adroit address, he had succeeded in performing services such as no other man in America could have rendered. For the young monarch of France he felt almost a paternal regard; and by appealing to the chivalrous instincts of both king and queen he had well supplemented his appeals to the lower motives of advantage and revenge entertained by Vergennes. He it was who first undertook to deal separately and secretly with Shelburne, proposing to give compensation to the Tories in return for the cession of all of Canada; but as negotiations progressed he was inclined to lay much stress on the instruction to consult France, and it was with genuine reluctance that he yielded to his colleagues when they concluded that the time had come to accommodate matters first with England. That he did so conclude was not his least service to his country.

Utterly unlike Franklin was John Adams, a most zealous patriot, in whom tact and judgment were often wanting. Lacking in the spirit of accommodation, he never could have accomplished all that Franklin secured; and yet his persistency and his undoubted genius for affairs political enabled him to obtain much. It was Adams's rough aggressiveness that caused the French minister Luzerne to have Congress associate with him as peace commissioners Franklin, Jay, Laurens, and Thomas Jefferson—a division of responsibility entirely agreeable to Adams. While Franklin and Jay were spending the better part of the year 1782 in negotiations with Oswald, the British representative, Adams successfully negotiated a treaty with Holland; and, fresh from this diplomatic triumph in October, he arrived in Paris to give to Jay the full support of his experience and decision of character. Friendly to France, indeed, he had no particular affinity for that country; hence it violated no feelings on Adams's part to come to terms with England while Vergennes was resting in fancied security that he had delayed indefinitely

LORD SHELBURNE

the negotiations he professed himself anxious to expedite.

From April 6 to June 23, 1782, Franklin and Oswald, the British commissioner, were trying to arrive at some satisfactory basis of negotiations. Jefferson was in America; Laurens was a prisoner in the Tower of London; Adams was busy in Holland. Satisfied that Jay was accomplishing nothing in Spain, Franklin called to his aid the young New York gentleman who, although only in his thirty-seventh year, had already achieved notable success as a member of Congress and as the chief-justice of the supreme court of his native State. Born of a Huguenot family, distinguished alike for social graces and for legal attainments, Jay was at once easy of approach, familiar with the usages of society, and strenuous in his Americanism. From his coming to Paris, late in June, till the signing of the preliminary articles of peace on the 30th of November, Jay pulled the laboring oar in all the negotiations. He it was who dared to disregard the instruction of Congress to deal only with the consent of France, who insisted on making the acknowledgment of independence a prerequisite to negotiations, and who stood out for the widest possible boundaries and the most ample rights to the fisheries and the navigation of the Mississippi. He persuaded Shelburne that it was for the interest of England to make a treaty that would be not only just but also conciliatory; and all this he accomplished with the hearty concurrence of Adams, who had but a month's part in the negotiations, and of Franklin, whose attachment to and confidence in Jay were shown afterwards by the fact that Franklin made Jay his executor.[1]

[1] "Our worthy friend, Mr. Jay, returns to his country like a bee to

The European fear of wide American boundaries was entirely natural. The depopulation of Europe, the loss of the fur-trade, the diversion of the product of the mines of New Mexico, and the use of the fisheries as a commercial and naval training-school, all were reasons impelling France and Spain to set the Alleghanies as the barrier which the too-enterprising Americans should not be allowed to cross; and in order to accomplish their purpose, these two nations did not scruple secretly to seek the participation of England. Employing as a medium of communication Vaughan, an intimate friend of Shelburne, Jay despatched to London the draft of a treaty comprising boundaries, the navigation of the Mississippi, and the fisheries. England was anxious to keep the back country as a means of settling the loyalists, or at least of compensating them for their losses by the sale of these lands; but on this point Shelburne was not strenuous. The two points on which he was decided were the payment of debts owed to British merchants by Americans, and the re-establishment of the Tories in their privileges and properties. On the first point there was no dispute; on the second, the commissioners were powerless to do more than to agree that Congress would recommend such action to the several States, which alone had the jurisdiction over matters of internal policy.

The repeated illnesses of Dr. Franklin caused the burden of the peace arrangements to fall on the shoulders of his younger and more vigorous colleague, John Jay, and although Oswald still regarded Franklin as the chief of the negotiators, he found that Jay's clear-cut and def-

his hive, with both legs loaded with merit and honor."—Adams to Barclay, quoted in George Pellew's *John Jay*, American Statesmen Series, p. 228.

inite demands must be met, because Franklin was determined to support his colleague at every point. Jay's experience in Spain had aroused a natural resentment towards that nation; and at the same time he had no such friendly feeling for France as had been engendered in Franklin by years of successful negotiation with Vergennes, and by that subtle flattery which the people of France willingly accorded to the distinguished scientific attainments, the profound knowledge, and the affable manners of the representative of the United States.[1] Towards England Jay's feelings were mixed. He was in sympathy with the best political thought of that country, but was not in sympathy with the government. Oswald found him polite, easy, well informed, but decidedly independent; and was disappointed in meeting such decided ideas so firmly held. In the end, however, the British negotiator came under Jay's influence, and became an earnest advocate with Shelburne and Townshend of Jay's views.

Of all the matters comprised in the peace treaty, there is no more obscure subject than that of the Northwest boundaries; and in the printed correspondence almost nothing is to be found to throw light on that perplexing question. In the manuscript correspondence that passed between Oswald and his principals, however, the matter is elucidated.[2] When the treaty of 1763 was proposed as a basis of negotiation, Jay maintained that Great

[1] For a brilliant exposition of Franklin's position in Paris, see Professor George W. Green's article on "The Diplomacy of the Revolution," in the *Atlantic Monthly*, vol. xv., p. 576. Professor Green does scant justice to Adams, and makes almost no mention of Jay, a fact which indicates the lack of available information on this subject in 1865.

[2] This correspondence, known as the Landsdowne Papers, is in the Library of Congress and in the State Department.

Britain had treated France with too little consideration at that time; and on Oswald's reply that it ill became an American to object to the enforced surrender of Canada, by means of which cession the American frontiers were protected from incursions of savages instigated by France, Jay retorted that the colonies were then a part of the British domain, and were therefore to be protected in common with other portions of the realm. What Jay now proposed was the cession of all that portion of Canada newly included in the Quebec act of 1774—that is, all the territory west of the Ottawa River and south of the lands of the Hudson Bay Company, and his argument was easy to be comprehended. The back lands, he said, were already occupied in part by the Americans, who were pushing over the mountains into that fertile territory; and for England to retain the Ohio country would simply be to invite trouble. Moreover, he pointed out a way in which England, while giving up the territory, could command its trade. Oswald professed anxiety over the honorable withdrawal of the British garrisons at New York and Charleston: let England use these troops to conquer the Spanish post at the mouth of the Mississippi; the United States would much prefer England to France as a neighbor; then with the free navigation of the great river, Great Britain would be able to control the two outlets of the back lands—New Orleans and Quebec. This reasoning seemed good to Oswald, for he was convinced that the plan of using the Ohio lands to furnish a fund to make good the losses of British loyalists and to pay for American property wantonly destroyed by the British was past hoping for. So he urged Jay's reasoning on his government; and in the dearth of authentic maps and other information in regard to

HENRY LAURENS

the Ohio, the wide boundaries of the Northwest were agreed to.[1]

The American commissioners offered a choice between the line passing through the middle of the Great Lakes, or the forty-fifth degree of latitude, which latter line would have left in Canada Lake Superior, Minnesota, and the northern half of Michigan, while it would have given to us the province of Ontario and all of Lakes Erie and Ontario. Fortunately for both parties, the more rational line was chosen and marked on Mitchell's map ; and on paper, at least, the two nations divided the navigation privileges of the great inland seas, and, without knowledge of the exact conditions, parted their respective territories along the Grand Portage from Lake Superior to the sources of the Mississippi. The triumph of Jay and his colleagues in obtaining these boundaries can best be appreciated when it is understood how persistently Vergennes, acting for both France and Spain, pushed the Spanish claims not alone at Paris, but also at London, and even at Philadelphia; and with what plausibility he argued that Spain should control the Mississippi, that the country between the Alleghanies and the Ohio should be maintained as Indian territory, under the control of Spain, and that Canada should reach south to the Ohio. Possibly England preferred to give up to the United States territory which she might hope to regain, rather than to yield to France what she would have to pay for by other and more important surrenders elsewhere. Be that as it may, the preliminary

[1] See Oswald's letters of August 8, September 2, and October 2, 1782. Also the letters in regard to Canada in vol. viii. of Wharton's *Diplomatic Correspondence of the Revolution*, and a very instructive article on "The International Boundary Line of Michigan," by Anna May Soule, in *Michigan Pioneer and Historical Collections*, vol. xxvi.

treaty was agreed to on November 30, 1782, with the saving provision that the peace should not become effectual until England had come to terms with France and Spain.

There was but one sentiment in regard to the treaty. D'Aranda wrote from Paris to his master, the King of Spain: "The federal republic is born a pigmy. A day will come when it will be a giant, even a colossus, formidable to these countries. Liberty of conscience, the facility for establishing a new population on immense lands, as well as the advantage of the new government, will draw thither farmers and artisans from all nations. In a few years we shall watch with grief the tyrannical existence of this same colossus." The chagrined Vergennes wrote to his secretary and companion in intrigue, Rayvenal, that England had rather bought a peace than made one; to which Rayvenal replied that the treaty seemed to him a dream. Luzerne wrote from Philadelphia to Vergennes that the boundary from Lake Superior to the sources of the Mississippi had surpassed all expectation. It gave the Americans four forts they had found it impossible to capture. Lands nearer the coast were already beginning to depreciate in value, owing to the new acquisitions; and that there was a belief that in pushing their possessions as far as the Lake of the Woods, the plenipotentiaries were preparing for their remote posterity a communication with the Pacific. Such words now seem prophecy; then they were but the legitimate deductions of statesmen.

A characteristic fate overtook the treaty in the British Parliament. Fox and North having combined to drive Shelburne out of power for making such a treaty, the new ministry sent Hartley to Paris to "perfect and establish the peace, friendship, and good understanding so happily commenced by the provisional articles"; and after intermittent negotiations these same provisional articles were adopted on September 3, 1783, as the definitive treaty between England and America. In Congress the negotiators were praised for their achievement, but were blamed for not consulting France!

In opposing the treaty in the House of Lords, Walsingham had asserted that the province of Canada had been made insecure, the fur-trade lost, several hundred million acres were ceded, and faith was broken with the Indians; and Lord Townshend deplored the fact that some one from Canada had not been brought in to arrange the matter of the boundaries. There was good reason to believe that the question of the Northwestern boundaries had not been well considered by the British; but they had made the treaty after due consideration and they were morally bound to live up to it.

Early in the autumn of 1782 Haldimand, having received orders from Shelburne to discourage hostile measures on the part of the Indians, and as much as possible to draw them from the American frontiers, instructed the commanders under him to carry out those orders; but to the Honorable Thomas Townshend he wrote that the safety of the province of Canada depended on the way in which the Indians should be managed. The savages, he said, had been great sufferers by reason of the war; from ease and affluence the Mohawks had been reduced to wanderers; and the Indians generally had so perpetually harassed the Americans that for them nothing short of abandoning England would secure a reconciliation with the United States. "Foreseeing the possibility of the Americans becoming an independent powerful people and retaliating severely upon them, they reproach us with their ruin." So long as the Six Nations remained faithful, Oswego, the key to Canada, was in security; but even the neutrality of those tribes would cause the gravest apprehension. On the friendship of the western Indians depended the safety of the trade and posts at Detroit and in the vicinity; so that the expense attending the Indian alliance, although enormous, must be borne. That was no time to retrench.[1] And again, two days later, Haldimand urged upon Townshend the absolute necessity that Niagara and Oswego be annexed to Canada; evidently he had no thought of the surrender of Detroit and Mackinac. His letters, however, came too late to be effective in the negotiation of the treaty, but his views were enforced in spite of the treaty, as will be seen.

It was small wonder that Haldimand was anxious to preserve the fur-trade; for the traffic in peltry was then, as it always had been, the life-blood of Canada. In 1765, two years after the massacre at Michilimackinac, the first English adventurer started northward from that post, only to have his canoes plundered by the Indians about Rainy Lake; nor was he more successful the next year; but in 1767 the traders penetrated beyond Lake Winnipeg, and, so far as the Indians were concerned, the battle was won. Competition, far from being the life of trade, became its bane, until the Frobishers combined with the other great Montreal house of Todd & McGill, and in 1774 the new company pushed its posts into territories unknown even to the French. At the date of the definitive treaty there were but twelve different interests engaged in the northern trade, and when the new boundaries were made known these twelve combined to form the Northwest Company,

[1] Haldimand to Townshend, October 23, 1782.

A FUR-TRADER IN THE COUNCIL TEPEE

in order to guard against American encroachments. The United States treaty commissioners had insisted on drawing the boundary-line through the Grand Portage of Lake Superior, then the only known water communication to the Lake of the Woods, and hence the key to the rich fur country of the north. To discover another convenient passage wholly within British lines became the first object of the monopoly, and to this end they sent out a strong exploring party under Umfreville and Venance St. Germain.

Even in 1784 the annual business of the Northwest Company amounted to £50,000, as the original cost of furs. Early in May, ninety long canoes, each of four tons burden and each navigated by eight or ten men, set out from Montreal bound for the Lake of the Woods. On reaching Michilimackinac their stock of provisions was replenished and off they paddled for the north shore of Lake Superior. There the goods were transferred to canoes carrying perhaps a ton and a half and navigated by four or five men especially trained for the combined work on stream and portage. Starting from the Portage early in July, two hundred and fifty bush-rangers made their way even to Lake Athabasca and Great Slave Lake, and throughout the entire country within a thousand miles or more from Lake Superior. Often provisions would fail and Indians be hard to come upon; then the tortures of hunger would bring men face to face with death, and not infrequently the close-following wolves would get their expected prey.[1] Such dangers and such hazards made the bottle pass quickly and the song wax hilarious when these forest-trampers

[1] Memorial of Benjamin and Joseph Frobisher to General Haldimand, October 4, 1784.—*Canadian Archives*, 1890, p. 50. Also James McGill to Henry Hamilton, *ibid.*, p. 56.

went into winter quarters and gathered about the great pine fires that defied the mercury-freezing cold and the high-piled snow. Such were the beginnings of the great Northwest Company, whose partners, making their annual voyage to Fort William, near the Grand Portage, ascended the mighty rivers in canoes freighted with every luxury known to civilization, and equipped with servants and cooks to serve banquets in the great hall of the council-house, that was hung with the richest of furs and the mightiest trophies of the chase. Opulence is a word that seems to belong to the Indies, but the opulence of the Lake Superior fur-trade in the closing days of the eighteenth century can be compared only with the opulence of the Lake Superior copper-trade in the closing years of the nineteenth.[1]

Great as was the fur-trade in the upper country, in value more than half of the furs came from countries within the new boundaries of the United States; and Montreal had practically the monopoly of the trade

[1] Compare the opening chapters of Irving's *Astoria*. The Boston and New York owners of copper-mines in Lake Superior are worthy successors of the Frobishers and the McTavishes of other days.

During a visit to Sault Ste. Marie, in October, 1899, I was entertained by Mr. Clergue, at his home in a blockhouse built on the foundations of a similar structure erected by the Northwest Fur Company, on the Canadian side of the rapids. In these closing days of the nineteenth century Mr. Clergue and the American capitalists whom he represents are realizing the dreams of the seventeenth and eighteenth centuries. The trade with Cathay that eluded Nicolet is now maintained by the daily shipments of wood-pulp to Japan; the copper that Joliet was unable to discover has at last been found, and with it nickel and iron; Radisson's overland path to Hudson Bay is being traversed by the Algoma Central railroad, now building; and the waters of St. Mary's River are being harnessed to build up a great manufacturing centre. Meanwhile the largest tonnage known to any waterway in the world annually passes to and from Lakes Superior and Huron.

from the St. Lawrence to the Ohio and the Mississippi. The Canadians rightly judged that inasmuch as the fur market was London and China, the United States would not be able to compete in this trade; and this estimate proved true until, in the person of John Jacob Astor, America was to have a merchant who could command trade in both London and China, who could maintain commercial rivalry at Mackinac even with the Northwest Company, and whose enterprise in the wilderness helped the United States to acquire by discovery and settlement the title to the Oregon country.

Haldimand, as a part of his plan for keeping control of the fur-trade, had forbidden building or navigating private vessels on the Great Lakes; because he conceived that, were the furs not carried in king's vessels, they would speedily find their way through the United States to tide-water. As may be supposed, this prohibition met with vigorous remonstrance not only from the Northwest Company, but also from the merchants of Detroit, and others who found their business almost ruined by lack of vessels and the usual naval disposition to take plenty of time to go from place to place. The merchants, however, got no satisfaction either from Haldimand or from his dual successors, General St. Leger and Lieutenant-Governor Hamilton.[1]

So soon as Sir Guy Carleton[2] had announced to General Washington that England had concluded a peace with France, Spain, and Holland, Congress authorized

[1] See correspondence in *Canadian Archives*, 1890, p. 63 *et seq.*

[2] Carleton to Washington, April 6, 1784. The documents relating to the attempts to get possession of the posts are given in connection with the message of the President of the United States of December 5, 1793. There is a Philadelphia and a London print of these documents. See also American State Papers, Foreign Relations, vol. i., p. 181.

the commander-in-chief to make the necessary arrangements with the British commanders for receiving the posts at Detroit, Michilimackinac, Erie, Niagara, Oswego, Oswegatchie, Point au Fer, and Dutchman's Point, occupied by the British and situated within the new boundaries of the United States. Thereupon Washington sent Baron Steuben to Quebec to arrange for the surrender. When, on August 8, 1783, Steuben met General Haldimand at Sorel, the British commander, with his customary suavity, made answer to the American demand, that his orders related solely to a cessation of hostilities, and that he had obeyed them to the letter, even to the extent of restraining the savages from committing the least hostile act; but that until he received explicit orders to turn over the posts, he conceived it to be his duty as a soldier to take no step in that direction.[1] Nor was Governor Clinton, of New York, more successful[2] when, during the next year, he endeavored to obtain possession of Fort Niagara. Still a third attempt was made by Secretary of War Knox, who, in the July of the same year, sent to Quebec one of the brightest and most successful of the younger officers of the Revolution, Lieutenant-Colonel William Hull; but again Haldimand pleaded his want of authority,[3] and there the army officials dropped the matter.

In so far as Haldimand himself was concerned, he acted as any prudent general would do in the absence

[1] American State Papers, Foreign Relations, vol. i., p. 181 *et seq.* Steuben to Haldimand, August 3, 1783; Haldimand to Steuben, August 13, 1783, and Steuben's report to Washington.

[2] *Ibid.* Clinton to Haldimand, March 19, 1784, and Haldimand to Clinton, May 10, 1784.

[3] *Ibid.* Hull to Haldimand, July 12, 1784, and Haldimand to Knox, July 12, 1784.

THE COUREUR DE BOIS AND THE SAVAGE

of definite instructions; but it is evident that, aside from the lack of positive orders, he was moved by his own personal knowledge of the enormous loss to British fur interests involved in the surrender of the posts. These facts are made evident by Haldimand's instructions to his successor, Brigadier General Barry St. Leger, to whom he wrote that he had thought it his duty "uniformly to oppose' the different attempts made by the American States to get possession of the posts in the upper country until his Majesty's orders for that purpose shall be received, and my conduct upon that occasion having been approved, I have only to recommend to you a strict attention to the same."[1]

On the arrival in Philadelphia of George Hammond, the first minister plenipotentiary of Great Britain to the United States, Secretary Jefferson promptly called his attention to the seventh article of the definitive treaty of peace, wherein it was stipulated that "his Britannic Majesty should, with all convenient speed, withdraw all his armies, garrisons, and fleets from the said United States, and from every post, place, and harbor within the same." Hammond rejoined that the posts were held because of the failure of the United States to secure from the several States the restitution of all confiscated estates, rights, and properties belonging to British subjects. To this Mr. Jefferson replied at great length to show that the States had acted in a spirit of conciliation towards British subjects, and that the treaty simply bound Congress to *recommend* such a course, that body having (as was clearly understood by the treaty-makers and by Parliament) no authority to compel the

[1] *Canadian Archives*, 1890, p. xxxii. Mr. Douglas Brymner, archivist, discusses the whole subject with his customary candor and accurate knowledge.

States so to act. In any event, Jefferson argued, Great Britain was not justified in exercising jurisdiction over the country and inhabitants in the vicinity of the posts, and in excluding citizens of the United States from navigating "even on our side of the middle line of the rivers and lakes established as a boundary between the two nations," and thus "intercepting us entirely from the commerce of furs with Indian nations to the northward, a commerce which has ever been of great importance to the United States, not only for its intrinsic value, but as it was a means of cherishing peace with those Indians and of superseding the necessity of that expensive warfare we have been obliged to carry on with them during the time those posts have been in other hands." [1]

Haldimand's apprehensions as to the results that must follow from the transfer of the sovereignty of the Indian country from England to the United States were entirely justified. Whether from ignorance or from carelessness, England had neglected to provide for her Indian allies, who had devoted themselves to her cause with such remorseless brutality as to inspire in Chatham feelings of repulsion that he poured forth in invective never surpassed even on this side of the Atlantic. In so far as he was able, Haldimand undertook to repair this neglect by seating the ruined Mohawks on the Grand River, that flows into Lake Erie some forty miles above the Falls of Niagara; but such a solution must of necessity be partial and unsatisfactory. Fortunately, however, Washington and Schuyler took up the subject with Congress, and attempted to arrange matters

[1] American State Papers, Foreign Relations, vol. i., p. 181. Jefferson to Hammond, November 29, 1791.

on the basis of blotting out the remembrance of the past hostility of the savages, and placing them under the care of the government of the United States, instead of leaving them to the mercies of the several States. In pursuance of this object, on October 22, 1784, the treaty of Fort Stanwix was negotiated by Oliver Wolcott, Richard Butler, and Arthur Lee with the Six Nations; and although the young chief Red Jacket was bitterly opposed to the surrender of lands, the more astute chief Corn-planter threw the weight of his age and experience into the scale in favor of the Americans. Unfortunately for our country, while this treaty was being negotiated, Brant, the great chief of the Six Nations, was in Quebec for the purpose of securing title to the British grant of twelve hundred square miles on the Grand River; and when he learned of the negotiations he not only opposed the results, but immediately he visited the western and Lake Indians to form a confederacy for the protection of the Indian lands as far south as the Ohio. The inception of this plan seems to have been entirely with Brant; its support came from England, not quickly, or as a matter of high official policy, but slowly, increasingly, and by the action of subordinates on the ground.[1]

Having engaged the northern and western tribes to act together, Brant set sail for England to obtain from the crown compensation for the losses incurred by the Mohawks in their support of the British during the Revolution; and his success created one more tie that bound the Indians to the cause of England. Arriving

[1] Stone's *Life of Joseph Brant* gives the best connected account of the intrigues and negotiations from the treaty of 1783 to 1790. It is to be read in connection with the correspondence in the Haldimand Papers.

in England in the December of 1785, Brant received a welcome such as that country ever accords to a foreign sovereign, no matter what his color or how limited his sovereignty. With many of the officers he was already acquainted; and king, queen, and prince, statesman and wit, men of fashion and ladies of quality, all gave him welcome. Nor did he prove an unworthy representative of the New World. Declining to kiss the hand of George III, he professed entire willingness to perform such homage to the queen. When at a masked-ball a Turkish diplomat attempted to feel of the texture of his painted nose, supposed to be false, Brant indulged his native Indian humor by giving vent to a war-whoop that curdled the blood in the dancers, and sent them fleeing before the gleaming tomahawk of whose prowess they had heard with horror. On his coming he was met by De Peyster; he was dined by Burke, Fox, and Sheridan; the Prince of Wales showed him the sights of the town; Haldimand did him honor in army circles; and Sir Guy Carleton, then on the point of returning to America, did not fail to cultivate the lion of the town, whose roar he was afterwards to invoke for purposes of state. Returning to this country in December, 1786, Brant called the chiefs of the Six Nations and of the western and Lake Indians to a council.

The first ice of winter was sealing the channels between the islands at the mouth of the Detroit, when, in the November of 1786, the United Indian Nations gathered for their first confederate council in the Huron village near the head of Lake Erie. The purpose of this most dignified and important assembly was to prepare an address to their " brethren of the thirteen United States of America." With absolute directness this state paper declares the disappointment of the Indians after having experienced three years of the peace made between the United States and England. They had hoped for a lasting friendship between themselves and their "oldest brethren." They had received two agreeable messages from the United States, and at the same time had been asked by the king whose war they had been engaged in to remain quiet. They now gave notice that in future no council would be held legal unless the entire confederacy gave its assent; and that they were ready to make a lasting treaty of peace, and for that purpose would meet the American commissioners in the spring, "to bury in oblivion the mischief that had happened, and speak to each other in the style of friendship." There was one condition. "Brothers," says the message, "we again request of you, in the most earnest manner, that you will order your surveyors and others that march on lands, to cease from crossing the Ohio until we shall have spoken to you; because the mischief that has recently happened has always originated in that quarter. We shall likewise preserve our people from going over until that time."

Such was the ultimatum. Then came this warning: "Brothers, it will be owing to your arrogance if this laudable plan which we so earnestly wish for is not carried into execution. In that case the result will be very precarious, and if fresh ruptures ensue, we are sure we will be able to exculpate ourselves, and most assuredly, with our united force, be obliged to defend those immunities which the Great Spirit has been pleased to give us; and if we should then be reduced to misfortune, the world will pity us, when they think of the amicable proposals we made to prevent the effusion of unnecessary blood."[1]

[1] Indian Speech to the Congress of the United States, *Michigan*

That the speech to Congress was the work of Captain Brant is made apparent by his remarks made six days later at McKee's council, held at the same Huron village.[1] With the same plain speaking he had used towards the Americans, Brant now told the king's representative that it was the devotion of the Indians to the cause of the British that had made the Americans their enemies; and that while the British were enjoying the blessings of peace the Indians were still involved in hostilities. Therefore, Brant, on behalf of the confederacy, demanded from "the great representative of the king, now arrived on this continent," an answer to the question whether the English would support them in their demand for the Ohio as a boundary. In this manner the vital question was referred to Lord Dorchester.[2]

While he was in England, Brant had attempted to learn from the Colonial Secretary, Lord Sidney, whether Great Britain would support the Indians in making war on the Americans. Lord Sidney evaded the question; and his example was followed by Sir Guy Carleton (now Lord Dorchester), who had arrived at Quebec, on November 23, 1786, to resume the office of Governor of Canada. Major Matthews, on his way to take command at De-

Pioneer and Historical Collections, vol. xi., p. 467. The tribes represented were the Six Nations, Hurons, Delawares, Shawanese, Ottawas, Chippewas, Pottawatomies, Cherokees, Wabash Confederates, and Miamis.

[1] On July 23, 1787, General Knox acknowledged the receipt of Brant's letter from Huron Town, dated December 18, 1786, the communication having been delayed by the Shawanese. Knox assured Brant that the matter had been laid before Congress, "who have taken the same into consideration, and will soon come to some decision thereon, which will be communicated to the superintendent (General Butler) in order to be transmitted to you."

[2] McKee's Report, *Michigan Pioneer and Historical Collections*, vol xi., p. 471.

GENERAL SIR GUY CARLETON

troit, wrote to Brant from Niagara that the British, so far from intending to surrender the posts, were, on the contrary, strengthening them, and would hold them so long as the Indians were ready to prevent the Americans from coming against them. Lord Dorchester, wrote the major, was sorry that the Six Nations had promised to aid the Americans to make roads for the purpose of approaching Niagara. "In future his lordship wishes them (the Indians) to act as is best for their interest; he cannot begin a war with the Americans because some of their people encroach and make depredations upon parts of the Indian country; but they must see it is his lordship's intention to defend the posts; and while these are preserved, the Indians must find great security therefrom."[1]

Nothing could have been more satisfactory to the English commanders in America than was the result of Brant's efforts to unite the Indians in a demand for the Ohio boundary. Sir John Johnson, the British superintendent of Indian affairs, expressed this satisfaction in a letter to Brant, in the course of which this significant passage occurs: "Do not suffer an idea to hold a place in your mind that it will be for your interests to sit still and see the Americans attempt the posts. It is for your sakes chiefly, if not entirely, that we hold them. If you become indifferent about them, they may perhaps be given up; what security would you then have? You would be left at the mercy of a people whose blood calls for revenge; whereas by supporting them you encourage us to hold them, and encourage the new settlements, already considerable, and every day increasing by num-

[1] Stone's *Life of Joseph Brant*, vol. ii., p. 270. Matthews to Brant, May 29, 1787.

bers coming in, who find they can't live in the states. Many thousands are preparing to come in. This increase of his Majesty's subjects will serve as a protection for you, should the subjects of the states, by endeavoring to make further encroachments on you, disturb your quiet."[1]

Had the British surrendered the Northwestern posts, as provided in the treaty of 1783, the Indians would have been dependent on the Americans for those markets which were the surest means of obtaining and maintaining peace. By holding the posts in order to protect the fur-trade and to secure the claims of the loyalists, England forced the United States into Indian wars that cost the lives of thousands of our people and long held back immigration and settlement.

Lord Dorchester found additional reasons[2] for the retention of the posts in the fact that the United States as a nation was still an experiment; that there were many elements of disunion, and great differences of opinion as to whether the new government should be a monarchy or a republic; and that France and Spain were anxiously watching every opportunity to strengthen and increase their influence and territory in North America. To be sure, the region west of the Mississippi nominally belonged to Spain; but in view of relations subsisting between the two nations, the secret transfer that was brought about in 1762 might well be reversed at any time without warning; and as a matter of fact Louisiana was transferred back to France in 1800.

[1] Stone's *Life of Joseph Brant*, vol. ii., p. 268.

[2] Dorchester to Sidney, January 16, April 10, 1787; October 14, 1788; and April 11, 1789.—*Canadian Archives*, 1890. Under the head of "Relations with the United States after the Peace of 1783," Mr. Brymner has grouped these letters.

In this critical situation Lord Dorchester's position was most delicate. The creation of a new nation out of the thirteen British colonies on the Atlantic had left the remaining English possessions in America but little better than a string of isolated towns and posts loosely held together by one industry—the fur-trade.[1] The great majority of the people were French, without ambition or initiative. Indeed, they seemed almost as much a part of their lands as were the very houses. Even the traders and wood-rangers kept the narrowest of paths as they performed their regular service for the great company which employed them. Out of these unpromising elements Lord Dorchester succeeded in laying the broad and deep foundations on which the Canada of to-day has been built. As Champlain was the father of New France, so Lord Dorchester became the father of Canada. A great administrator, his character is sullied by no act of personal greed; and although he lived during the most openly corrupt period of British politics, the utmost that can be said against him is that a slender purse and a large family led him to strive for continuance in official position. Trained to war, he won distinction by bestowing on a discordant and unreconciled people the blessings of peace and tranquillity.[2] To the loyalists, driven from the United

[1] The best discussion of the question of the retention of the posts is to be found in Professor Andrew C. McLaughlin's paper on "Western Posts and British Debts," printed in the *American Historical Society Report* for 1894; and subsequently in the New England *Yale Review*.

[2] Lord Dorchester, the third son of General Sir Guy Carleton, of Newry, County Down, Ireland, was born in 1724; he served in Flanders, and was wounded at the siege of Bergen-op-Zoom. He was quartermaster-general in Wolfe's expedition against Quebec, and was wounded twice in the operations about that city. A fourth wound was received at the capture of Havana. His success in driving the

States because of their fealty to the crown of England, he extended every opportunity to make settlements within the broad regions that still remained of England's transatlantic empire. His efforts on behalf of Canada often resulted to the detriment of the United States; for it was inevitable that the violent feelings engendered by the Revolution, and especially by the treatment — justly, as we believe — accorded to the Tories, should continue to find expression whenever provocation offered.

Even while advocating the passage of the Quebec act before the House of Commons, he was frank to state that the Indians regarded the country between the Ohio and the Great Lakes as their own territory, within which no European monarch had rights. It is not strange, therefore, to find him willing to give countenance to this position, when it was maintained in opposition to the United States by Brant and the Indians over whom that powerful chief had influence. This theory of Indian monarchy had been asserted against the French and English at the outbreak of the French and Indian War, and against the English and Americans at the beginning of the Revolution; but it never was acquiesced in by the whites. Indeed, the Indians themselves had repudiated it repeatedly by placing them-

Americans from Canada should have been rewarded by the command of the expedition led by Burgoyne. It is fortunate for our country that a less capable man was selected. As governor of Canada he won the reputation of "having the cleanest hands of any person ever intrusted with public money." As commander of the British forces in New York he managed the withdrawal of the English troops. He was one of Wolfe's executors and legatees. In 1786 he was raised to the peerage as Baron Dorchester. For a sketch of his life, see *The English Political Magazine* for 1782, p. 351; and Kingsford's *History of Canada*, vol. v., p. 191.

selves under the protection of France or of England. Moreover, the treaty of 1783 left Dorchester no right to interfere beyond the line of the British possessions; although as a practical ruler he doubtless felt himself bound to take advantage of any circumstance that would aid England to regain the Western country, in case the uneasy settlers should incline to seek an alliance with Spain in order to gain an outlet for their products.

In all the intrigues of those most troublous times, Quebec was the headquarters for British influence, as New Orleans was for Spanish and French designs on the new nation. To aid Lord Dorchester to understand the problem with which he had to deal, an emissary who had proved himself valuable during the Revolution was sent from England, and, at the munificent salary of £200 a year, was despatched to the Northwestern country[1] as a spy. The observations of this "cool and temperate man" throw a strong light on the manner in which the beginnings of our national existence were regarded in British ministerial circles, and prove conclusively that England acted deliberately in supporting the Indians while they carried on the warfare against the armies of the United States. To the English the Indians were part and parcel of the fur-trade, which was to be maintained at every cost. Therefore it was essential that the savages be protected in their hunting-grounds. Dorchester apprehended that the United States meant to take the posts by force, and, however indifferent England might be about retaining them, he was prepared to repel war by war.[2]

[1] Brymner identifies this agent as Major George Beckwith, but the facts concerning him are obscure.—See *Canadian Archives,* 1890, p. xi. *et seq.*

[2] Dorchester to Sir John Johnson, December 11, 1786; Dorchester to Sidney, January 16, 1787.—See *Canadian Archives,* 1890.

Making his headquarters at Detroit, the British emissary put himself in communication with Pittsburg and Kentucky, and made systematic reports to Dorchester. The emigration to Kentucky and the Ohio regions he declared to exceed the bounds of credibility. "The enterprising people of New England, checked in their commercial pursuits, turn with wonderful facility to this tempting though remote country, and without being deterred by the danger, or prevented by the difficulty of finding means of subsistence for themselves and families until they can form an establishment in those distant settlements, they travel in hordes to the Southwest, threatening the weak Spanish provinces with early hostilities." As a preliminary step, Colonel Sherman, of Connecticut, was preparing to cross the Mississippi with five hundred armed men, and to establish a post at the mouth of the Missouri. The Kentuckians, too, were bent on forcing the free navigation of the Mississippi, and plans were maturing to reach the Michilimackinac fur-trade along the water-route discovered by Joliet and Marquette more than a century before. All these schemes were being prosecuted without regard to Congress, a body as yet too feeble to exercise authority over any part of the Western country.[1]

The situation in the Western country had indeed become critical for the United States. Separated from the Atlantic seaboard by a difficult range of mountains,

[1] In October, 1786, Clark led a feeble expedition against the Indians in the neighborhood of Vincennes, the people of which place had written to him that they considered themselves British subjects. Clark placed a garrison in fort; but his own habits had now become so bad that he had no control over his men, and both Virginia and Congress were compelled to repudiate his action in seizing property belonging to a Spanish trader.—See English's *Life of George Rogers Clark*, vol. ii., p. 796.

the Northwest was still in possession of numerous bands of hostile Indians fed and clothed by Great Britain, and thus enabled to carry on a warfare of extermination against the settlers. On the north the outlet for the fur-trade was by the St. Lawrence. On the west the Kentucky and Illinois countries must find an outlet for their trade by way of the Mississippi, and the navigation of that stream was in control of the Spanish, who were using this advantage to alienate the Western people from their remote kinsmen east of the mountains. No one appreciated this situation better than President Washington, who was himself a large owner of Ohio lands, but whose concern for the expansion and strengthening of the nation was of such a character as to make his personal interests not a bias but simply a means of knowledge. More closely than any other man then living he had been identified with the beginnings of Western conquest. As a young man he had played a large part in wresting the Northwest from France; and now in his maturer years he was to direct those forces which were forever to bind that territory to the United States.

Five years before the outbreak of the Revolution, Washington had urged upon Governor Thomas Johnson of Maryland the necessity of an enlarged plan for reaching the Ohio, "as a means of becoming the channel of conveyance of the extensive and valuable trade of a rising empire."[1] Before resigning his commission as commander-in-chief, Washington had made a tour of western New York, in company with Governor Clinton, and the two made a joint purchase of six thousand acres; for he

[1] House of Representatives Report No. 228, Nineteenth Congress, first session.

rightly apprehended that "the Yorkers will delay no time to remove every obstacle in the way of other communication, so soon as the posts of Oswego and Niagara are surrendered."[1] In 1784, Washington spent a month riding through the Ohio country to examine the routes for penetrating the mountains; and it was on this trip that he first met Albert Gallatin, who has left on record a description of the scene. The great soldier seated at the head of a rough table in a frontier cabin, called one after another from the crowd of frontiersmen and examined each at length as to trails and gaps, pursuing the question long after the nimble-minded young Swiss had decided on which side the weight of testimony lay. The extreme patience and care that the general took to get to the bottom of the matter before allowing his own mind to reach a decision greatly impressed Gallatin with the force and strength of Washington's character.[2] Returning from this horseback journey of nearly seven hundred miles, Washington laid before Governor Harrison of Virginia a great scheme for bringing the trade from Detroit and the West to tide-water by way of Fort Pitt and the Potomac, a route more than a hundred miles shorter than that by way of Philadelphia, and three hundred miles shorter than the Albany route.[3] Calling Harrison's attention to the fact that "the flanks and rear" of the United States were possessed by Spain and England, he argued that unless shorter and easier channels were made for the trade of the West, "the stream of commerce will glide gently down the Mississippi"; while by opening these new communications, all parts of the Union would be cemented together by common in-

[1] Washington's will.

[2] Henry Adams's *Life of Albert Gallatin*, p. 57.

[3] Pickell's *History of the Potomac Company*, p. 174.

GEORGE WASHINGTON

(After a painting by Gilbert Stuart.)

terests. By opening the eastern water communications to the Ohio, and by opening the Ohio to Lake Erie, was Washington's method to "draw not only the produce of the Western settlers, but also the peltry and fur-trade of the lakes to our posts: thus adding an immense increase to our exports, and binding these people to us by a chain which can never be broken."[1] In 1785 Washington became the first president of the Potomac Company, but when he was elected President of the United States, in 1788, he turned the office over to Thomas Johnson. The costly national road to Wheeling, and the Chesapeake and Ohio Canal, whose crumbling masonry and still used but almost overgrown towpaths are now more picturesque than useful, were the direct results of Washington's enthusiasm for Western communications; while the Baltimore and Ohio Railroad trains now thunder along the Cumberland turnpike from Pittsburg to the Potomac.[2]

As at the end of the old plays the actors one by one step to the foot-lights to make their parting speeches, so we take leave of the more prominent British players in the drama of the Revolution in the Northwest. On June 23, 1782, the *Dædalus* arrived

[1] Marshall's *Life of Washington*, vol. v., p. 14.

[2] For Washington's connection with Western lands and the Potomac Company, see the very suggestive papers by Herbert B. Adams, Ph.D., in Johns Hopkins "Historical Studies," third series. Dr. Adams figures that Washington owned in 1799 about 70,000 acres of land which he had originally bought for speculative purposes; his lands were valued at $488,339; and in the Northwest Territory on the Little Miami he held 3051 acres valued at $5 an acre. The father of his country was at once a man of the highest personal and political probity; and yet he was a speculator! As Henry Adams points out (*Life of Albert Gallatin*, p. 53), all America was engaged in land speculations. Robert Morris closed his public career a bankrupt and in prison as the result of his speculations in lands; and no one seems to have made a fortune by such investments.

from England bearing the news that Henry Hamilton had been appointed lieutenant-governor at Quebec, and that his fellow-prisoner Jehu Hay had been commissioned to the same office at Detroit.

Hamilton's sufferings in his Virginia "dungeon" excited a great amount of sympathy for him, both in England and among the Tories in America.[1] The position in which he now found himself, however, so far exceeded his abilities that, after scarcely more than a year at Quebec, the government notified him that there was no further need of his services. His friends succeeded, to use his phrase, "in forging for him on the public anvil" an appointment as governor of Bermuda, where his name is still perpetuated in the capital city of those islands. Tradition in Bermuda has it that he was a homely man, of quiet, unpretentious habits, not given to display or ostentation.[2] After four years of service

[1] In Winthrop Sargent's *Loyalist Poetry of the Revolution*, p. 50, is this stanza on Jefferson and Hamilton:

> "Virginia caitiff! Jeff by name,
> Perhaps of Jeffries sprung, of rotten fame;
> His savage letter all belief exceeds,
> And Congress glories in his brutal deeds.
> In the dark dungeon Hamilton is thrown;
> The virtuous hero there disdains to groan!
> There, with his brave companions, faithful friends,
> Th' approaching hour in silence he attends,
> When, with his council, shall the wretch expire
> Or by the British or celestial fire!"

Hamilton was exchanged for Captain James Willing, of Philadelphia, a younger brother of Bouquet's friend and correspondent. See *ante*, p. 156.

[2] For this bit of tradition, extant in the family of Chief-justice Leonard, of Hamilton, Bermuda, as well as for copies of Hamilton's letters and the records of his governorship, I am under obligations to Mrs. Mary K. Bosworth Smith. In a letter to Lieutenant Jacob

there he was transferred to the governorship of Dominica, where in 1796 he died, full of years, and not without public esteem and honors.[1]

Although Lord Shelburne professed that in appointing Hamilton and Hay he had acted entirely on Haldimand's recommendations, as he himself was unacquainted with either of the gentlemen, Haldimand was not willing to see so faithful and efficient an officer as De Peyster placed under a half-pay lieutenant like Hay. Accordingly the commander-in-chief detained Detroit's new lieutenant-governor until he secured De Peyster's promotion and transfer to Niagara. Hay reached his new station in the July of 1784, much broken in health and spirits; and after a year of peaceful occupation of the governor's palace, on August 2, 1785, he was carried thence to his grave.[2] In September, 1785, De Peyster returned to England with his regiment, and eventually settled in Scotland, in the town of Dumfries, relinquishing the pursuit of arms for the gentler occupations of domestic life. Yet his martial vigor only slumbered; for when the Napoleonic wars made it necessary to embody the militia to defend Great Britain's coasts, Colonel de Peyster became commander of the Dumfries Gentlemen Volunteers, which organi-

Schieffelin, of New York (the original of which was presented to the Hamilton Library in 1897 by a son of Henry Hamilton Schieffelin), the governor says: "Everything at this place goes on very harmoniously; and tho' I had a strong desire to have remained in Canada, and had many valuable acquaintances there whom I highly esteem, yet I think my lot is cast in a fair ground, and am satisfied." Hamilton was the fourth son of Gustavus Frederick, seventh Viscount Boyne.

[1] There is a short obituary notice in *The Gentleman's Magazine* for 1796.

[2] Ford's Moravian Settlements at Mt. Clemens, *Michigan Pioneer and Historical Collections*, vol. x., p. 107.

zation he drilled with the thoroughness of a martinet. The commander, however, saw but one contest. In the columns of the local paper he essayed a combat in verse, only to be badly worsted by one of his own soldiers—Robert Burns.[1] In November, 1822, De Peyster mounted his great charger for the last time, riding about the country with the vigor of middle age; on the 26th of that month an accident brought him to his death, at the ripe age of eighty-six years.[2] In November, 1784, Haldimand sailed from Quebec for London, where he was well received by Lord Sidney, and was presented to the king and queen; with all due pomp and circumstance he was made a Knight of the Bath;[3] and as Sir Frederick Haldimand he died in May, 1791, at his birthplace, Yverdon, Switzerland, leaving an ample fortune to his nephew and his nieces.[4] On March 17, 1785, Pat Sinclair was released from Newgate Prison, in London, on payment of the Mackinac bills protested by Haldimand.[5]

[1] See Burns's *Poem on Life*, addressed to Colonel De Peyster.

[2] *De Peyster's Miscellanies*, p. clxxi.

[3] Haldimand's Diary, *Canadian Archives*, 1889, p. 145.

[4] *Canadian Archives*, 1889, p. xxv.

[5] Haldimand's Diary, *Canadian Archives*, 1889, p. 147; Sinclair to Haldimand, *Michigan Pioneer and Historical Collections*, vol. xi., p. 456.

CHAPTER IX

THE NORTHWEST TERRITORY

SILAS DEANE of Connecticut, sent to France as one of the agents of the Continental Congress in order to obtain supplies for the army and loans for the United States, not meeting with all the success that his principal desired, repeatedly suggested that the Western lands be sold to obtain the money that came so grudgingly without real-estate collateral. He had no doubt that he could place a very considerable quantity of these lands among the Germans, at a fair price; and apparently it never occurred to him that the lands he was so ready to sell were already occupied by savage bands of Indians; or that beyond this wide belt of hunting-grounds were forts and garrisons so commanding as to make an attack on them not less hazardous than was England's task of crossing the Atlantic to fight the colonists along the sea-coast.

In Congress the question of jurisdiction over the lands of the Northwest did not receive attention until, on October 15, 1777, Maryland proposed that "the United States in Congress assembled shall have the sole and exclusive right and power to ascertain and fix the western boundary of such states as claim to the Mississippi or South Sea, and lay out the land beyond the boundary, so ascertained, into separate and independent states, from time to time, as the numbers and circumstances of the people may require."[1] Squeezed in between the states of Pennsylvania and Virginia (each quarrelling with the other about their respective territories while still reaching farther and farther into the West,) Maryland was in a position to see and to feel how passion for expansion might easily lead to other Dunmore wars. So far were the other states from agreeing with their sister, that Congress even took occasion to provide in the articles of Confederation that no state should be deprived of territory for the benefit of the United States, although the three smaller states desired to be allowed to share in the proceeds of the sales of Western lands.[2]

In December, 1779, while George Rogers Clark, at the head of Virginia troops paid from the Virginia treasury, was conquering the Illinois country, Maryland was forbidding her delegates to ratify the Articles of Confederation before the several states should waive their claims to territory beyond the mountains; for, said Maryland, Virginia might sell the territory thus gained, and by making her own taxes low might quickly drain Maryland, where taxes would be higher and land less cheap.[3] Besides, a country "wrested from the common enemy by the blood and treasure of the thirteen states should be considered as a common property, subject to be parcelled out by Congress into free, convenient, and

[1] Journals of Congress, from 1774 to 1788, vol. ii., p. 290.

[2] Donaldson's *Public Domain*, p. 61.

[3] In his exhaustive treatment of the subject of the Northwestern cessions, Dr. B. A. Hinsdale, of Michigan University, adverts to the fact that "the fallacy that there is value in wild lands appears to have been universally accepted in Congress and the states one hundred years ago. . . . In the long run the national government has not found the public domain a source of revenue."—*The Old Northwest* (New York, 1899), pp.197 *et seq.*

independent governments." In the same month of May, 1779, that Maryland was pressing on Congress the restrictions she sought to impose on Virginia, the latter state established a land-office to obtain the money necessary to enable her to pay Clark's expenses and to support his army on its way to Detroit, a self-imposed task indeed, so far as Virginia was concerned, but one that served Maryland well by protecting her frontiers from Indian raids. In October of the same year, while the British-paid Indians were watching every opportunity to wipe out the slender Virginia settlements in the Kentucky region, and to recover the valley of the Wabash, Maryland secured the passage by Congress of a resolution recommending that Virginia close her land-office. Maryland absolutely refused to join the Confederation until the land matter was settled; and during the Revolution she stood technically as an ally and not as a member of the United States. Virginia entered a vigorous remonstrance to this selfish policy of her neighbor, at the same time stating her readiness to listen to any just and reasonable propositions for removing the *ostensible* causes for delaying the ratification of the Confederation.[1]

At this juncture the New York Assembly, acting under the advice of General Schuyler, then one of the delegates in Congress from that state, passed an act authorizing either an unreserved or a limited cession of

[1] "Maryland's Influence upon Land Cessions to the United States," by Herbert B. Adams, Ph.D., Johns Hopkins University Studies in Historical and Political Science, third series. This monograph is a most painstaking presentation of a novel subject. The facts are as Professor Adams states them; in his admiration for the results obtained by Maryland's stubbornness, however, he seems to me to do an unjustice both to Virginia's sacrifices and also to her graceful action in ceding her territories to the United States.

her Western lands, according as her delegates should deem it expedient. The western and northern boundaries of New York had been fixed in the Quebec act by her London agent, Edmund Burke, who had the bill amended on the floor of the House of Commons; and General Schuyler had ascertained that there was no purpose in Congress to curtail these extensive limits. What New York gave up, therefore, was a claim to the Ohio country based on ancient and unacknowledged conquests by her former allies, the Iroquois. Without impugning New York's magnanimity in making a surrender of lands that Virginia had just conquered, the fact remains that she had nothing to give: this nothing she gave so gracefully as to win much credit, and to exert no little influence on other states similarly circumstanced, and also on Congress. To that body, on September 6, 1780, report was made on the Maryland Instructions, the Virginia Remonstrance, and the New York Cession; and in that report the several States were urged to remove the embarrassments respecting the Western country by a liberal surrender of a portion of their territorial claims, and thus "establish the Federal Union on a fixed and permanent basis, and on principles acceptable to all its respective members." Connecticut, on September 10th, offered to give up her title to the lands on the condition that she retain jurisdiction over the territory, a principle for which Alexander Hamilton contended, possibly because he objected to the formation of new states, especially on the frontiers. A month later Congress provided for the sale of such lands as should be ceded, and also declared that separate governments would be erected west of the mountains, as proposed by Franklin in 1755. Moreover, the necessary and reasonable expenses incurred by any particulár state in subduing any British posts, or in maintaining forts or garrisons within or for the defence, or in acquiring any part of the territory that might be ceded or relinquished to the United States, would be reimbursed. Thus a way was opened for Virginia to yield her conquered lands without great financial loss; and her services found Congressional acknowledgment.

Virginia, the only one of the states which had an equitable title, now came forward, and on January 2, 1781, offered to cede her lands northwest of the Ohio, on condition that her possession of the lands south of that river be guaranteed, and that the claims of other parties to the Northwestern lands be annulled. These conditions were declared by Congress to be incompatible with the honor, interests, and peace of the United States. Maryland, perceiving that her point against territorial acquisitions by individual states was now virtually made, on March 1, 1781, joined the Union. The United States being now an accomplished fact, suitable announcement was made to the respective states, to foreign courts, and to the army.

A committee of Congress, thinking to overreach both Virginia and Connecticut, reported in favor of accepting New York's cession, because by so doing the United States would acquire all the lands on both sides of the Ohio, on the theory that the territories of the Six Nations and their allies extended from Lake Erie to the Alleghanies and westward to the Mississippi.[1] This theory was not true in fact even at the outbreak of the French and Indian War; much less was it true in 1782.[2]

[1] Hinsdale says that New York's claim appears the most flimsy of all the Western claims. The original report in manuscript is preserved in the Department of State.

[2] Johnson *vs.* McIntosh, 8 Wheaton.

Moreover, nations do not derive jurisdiction from savages, but in spite of them.[1] Congress, as is often the case, grasped both horns of the dilemma, by accepting New York's unqualified cession, and then asking Virginia to remove the restrictions from her offer. On October 20, 1783, Virginia, ever loyal to the establishment of the new nation, authorized her delegates to make the cession. As governor, Jefferson had written to Washington that the state would give up her claims for the sake of harmony; and as a delegate in Congress he, with his colleagues, Samuel Hardy, Arthur Lee, and James Monroe, completed the transfer. Virginia, however, made two reservations of territory—the first of 150,000 acres promised to George Rogers Clark and his officers and soldiers; the second a tract between the Scioto and Little Miami, to be used as bounty lands for the Virginia soldiers of the Revolutionary War.

Ten years from the date of the battle of Lexington, Massachusetts ceded her Western lands, embracing the lower portions of Michigan and Wisconsin. At the time these lands were absolutely under British control, although nominally they were within the boundaries of the United States. Robert Rogers, the New Hampshire Ranger, had received the surrender of Detroit from the French, and Jonathan Carver, a native of Connecticut, had once been an unsuccessful trader at Mackinac; but the only connection that any resident of

[1] The report also held that the proclamation of 1763, which fixed Virginia's boundary at the mountains, and the Walpole grant were still effective. This was a flagrant case of injustice; for Congress itself had repudiated the boundaries of 1763, and the Walpole grant was clearly ineffective when hostilities broke out. The Illinois and Wabash grants made to Lord Dunmore and his friends were brushed aside by the committee, and were afterwards declared invalid by the supreme court.—Johnson *vs.* McIntosh, 8 Wheaton.

Massachusetts had with this territory was the vain demand made by Colonel William Hull for the surrender of the posts, as has been related. Connecticut, whose claims were equally shadowy with those of Massachusetts, secured the best bargain of any of the yielding states, by retaining in the Connecticut Reserve a tract of three and a quarter million acres, over which she claimed jurisdiction till 1800.[1] Reserving five hundred thousand acres for those of her citizens who had suffered from the wanton and piratical raids of the British on her coasts during the Revolution, Connecticut sold the remainder for $1,200,000, and devoted the money to schools and colleges.

The moral of the land cessions to the nation would seem to be this: Maryland, by standing out for the national ownership and control of the Northwest, brought about a result of tremendous benefit to the United States; New York, by giving up early what she never had, won for herself great credit; Virginia generously made a distinct sacrifice of dearly conquered territory over which she was actually exercising jurisdiction; Massachusetts quit-claimed a title she could not defend; and Connecticut gained an empire to which she was not entitled, but which she put to the very best of uses.[2] Moreover, from the very nature of things, Virginia could not have held control over far-distant

[1] For a succinct statement as to the rise of the Northwest Territory and Western Reserve, see James A. Garfield's Address before the Historical Society of Geauga County, Ohio, September 16, 1873.—"Old South Leaflets," General Series, No. 42.

[2] A brief but of course perspicuous statement of the facts relative to the land cessions, by Justin Winsor and Professor Channing, is given at the beginning of their article on "Territorial Acquisitions and Divisions," in the appendix to vol. vii. of the *Narrative and Critical History of America.*

territory, any more than Henderson & Company could have continued to rule Transylvania as a proprietary colony; or than Connecticut could have held the Western Reserve after it became populated. Franklin had foreseen the necessity of new jurisdictions beyond the mountains, even before the French war broke out; and no power could have thwarted this manifest destiny.

How the French discovered and possessed the Northwest; how England wrested New France from her ancient enemy; how George Rogers Clark made partial conquest of the territory for Virginia; how the treaty-makers won extensive boundaries for the new nation; and how at the instance of Maryland the claimant state, and especially Virginia, by "the most marked instance of a large and generous self-denial," made cession of their lands to the general government—all these things have been told. It now remains to discover how this vast empire, larger than any country in Europe save Russia, was to be governed and peopled. For the most part this immense region was an unbroken wilderness; but tales of the richness of its alluvial soil, and its accessibility by means of noble streams and great inland seas, had caught the ear of people made restless by the possibilities opened up by a magnificent peace attained after a prolonged and wasting war.

On the very day that Virginia made cession of her claims, Thomas Jefferson came forward in Congress with a plan for the government of the ceded territory. There were still three obstacles in the way of exercising jurisdiction: first, there were controversies with Spain as to the western boundary and the navigation of the Mississippi; second, England still held military possession of the frontiers; and third, the ceded territory was occupied by numerous hostile tribes of Indians. With the exception of the reservations made as to territory by Virginia, and as to both territory and jurisdiction by Connecticut, the United States succeeded alike to the jurisdiction and to the title to unoccupied lands. That is to say, the power to grant vacant lands within the ceded territory, a power that had formerly resided in the crown, or the proprietary governments created by the crown, now passed, by reason of the state cessions, into the possession of the Government of the United States; and to the general government belonged the exclusive right to extinguish, either by purchase or by conquest, the Indian title of occupancy. It is important to remember this fact, as it is the key to the otherwise perplexing subject of Northwestern affairs.[1]

Since June 15, 1779, Virginia had been exercising jurisdiction over so much of the Northwest as was included in Clark's conquest. John Todd, Virginia's commandant of the County of Illinois, appointed officers and organized courts both at Kaskaskia and at Vincennes. Todd and the officers under him made their first business not justice but land-titles; and had the grants made by these industrious officials been held valid, probably there would have been little land left for disposal by the United States. Called to Virginia by land matters, Todd was returning through Kentucky when, on August 18, 1782, he was killed at the battle of Blue Licks. The government which he set in motion answered the demands of the sparse settlements,

[1] In Johnson *vs.* McIntosh, 8 Wheaton, Chief-justice Marshall makes luminous exposition of the title to unoccupied lands. He never questioned Virginia's title to all the lands included within her charter-lines from the Atlantic first to the "South Sea," and, after the treaty of 1763, to the Mississippi; nor did he think that Virginia was yielding but a nominal title when she made cession to the United States.

and for five years the French inhabitants governed themselves according to the "custom of Paris," which had come to mean that when disputes arose, the priest, the commandant, or some one in authority was appealed to for a decision.[1]

Two great principles were embodied in the ordinance reported by Mr. Jefferson: first, the Northwest Territory was forever to remain a part of the United States; and second, that vast region, to be divided into sovereign states, was to be dedicated to freedom. Thomas Jefferson, at the age of forty-one years, had in his mind no thought of the day when he should inspire the Virginia and Kentucky resolutions; at that time his one fear was lest, beguiled by England or Spain, the new region should break away from the Union and either set up a government of its own, or else cast its lot with the

[1] John Reynolds, in his *Pioneer History of Illinois*, says that after the departure of Todd, "there was a mixture of civil and British law in the country, administered by the courts, down to 1790, when Governor St. Clair came to Kaskaskia and set in motion the territorial government under the ordinance or act of Congress of 1787." At Vincennes, Todd appointed M. Legrass "lieutenant-governor"; but in 1787 General Harmar, as civil governor and superintendent of Indian affairs, took charge of matters, either personally or by deputy.—Law's *Vincennes*, p. 41.

David Todd and Hannah Owen, his wife, were Scotch-Irish immigrants who settled in Lancaster County, Pennsylvania, before the Revolution. Their three sons, John, Robert and Levi, emigrated to Fayette County, Kentucky, in 1778. Levi was with Clark at Kaskaskia, and took charge of the abusive Rocheblave, on that prisoner's journey to Virginia. His granddaughter became Mrs. Abraham Lincoln.

At Vincennes, the judges, F. Bosseron, L. E. Deline, Pierre Gamelin, and Pierre Querez (who used his mark by way of expedition—or illiteracy), took turns in leaving the bench so that their fellows could make grants of land to one another. One of these grants was ten miles square.—See Law's *Vincennes*, chapter on Public Lands.

nations through whose territories the products of the rich and fertile country must find an outlet. Again, Jefferson was always a consistent opponent of slavery, and by providing that throughout the Northwest human bondage should cease after the year 1800, he hoped and expected that within the time named what little slavery then existed in the new region would be wiped out.[1] Having laid down two such broad principles, Mr. Jefferson might be permitted to indulge his well-known taste for minute details and for classical appellations by providing the exact boundaries for seven States, to be known as Sylvania, Michigania, Chersonesus, Assenisipia, Metropotamia, Polypotamia, and Polisipia.[2] Congress, however, recommitted the report, and, when it was again submitted, the provision for the names of the states was stricken out. Then Congress struck out the provision relating to slavery, and the ordinance of April 23, 1784, became a law. As supplementary to the ordinance, Congress, also, at the instance of Jefferson, provided

[1] The first proposition for the exclusion of slavery from the Ohio country is to be found in a petition presented to Congress by certain disbanded New England soldiers, who in 1783 asked for a grant of lands in that region. The author of the petition probably was Timothy Pickering. Jefferson's proposition would have excluded slavery from Kentucky, whither the Virginians with their slaves were already settling in great numbers; and for this reason the slavery clause met successful opposition. The State Department manuscripts relating to the Northwest Territory show by the amendments written on the broadside reports how carefully the later ordinances were confined to "the country northwest of the river Ohio."

[2] Washington's plan for the Northwest was first to secure the Indian titles to a portion of the territory and erect a state that would include the region from Pennsylvania to the mouth of the Great Miami, and stretching northward to include Detroit. But for the necessity of including Detroit, he would have preferred smaller boundaries, as less likely to meet Indian opposition.—See Sparks's *Washington*, vol. viii. p. 483.

for a system of government surveys, by which the lands were to be divided into townships six miles square; and also provided that the surveyed lands should be the first to be offered for sale. Under this rectangular system, the whole Western country has been regularly laid off; the old "tomahawk rights" found no place; and as a consequence there were no overlapping claims.[1]

The subject of slavery in the Northwest would not down. On March 16, 1785, Mr. King brought up the subject by a motion to refer to the committee of the whole House a proposition totally preventing slavery in the Northwest, and the motion prevailed, but there the matter rested.[2] During the first half of 1786, Mr. Monroe struggled with the question of a temporary government, but without accomplishing results. In September, however, a new committee, consisting of Mr. Johnson of Connecticut, Mr. Pinckney of South Carolina, Mr. Smith of New York, Mr. Dane of Massachusetts, and Mr. Henry of Maryland essayed the task, and on the 26th of April, 1787, reported "An ordinance for the government of the Western Territory." On the 10th of May this colorless measure was ordered to a third reading; but Congress, being dissatisfied, on July 9th referred it to a new committee, made up of Mr. Carrington of Virginia, Mr. Dane of Massachusetts, Mr. R. H. Lee of Virginia, Mr. Kean of South Carolina, and Mr. Smith

[1] As Jefferson reported the bill the townships were to be ten miles square. On motion of Mr. Grayson, of Virginia, supported by Mr. Monroe, the size was reduced to six miles square, and on May 20, 1785, the bill was passed.—See Thomas Donaldson's *Public Domain*, pp. 178, 197.

[2] This action on Mr. King's part was the result of a letter written to him by Timothy Pickering, who implored him to make one more effort for the exclusion of slavery, before the constitutions to be adopted by the new states should make such exclusion impossible.

of New York—a majority being new members. After a deliberation of forty-eight hours the committee brought in a radically new measure, which, after being debated and amended on June 12th, was passed by a unanimous vote on the 13th. The amendment adverted to was the provision prohibiting slavery, to which was attached a proviso permitting the reclamation of fugitive slaves. Mr. Dane of Massachusetts proposed the amendment, and it was agreed to with but one dissenting vote. On the same day, in the Constitutional Convention, a provision was agreed to giving the slave-owning states a representation in Congress based on the whole number of free persons (including those bound to service for a term of years, and excluding Indians not taxed) plus *three-fifths of all other persons.*

Four days covers the legislative history of the "immortal" Ordinance of 1787 for the government of the territory northwest of the Ohio—legislation comparable only to the Constitution of the United States, which was being written at the same time in a neighboring city. In his tremendous reply to Hayne, Daniel Webster doubted "whether one single law of any lawgiver, ancient or modern, had produced effects of more distinct, marked, and lasting character than the Ordinance of 1787." Senator Hoar, in his splendid tribute[1] to the founders of the Northwest, speaks of the ordinance as belonging with the Declaration of Independence and the Constitution—"one of the three title-deeds of American constitutional liberty." Judge Cooley, after a life spent under its beneficent influences, stamped it as "immortal for the grand results

[1] George F. Hoar's oration at the centennial of the founding of the Northwest at Marietta, Ohio, April 7, 1888 (Worcester, Massachusetts, 1895), p. 40.

which have followed from its adoption, not less than for the wisdom and far-seeing statesmanship that conceived and gave form to its provisions. No charter of government in the history of any people," continues the great jurist, "has so completely withstood the tests of time and experience; it had not a temporary adaptation to a particular emergency, but its principles were for all time, and worthy of acceptance under all circumstances. It has been the fitting model for all subsequent territorial government in America."[1]

This monumental compact between thirteen existing states, and five states yet to be born, provided for that freedom of religion without which Virginia's growth had been retarded; for the inviolability of contracts, a principle then being fought out in Shay's rebellion; for the fair and just treatment of the Indians, and the abolition of private wars against the savages; for the permanence in the Union of the States to be created within the new territory; for the absolute freedom of all their waters and portages; for the perpetual encouragement of schools and the means of education; and for the freedom of every person within the territory excepting fugitive slaves from the original states. Possibly to many of those who voted for the measure some of its provisions appeared to be "glittering generalities"; yet not even the slavery provision itself was of more substantial benefit to the Northwest than has been and still is the pregnant sentence: "Religion, morality, and knowledge being necessary to good government and the happiness of mankind, schools and the means of education shall forever be encouraged." Those twenty-four words were to the Northwest at once the charter

[1] Cooley's *Michigan*, p. 127.

and the endowment of that novel and wide-spread system of public education, beginning at the primary school and extending through the university and professional schools, which speedily created in the new West a body of educational institutions to take the place of the endowed academies and colleges of the East. For more than a century that phrase has been both the incentive of the friend of learning in urging and the justification of the penurious legislator in granting those appropriations from the public treasury by means of which the Northwest has provided herself with a well-educated body of citizens. Taking the ordinance in its entirety, it would seem as if the nation, wearied by its own struggles to obtain freedom from the laws and customs of the past, had determined that its children should step forth into the world free from their very birth.

Who shall trace the origin of the Ordinance of 1787? Like a tree, its roots were deep down in a free soil, and its leaves drank nourishment from an air filled with the makings of constitutions. Jefferson had planted, and Monroe and Rufus King had watered, the tender plant. The vital force, however, came from neither earth nor air; from neither the planting nor the nurture of the fathers of the republic. Up to the 6th day of July, 1787, the government of the Northwest had been almost purely an academic question; on that day it became the most tangible of all the measures before Congress. This marvellous change was wrought by Manasseh Cutler, a Massachusetts minister, who appeared in New York with a proposition to buy a million dollars' worth of Western lands. The coming of Cutler signified that both the men and the money were at hand to develop the Northwest, and that the time had come to legislate to meet not a theory but a condition. The undertaking had been long in preparation, and the men behind it were of proved ability and worth.[1]

Into the camp at Cambridge, just after the battles of Concord and Lexington, came Rufus Putnam, a tall, sturdy, self-reliant but modest lieutenant-colonel of a Worcester County, Massachusetts, militia regiment. At

[1] The literature on the subject of the authorship of the Ordinance of 1787 is voluminous, and the majority of writers give the credit almost exclusively to Cutler. This list comprises, among others, Senator Hoar, Edward Everett Hale, and the late Dr. William F. Poole. In controversial historical literature of recent times it would be difficult to find a more ruthless assault on author and theory than Dr. Poole made on the argument of the late Henry A. Chaney, attributing the authorship of the measure most largely to Nathan Dane. Dr. Poole's address before the American Historical Society in 1888 sets forth his theory that Cutler brought the ordinance from New England and forced it on the committee of Congress as a prerequisite to the land purchase he proposed. Mr. Frederick D. Stone, librarian of the Historical Society of Pennsylvania, in a calm review of the different arguments (*The Ordinance of* 1787), reaches the conclusion that there is no evidence to show that Cutler had anything to do with the essential features of the measure. On the contrary, he went to New York prepared to purchase lands under the Ordinance of 1784, provided he could make suitable arrangements with the Board of Treasury. Mr. Stone gives Dane the credit for making up the bill from the existing law, and taking the opportunity on the floor of the House to insert the slavery clause with a proviso satisfactory to the South. After a careful study of the diary and letters of Cutler, of the State Department MSS., and of the documents in the library of the Massachusetts Historical Society, I am convinced Cutler's appearance with the money to purchase, and the organization to people, the Western lands made it possible to secure from Congress a fundamental law in accord with the repeatedly expressed desires of the New England promoters. So long as slavery was prohibited only north of the Ohio, the Southern members might well have acquiesced in that provision, because they might have foreseen what actually came to pass—that the prohibition of slavery north of the Ohio would hasten the settlement of Kentucky and the Western lands of the Southern States, and would retard emigration to the country north of the great river.

RUFUS PUTNAM

GENERAL RUFUS PUTNAM'S LAND-OFFICE

the age of nineteen he had entered the old French war, and at the age of thirty-seven he had acquired such a reputation as an engineer that Washington fixed upon him as the man to construct the works that were to force the evacuation of Boston. By one of those chances which are the raw material of genius, this self-taught engineer, while pondering over the difficulties presented by frozen ground, stumbled on *Muller's Field Engineer*, and from the book learned how to make a "chandelier" of timber and bundles of brush. On the morning of March 5, 1776, Sir William Howe saw himself hemmed in by long lines of intrenchments framed in a night, and so extensive that a month would scarcely have sufficed his army to build them. There was no escape but in evacuation; and as the result of his labors, Rufus Putnam had the satisfaction of seeing his cousin Israel, at the head of the first victorious army, march through the winding streets of Boston. Such was the first great triumph of one whom Washington called the ablest engineer officer of the war, whether American or Frenchman; his second notable work was fortifying West Point.

The Revolution ended, Putnam returned to the little Rutland, Massachusetts, farm-house, that to-day stands as a memorial of him, there to scheme and plan the building, not of fortifications but of a state—"a new state westward of the Ohio," as Timothy Pickering puts it.[1] In 1783 Putnam sent to Washington a pe-

[1] Senator George F. Hoar has told the story of Putnam in his oration at the Marietta centennial; and also in his address on "Rufus Putnam, Founder and Father of Ohio," on the occasion of placing a tablet to the memory of Putnam, upon his dwelling-house in Rutland, September 17, 1898. I am much indebted to Senator Hoar for copies of these excellent examples of his eloquence and scholarship.

tition to Congress signed by 288 officers, who prayed for the location and survey of the Western lands; and the next year Washington writes his old friend that he has tried in vain to have Congress take action. Appointed one of the surveyors of the Northwestern lands, Putnam sent General Tupper in his stead; and on the return of the latter from Pittsburg, the two spent a long January night in framing a call to officers and soldiers of the war, and all other good citizens of Massachusetts who desired to find new homes on the Ohio. On March 4, 1786, the Ohio Company was formed at the "Bunch of Grapes" tavern in Boston; and Putnam, Reverend Manasseh Cutler, and General Samuel H. Parsons were made the directors.[1] The winter was spent in perfecting the plan; then Parsons was sent to New York to secure a grant of lands and the passage of an act for a government. He failed. Putnam now turned to his other fellow-director, Cutler. On July 6, 1787, the polished and courtly ex-chaplain, and the greatest naturalist of his day in America, entered the chamber where Congress was sitting, and in his most felicitous manner laid before the statesmen his proposition. He promised much, and he demanded much. The restless veterans of the war were to be provided for; a large portion of the bothersome and burdensome public debt was to be extinguished; this sale of lands would lead to others, and the value of all would be increased; the frontiers of Virginia and Maryland would be protected against the savages; and Spain and England would intrigue in vain

[1] A copy of "The Articles of an Association by the name of the Ohio Company, printed in Worcester, Mass., by Isaiah Thomas, 1786," is preserved in the library of the Massachusetts Historical Society. Article II. recites that the purchase of lands is to be made under the law of May 20, 1785, "or other legislation.'

for the control of the Western country. In return he asked for a free soil, for the promotion of education, and for the machinery of government.

Having secured the passage of the Ordinance, Dr. Cutler next turned his attention to a law for the sale of lands. The first committee having been made up largely from the Committee on Lands, there was little difficulty in securing a favorable report, for the Ordinance had been based on the land scheme. In order to carry the project through Congress, however, it was expedient to parcel out the offices. General Parsons, one of the directors of the Ohio Company, having been selected privately for the office of governor, Cutler shifted him to a judgeship; the governorship was promised to General Arthur St. Clair, the President of Congress; and Major Sargent was slated for the place of secretary. Ten days after the passage of the ordinance, the land-contract measure was adopted; but inasmuch as its provisions were not satisfactory to Dr. Cutler he suggested modifications, and enforced his views by a threat to leave New York unless they were acceded to. Again he was successful, and on July 27 he found himself the possessor of a grant of five million acres of land, one half for the Ohio Company, and one half for a private speculation which became known as the Scioto Purchase. Congress on its part was able to retire some three and a half millions of outstanding script, and to reduce the public debt by that amount.

While the officers of the new territory were virtually settled upon at this time, it was not until October 5th that Congress elected Arthur St. Clair governor; James M. Varnum, Samuel Holden Parsons, and John Armstrong judges; and Winthrop Sargent, secretary;

subsequently John Cleves Symmes took the place of Mr. Armstrong, who declined the appointment.[1]

On August 29th, Dr. Cutler met the directors and agents of the Ohio Company at the "Bunch of Grapes" to report that he had made a contract with the Board of Treasury for a million dollars' worth of lands at a net price of seventy-five cents an acre; that the lands were to be located on the Ohio, between the Seven Ranges platted under the direction of Congress and the Virginia lands; that lands had been reserved by the government for school and university purposes, according to the Massachusetts plan; and that bounty lands might be located within the tract. The next day the plat of a city on the Muskingum was settled upon, and proposals for saw-mill and corn-mill sites were invited from prospective settlers.[2] So it happened that the future State of Ohio was planned in a Boston tavern.

"It would give you pain, and me no pleasure," writes the founder of Ohio to his co-laborer, Dr. Cutler, "to detail our march over the mountains, or our delays on account of bad weather, or other misfortunes." A number of ship-carpenters from Danvers were sent ahead; but when, on the 14th of February, 1778, the main party of New England pilgrims arrived at the Youghiogheny they found no boats and no boards or planks to build any, no persons able even to hollow out a canoe, the saw-mill frozen up, and small-pox prevailing. The ablest engineer of the Revolutionary army, however, was not to be discouraged. On April 1st the party embarked, and seven days later they ran upon the banks of the Muskingum the prows of the forty-five ton galley *Adventure*,

[1] In July, 1789, the first Congress of the United States gave its sanction to the new government.

[2] *Life of Reverend Manasseh Cutler*, vol. i., p. 321.

MANASSEH CUTLER

afterwards appropriately rechristened the *Mayflower;* also the *Adelphia,* a three-ton ferry; and three log canoes. First to greet them was the famous Captain Pipe, a Delaware of unlimited curiosity, who was quite accustomed to speak his mind plainly to white men, whether Englishmen or Americans.[1] With the Indians came the garrison from Fort Harmar to give a Continental welcome to the home-makers; and speedily all was activity. Lands were cleared, a hundred acres were planted with corn, and maple-sugar making added jollity to the toil. The site selected for the town was a level thirty feet above the Muskingum and on the eastern side of that stream at its junction with the Ohio, where once the Mound-builders had made a resting-place, setting up an arrow factory and heaping up piles of dirt for scientists to battle over to this day. For a name, Marietta was chosen by way of compliment to Marie Antoinette, gracious friend of the struggling colonies. We of to-day laugh at the pseudo-classicism of times that rejected the unpronounceable Indian names in favor of Latinized appellations; but the Campus Martius, the Via Sacra, the Capitolium, and the Quadranaon of Marietta, like the names under which Jefferson would have smothered the states of the Northwest, soon disappeared, leaving as the memorials of that period an architecture, both public and domestic, that is pure, simple, graceful, and stately. They were not pedants, but idealists, who named the seat of their backwoods university Athens!

On the morning of the 9th of July the boom of a boat's gun awoke the echoes between the forest-lined

[1] Had the settlers known that Captain Pipe was one of the murderers of Crawford, his greetings would not have been so warmly reciprocated.

banks of the broad Ohio, and soon a barge, hurried by the swift current and twelve stalwart watermen, turned into the Muskingum and swung up to the rude landing-place at Marietta. The Governor of the Northwest Territory had arrived at the capital. It was a great day for the new colony; and with the true New Englanders' love of dignity and order, they were determined to make the most of it. The Revolutionary veteran General Harmar and his handful of soldiers from the fort were drawn up in line, the burnished gun-barrels glistening in the July sun; there too was Rufus Putnam, unwearied surveyor, matchless engineer, veteran soldier and founder of the great state that was to be; and Judge Varnum, who, apostrophizing the new governor in sonorous periods on the nation's birthday, had called on the gently flowing Ohio to "bear him, oh bear him safely to this anxious spot," and on the "beautiful, transparent Muskingum to swell at the moment of his approach and reflect no objects but of pleasure and delight!" Amidst the ruffle of drums and the booming of the federal salute of fourteen guns, the commanding figure of Governor Arthur St. Clair stepped from the barge of state, closely followed by Judge Parsons and Secretary Sargent. Attended by the towns-people, they advanced to the Campus Martius, where the secretary read the ordinance and the commissions of the officers, and the governor expatiated to his New England hearers on the advantages of good government! Great results often follow upon unheralded beginnings; but there was no lack of appreciation of this auspicious occasion. "During the address of his Excellency," writes an eye-witness, "a profound veneration for the elevated station and exalted benevolence of the speaker; the magnitude of the subject; the high importance of the occasion; the

GENERAL ARTHUR ST. CLAIR

immense consequences resulting ; the glory, the grandeur of the new world unfolding ; heaven and earth approving, called forth all the manly emotions of the heart."

Indeed, the good people of Marietta had reason to be proud of their new officials, and particularly of their governor. Born in Caithness, of an ancient Scotch family, the early death of his pleasure-loving father had left Arthur St. Clair to the care of a mother as intelligent as she was devoted ; and after a course of study at the University of Edinburgh, and a short indenture as a student of medicine, at the age of twenty-three he was commissioned an ensign in the Royal Americans, the regiment of his friends Henry Bouquet and Haldimand. With Amherst, in the siege of Louisburg, he had earned a lieutenancy even before he climbed the Plains of Abraham, and, inspired by the undaunted courage of Wolfe, had caught up the colors from the hand of their dying defender and had borne them where the battle raged fiercest. From war to love is the shortest of steps; and no sooner had the British ships appeared before Quebec, bringing the aid that made the romantic New France into the prosaic Canada, than the dashing young soldier betook himself to Boston to marry Phœbe Bayard, the niece of Governor James Bowdoin.

With the remains of his own fortune added to the abundant patrimony of his wife, St. Clair purchased in the beautiful Ligonier valley a large estate to add to the lands he had located under the king's grant; and there, in the year after Bouquet's victory over the Indians at Bushy Run, St. Clair settled. He built a substantial house and a grist-mill, became a state surveyor, a justice of the court of quarter-sessions, a member of the Proprietary, and afterwards recorder of deeds, clerk of the orphans' court, and prothonotary. In his capacity as a Pennsylvania magistrate, St. Clair had Lord Dunmore's commandant, Dr. Conolly, arrested and placed in jail for usurpation at Pittsburg, and when his lordship demanded that St. Clair be punished, Governor Penn told the Governor of Virginia that he was dictatorial. At the outbreak of the Revolution St. Clair acted as secretary at the Indian council held at Fort Pitt, and while there engaged between four and five hundred young men for an expedition against Detroit. Delayed for the want of powder, an application was made to Congress, only to receive the reply that Arnold would soon capture Quebec, and Detroit would fall with the capital, so the expedition would be unnecessary! The difference between St. Clair and George Rogers Clark was that Clark got the powder. Meantime St. Clair's Boston relatives had not forgotten him. In December, 1775, President Hancock called him to Philadelphia; he was instructed to raise a regiment and start for Quebec; he did so, and arrived just in time to cover Arnold's retreat. Elected a brigadier by Congress, St. Clair joined Washington on his retreat through New Jersey, and until the close of the Revolution was an active, faithful, and even brilliant commander. Returning to civil life impoverished in fortune, he was chosen to the Continental Congress, over the last session of which he presided. And now, at the age of fifty-four, his chestnut hair but little touched with white, and his polished manners winning favor from every one on whom his blue-gray eyes smiled, he had come to preside at the making of a state.

His companions in office were not unworthy associates. Winthrop Sargent had been born in rocky Gloucester thirty-five years before, had graduated from Harvard College, had served through the Revolution

SITE OF MARIETTA IN 1788

as captain of artillery and as major on staff duty, had tramped through the country on the upper Ohio while surveying one of the Seven Ranges laid out in 1786 by order of Congress, and now was entering on a long and honorable career in civil life. Like Sargent, Judge Samuel Holden Parsons was a Harvard graduate, and had seen distinguished service in the Revolution, rising to the grade of major-general. He had been active in promoting the interests of the Ohio Company, and, as has been said, was Cutler's original choice for governor. Unfortunately for the colony this sagacious and influential founder was drowned the next year at the rapids of the Big Beaver. The second judge, James M. Varnum, a Dracut man, a brigadier-general at twenty-eight, a member of the Continental Congress at thirty-one, and a judge at thirty-nine, was one of the directors of the company during the remaining six months of his short life.[1]

Either human ingenuity never devised a more contentious form of government than that known as "The Governor and Judges," or else Revolutionary officers were not the best stuff out of which to make executive and judicial officials.[2] No sooner had the judges begun to make a patchwork of pieces from the laws of the states—as they were restricted to doing—than they of necessity began to stretch their quilt by enacting origi-

[1] Rufus Putnam succeeded Varnum, serving until 1796, when he was made surveyor-general, and was succeeded by Joseph Gillman, of Point Harmar. Parsons was succeeded by George Turner, who resigned in 1796, Return Jonathan Meigs succeeding him. No other changes were made before Ohio became a state.—See *St. Clair Papers*, vol. i., p. 145.

[2] General William Hull was so badgered by the judges of Michigan Territory that it is small wonder he lost all vigor and stamina before the War of 1812.

nal legislation; and when the cautious governor would have interposed his veto, they told him he had no such prerogative under the law. To the governor this seemed to smack of tyranny. In his strictures on the militia bill, General St. Clair made it plain to Major-general Parsons and Brigadier-general Varnum that they knew very little about military matters; but a militia law was passed, as were also laws establishing courts, punishing profanity, regulating marriages and ministers, and providing for a Christian Sabbath.[1]

Colonel John May, of Boston, one of the members of the Ohio Company, has left on record a graphic description of early days on the beautiful river. In the year 1788 it was no light matter to undertake a journey from the capital of Massachusetts to the seat of government of the Northwest. On May 5, after a tedious and fatiguing horseback journey of twenty-two days, Colonel May arrived at Pittsburg, "a place by no means elegant, and the people not so industrious as he had seen." The river was fairly alive with great boats carrying home-seekers to the fertile regions below. No fewer than two hundred and fifty of these craft had been counted that spring, and probably as many more went down by night, when no tally was kept. On one of these boats Colonel May counted twenty-nine whites, twenty-four negroes, nine dogs, twenty-three horses, cows and hogs, besides provisions. It went to the heart of the thrifty Bostonian that this enormous emigration was bound for Kentucky, where there were no restrictions as to slavery, and that his own party was only the second one destined for the region of freedom.

While a great majority of the boats passed down the

[1] State Department MSS. relating to the Northwest Territory.

FORT HARMAR, BUILT IN 1785

CAMP MARTIUS, THE FIRST HOME OF THE PIONEERS

river safely, yet Indian attacks were so frequent as to give hazard to the journey. Indeed, while Colonel May was waiting at Pittsburg, news came that on the 20th of March three Kentucky-bound boats were attacked by the savages near the Big Miami; and that among those killed were Samuel Purviance, a Baltimore patriot, and three French scientists who were bent on exploring the country. After a fortnight spent in the society of those hospitable soldiers of the Revolution who were making their homes at Pittsburg, Colonel May cast-off the fasts of his flat-boat and committed himself to the current of the Ohio. Without wind or waves, at a speed of five miles an hour, the party of twenty-seven men (besides cows and calves, dogs and hogs) were borne towards their wilderness home. Through thunder-storm and sunshine the boat drifted on its course, now between high banks, and again past broad stretches of fertile bottom-lands. On the Virginia bank the house of some settler, like Ebenezer Zane, occasionally gave human interest to the prospect, and after a voyage of scarcely fifty hours they had the good fortune to reach the Muskingum in safety.

By day there was work in plenty for all. Speedily the axe was laid at the root of the trees, and an acre and a half of clearing was reckoned a good day's work. So the week would pass, and on Sunday General Harmar would send his barge to bring to his hospitable board the veterans of war and the pioneers of peace. "As elegant a table as any in Boston" was spread at Fort Harmar: for solids there were bacon gammon, venison tongues, roast and boiled lamb, barbecued and *à la mode* beef, perch and catfish, lobsters and oysters—or what passed as such; for vegetables there were green peas, radishes, and salads; and "for drink, spirits, excellent wine, brandy, and beer." With stories of the camp and plans for the field the short afternoon was spent; and after a cup of tea, the refreshed settlers were rowed across the Muskingum to their stockade home.[1]

September 2d was set apart for the formal installation of the judges of the newly created courts for the new county of Washington, then consisting of one hundred and thirty-two people. Again General Harmar had the muskets of the garrison polished for the occasion; the governor and judges were on hand; and Sheriff and Colonel of Militia Ebenezer Sproat, with drawn sword and wand of office, marched at the head of the procession with all the dignity and impressiveness of his prototype, the Sheriff of Middlesex, at a Harvard commencement. Persons being more limited than offices, Rufus Putnam was made both justice of the peace and also judge of probate, and on Return Jonathan Meigs two clerkships were bestowed. To add lustre to the occasion, the Reverend Manasseh Cutler was present to offer prayer. In response to Sheriff Sproat's stentorian declaration that the court of common pleas was "open for the administration of even-handed justice to the poor and the rich, the guilty and the innocent, without respect to persons," Paul Fearing presented himself to be admitted as the first lawyer in the Northwest Territory; then the court adjourned to await the commission of crime. One smiles to note the seriousness with which these six-score-and-ten pioneers transplanted to the wilderness a system of government so complete that it would answer the manifold necessities of a nation—at least, in so far as internal relations were concerned; but wisdom was justified by her children.

[1] *Journal and Letters of Colonel John May* (Cincinnati, 1873).

While the Marietta settlers were busy among the buckeyes and the maples, another colony was planting itself farther down the river. While Cutler was in New York lobbying the ordinance and land grant through Congress, he found that in order to obtain the requisite number of votes he would be compelled to make terms with Colonel William Duer, who promised that the bills should pass provided the Ohio Company would stand sponsor for twice the amount of land needed, and allow Colonel Duer's friends to take the other half. The result was that Dr. Cutler and Winthrop Sargent made contracts with the Treasury, not only for the Ohio Company's lands but also for the lands they afterwards ceded to the Scioto Company, in which latter corporation they retained an interest that they shared with Putnam, Parsons, and other friends, including Barlow the poet and Apothecary-general Craigie, whose house in Cambridge Washington and Longfellow have made famous by occupying it. Barlow, acting as agent in Paris, disposed of Scioto lands to a French company, which in turn sold in small parcels before making payment to Barlow. On October 20, 1790, the first of the French immigrants arrived at Gallipolis, where by Putnam's energy houses had been built for them. There was dissatisfaction on the part of the leaders, questions as to good faith on the part of the American promoters, incompetency on Barlow's side, and fraud in the French company; there were Indian wars, and a financial panic in which Duer, Craigie, and the moneyed men of the Ohio Company went to the wall; but in spite of all the settlement at Gallipolis persisted.[1]

[1] For the intricate history of the Scioto Company, see the appendix to *Life of Manasseh Cutler*, vol. i.

For the first two years at Marietta the settlers suffered comparatively little from Indian attacks, a fact due not only to the practice of planting with a hoe in the right hand and a rifle in the left, but also to the protection afforded by the guns and garrison of Fort Harmar.[1] This group of seven or eight buildings clustered about a strong block-house and surrounded by a palisade, had been constructed in 1785 by Major Doughty, the first commander of the artillery of the United States under the Constitution. Commanding both the Ohio and the Muskingum rivers, the post was at this time the most important military station in the country; for while West Point and Springfield each had but a single company of artillery, the Ohio River posts were garrisoned by 596 men out of the entire United States army of 672 men; and of this remnant General Josiah Harmar was the commander. So sweeping had been the reduction of the Continental army. As settlers increased and cabins came to be located on the watercourses, the savages grew more and more restless, while the British became apprehensive lest an attempt should be made to seize the frontier posts.[2]

[1] *Life of Manasseh Cutler*, vol. i., p. 389.

[2] Soley's "Wars of the United States," in *The Narrative and Critical History of America*, vol. vii., pp. 357, 449.

PLANTING IN THE NORTHWEST TERRITORY

CHAPTER X

THE UNITED STATES WIN THE NORTHWEST POSTS

A NATIONAL domain implies national defence. When the general government came into the title to the Northwest and made laws and appointed officers for its government, the duty of protecting settlers and enforcing law and order devolved on the nation. With Washington as the Chief Executive, there could be no question that patiently, persistently, surely the national boundaries would be rounded out until the stars and stripes should float over every frontier post and the power of the United States be made supreme throughout the whole territory. The Indians were becoming reconciled to the sovereignty of the United States, and even Joseph Brant was looking forward to the inevitable day when the British should no longer be able to maintain the frontier posts. Indeed, that chief's allegiance to the English had been shaken for the time being by a council of his enemies, who filled Lord Dorchester's mind with charges and complaints against the chief of the Mohawks in his dealings with the Grand River lands. After repelling these attacks he relapsed into literary labors, translating the liturgy of the Church of England into the Mohawk language.[1] In January, 1789, however,

[1] On July 20, 1789, President Joseph Willard, of Harvard College, acknowledged the receipt of a copy of this work.—Stone's *Life of Joseph Brant*, vol. ii., p. 287.

Brant was present at the treaty of Fort Harmar negotiated by Governor St. Clair, at the mouth of the Muskingum.[1]

By this treaty the Lake Indians ratified the treaty of Fort McIntosh in 1785, by the terms of which the Indians kept the country south of Lake Erie, from the Cuyahoga to the Miami, and extending south to about the fortieth degree of north latitude, the Indians retaining the right of hunting throughout the entire country north of the Ohio, and the Americans reserving sites for trading posts within the Indian reservation. The lands along the west bank of the Detroit, and a tract twelve miles square at Michilimackinac also were granted to the Americans; and the two parties to the treaty mutually agreed to give each other warning of hostile intentions against either. A copy of this treaty fell into Lord Dorchester's hands, and he immediately communicated its provisions to Lord Sidney, with the further information that those Indian nations not parties to the treaty "seem now determined to remove and prevent all American settlements northwest of the Ohio." In consonance with this plan a large party of Wabash and Miami Indians appeared at Detroit, with the intention of presenting the war-pipe to the commanding officer; but the execution of this design was prevented by the prudent management of McKee, who privately discovered the plan and convinced the chiefs of the impropriety of such action.[2]

The Indians, however, had begun to feel the pressure of the white settlements on the Ohio. Five hundred savages from the Great Miami removed to the Glaize,

[1] *Haldimand Papers.* Dorchester to Sidney, January 10, 1789.
[2] *Haldimand Papers.* Dorchester to Sidney, June 25, 1789.

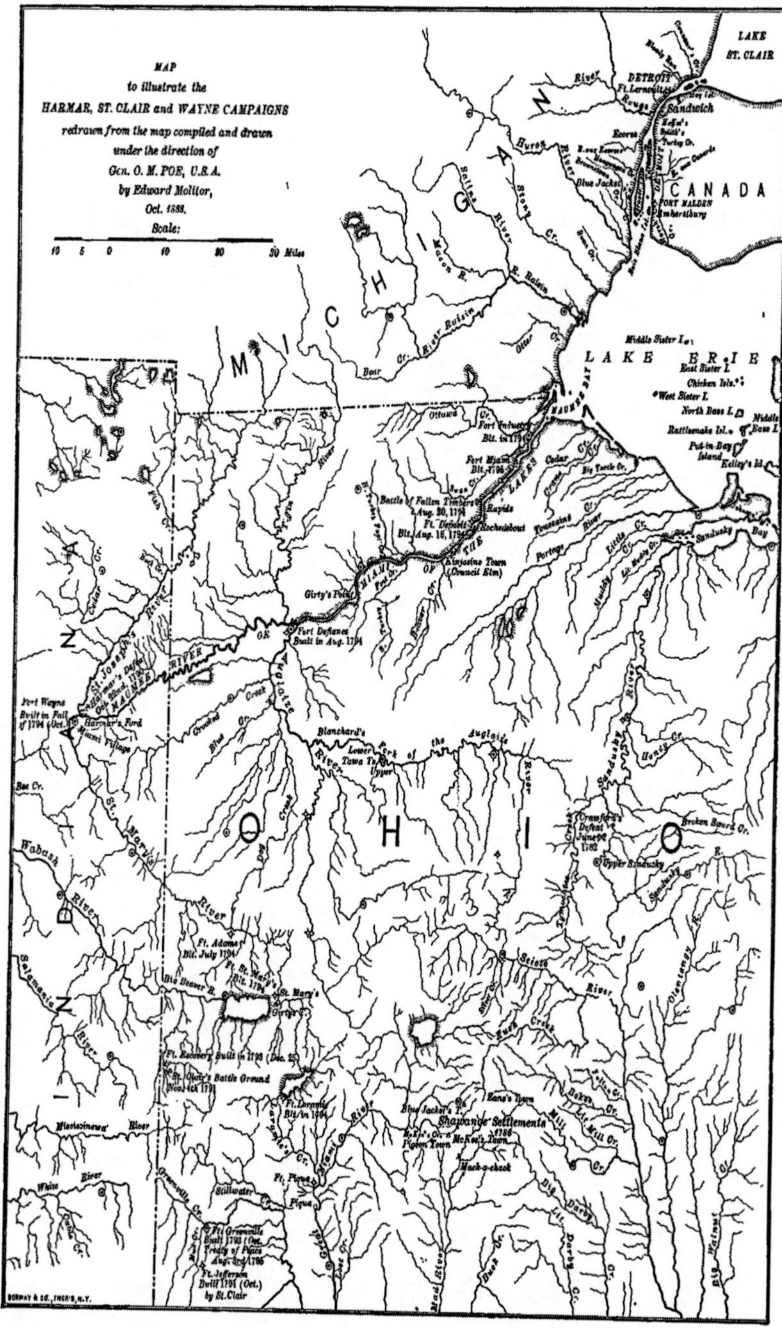
MAP
to illustrate the
HARMAR, ST. CLAIR and WAYNE CAMPAIGNS
redrawn from the map compiled and drawn
under the direction of
Gen. O. M. POE, U.S.A.
by Edward Molitor,
Oct. 1888.
Scale:
10 5 0 10 20 30 Miles
LAKE ST. CLAIR
DETROIT
Sandwich
CANADA
FORT MALDEN
LAKE ERIE
MAUMEE BAY
MICHIGAN
OHIO
Fort Defiance Built in Aug. 1794
Girty's Point
Battle of Fallen Timbers Aug. 20, 1794
Fort Miami Blt. 1795
Fort Wayne Built in Fall of 1794 (Oct.)
Harmar's Ford
Miami Village
Wabash River
Blanchard's Fork of the Auglaize
Ft. Adams Blt. July 1794
Ft. St. Mary's Blt. 1794
Ft. Recovery Built in 1793 (Dec. 25)
St. Clair's Battle Ground Nov. 4th 1791
Shawanoe Settlements
Ft. Piqua
Piqua
Stillwater
Ft. Greenville Built 1793 (Oct.) Treaty of Peace Aug. 3rd 1795
Ft. Jefferson Built 1791 (Oct.) by St. Clair
Scioto River
Sandusky Bay
Upper Sandusky
Crawford's Defeat June 1782
Mississinewa River
Mad River
BORMAY & CO., ENGR'S, N.Y.

a stream falling into Lake Erie near its head; and others had already begun to look to the Spanish side of the Mississippi for new hunting-grounds. Dorchester was disturbed by these indications, and he viewed with apprehension the efforts of St. Clair and Congress to gain control over the Indians. Particularly was he concerned over the gathering of a large body of troops on the Ohio. "The pretence to the public," he wrote to Sidney, "is to repel the Indians; but those who must know better and see that an Indian war does not require so great a force, nor that very large proportion of artillery, are given to understand that part of these forces are to take possession of the frontier, as settled by treaty, to seize the posts and secure the fur-trade; a more secret motive, perhaps, is to reduce the state governments and crush all internal opposition."

Dorchester, however, had little fear of a successful attack on the upper posts, all of which had been repaired and provisioned during the previous year. Yet he admitted that Detroit could be defended only against Indians, and must depend on their fidelity together with that of the militia, and on the ability of the commandant; that Niagara could make a good defence, provided the militia behaved well; that Michilimackinac could keep out only Indians; that Fort Ontario was not and could not be defended at all; and that the works on the Sorel were all very bad.[1]

That the British had no intention of yielding the posts immediately is made evident from the fact that those in the upper country were repaired during 1789. In preparation, however, for ultimate surrender, Captain Gother Mann, of the Royal Engineers, made a tour of

[1] *Haldimand Papers.* Dorchester to Sidney, March 8, 1790.

the lakes during the summer of 1788, for the purpose of a detailed examination of forts and channels. At Detroit he found Fort Lernoult in a fair state of repair, the inhabitants having furnished the pickets for a new palisade about the town; but the navy-yard, being beyond the defences, was hopelessly open to attack. He selected as the site for the new post a location opposite Bois Blanc, whence the guns could command the channels on either side of that island; and the opening events of the War of 1812 amply justified his foresight. Sinclair's fort on the island of Michilimackinac he found on too extensive a scale for defence against the Indians, and "far too little against cannon, and most of that ill-judged." At Sault Ste. Marie the lands on the American side of the line were the better; but for business purposes there was room enough on the eastern shore; and, besides, the white-fish resorted to that bank, and the fish-packing business was already extensive. Further, he recommended vessels of fifty tons for the navigation of the upper lakes, that limit being fixed because of the bars at the mouth of the St. Clair River and the rapids at the head of that stream; and he strongly advised against continuing the practice of building flat-bottomed vessels for lake navigation.[1] Beyond this, the Indian agent McKee negotiated the purchase from the savages of the lands on the east side of the Detroit River.[2]

Meanwhile the Indians of the Wabash and the Miami, joined by the Shawanese on the Scioto (whose regular occupation, according to Brant, was horse-stealing),

[1] Gother Mann to Dorchester, December 6, 1788. This letter is printed out of its order in the Haldimand Collection given in the *Michigan Pioneer and Historical Collections*. See vol. xii., p. 35.

[2] *Ibid.*, Colonel McKee to Land Board, p. 28.

made the passage of the Ohio a voyage of apprehension and peril. In June, 1790, information came to Detroit that the Indians on the Ohio, in the course of hostilities, had gone so far as to burn one of their white prisoners, a proceeding that brought a message of remonstrance from that post. That same month eight Americans who had escaped from the Indians, and in September thirteen prisoners brought to Detroit by the Ohio raiders, were sent back to Fort Pitt by the British, and pains were taken to express to the savages the king's displeasure.[1] So aggressive had these Indian attacks become that President Washington decided that the time was ripe to use something stronger and more tangible than treaties. In pursuance of this idea a call was made on Kentucky for 1000 and on Pennsylvania for 500 militia to join the regulars at Fort Washington, built on the present site of Cincinnati.

During the latter half of September, 1790, the militia came in: not the smart, active backwoodsmen on whose trusty rifles Washington had been accustomed to rely during the Revolution, but old and infirm men and even boys, substitutes, many of whom had never fired a gun. Indeed, the arms they brought represented a greater variety and quantity of useless weapons than it was supposed all Kentucky could produce; there were guns without locks and barrels without stocks, carried by men who did not know how to oil a lock or fit a flint. Added to this were the disputes as to who should command the Kentuckians; and these were calmed only by

[1] *Haldimand Papers.* Dorchester to Grenville, June 21 and September 25, 1790. Possibly some of these captives were taken at Big Bottom in January, when the Ohio Company's town, forty miles up the Muskingum, was cut off, with a loss of fourteen killed and three captured.

placing the popular Colonel Trotter over the Blue-grass battalions and giving to his senior, Colonel Hardin, the command of all the militia. On the 3d of October the march to the Miami villages began; and so far as regulations and foresight could go with such a body of men, General Harmar seems not to have been wanting. But the pack-horses escaped, as it was for the financial advantage of their drivers to have them lost; and general inefficiency begot demoralization everywhere save among the little band of 320 regulars,[1] with whom, unfortunately, the militia were too jealous to serve effectively.[2]

On October 13th a patrol of horsemen captured a Shawanese Indian, who reported that the savages were nowhere in force; thereupon Colonel Hardin was detached with six hundred light troops to push for the Miami villages, on the present site of Fort Wayne, and to surprise the Indians. Instead of the enemy he found their deserted and still burning towns. The main body of the army having come up, Colonel Trotter with a small force was sent out for a three days' scout; but, having satisfied himself by killing two Indians, he returned the first evening. Then Hardin, anxious to retrieve the disgrace brought upon the militia by Trotter's failure, sought and obtained permission to discover the enemy. Confident that the Indians would not fight, Hardin proceeded carelessly until, coming upon a party of perhaps a hundred savages, the militia, all save nine, broke and fled at the first fire, more scared by the warwhoop than hurt by the bullets of their foes. The regulars stood their ground, and twenty-four of them, with

[1] American State Papers, Military Affairs, vol. i., Proceedings of the Court of Inquiry on General Harmar.

[2] Perkins's *Western Annals* (Cincinnati, 1846), p. 342.

the nine militia-men, met death; but of the retreating militia some never stopped until they had crossed the Ohio.[1] The army having burned the houses in five villages, and corn to the amount of twenty thousand bushels, began its homeward march. General Harmar, anxious to achieve some success, now detached four hundred choice men — militia and regulars — to return to the burned villages in the hope of finding some Indians at the scene of disaster. Major Wyllys, of the regulars, was placed in command; but he was absolutely unable to control the militia, who ran off in pursuit of small parties of the enemy, leaving the brave major and his band of regulars to meet death at the hands of Little Turtle's braves. The best of the militia and of the regulars were now dead; and nothing was left for the army but to struggle homeward as best they might. Probably not more than 150 Indians were engaged in the rout of an army of 1453 men.[2]

To Harmar and his friends the expedition was hailed as a success; to the elated Indians it was an encouragement to renewed aggressions. Rufus Putnam was under no misapprehensions as to the result of the campaign. He knew that unless measures were taken speedily to punish the savages, the fate of the Ohio settlements was sealed. Already there were eighty houses at Marietta; twenty-two miles up the Muskingum some twenty fami-

[1] Testimony of Lieutenant Armstrong, who says that Hardin ran with the militia. Armstrong was saved by dropping into a swamp. It was his opinion that Trotter might have surprised and captured the enemy the day before, had he persisted. Hardin was personally a brave man, but was not a good officer.

[2] Testimony of Lieutenant Denny. It appears from a letter to Brant, quoted by Smith (*Life of Joseph Brant*, vol. ii., p. 294), that the Indian loss was between fifteen and twenty. The Americans lost three regular and ten militia officers, and about five hundred men.

lies had settled; on Wolf and Duck creeks mills had been built; at Belle Prairie, opposite the Little Kanawha, between twenty and thirty houses were scattered along twelve miles of shore; and there were various other little settlements at the mercy of Indian attacks.[1] Moreover, the excited Indians now dared to push their way into the Pennsylvania settlements on the Alleghany, murdering women and children and taking away captives and horses. It is estimated that from 1783 to October, 1790, no fewer than fifteen hundred men, women, and children were slain or captured by the Indians in the Ohio country.

It is necessary here to understand the theory on which the British were acting in regard to Indian troubles; for much misapprehension exists on this point. In a letter to Brant, dated February 22, 1791, Sir John Johnson writes that he and Lord Dorchester held that "the Americans had no claim to that part of the country beyond the line established in 1765, at Fort Stanwix, between the Indians and the governors and agents of all the provinces interested, and including the sales made since the war." Not being able to afford the Indians assistance in arms, Johnson thought the British should offer their mediation to bring about a peace on terms just and honorable.[2] To a deputation of Indians who visited him, Lord Dorchester replied that the King of England had never given away the Indian lands, because he never possessed them; that the posts would be retained only until England and America could adjust their differences; and that although the Indians had the friendship and good-will of the English, the latter could

[1] Putnam to Washington, quoted in Perkins's *Western Annals*, p. 345.

[2] Stone's *Life of Joseph Brant*, vol. ii., p. 297.

not embark in war, but could only defend themselves if attacked.[1]

Chagrined and humiliated by Harmar's failure, Washington called Governor St. Clair to Philadelphia, placed him in command of an army to be organized for a new expedition; and, after impressing upon him the peril of ambush and surprise, sent him against the hostile tribes. The expedition was to be on an extensive scale; but then as now the organization of the War Department was thoroughly unfitted to deal with war.

On March 3, 1791, Congress had authorized the organization of the Second Regiment of Infantry, and at the same time had given to the President the power to enlist not more than 2000 men for six months, thus providing for an army of 4128 non-commissioned officers, privates, and musicians. A portion of this force was needed for garrison duty at Venango and Forts Harmar, Washington, Knox, and Steuben; with the remainder General St. Clair was ordered to march to the site of the Miami towns and there establish himself. Recruiting was slow; but on August 1st General Wilkinson with a body of Kentucky horse advanced from the headquarters at Cincinnati, and on the 14th such of the First and Second Regiments as had arrived, together with Rhea's, Gaither's, and Patterson's levies, pushed on to Ludlow's Station, five miles from Cincinnati, the object of the movement being to withdraw the men from the debaucheries of the town and to acquaint them in some degree with camp duties, of which both officers and soldiers were very generally ignorant. Eighteen miles from Ludlow's Station Fort Hamilton was built.

General St. Clair being absent on recruiting duty, the

[1] Stone's *Life of Joseph Brant*, vol. ii., p. 299.

command devolved on Major Hamtramck, or some other officer detailed for that duty; and it was not until October 4th that the advance movement began, under the command of General Butler. It was a sorry army. "Picked up and recruited from the offscourings of large towns and cities; enervated by idleness, debaucheries, and every species of vice, it was impossible they could have been made competent to the arduous duties of Indian warfare." At least such was the opinion of Adjutant-general Winthrop Sargent. He found, further, an extraordinary aversion to service, demonstrated by the most repeated desertions, in many instances to the very foe they were to combat; the late period at which they were brought into the field left no leisure or opportunity to attempt to discipline them; and, moreover, they were badly clothed, badly paid, and badly fed. The powder was bad, and "the military stores were sent on in the most infamous order." All these matters so worried St. Clair that he was worn out at the beginning of the campaign;[1] and the continued delinquencies of the contractor were "one among the many primary causes" of defeat.

On the 8th of October, when forty-four and one-quarter miles from Fort Washington, the flank guards fired unsuccessfully upon an Indian, the first one seen upon the march; four days later the marksmen killed the savage

[1] *Diary of Colonel Winthrop Sargent*, Adjutant-general of the United States army during the campaign of 1791. The original manuscript of Colonel Sargent's diary was printed in 1851 in an edition of forty-six copies, with two plates, for George Wymberley-Jones, as the fourth of the series of Wormsloe quartos. The diary was then in the possession of Winthrop Sargent, of Philadelphia, a grandson of Colonel Sargent. The above quotations are made from the copy presented to Peter Force by Mr. Wymberly Jones, and now in the Library of Congress.

ST. CLAIR'S ADVANCE DISCOVERED

they encountered, and secured a quantity of fresh peltry and four or five horses. So plentiful was the game and so great the temptation to kill it, that even the penalty of a hundred lashes could not keep the militia from firing, thus demoralizing discipline. On the 14th, sixty-eight and a half miles from Cincinnati, Fort Jefferson was laid out as a square log fort with four bastions, on "a pretty rising ground, terminating in gentle and low descents to east and west to a prairie." By the 17th, but one day's rations and one day's allowance of liquor remained; the forage was nearly exhausted, and even had the troops been well disciplined matters would have been extremely serious. As it was the militia were discontented and insubordinate; and, as the terms of their enlistment were about to expire, they were beginning to prepare to go home. Heavy rains and snow flurries added to the discomfort. The troops were put first upon half rations and afterwards upon quarter rations of bread; and three hundred and fifty pack-horses with a company of much-needed riflemen were sent back for supplies. On the 23d three soldiers were executed—one for shooting an officer, and two for desertion.

On November 3d, the army having proceeded ninety-seven miles from Cincinnati, camp was made "on a very handsome piece of rising ground," with a stream of forty feet in front, "running to the west." The army was in two lines, with four pieces of artillery in the centre of each; Faulkner's company of riflemen upon the right flank with one troop of horse, and another troop of horse on the left. The militia encamped across the stream, three hundred yards away, "upon a high, extensive, fine flat of open woods." From abundant evidences the place was known to have been one of general resort for the Indians; and indeed a party of fifteen departed as the troops advanced.

This position, very defensible against regular troops, "was feeble to an Indian attack," because of the close woods near by, of the underbrush and fallen timber at hand, and of "an unfortunate ravine" and small swamps on the borders. A chain of sentinels around the camp, at a distance of fifty paces apart, constituted the principal security against surprise. The militia detailed to explore the country pleaded fatigue, and such was the temper of the troops that the command could not be enforced. At midnight Captain Stough, of the levies, sent out with a small force to prevent the horses from being stolen, was driven in by the Indians, but no report was made to headquarters. Occasional shots exchanged during the night led St. Clair to keep the men under arms; and on the morning of the 4th the army was turned out earlier than usual, and continued on parade until day began to break. A half hour before sunrise came the Indian yell, like "an infinitude of horse-bells," followed by an attack on the militia. Although occupying a defensible position, the levies made no defence, but indulged in "a most ignominious flight." Dashing helter-skelter into the camp of the regulars, the militia threw the forming battalions into some confusion; the fugitives even passed through the second line, and were checked only by the Indians completely surrounding the camp. Close upon the heels of the flying militia followed the Indians, who for a moment seemed as if determined to enter the camp; but the array of fixed bayonets having cooled their ardor, they dropped behind logs and bushes, and at a distance of seventy yards began to pour a deadly fire into the closed ranks of the soldiers. Probably there were 1500 Indians;

while of St. Clair's total army, aside from the militia of 1380, not more than 1080—and those raw and undisciplined troops—were available for battle. For two hours men who never before had fired even a blank-cartridge stood up against the unseen foe; officers and men dropped fast, save in Clark's battalion and the riflemen on the right flank, who gave a good account of themselves, fighting after the Indian fashion. Butler's battalion charged with spirit, and "the artillery, if not well served, was bravely fought, every officer and more than two-thirds of the men being killed or wounded." The Second Regiment made three charges, until but two officers were left alive, and one of the two was wounded.[1]

With daring spirit the savages rushed on the artillery, and twice gained the camp, plundering the tents and scalping the dead and dying, but both times they were driven back. The loss of officers and comrades, however, demoralized the men, so that they huddled together and became targets for the savages, and neither threats nor entreaties could bring order out of the chaos. It was only when the troops had almost ceased firing in their demoralization that the gout-ridden St. Clair, cool and brave in disaster, ordered a retreat. Only the Indian madness for plunder left alive a single man to tell the tale of disaster. Such of the wounded as could travel at all were mounted on horses; the others, though few, charged their pieces, and with what fortitude they could muster awaited the barbarities in store for them.

[1] The regulars and levies lost of men and non-commissioned officers 550 killed and 200 wounded; of officers, 31 killed and 24 wounded, out of 95. The militia had 29 officers and 290 men; their loss was 4 officers killed and 5 wounded, 38 men killed and 29 wounded, besides 14 camp men killed and 13 wounded. The Indians, led by Blue Jacket, numbered 1500, of whom but 30 were killed.

The scattering discharge of fire-arms told to the fugitives the agonizing story of lives dearly sold. At half-past nine the retreat began, officers and men throwing away arms, ammunition, and accoutrements in their precipitate and ignominious flight; and at seven that evening the friendly gates of Fort Jefferson, twenty-nine miles from the battle-field, opened to the fugitives. But at five o'clock next morning the march was resumed, lest famine should complete the work left by the savages. On the 8th, the remnant of the army reached Cincinnati.[1]

Three months after St. Clair's defeat, Colonel Sargent visited the scene of action. Although twenty inches of snow covered the ground, at every tread of his horse's feet dead and mangled bodies were brought to view; every twig and bush was cut down by bullets, and the trees were riddled by Indian shot, while the fire of the troops, even of the artillery, appeared to have been ineffective. So far as possible, the mutilated bodies were suitably buried in the frozen ground; and several tons of iron-work was recovered, but the artillery had disappeared.

In all the story of Washington's life there is no more

[1] See also "Causes of the Failure of the Expedition against the Indians, in 1791, under the Command of General St. Clair," *American State Papers*, vol. i., Military Affairs, p. 63. Mr. Fitzsimons, as the result of the inquiry by a committee of the House of Representatives, reported the causes of failure to be: delays in furnishing material, mismanagement and neglect in the quartermaster's and contractor's departments, lateness of the season, and want of discipline and experience of the troops. St. Clair was completely exonerated, "as his conduct in all the preparatory arrangements was marked with peculiar ability and zeal, so his conduct during the action furnished strong testimonies of his coolness and intrepidity." See also the report of Mr. Giles, Second Congress, second session.

ANTHONY WAYNE

human passage than that which relates how the news of disaster was brought to him one December day while he was at dinner; how the messenger would confide his despatches to none but the commander-in-chief; how the President got their purport, then quietly returned to the table and afterwards went through the appointed function for the evening; and how, after all was over, Washington, in the presence only of Tobias Lear, his secretary, poured forth one of those torrents of rage and passion that on rare occasions passed over him as a squall lashes a mountain lake, leaving it placid and serene. There is reason to believe that on this occasion Washington swore! But the end was the determination that St. Clair should not be prejudiced, but should have justice.[1]

Realizing from his own bitter experiences with militia at the outbreak of the French and Indian War, that the failures of Harmar and St. Clair were due quite as much to the insubordinate character of the troops as to the lack of capacity on the part of their commanders, Washington now selected for general of the army a soldier of proverbial bravery, Mad Anthony Wayne, one of those rare men whom prudence teaches when to be rash successfully. The grandson of a Yorkshireman who had removed first to County Wicklow, in Ireland (where he fought gallantly at the battle of the Boyne), and then had come with the Scotch-Irish to settle in Chester County, Pennsylvania, young Anthony Wayne inherited also from his Indian-fighting father such a love of arms that the teachers of Philadelphia were unable to put their kind of learning into his head. He was ten years old the year Braddock was defeated, and fifteen

[1] Irving's *Life of George Washington*, vol. v., p. 103.

when Montreal capitulated. The British army being closed to the son of a Pennsylvania frontier farmer, he chose the life nearest the soldier's—that of a surveyor. He was twenty years old when Benjamin Franklin and his associates selected him to lead a band of settlers to Nova Scotia, where for a year the enterprising post-master-general of the colonies hoped to make a fortune out of a great land speculation. The troubles with England quickly stopped emigration, and Wayne returned to Pennsylvania to take a small but busy part in the conventions and assemblies that led up to the Revolution.

Entering the service as a colonel in the Pennsylvania line, Wayne and St. Clair were fellow-officers in the unsuccessful Canada expedition, and afterwards they became not altogether ungenerous rivals. At Brandywine, Germantown, Monmouth, and Stony Point, Wayne led his Pennsylvania troops with unsúrpassed gallantry; and after Yorktown he won a major-general's commission in Greene's campaign in Georgia, from which state he was sent to Congress with credentials that were not approved by the House of Representatives. In April, 1792, at the end of Wayne's unsuccessful contest for a seat in the House, Washington appointed this bankrupt Georgia planter and Pennsylvania farmer to command the army. Wayne's task was to retrieve the failure of St. Clair, his former rival, and to avenge the death of his campmate and friend, General Richard Butler, who after winning glory in the Revolution died the death of a Bayard on St. Clair's bloody field.[1] The first necessity was

[1] There were three brothers Butler in this battle. Captain Edward Butler removed the wounded general from the field; returning he found his other brother, Major Butler, shot through both legs, and carried him to the same tree under which the general was placed.

to get into shape the enlarged army that Congress had authorized for the campaign, and had named the Legion of the United States.

Arriving at Pittsburg in June, Wayne began the arduous task of recruiting and drilling men who were so terrified at the name of Indian that while yet in Pennsylvania on one occasion the mere report of savages in the neighborhood caused one-third of the sentinels to desert their posts. So thorough was the drill that by St. Patrick's day the sons of that saint could manœuvre and shoot in a way to astonish the observant Indians. In May, 1793, Wayne with his legion dropped down the Ohio from his camp near Fort McIntosh to Fort Washington, and there kept up the daily drills while he grimly awaited the results of the council to be held with the Indians at the mouth of the Detroit.

Desiring above all things to reach, if possible, a harmonious understanding with the Western Indians before resorting to hostilities, Washington, early in 1793, appointed as commissioners General Benjamin Lincoln, of Massachusetts, who had been Secretary of War, and had suppressed Shay's rebellion in 1787; Beverly Randolph, of Virginia; and Colonel Timothy Pickering, then of Pennsylvania, the Postmaster-general, and shortly afterwards the Secretary of War. After a private council with the British agents, Colonel Brant,[1] on behalf of the Confederated Indians, sent to the commissioners an ultimatum stating that the southern boundary of the Indian lands must be the Ohio River; and when

When retreat became necessary General Butler said, "Edward, I am mortally wounded. Leave me to my fate and save my brother!" It is to be hoped that he died before the coming of the Indians. See Stille's *Life of Wayne*, p. 370.

[1] *Canadian Archives.* Brant to Colonel McKee, May 17, 1793.

the council met on July 31, in the little council-house at the mouth of the Detroit, this message was repeated in emphatic form. "We shall be persuaded that you mean to do us justice, if you agree that the Ohio shall be the boundary-line between us," said the message; "if you will not consent thereto our meeting will be altogether unnecessary." To this the commissioners made reply that it was impossible to fix the Ohio as the boundary, and that the negotiation was therefore at an end.[1] So the commissioners returned to report their failure; and the chiefs of the Western Nations informed Simcoe that the Americans insisted on keeping the whole Indian country, and in payment offered money, which was useless to them. "We expect," they said,[2] "to be forced again to defend ourselves and our country, and we look up to the great God, who is a witness of all that passes here, for His pity and His help." McKee, reporting the results of the council to Simcoe, professes that he did all he could to bring about a better result; but that the Western Indians would not agree with the Six Nations, but insisted on the Ohio boundary. "The nations that have not sold," he says, "will enjoy without dispute the lands belonging to them; these will form an extensive barrier between the British and American territory. Although I have used no influence to prevent a peace, which would have afforded me gratification, I expect to be blamed by the malevolent."[3] One need not necessarily be malevolent in assuming that a result so entirely satisfactory to his masters was brought about through the efforts of the wily Indian agent. Indeed, a contrary view would be an aspersion on Mc-

[1] *Canadian Archives*, 1891, p. 54.
[2] *Ibid.*, 1891, p. 55.
[3] *Ibid.*, 1891, p. 55.

DRAWING-ROOM, WAYNE HOMESTEAD

Kee's undoubted abilities and influence over the savages whom he fed and clothed.[1]

It was September before Secretary Knox countermanded the orders against an Indian campaign. "Every offer has been made to obtain peace by milder terms than the sword," wrote Knox; "but the efforts have failed under circumstances that leave us nothing to expect but war." In short, the Indians had stipulated for the Ohio boundary-line, and that was an impossibility. On receipt of this letter Wayne replied from Camp Hobson's Choice: "I will advance to-morrow with the force I have." On October 13th the army encamped on a branch of the Miami eighty miles north of Cincinnati, a spot to which Wayne gave the name Greenville, in honor of his commander and friend in the South Carolina campaign. There he passed the winter, sending forward a large detachment to build upon St. Clair's fatal field a post euphemistically called Fort Recovery.

The Indians know a soldier. They quickly took the measure of Braddock and of Bouquet, of St. Clair and of Wayne. The way in which the Swiss colonel and the Pennsylvania general handled their men on the wilderness march showed to the savages that ambush was out of the question; and that a battle or else submission were the alternatives. While the administration had no desire to get into difficulties with Great Britain, still Secretary Knox instructed Wayne that if in his operations against the Indians it should be found necessary to dislodge the British garrison in Governor Simcoe's fort at the rapids of the Miami, he was author-

[1] A brief reference to the council will be found in Charles Wentworth Upham's *Life of Timothy Pickering* (Boston, 1873), vol. iii., p. 49 *et seq.*

ized in the name of the President to do so. On the 30th of June, 1794, a force of riflemen were attacked suddenly under the guns of Fort Recovery; but the savages, although they appeared in force, were beaten off.

Making feints towards the Miami villages on the left and Roche de Bout on the right, Wayne's army, on August 8th, advanced to the Auglaize to find that by reason of the timely warning of Newman, a deserter, the Indians had precipitately abandoned their settlements and towns. Thus without loss Wayne gained possession of "the grand emporium of the hostile Indians of the West," with its very extensive and highly cultivated fields and gardens, showing the work of many hands. The margins of those beautiful rivers, the Miami of the Lakes (Maumee) and the Auglaize, appeared like one continuous village for miles up and down the streams; while for immensity the fields of corn were unrivalled from Canada to Florida. In the midst of this beautiful prospect, at the confluence of the two rivers, Wayne set a strong stockade fort bastioned with four good block-houses, and called it Fort Defiance. Thence he sent to the Delawares, Shawanese, Miamis, and Wyandottes and their allies an offer of a lasting peace, which should restore them to their lands and villages and preserve their helpless and distressed women and children from hunger and famine. This message he sent by Christopher Miller, an adopted Shawanese; and he warned the Indians that injury or delay to his messenger would be followed by the death of the prisoners, some of whom were known "to belong to the first families of their nations."

Wayne's offer met an evasive response. On August 20th, the Indians, assembled near the British post on McKee's farm at the falls of the Miami, received the

American army. Into Price's battalion of mounted volunteers the savages, secreted in the woods and the tall grass, poured a murderous fire. The tornado-swept ground was covered with fallen timber, which gave the Indians a great advantage; and the savages attempted to execute their favorite manœuvre of turning the enemy's flank. Sending Major-general Scott to turn the Indian right, Wayne ordered his front line to advance and charge with trailed arms, to arouse the Indians from their coverts at the point of the bayonet, and when up, to deliver a close and well-directed fire on their backs, followed by a brisk charge, so as not to let them load again. So sharp was this attack and so precipitate the retreat of the savages that the detachments sent to turn the flanks of the Indians could not catch up with their comrades who took the straight road to the British post.

During the three days that he remained on the Miami, Wayne treated the British garrison to huge bonfires of standing corn, and of the houses and farm buildings of the British Indian agent, Alexander McKee, "the principal stimulator of the war now existing between the United States and the savages," as Wayne justly characterized him. The British commandant Major William Campbell, as in duty bound, protested against Wayne taking post "almost within reach of the guns of this fort"; to which the American general replied that his "fullest and most satisfactory answer was announced to you from the muzzle of my small-arms yesterday morning in the action against the hordes of savages in the vicinity of your post, which terminated gloriously for the Americans; but had it continued until the Indians, etc., were drove under the influence of the post and guns you mention, they would not much have impeded the progress of the victorious army under my command; as no such post was established at the commencement of the present war between the Indians and the United States." Major Campbell prudently forebore to resent the insults which Wayne offered to the British flag by sending his light infantry[1] within pistol-shot of the fort. Then Wayne ordered the British commandant to withdraw from that post; and after destroying everything even under the muzzle of his guns, the American army, its purpose accomplished, began its homeward march. On his way Wayne set the iron heel of war on the paradise of Grand Glaize, and that winter there was want and suffering in the Indian towns and depletion in the stocks of British provisions.

After the battle of Fallen Timbers, General Wayne retired to Greenville, where the remnant of the Legion that was retained in service went into winter-quarters. There he was visited by various chiefs and warriors, to whom he explained that the United States, having conquered Great Britain, were entitled to the possession of the Lake Posts; and that the new nation was anxious to make peace with the Indians, to protect them in the possession of abundant hunting-grounds, and to compensate them for the lands needed by the white settlers. The Indians, on their part, had lost a number of their most warlike chiefs; they were deeply incensed at the action of the British, both in closing Fort Miamis to them at the time of their great defeat, and also in not coming to their aid with the soldiers from Detroit, as McKee and the other agents had promised; and already the Shawanese were

[1] *Daily Journal of Wayne's Campaign*, by Lieutenant Boyer (Cincinnati, 1866), p. 9.

WAYNE HOMESTEAD

planning to remove across the Mississippi. In the midst of these prolonged negotiations a copy of the Jay Treaty arrived, and when the Indians found that a definite date was fixed for the surrender of the posts, they no longer hesitated to draw a boundary line which surrendered the territory embraced in the land grants already made by Congress, together with other lands about the various posts as set forth in the treaty of Muskingum or Fort Harmar. On August 3, 1795, General Wayne was able to announce that he had concluded "a permanent peace" with the ten great nations dwelling within the Northwest; and nothing now remained but to await the day set for the delivery of the posts.[1]

While General Wayne was preparing for his campaign against the Indians, the Chief-justice of the United States appeared in London as a special envoy from President Washington to compose those differences that had brought the two countries to the verge of war. There were aggravations on both sides. England had been thrown from her balance by the French Revolution, which then was shaking every government in the civilized world. In the United States a numerous and noisy party espoused the cause of France; and Minister Genet had even presumed to take an appeal from the conservative Washington to the excitable American people. In the end the dignity and individuality of this nation were preserved; but it took time for the sober sense of the people to make itself felt. England, revolting from the cruelties and horrors of Robespierre, had joined Austria, Russia, Spain, and Sardinia in a war with France; and in her efforts to crush her rival had no

[1] The full proceedings of the Treaty of Greenville are given in Jacob Burnet's *Notes on the Early Settlement of the Northwestern Territory* (Cincinnati, 1847), chapters ix. to xii.

scruples about seizing American ships trading to French ports. Moreover, eleven years had elapsed since the treaty of 1783, and still the posts were not surrendered; and the tates were aggravating matters by legislation to prevent the collection of debts owed to English merchants. Such was the inauspicious condition of affairs, when, on June 15, 1794, John Jay informed Lord Grenville of his coming to negotiate a treaty of friendship and commerce.

Fortunately for both countries, the negotiators were men of more than the ordinary calibre, and as a consequence in their informal discussions they speedily came to terms that were mutually conciliatory. The British spoliations on American commerce; the debts due to English creditors and for any reason not collectable in the courts, and the damages due England on account of depredations of French cruisers fitted out in the United States, were to be settled by commissions; the negroes carried away by the British in 1783 were not to be paid for; the Northwestern posts were to be surrendered on or before June 1, 1797, but there was to be free intercourse across the border, and free navigation of the Mississippi, the duties on goods to be uniform with those paid at the sea-coast ports of entry; all ambiguities in the boundaries were to be removed by a commission of survey; American vessels were to be allowed to trade, under restrictions, with the British West Indies; and there were other provisions of decided advantage to this country. This treaty, although bitterly assailed at first, was ratified by the Senate; and the House, on April 30, 1796, agreed to the appropriation required to carry out its provisions, in spite of the opposition of Madison and Gallatin.[1] The Senate, however, provided for the sus-

[1] For a discussion of the treaty see Dr. James B. Angell's judicial

JOHN JAY

pension of the article relative to West Indian trade, and, pending the agreement of England to the amendment, the execution of the treaty was delayed.

In the spring of 1796 a second New England colony, led by Moses Cleveland, Augustus Porter, and Seth Pease, assembled at Schenectady, New York, to make a wilderness journey and to plant on the shores of Lake Erie the colony of New Connecticut. From the Connecticut legislature of 1792 came grants of a half million acres of Fire Lands, to be located at the west end of the territory reserved in the cession of the state to compensate the sufferers from the British ravages on its coasts; and in September, 1795, the state had sold to John Caldwell, Jonathan Brace, and John Morgan, as trustees for the Connecticut Land Company, three million acres of its reserve at forty cents per acre. Provided with quit-claim deeds, the Connecticut immigrants met, near Buffalo, Red Jacket and the principal chiefs of the Six Nations, and from them purchased the Indian rights of occupancy to the entire reserve for £500 worth of goods, to be paid to the Western Indians; two beef cattle, and one hundred gallons of whiskey, together with the usual gifts and feasts. On the nation's anniversary the band of fifty home-makers came to Conneaut Creek; there they celebrated the day with a federal salute of fifteen rounds and a sixteenth for New Connecticut; then they drank

article on the "Diplomacy of the United States" in vol. vii. of the *Narrative and Critical History of the United States;* also William Jay's *Life of John Jay* (New York, 1833), vol. i., p. 322 *et seq.* President Angell is convinced that "looking back from our present point of view, we must admit that the completion of the negotiation was wise and fortunate." Henry Adams, in his *Life of Albert Gallatin*, says that Jay's treaty "thrust a sword into the body politic," and he regards the treaty as having forced the division of parties. See p. 159.

"several pails of grog," and "supped and retired in good order."

Beginning at once the surveys, General Cleveland's party coasted along the lake to the Cuyahoga, where, on July 22d, they began the city that bears the name of its founder; and by the year 1800 there were thirty-two settlements on the Reserve.[1]

No sooner had the ratifications of Jay's treaty been exchanged than, on May 27th, General Wilkinson, left in command of Wayne's army at Greenville, sent his aide-de-camp, Captain Schaumburg, to Colonel England at Detroit, to demand the surrender of the posts under his command. Colonel England regretted—so he said—that a lack of orders from Lord Dorchester would prevent him from complying with General Wilkinson's request; and the condition of the new post at the mouth of the Detroit was not sufficiently advanced to enable him to name a date for evacuation.[2] This was the last ineffectual demand.

In June, 1796, Captain Lewis, despatched from Philadelphia on the day that the Senate took final action on the Jay treaty, presented to Lord Dorchester a demand for the surrender of the Northwest posts. Nothing could exceed the civility that was bestowed upon the representative of the War Department by Lord Dorchester's family; his lordship, then about seventy years old, made particular inquiries as to Washington's health, and "seemed pleased to learn that he was well and looked well." Captain Lewis could have dined out for a month at Quebec. At every gathering "the first toast was the King of Great Britain and the second

[1] Whittlesey's *History of Cleveland.* See also Garfield's Oration on the Northwest Territory, "Old South Leaflets," No. 42.

[2] *Michigan Pioneer and Historical Collections,* vol. xii., p. 220.

invariably the President." The people, too, seemed pleased at the prospect of friendly intercourse with the Americans.[1]

On his way back to Philadelphia, Captain Lewis delivered to Captain Bruff at Albany the orders for the evacuation of Niagara and Oswego.[2] He brought to Secretary McHenry the British commander-in-chief's order addressed to the officers commanding the guard left for the protection of the works and buildings at Forts Miami, Detroit, and Michilimackinac,[3] and commanding each to vacate his post "to such officer belonging to the forces of the United States as shall produce this authority to you for that purpose, who will precede the troops destined to garrison it by one day, in order that he may have time to view the nature and condition of the works and buildings." Congratulating the President on "the event which adds a large tract of country and wide resources to the territory of the United States," the secretary immediately despatched a special messenger to put General Wayne in possession of the precious documents.

The orders for the surrender of Fort Miami and of Detroit were sent from General Wilkinson at Greenville to Lieutenant-colonel Hamtramck, at Camp Deposit; and the latter lost no time in putting them into execution. Sending Captain Henry de Butts to Detroit to purchase a vessel, Hamtramck himself, on June 11th, "actually displayed the American stripes at Fort Miami,

[1] State Department MSS., McHenry to Washington, June 23, 1796.

[2] State Department MSS., McHenry to Washington, June 27, 1796. Niagara was surrendered August 11, 1796. See *Canadian Archives*, 1891, p. 75.

[3] State Department MSS., Adjutant-general George Beckwith's letter of June 2, 1796. The Lake Champlain posts and Oswegatchie (Ogdensburg) had previously been given up without formality. See also *Canadian Archives*, Beckwith to McHenry, June 3, 1796.

and embarked the same day with about four hundred men for Detroit."[1]

Captain Moses Porter,[2] despatched by Hamtramck with a detachment of artillery and infantry, comprising sixty-five men, embarked at the mouth of the Maumee in a schooner of fifty tons burden and in a dozen bateaux. Entering the Detroit River on the 11th of July, 1796, they discovered first a few widely scattered houses set along the low-lying shores, but as they progressed they found clustered about the new British post some twenty houses, in all stages of completion. The region was known as the district of Malden, but as yet the name of Amherstburg had not been given to the town, and for months it was known simply as "the new British post and town near the island of Bois Blanc," an island, by-the-way, that was claimed to be within the United States, greatly to the disturbance of Governor Simcoe.[3] The most considerable establishment in the place belonged to the Indian agent, Captain Elliott; the lands, comprising two thousand acres, were cultivated in a manner that would not have been "thought meanly of even in England"; the house, standing about two hundred yards from the river, commanded a full view of that noble stream and of Lake Erie. At the edge of the water stood the council-house, in which matters were discussed and decisions were reached the echoes of which were heard in the councils of nations

[1] *American Telegraph*, August 24, 1796. Letter of General James Wilkinson to the Secretary of War, dated Greenville, July 16, 1796.

[2] *American Pioneer*, vol. ii., p. 394. Hamtramck to Wilkinson.

[3] The ownership of the island was not settled until after the treaty of Ghent in 1817. After the War of 1812 the question was again raised.—War Department MSS.; Protest of Colonel Anthony Butler, July 1, 1815; and Andrew J. Dallas to Colonel Butler, May 31, 1815.

at New York and London. On Bois Blanc were encamped hundreds of Indians, curious and intent spectators of the changes then in progress. Ahead, the broad water was dotted with the swift-darting Indian canoes, with here and there the pleasure-boat of some thrifty trader; islands of all sizes and shapes, their shores lined with marshes, were strewn along the river; and the banks were without habitation save here and there little knots of miserable Indian huts. As the flotilla came within four miles of Detroit the houses became numerous; there were smiling orchards of peach and cherry; and tall trees of the pomme-caille, the favorite apple of the country. Sailing up to the great wooden wharf, the detachment disembarked, and marched up one of the narrow, unpaved streets, with its footway of squared logs laid transversely, thence through one of the two gates on the water side of the strong stockade, and through the town and up the slope to Fort Lernoult, with its bastioned corners from which the cannon had been removed to supply the new post at Malden. As the troops passed up the street crowds of barefooted Frenchmen greeted them in a language they did not understand, and bevies of dark-eyed French girls gazed demurely from under the wide brims of their straw hats, anxious to discover whether the homespun-clad newcomers were fitted to take the place of the gorgeous-hued soldiers and sailors whom the fate of war had relegated to the mouth of the river. Nor were Indians wanting; old squaws leading their daughters leered at the soldiers; chiefs and warriors of many tribes, hideous in their paint and more hideous in the wounds received in drunken orgies, moved about with what dignity they could command, or sat in the sun smoking their stone pipes, waiting for General Wabang (General

To-morrow) to distribute the presents he was ever promising and never bestowing.

At the hour of noon[1] the last of Colonel England's troops made their way to the ramparts, and, loosing the halyards, the flag that for thirty-four years had floated over the town of Cadillac's foundation dropped slowly to the ground. While the British soldiers gathered up the dishonored ensign, eager Americans bent the Stars and Stripes, and as the joyous folds of the beautiful banner streamed out on the July breeze a cheer went up from the little band of United States soldiers, whose feet at last trod the soil made theirs by the conquest of Clark, seventeen years before. Standing among the indifferent crowd that watched the change of flags were many besides the Detroit-born Reynolds[2] who would live to see and to rejoice in the day, sixteen years distant, when the then despised flag of England would again for a few months wave over that town and people. Detroit was essentially a foreign city, a small part English, the greater part French, but not in any degree or sense American.

[1] *Columbian Sentinel*, Boston, August 24, 1796; extract from a letter of Captain Henry de Butts to the Secretary of War, dated Detroit, July 14th: "It is with great pleasure I do myself the honor of announcing to you that on the 11th instant, about noon, the flag of the United States was displayed on the ramparts of Detroit, a few minutes after the works were evacuated by Colonel England and the British troops under his command, and with additional satisfaction I inform you that the exchange was effected with much propriety and harmony by both parties."

[2] 1812; *The War and Its Moral*, by William Coffin (Montreal, 1864), p. 196. Reynolds was born in Detroit, in 1781; his father was the British commissary. To Coffin, who visited him at his home in Malden in 1863, he said: "I saw the British flag hauled down from the flag-staff of Detroit at noon, 11th July, 1796. I saw it again hoisted by Brock, at noon of Sunday, 16th August, 1812."

On July 25th the twenty-ton American sloop *Detroit*, Captain Curry, arrived at Presque Isle for provisions and stores, and returned to Detroit for the garrison intended for Michilimackinac.[1] On the 16th of that month, fifty-eight of the merchants, traders, and inhabitants of the post had united in an address to the retiring British commandant, Major William Doyle, commending him for the impartial manner in which he had supported and protected the trade of that place, and for the "invariable propriety" with which he had acted as magistrate. Before taking passage for the lower lakes, he had replied, on July 26th, acknowledging for himself and his officers the uniform support they had always experienced from the signers of the address, and wishing every prosperity to the Canadian fur-trade.[2] The actual evacuation of the post took place early in August, and before the first of September the strange flag of the United States was snapping in the brisk breezes at the meeting-place of lakes Huron and Michigan.[3]

On the evening of August 10th, the Americans appeared at Fort Niagara, where they were politely and attentively received by the British Captain Sheafe, who turned over the fort, and possession was formally taken by mounting a sergeant's guard. Next morning the artillery, stores, and the remainder of the garrison disembarked; at three o'clock in the afternoon of the 11th the

[1] *Massachusetts Spy*, August 24, 1796.

[2] *Quebec Gazette*, August 25, 1796. A similar address, dated July 6th, was made to Colonel England by the people of Detroit, and was replied to by him.

[3] *Albany Gazette*, September 30, 1796: "A letter from Detroit, of August 15th, says that Michilimackinac is evacuated by the British, and will in the coming two weeks be occupied by our troops."

Stars and Stripes were run up under Federal salute, and the United States came into possession of the last of the frontier posts.[1]

Colonel John Francis Hamtramck, with his command, arrived at Detroit on the 13th of July, and immediately began to mount his artillery in the places made vacant by the removal of the British cannon, and in all possible ways to Americanize an old French town filled with British traders. Born in Canada, Hamtramck was one of some seven hundred American sympathizers who crossed the border to join the Revolutionary forces.[2] Entering the army at the age of twenty-one, he won a captaincy during the war; on the organization of the First Regiment of Infantry he was appointed a lieutenant-colonel by Washington in 1790, and as colonel he was with both St. Clair and Wayne in their Indian campaigns, having command of the left wing of the army at the decisive battle of Fallen Timbers. At Detroit he entered at once into the spirit of the situation, and became popular both with his command and with the towns-people. With his wife he occupied a comfortable house in the town, and until his death in 1803, at the early age of forty-eight years, he enjoyed a popularity that has kept his memory green to this day.[3]

[1] *Albany Gazette*, September 9, 1796.

[2] The birthplace of Hamtramck is unknown. He was born August 14, 1754, and died April 11, 1803, leaving an estate valued at $2138.47, which descended to his widow Rebecca Hamtramck. His home was above the old city of Detroit, in the suburb afterwards known as Hamtramck. His body was buried in St. Anne's Cemetery, then occupying the block on Jefferson Avenue bounded by Jefferson Avenue, Larned, Shelby, and Griswold streets, whence it was removed in 1817 to the new St. Anne's grounds on Congress Street, and in 1866 was removed a second time to Mount Elliott Cemetery. With more of truth than is commonly found in such a connection, the

In the wake of the army of occupation came General Wayne himself. After enjoying at his home-city of Philadelphia the honors and triumphs of his victory; after having experienced the gratification of being mentioned in eulogistic terms in President Washington's special message to Congress; and after incurring the persistent hostility of the anti-Federalists and the secret enmity of General Wilkinson, General Wayne was despatched to the frontier with the combined powers of a civil commissioner and a military commander. On August 13th he reached Detroit, to find that before his coming and without orders from Congress, the secretary of the Northwest Territory, Winthrop Sargent, had visited Detroit and erected the county of Wayne. Availing himself of the absence from the territory of Governor St. Clair, Sargent, as acting governor, had started for the North, and on August 15th had drawn the boundaries of Wayne County, from the present site of Cleveland, south to Fort Laurens, thence westward through Fort Wayne and the Chicago portage, thence north through the sources of the streams

stone erected by the officers of his command bears record that, "true patriotism and a zealous attachment to rational liberty, joined to a laudable ambition, led him into military service at an early period of his life. He was a soldier before he was a man; he was an active participator in all the dangers, difficulties, and honors of the Revolutionary War; and his heroism and uniform good conduct procured him the attentions and personal thanks of the immortal Washington. The United States in him has lost a valuable officer and a good citizen, and society a useful and pleasant member: to his family the loss is incalculable; and his friends will never forget the memory of Hamtramck."—See *Michigan Pioneer and Historical Collections*, vol. xiii., p. 493; and an address, on the occasion of marking the grave of Colonel John Francis Hamtramck, at Mount Elliott Cemetery, Detroit, Michigan, by the Sons of the American Revolution, October 18, 1897, delivered by Mr. R. Storrs Willis.

flowing westerly into Lake Michigan, to the national boundary-line north of Lake Superior. Making Peter Audrain prothonotary at Detroit, Sargent continued his way to Michilimackinac, where he established the civil authority of the government. Of these acts the chagrined St. Clair learned most casually, but he contented himself by merely intimating surprise that he had been forestalled in making the journey to the northern limits of his government.[1]

After a fatiguing, difficult, and dangerous journey of twelve hundred miles, over mountains, rivers, swamps, and lakes, General Wayne was flattered by his reception on the part of both the garrison and the inhabitants of Detroit. On his approach he was met by the chiefs and warriors of numerous tribes of Indians, who welcomed their "father" by repeated volleys of musketry, ear-piercing yells, friendly shakes of the hand, and other demonstrations of joy, "agreeably to the customs and usages of those hardy sons of this wilderness." When he entered the stockaded town the guns boomed a federal salute, and music attended his progress to the fort.

As Hennepin the Frenchman and Hamilton the Englishman gave expression to their appreciation of the beauty of Detroit's situation, so this first American commander found much to admire in a town that had "formerly filled an interesting place in history." "Here, in the centre of the wilderness of the West," he writes, "you see ships or large vessels of-war and merchantmen lying at the wharves or sailing up and down a pleasant river of about one mile wide, as if passing and repassing

[1] *St. Clair Papers.* St. Clair to James Ross, September 6, 1796; St. Clair to Roger Wolcott, August 30, 1796.

to and from the ocean. The town itself is a crowded mass of frame or wooden buildings, generally from one to two and a half stories high, many of them well finished and furnished, and inhabited by people of almost all nations. There are a number of wealthy and well-informed merchants and gentlemen, and elegant, fashionable, and well-bred women.

"The streets are so narrow as scarcely to admit two carriages to pass each other. The whole place is surrounded with high pickets, with bastions at proper distances, which are endowed with artillery; within the pickets is also a kind of citadel, which serves for barracks, stores, and for part of the troops. You enter the town by one main street, which runs parallel with the river and has a gate at each end, defended by a block-house; these gates are shut every night at sunset, and are not opened again until sunrise, in order to protect the citizens and their property from insult or injury by drunken, disorderly, or hostile Indians. At particular seasons large bodies of Indians assemble at this place. Upon my arrival I found about twelve hundred, whom we have been obliged to feed from principles of humanity as well as policy at this crisis. In the daytime these Indians appear to be perfectly domesticated, and pass and repass along the streets in common with the white inhabitants, but regularly retire at retreat-beating without aversion, from long habit. It is probable that this precaution of clearing the town of the savages and closing the gates originated from the attempt made by the Indians to destroy the garrison and place in the year 1763, under the conduct of the famous chief Pontiac.

"The fort, which has been built since, stands upon an eminence in the rear of the town and citadel, and commands both, as well as all the country in its vicinity. It's a regular earthen work, consisting of four half-bastions, with twenty-four platforms and embrasures suited to heavy artillery, with barracks, bomb-proofs, stores, etc., surrounded by a wide, deep ditch, with pickets set perpendicular in the bottom, and a fraise projecting from the beam of the parapet over the ditch. The whole is encompassed by an abatis, but now generally in a state of ruin, from the effect of time only, and not from any wanton destruction; on the contrary, every precaution was used to prevent any injury or damage to the works or buildings. In fact, all the works and buildings on the American side of the line of demarcation have been surrendered up by the several British commandants to the troops of the United States, agreeable to treaty, and in the most decent, polite, and accommodating manner, in virtue of the arrangements previously made with Lord Dorchester.

"This event must afford the highest pleasure and satisfaction to every friend of government and good order, and in particular to that great and first of men, the President of the United States, and I trust it will produce a conviction to the world that the measures he has uniformly pursued to attain this desirable end were founded in wisdom, and that the best interests of his country have been secured by that unshaken firmness, patriotism, and virtue for which he is universally and justly admired and celebrated; a few *Demon-crats* excepted."[1]

[1] Pennsylvania Historical Society's collections of Wayne MSS.; General Anthony Wayne to Isaac Wayne; Detroit, September 10, 1796. I am indebted to Mr. John W. Jordan, the secretary of the society, for furnishing me a copy of what is believed to be the only extant communication written by Wayne while at Detroit.

GENERAL WAYNE'S GRAVE

General Wayne remained at Detroit until November 17th, when he set sail for Presque Isle, on his homeward way. Tossed on the fitful billows of that shallow lake, Wayne's gout returned in violent form, and it was with difficulty that he was transferred to the block-house. There he remained under the devoted ministrations of Captain Russell Bissell and Dr. George Balfour until, on December 15th, death released his indomitable spirit from the racked body. A log block-house, copied from the one Wayne himself had built there in 1790, marks the spot where the brave soldier was laid at rest; his remains, however, were removed in 1809 to the church-yard of St. David's, at Radnor, Pennsylvania.[1]

The surrender of the posts by no means involved the surrender of the fur-trade. Oswego had been founded by Sir William Johnson for the purpose of drawing the trade away from the French on the St. Lawrence; and the New York traders had continued to enjoy this market in spite of the British garrison; but at best the traffic was meagre. At Niagara the trade was of considerable volume; but Newark, the town in which the traders lived, was on the Canadian side of the river; and when news came that the post was to be surrendered the few merchants within the fort limits crossed the line, leaving for the time being an empty fortress. Mackinac was indeed an important station of the Northwest Company of Montreal, and several independent traders were there; but on the surrender of Sinclair's fort the British established themselves near by, on the Island of St. Joseph, in the highway between lakes Huron and Superior; and although a number of American traders came to take the vacant places, the intelli-

[1] Stillé's *Life of Wayne*, p. 344.

gence, the trade connections, and the capital of an Astor were necessary before competition with the Montreal merchants could become effective.[1] Of all the posts given up, Detroit was the most important. At the time of the surrender the town contained upward of twelve hundred people; but many of the traders removed to the new British post at the mouth of the river, and many of those who remained hesitated to become American citizens. Indeed, the Jay treaty made it of no advantage to change one's nationality. The departure of the traders and garrison gave house-room to the United States officers, not a few of whom appropriated to their own use houses and stores that had been built on lands granted illegally by the various post-commanders; and the Americans even went so far as to compel the subjects of Great Britain to serve in the militia, a burden that caused them to appeal to the British minister.[2]

Tradition has it that on the appearance of the Americans at Detroit, Simon Girty, in his haste to escape from possible vengeance, swam his horse across the river, and galloped to his farm near the mouth of that stream. As an employé of the British Indian department he continued to urge the savages to withstand the encroach-

[1] The romantic side of the American fur-trade at Mackinac has been related in Constance Fenimore Woolson's novel, *Anne;* while the charm and witchery of the Lake region finds its subtlest expression in Miss Woolson's *Castle Nowhere: Lake-country Sketches.*

[2] *Travels through the States of North America, and the Provinces of Upper and Lower Canada, during the years* 1795, 1796, 1797; by Isaac Weld, Jr. Fourth edition (London, 1807), vol. ii., letters xxxii. and xxxiii. These letters contain the acute observations of an Englishman who, with all his prejudices, saw matters in a truer light than did Judge Jacob Burnett, whose often-quoted description of Detroit at this time is as near the truth as a clever caricature is like the original.

ments of the Americans on the territory north of the Ohio; in January, 1791, he led the Indians in their attack on Dunlap's Station, on the Great Miami; and he was a participant in the frightful tortures inflicted by the Indians on Abner Hunt, by way of revenge for their ill success. At St. Clair's defeat Girty led the Wyandottes, looking on at the scalping of General Butler, and sharing in the booty and prisoners. It is said that he saved the life of William May, a soldier who bore a flag of truce to the Indians, and that May afterwards became a vessel-captain in the service of McKee and Elliott. In June, 1794, Girty aided McKee in planning the unsuccessful Indian attack on Fort Recovery; and on August 20th the three renegades—Girty, McKee, and Elliott—watched from a safe distance Wayne's crushing defeat of the savages at Fallen Timbers. For the time being the Indians were whipped into submission; and it was all in vain that the British agents fed and clothed the homeless savages, and loaded the chiefs with presents. The utmost that they and Captain Brant could do was to prevent several tribes from joining in the treaty of Greenville; but in so doing they covered the embers for future use. Girty himself continued to be employed as the king's interpreter; he had family troubles caused by his drunkenness; he lived through the War of 1812, but by reason of blindness he could take no part in the struggles that went on about him; and on February 18, 1818, he died in the arms of his forgiving wife, and was buried on his farm in Malden.[1]

The British retained command of the Grand Portage of Lake Superior, and of the Ottawa River route to and from the upper country; their new fort at Malden and

[1] Butterfield's *History of the Girtys*, p. 322.

the block-house on Bois Blanc Island commanded the channels of the Detroit River, as General Hull was to discover to his cost; and the British fort at Niagara was built so as to toss shot down into the American fortress. All these points were to prove of decided advantage to the British when the aggravations that never were wanting finally provoked the War of 1812.

During the twenty-two momentous years that elapsed between Lord Dunmore's war in 1774 and the surrender of the Northwest posts in 1796, the Revolution had been fought through eight trying years; the Northwest had been conquered by George Rogers Clark, and through the efforts of Jay and Franklin and Adams had been made the first addition to the territories of the new nation of the United States; the land claims of the states had been surrendered to the federal government, and the new territory had been dedicated to freedom, with large provisions for education; the Ohio had become a highway of traffic and of immigration; on the Muskingum and on Lake Erie New England colonies had been planted under such conditions and with such strength as to make New England ideas the dominant force throughout Ohio even to this day; after two disastrous failures the Indians had been conquered though not subdued; and the forces of England had been removed across the boundary-line. It was perhaps natural that there should be a reaction after such rapid expansion. England, made sullen and vindictive by the rapid growth of the United States, by presents and subsidies kept a hold over the savages of the Northwest; and the tremendous power of that rich and proud nation was felt particularly along the frontier, where the poverty and the meagre resources of the new nation were most apparent. When in 1812 England and America for a second time grappled with each other in war, the northwestern frontier from Niagara to Mackinac was called to receive the first shock of combat, and to experience the horrors of savage warfare to an extent unparalleled during the Revolution. Far-off Kentucky was made to "Remember the River Raisin"; and the ignominious surrender of Detroit and the massacre at Mackinac were to be atoned for by Perry's victory of Lake Erie and Harrison's triumph on the Thames.

INDEX

ABBOTT, EDWARD, Lieutenant-governor, at Vincennes, 211.
Abercrombie, Defeat of, 100, 245.
Adams, Dr. Herbert B., 317.
Adams, Henry, 310, 369.
Adams, John, elected peace commissioner, 281, 283, 284, 384.
Aix-la-Chapelle, Treaty of, 74, 75, 154.
Albany convention of June, 1754, 90.
Alexandria, Braddock's army at, 95, 115.
Algonquin Indians, 3, 7, 15.
Allen, Ethan, 245.
Allouez, Claude, 21.
Amherst, General Jeffrey (Baron Amherst), 100, 106, 131, 147, 148, 149, 152.
Amherstburg, 372.
Andrain, Peter, 378.
Angell, Dr. James B., 368.
Arkansas River, Discovery of, 26.
Armstrong, John, 33.
Army of the United States, Size of, in 1787, 344.
Asatanik goes overland to Hudson Bay, 12.
Ashland, Wisconsin, 21.
Astor, John Jacob, 295, 382.
Aubry, Spanish commandant at New Orleans, 172.
Aveneau, Father, 47.

BABY, M., warns Gladwin of Indian treachery, 130.
Baltimore and Chesapeake Canal, 311.
Baltimore and Ohio Railroad, 311.
Bancroft, George, 24, 25.
Barlow, Joel, 343.
Barré, Colonel Isaac, opposes Quebec Bill, 201.
Barthe, Pierre, 132.
Baton Rouge, 258.
Bay des Puants. (*See* Green Bay.)
Beaubien, Charles, 209.
Beaubien family, Origin of, 122.
Beaujeu commands French at Braddock's defeat, 96.
Beauvais, the richest man in Illinois country, 170.
Beaver, Pennsylvania, 157.
Beckwith, Major George, British spy, Reports of, in regard to the United States, 307, 308.
Bedford, Pennsylvania, 129.
Belestre (or Belêtre), 102, 103.
Belle Prairie, 352.
Benton, Thomas H., 189.
Bienville. (*See* Céleron.)
"Big Knives," 219.
Billon, F. L., 256.
Bird, Lieutenant Henry, plans fort at Detroit, 250; expeditions of, 250, 252.
Birney, Thomas, 77.
Black Hawk War, 40.
Blair, Francis P., 76.
Blair, Montgomery, 76.
Blue Licks, Slaughter at, 275.
Bogy, Colonel L. V., 173.
Bois Blanc Island, 31, 59, 348, 372, 384.
Bolivar, 251.
Bolton, Colonel, 228.
Bonne, Louis de, 61.
Boone, Daniel, 185, 193; at Detroit, 209.
Boone, Squire, 185.
Bosseron, 208.
Boston, Troubles at, 186, 280; evacuation of, 331.

INDEX

Botetourt, Lord, 186.
Boundaries in treaty of 1783, 282–9.
Bouquet, Colonel Henry, arrives in America, 100; at Fort Pitt, 106, 131; invited to join Ohio Company, 146; attempts to remove settlers, 149; his proclamation, 147, 148, 151; thinks Ohio project a bubble, 150; proposes separate colony on the Ohio, 147, 161; his victory at Bushy Run, 152; early life of, 154, 155; his acquaintance with Miss Willing, 155; his expedition to the Muskingum, 156–165; his promotion and death, 162, 183, 247, 337, 363.
Bouquet expedition, Accounts of, 155, 245.
Bouquet Papers, 276.
Bowman, Major John, 219, 220, 234, 251.
Brace, Jonathan, 369.
Braddock, General Edward, appears on the Potomac, 92; summons the royal governors to meet him at Alexandria — his character and training, 93; his boast, 94; defeat and death of, 97, 115, 167, 290, 363.
Braddock's road, Dispute between Washington and Bouquet as to, 101, 150.
Bradstreet, Colonel John, makes peace with Lake Indians—the peace repudiated, 139; reaches Detroit, 139, 156.
Brady, Thomas, 258.
Brandy, Indian demand for, 44; price of, at Detroit, 53.
Brant, Joseph, 262, 275; forms conspiracy against Americans, 299; a social lion in England, 300; holds council at Detroit—his ultimatum, 301; his Indian policy acceptable to England, 303, 306, 345, 348, 351, 352, 361, 383.
Brebœuf, Jean de, 4.
Brodhead, Colonel Daniel, 242, 264, 267.
Brown, B. Gratz, 76.
Bruff, Captain, receives surrender of Niagara and Oswego, 371.
Brulé, Étienne, his wanderings, 2.
Brymer, Douglas, 297.
Buffalo, New York, 369.
Bullitt, Thomas, 184.
"Bunch of Grapes" tavern, The, 333, 334.
Burgoyne's defeat, 226, 281.
Burke, Edmund, 64, 70, 141; opposes Quebec Bill — fixes boundaries of New York, 202, 283, 300, 318.
Burke, William, argues for retention of Guadaloupe instead of Canada, 141.
Burnett, Judge Jacob, 231, 382.
Burton, Clarence M., his Cadillac papers, 50, 112.
Bushy Run, Battle at, 152, 154.
Butler, Captain Edward, 360.
Butler, General Richard, 299, 360.
Butler, Indian trader, 188.
Butler's Rangers, 262.
Butterfield, Consul Willshire, 6; as to Crawford expedition, 269.

Cabots, Voyages of the, 63.
Cadillac, Antoine de Lamothe, 40; character of, 41; puts Iroquois messengers to death, 42; plans for a settlement on the Detroit, 43; opposition of the Jesuits, 44; persuades Count Pontchartrain to grant concessions at Detroit, 44; founds Detroit, 46; objects to enforcing liquor regulations, 50; his early life, 50; his marriage, 50; children of, 51; prosperity of his enterprise, 52; excessive charges for land, 52; obtains trading privileges, 55; his appearance, 55; ordered to Louisiana, 55, 374.
Cadillac, Madame, joins her husband at Detroit, 49, 55.
Cahokia, 169, 215, 220, 257, 258, 261.
Caldwell, John, secures religious toleration in Virginia, 72, 369.
Caldwell, Lieutenant, 211.
Calhoun, John Caldwell, 72.
Callières, Governor of New France, 43.
Calvé, a French trader, 256.
Camp Hobson's Choice, 363.
Campbell, Captain Donald, commandant at Detroit, 107; detained by Pontiac, 122; murder of, 131.
Campbell, Henry Colin, 11, 13, 16.

INDEX

Campbell, Major William, British commander at Fort Miami, 365.
Canada, Character of settlers in, 196; justice in, 197; loyalty to the crown, 198; population of, 203; invited to join the American colonies in the Revolution, 205; cession, of proposed, 288; friendly feeling in, towards the United States, 371.
Canadian Pacific Railway, 29.
Carheil, Father Stephen de, refuses to leave Michilimackinac, 47; on the liquor question, 48.
Carleton, Sir Guy, succeeds Murray as Governor at Quebec, 196; revives old laws of Canada, 197; approves Quebec Bill, 199; testimony of, before House of Commons, 202; recalled, 215, 222, 228, 247, 254, 295. (*See also* Lord Dorchester.)
Carlisle, Fred., 132.
Carlisle, Pennsylvania, 129.
Carlyle, Colonel John, his opinion of Croghan, 167.
Carrington, Edward, 326.
Carroll, Charles, 205.
Carroll, Rev. John, 205.
Carteret, Sir George, 13.
Cartier, Jacques, explores the St. Lawrence, 2, 63.
Carver, Jonathan, his story of the Pontiac conspiracy, 113; his travels through North America, 113, 320.
Cass, General Lewis, 18, 45; secures documents relating to the Northwest, 49, 113.
Casse family, 59.
Castel Sarrasin, 55, 223.
Catharine II. of Russia, 282.
Cathay, 5, 294.
Catherwood, Mary Hartwell, 129.
Cavendish, Sir Henry, reports debates on Quebec Bill, 144.
Cealle, Carrigan de, 60.
Céleron de Bienville takes possession of the Ohio country, 74; ordered to drive the English from the Northwest, 82, 83.
Chacornacle, Cadillac's lieutenant, 45.
Champigny, Intendant of New France, 43.
Champlain, 2, 5.
Chaney, Henry A., 330.
Channing, Professor Edward, 321.
Chapoton, Jean Baptiste, 208.
Chapoton family, 59.
Chase, Samuel, 205.
Chatham, Earl of, opposes Quebec Act, 199; opposes American independence, 279. (*See also* Pitt, William.)
Chequamegon Bay, 20, 22.
Cherokees, 177, 181, 188, 216.
Cherubin, Father, 56.
Chevalier, Louis, 257, 259, 261.
Chickasaws, 166, 241.
Chillicothe, 251.
Chippewas capture Michilimackinac, 122, 128, 158, 210, 270.
Choctaw Indians, 241.
Choiseul encourages colonies to revolt, 280.
Chouart, Médard, comes to New France, 9. (*See also* Radisson and Grosseilliers.)
Chouteau, Auguste, a founder of St. Louis, 169, 173, 256.
Christinos Indians, 21, 23.
Christmas celebrated in the Ohio country, 77.
Cincinnati, 348, 355, 363.
Clapham, John, Murder of, 107.
Clara d'Assisi, Saint, 32.
Clark, George Rogers, with Cresap at Wheeling, 191; in Dunmore war, 193; early life of, 216; plans conquest of the Northwest, 217; sends spies to Illinois country, 218; captures Kaskaskia, 219; capture of Vincennes, 232-237; plans to march on Detroit, 238; Pickaway raid, 253, 261; leads force to Vincennes, 308; his bad habits, 308, 316, 322, 338, 374, 384.
Clay, Henry, 37.
Clergue, F. H., 294.
Cleveland, Moses, 369.
Cleveland, Ohio, 167; founded, 370.
Clinch River, 185.
Clinton, Governor George, 296, 309.
Coal in the Ohio country, 92.
Coffin, William, 374.
Colonies, Jealousies among, 142.
Company of the Colony, 46, 51, 53.
Condé, Prince, 30.
Congress, recommends that Virginia

close her land office, 317; declaration of, as to new States in Western territory, 318; provides for sale of ceded lands, 318; asks Virginia to make more favorable offer of cession, 320.
Connecticut, 8; boundaries of, 66; offers to cede her Western lands, 318; sells reserved lands, 321; gains by her cession, 321.
Connecticut Land Company, 369.
Connecticut Reserve, 321, 322.
Conolly, Dr. John, in command at Fort Pitt, 186; calls on settlers to repel Shawanese raids, 188, 195, 212, 338.
Contrecœur captures fort at forks of the Ohio, 89.
Cooley, Thomas M., 327.
Copper, 2, 22, 25, 47.
Corn-planter, 299.
Cornstalk, Shawanese chief, at the battle of Point Pleasant, 190; assents to Dunmore peace, 192.
Cornwallis, Lord, Surrender of, 279.
Coureurs de bois, 21.
Craigie house, 343.
Cramahé, Lieutenant-governor, at Quebec, 197.
Crawford, Colonel William, with Washington on the Ohio, 184; friend of Washington, 270; defeat of, 272; torture of, 274.
Cresap, Captain Michael, 188; early life of, 189; joins Washington at Cambridge, 193; his death, 193.
Cresap, Colonel Thomas, 72, 76, 145, 146, 147, 150, 153; sketch of, 188.
Croghan, George, 76, 106, 151; his journey to Illinois country, 162; his journals, 163; sketch of, 167, 168, 172, 180; with Washington, 184.
Cromwell, 68.
Crown Point, 94.
Cuillerier, the family, 60, 122, 126; M. Cuillerier, French trader at Detroit, 122, 126; Mademoiselle Cuillerier, 108, 112.
Culpeper grant, 69.
Cumberland River, 185.
Curran, Barnaby, 76, 85.
Custom of Paris, 324.
Cutler, Rev. Manasseh, proposes to buy Western lands, 329, 330, 332; secures passage of Ordinance of 1787, 333, 342, 344.
Cuttawa River. (*See* Kentucky River.)
Cuyler, Lieutenant, 127.

D'Abbadie, French Governor at New Orleans, 172.
Dablon, Claude, 22, 24.
D'Aigrement, Report of, as to Detroit, 48, 52.
Dalyell, Captain, reinforces Detroit, 132; killed at Bloody Run, 133.
Dane, Nathan, 326; proposes amendment excluding slavery from Northwest, 327; his work on Ordinance of 1787, 328.
D'Aranda's opinion of treaty of 1783, 290.
Dartmouth, Lord, 198; prepares Quebec bill, 199, 205; succeeds Hillsborough, 183.
Daumont, Simon François. (*See* Saint Lusson.)
Davers, Sir Robert, 110, 119.
Davis, Andrew McFarland, 276.
Deane, Silas, suggests sale of Northwest lands, 315.
De Butts, Captain Henry, 371.
Dejean, Philip, judge at Detroit, 229, 235, 236, 237.
Delawares, 78, 85, 156, 157, 160, 162, 177, 180, 185, 210, 212, 263; villages burned, 267, 270, 272, 273, 277, 364.
Deniaux, Cherubin de, 54.
De Peyster, General J. Watts, 223.
De Peyster, Major Arent Schuyler, 211, 221; early life of, 221; his appearance and character, 221; his marriage, 222; his poems, 222; commands at Detroit, 253, 260; kindness to American prisoners, 260; furnishes men and ammunition to oppose Crawford's expedition, 270; his opinion of the Moravian massacre and Crawford torture, 274; thinks peace in the Northwest impossible, 277; meets Brant, 300; transferred to Niagara, 313; returns to England, 313; his life in Scotland, 313; his poetical contest with Robert Burns, 314; death of, 314.

INDEX

Derruisseau, 60.
De Soto, 25.
Detroit, founded by Cadillac, 45; Jesuit hostility to, 47; fire at, 51; besieged by Indians, 56; surrendered to English, 102; society at, 107; attacked by Pontiac, 119; capital of the Northwest, 205; Hamilton's description of, 206; fort at, 208, 218; Clark plans capture of, 238, 242; Indians at, 249; Fort Lernoult built, 250; attack on, planned, 269; outlet for trade of, 310, 346; surrendered, 371; description of, by General Wayne, 378, 379, 380.
Detroit country, Conferences in, 39.
Detroit River discovered, 25, 31.
De Vierville, 227.
Dieskau at Lake George, 98.
Dinwiddie, Governor, 81; defends Virginia frontiers, 84; seeks aid against the French, 89.
Dongan, Governor of New York, attempts to capture Michilimackinac, 39.
Dorchester, Lord, assumes governorship of Canada, 302; insists on holding Northwestern posts, 303, 304; his high character, 305; his friendship with Wolfe, 305; his Indian policy, 306, 307, 345; disturbed at United States military preparations, 347, 352; orders surrender of Northwest posts, 370.
Doughty, Major, builds Fort Harmar, 344.
Doyle, Major William, surrenders Michilimackinac, 375.
Draper, Lyman C., 173, 186, 213, 224.
Dubuisson, Joseph Guyon, defends Detroit against Indians, 55.
Ducharme, M., 256.
Duer, Colonel William, 343.
Duff, John, 218.
Dugué, M., 45.
Du Juanay, Father, 24.
Du Lhut builds Fort St. Joseph on St. Clair River, 39.
Dunmore, Earl of, 185; his perplexity, 185; interested in Western lands, 187; marches against Indians, 189; makes peace, 191; honors to, 192, 193, 212, 216, 217, 320, 338.
Dunmore, The, sloop-of-war, 222.
Dunmore's war, Causes of, 188; results of, 194, 212, 384.
Duquesne, Governor of New France, prepares to drive the English from the Ohio country, 84, 88.
Durantaye, 39.

Easton, Treaty of, 101, 146, 147, 151.
Edison, Thomas A., begins experiments at Fort Gratiot, 40.
Education in the Northwest, 329.
Eel River, 174.
Elizabeth, Queen, 64.
Elliott, Matthew, 214, 262, 372.
Elliott, Richard R., 51, 60, 115.
Embarrass River, 231, 233.
England, Colonel, commandant at Detroit, declines to surrender the post, 370, 374.
England, Strength of, in America, 8; attempts to gain the Northwest, 38, 39; furnishes cheapest markets, 44, 53; her title to the Northwest, 64, 90; English traders in Ohio country, 82; English and French policies contrasted, 86; makes national issue of French invasion of the Northwest, 92; defeats of, 99; victories of, 100; gains in Seven Years' War, 141; prefers to give up territory to United States, 289; effects of retention of Western posts, 304; prepared to go to war to retain Northwest posts, 307.
English, William Hayden, 220.
Established Church, Opposition to, 80.
Etherington, Captain George, 128, 225.

Fairfax, Honorable William, 69.
Fairfax, Lord, 69.
Fallen Timbers, 213; battle of, 366.
Falls of the Ohio, 76.
Farmer, Silas, 50.
Farquier, Lieutenant-governor of Virginia, 148, 149, 150.
Fearing, Paul, first lawyer in the Northwest territory, 342.
Field, Colonel John, 213.
Finley, John, explores Kentucky, 185.
Fitzhugh, Henry, 184.
Floridas, The, exchanged for Cuba, 141, 144.

INDEX

Forbes, General John, forces the evacuation of Fort Duquesne, 100; success and death of, 102, 147, 150, 115, 270.
Force, Peter, 354.
Ford, Captain Henry A., 266.
Forts:—Chartres, 82, 101, 164, 168, 170, 171; surrendered to the English, 255; Crèvecœur, 36, 168; Defiance, 364; Duquesne, 100, 101; Frontenac, 35; Gage, 170, 215, 219; Gower, 193; Gratiot, 40; Hamilton, 353; Harmar, 335, 344, 353; treaty of, 346, 367; Jefferson, 239; Knox, 353; Laurens, 251, 252; abandoned, 267; Lernoult, 249, 348; Mackinac, 254; McIntosh, 251; abandoned, 267; treaty of, 346; Miami, 126, 366; surrendered, 371; Necessity, 151; Ontario, 347; Orange, 10; Ouiatanon, 166, 167, 168, 174; Patrick Henry, 238; Pitt (*see also* Pittsburg), invested by Indians, 152, 185; name changed to Fort Dunmore, 212; Pontchartrain, 82; Recovery, 363; Sackville, 234, 235; Sandusky captured, 126; Stanwix, treaty of, 180, 182, 299, 352; Steuben, 353; St. Charles, 256; St. Joseph captured, 127; St. Joseph, on the St. Clair, 40; Washington, 348, 353; Wayne, 350; William, 294.
Fox, Charles James, opposes Quebec bill, 201, 283, 290, 300.
Fox River, 5, 25.
France, Numerical strength of, in America, 8; assumes the aggressive in the Northwest, 38; economic policy of, 46; her claims to the Northwest, 63; takes possession of Ohio country, 74; losses in Seven Years' War, 141; opposes American extension, 280.
Franklin, Benjamin, his plan for union of the colonies, 91; plans colonies on the Ohio, 92; secures supplies for Braddock, 94; argues for retention of Canada, 141; says American independence improbable, 142; promotes Walpole grant, 175; answers Lord Hillsborough, 182; at Quebec, 205, 222, 270; his services in Paris, 280–283; in peace negotiations, 281, 318, 322, 384.
Franklin, Governor William, 175, 180, 183.
Fraser, Lieutenant, sent to Illinois country, 164, 172.
Frazer, John, 87.
Frederick the Great, 282.
French and Indian War begun, 89.
French proper names, Confusion in the, 59; aid the Indians during the Pontiac war, 125; assist Gladwin, 130; traders become British subjects, 163.
Friedenwald, Dr. Herbert, 184.
Frontenac, Count, 27, 34; he celebrates his victories, 38.
Fry, Colonel Joshua, 89.
Fur-trade, accessibility of, 143, 286; description of, 293, 295, 304, 347, 381.

Gage, General Thomas, repudiates Bradstreet's peace with Indians, 139, 172, 183.
Gallatin, Albert, meets Washington on the Ohio, 310.
Gallipolis, settlement of, 343.
Galvez, 261.
Garfield, James A., 321.
George, Captain Robert, 238.
George III., Gladwin presented to, 139, 193, 198; Brant refuses to kiss the hand of, 300.
Georgian Bay, 11, 45.
Gere, Amable de, 96.
Germain, Lord George, 228, 248, 253.
Germain, Père, 49.
Germans in the Shenandoah Valley, 72; in the Northwest, 86; in New York, 178.
Gibault, Father, receives surrender of Vincennes, 215; Hamilton's opinion of, 232, 235; at Michilimackinac, 254; Sinclair's opinion of, 255; baptizes first child at St. Louis, 256.
Gibraltar the price demanded by Spain, 258, 282.
Gibson, Colonel John, writes out Logan's message, 192, 194, 252, 268, 269.
Gillman, Joseph, 339.
Girty, George, 211.
Girty, James, 211.

INDEX

Girty, Simon, translates Logan's message, 192; his early life, 212; escapes to Detroit, 214; witnesses torture of Crawford, 274; escapes from Detroit, 382.

Gist, Christopher, his explorations, 75–80; removes to the Ohio, 85; accompanies Washington to the French, 85; his sons, 75.

Gladwin, Major Henry, explores Lake Erie, 146; with Sir William Johnson at Detroit, 109; Indian complaints against, 110; military training of, 115; his marriage, 116; forces French to refuse aid to Indians, 136; advises free sale of rum to Indians, 137; his course approved by Amherst, 138; promoted, 138, 139; returns to England and is presented to George III., 139; death and burial, 140.

Gladwin, The, strange escape of, 135.

Gooch, Governor of Virginia, welcomes Scotch-Irish, 72.

Gorrell, Lieutenant J., commands at Green Bay, 129.

Gouon, M., warns Gladwin, 112.

Gouon family, 59, 60.

Grand Company. (*See* Walpole Grant.)

Grand Portage, 289, 293.

Grand Portage of Lake Superior, 383.

Grand Sables, 17.

Grant, Major, his force slaughtered, 101.

Gratiot, Captain Charles, 40.

Great Kanawha River, 181.

Great Slave Lake, 293.

Greathouse murders, 186, 188.

Green, George W., 287.

Green Bay, 4, 11, 12, 21, 22, 23, 34, 129.

Greenbrier River, settlements on, 148.

Greenville, 366.

Grenada, Government of, 144.

Grenolle, companion of Brulé, 2.

Grenville, Sir Richard, founds Roanoke colony, 65.

Griffin, The, first ship on the upper Lakes, 27.

Grigon, Captain, 224.

Grosse Isle, 31.

Grosse Pointe, Indian defeat at, 58.

Grosseilliers, Médard Chouart, Sieur des Grosseilliers. (*See* Radisson and Grosseilliers.)

Guadaloupe, 141.

Guerin, Jean, companion of Menard, 15.

Guyon, Marie Thérèse, wife of Cadillac, 50.

HALDIMAND PAPERS, 276.

Haldimand, Sir Frederick, 154; succeeds Carleton, 215, 235, 256, 259; shocked by news of Crawford's torture, 275; withdraws war parties, 291; opinion as to boundaries, 292; refuses to surrender posts, 296; seats Mohawks in Canada, 298; entertains Brant, 300, 337.

Hale, Edward Everett, 330.

Half-king of the Six Nations demands the retirement of the French, 85.

Hamelin, Louis, 96.

Hamilton, Alexander, objects to formation of new States, 318.

Hamilton, Governor of Pennsylvania, 89.

Hamilton, Henry, Lieutenant-governor and Superintendent at Detroit, 205; prepares to invade the Illinois country, 216; accused of usurpation, 227; sets out for the Illinois country, 229; repairs fort at Vincennes, 230; ignorant of Clark's approach, 234; surrenders Vincennes, 235; his journey to Williamsburg, 236; placed in irons by command of Jefferson, 237; returns to England, 237; his proclamation, 263, 295; appointed Lieutenant-governor of Canada, 312; removed, 312; Governor of Bermuda, 312; town of Hamilton named for, 312; Governor of Dominica, 313; death of, 313, 378.

Hammond, George, British Minister, 297.

Hamtramck, Lieutenant-colonel, 354; receives surrender of Fort Miami, 371; arrives at Detroit, 376; sketch of, 376, 377.

Hanbury, Thomas, 73, 81.

Hand, General Edward, 213, 214, 267.

Harding, Colonel, 350.

Hardy, Samuel, 320.

Harmar, General, takes control of

matters in the Northwest, 324, 336; gives Sunday dinners to Ohio settlers, 341, 344; expedition of, against the Indians, 350.

Harris, Mary, Indian captive, 78.

Harrisburg, Pennsylvania, 167.

Harrison, William Henry, 231; Governor of Virginia, 310.

Harrod, William, 251.

Hartley, David, perfects treaty of 1783, 290.

Harvard College, 338, 339, 342, 345.

Havana captured by the English, 141.

Hay, Jehu, Lieutenant-governor at Detroit, 130, 211, 237, 312; death of, 313.

Hay, Major, 230.

Hayet, Margaret, sister of Radisson and wife of Des Grosseilliers, 10.

Helm, Captain Leonard, 230, 236, 238.

Henderson, Colonel Richard, proprietor of Transylvania, 216, 218.

Henderson & Company, 322.

Hennepin, Louis, longs to go to New France, 30; assists at building of the *Griffin*, 30; desires to remain at Detroit, 35; names Lake Ste. Claire, 32; is sent on a voyage down the Illinois, 35, 168, 378.

Henry, Alexander, British trader, 129.

Henry, Patrick, Governor of Virginia, 185, 186, 217, 218.

Henry, William Wirt, 72.

Hey, Chief-justice, 197, 199.

Hillsborough, Lord, opposes Ohio Colony project, 175, 181; Franklin forces resignation of, 182, 196.

Hinsdale, Dr. B. A., 316.

Hoar, Senator George F., 327, 330.

Hocking River, 193.

Holmes, Ensign, commandant at Fort Miami, 126.

Howard, Jacob M., 62.

Howard, John, on the Ohio, 90.

Hubbard, Bela, 18.

Hudson Bay, 12, 21.

Hudson Bay Company, 21, 144.

Hull, Lieutenant-colonel William, 296, 321, 339, 384.

Huron country, 6.

Huron Islands, 19.

Hurons, 9, 12, 24, 34, 56, 57, 210, 211, 300.

ILLINOIS, County of, 220.

Illinois country, French in, 168; surrendered to the English, 173, 203.

Illinois Indians, 23, 36, 56, 169, 208.

Illinois River, 26, 36.

Indians, Trade with, cut off by Iroquois, 38; allotted lands at Detroit, 46, 52, 54; their claims to the Northwest, 86; lands of, in 1763, 145; treatment of prisoners, 161; trade with, at Fort Chartres, 169; discipline of, in battle, 190; orgies of, 207; councils of, 210; terrorized by Clark, 238; not to be employed against whites, 241; after Revolution, 291; expense of, 292; number of captives taken by, 352; insist on the Ohio as the boundary, 362.

Ireland, religious persecutions in, 71.

Iroquois, 6; friends of the English, 8, 12, 17, 23, 28, 39, 41, 42, 66, 135, 178, 221; claims of, 318; claims to Western lands not valid, 319.

Irvine, William, 268.

Isle au Cochon, 107.

Isle Royale, 20.

JACKER, Father Edward, 16; discovers Marquette's remains, 27.

Jamestown founded, 65.

Jamet, Lieutenant, 128.

Jay, John, peace commissioner, 281, 283; failure of, in Spain, 285; Franklin's confidence in, 285; takes leading part in treaty, 286; his argument as to the Northwest, 288; triumph of, 290; negotiates treaty with England, 367.

Jay Treaty, 367, 368, 370, 382, 384.

Jebb, Rev. Henry Galdwin, 107.

Jefferson, Thomas, his report of Logan's message, 191, 218; his treatment of Hamilton, 237; assures Clark of aid against Detroit, 238; opposes Spain on the Mississippi, 239; his policy as to the employment of Indians, 241, 242; peace commissioners, 284, 285; negotiates for surrender of the Northwest posts, 297; loyalist poetry as to his treatment of Hamilton, 312, 320; his plan for ceded territory, 322, 324; would exclude slavery

INDEX

from the Northwest, 325; proposes classical names for States of the Northwest, 325, 329, 335.
Jenkins, William, 85.
Jesuit Manuscript, The, 60.
Jesuits, Claims of, 28; traffic in furs, 43.
Jogues, Isaac, at Sault Ste. Marie, 6; death of, 8.
Johnson, Guy, 180.
Johnson, Sir John, British superintendent of Indian affairs, 303; his significant letter to Brant, 303, 352.
Johnson, Sir William, 91; in charge of Indian affairs, 94, 106; made a baronet, 98; at Lake George, 98; at Detroit, 108, 160; exceeds his instructions, 153, 181, 188, 213, 245; sends Croghan to Illinois country, 162; his plan for Ohio colony, 174; ordered to perfect Indian boundary, 177; early life of, 179, 180; death of, 247.
Johnson, Thomas, president of the Potomac Company, 311.
Johnson *vs.* McIntosh, 64, 187, 319, 320, 323.
Joliet, Louis, Birth of, 6; on the Detroit, 25; discovers the Mississippi, 38, 294.
Joncaire, Captain, 87.
Jones, Gabriel John, 216.
Jones, Rev. Arthur E., 6.
Jordan, John W., 380.
Jouan, Henri, 6.
Juniata River, 76.

KALLENDAR, ROBERT, 78.
Kaskaskia, 26, 170, 215, 218, 323.
Kenton, Simon, 185, 193.
Kentucky country, Gist in, 80, 178; Indian title to, 180; first settlements in, 185, 216; raids into, 244, 248, 262, 275; influx of settlers, 262, 308; isolation of, 309; emigration to, 340; emigrants to, attacked by Indians, 341, 385.
Kentucky River, 80, 209.
Kerlerec, Governor at New Orleans, 169.
Keweenaw Bay, 15.
Keweenaw Point, 20.
Kickapoos, 164, 165, 166, 167, 241.
Kidd, Benjamin, 44.
King, Rufus, moves to exclude slavery from the Northwest, 326, 329.
King Philip's War, 9.
King's Mountain, Battle of, 75.
Knight, Dr. John, 273.
Knox, Henry, Secretary of War, 363.

L'ANSE, 15.
L'Arbre Croche, Indian council at, 227.
La Chine, 29, 45.
La Forest, Lieutenant, 39.
La Fortune, 96.
La Hontan, on the Detroit River, 39.
La Jaunay, Father, missionary at Mackinac, 128.
La Pointe d'Esprit, 22, 23.
La Salle, René Robert Cavelier, Sieur de la Salle, friend of Count Frontenac, 27; builds the *Griffin*—his purposes—his creditors, 28; discovers the Ohio, 29; early life of, 29; reaches St. Ignace, 33; builds Fort St. Joseph, 35; builds Fort Crèvecœur, 37; returns to Fort Frontenac, 37; murder of, 37, 38, 55, 87, 168.
La Tour, store-keeper at Detroit, 60.
Labrador fisheries, 200.
Labutte, Interpreter, 114.
Laclede. (*See* Liguest.)
Lafayette, Indiana. (*See* Fort Ouiatanon.)
Lakes:—Athabaska, 293; Chautauqua, 74; Erie, 25; Maurepas, 55; Michigan, discovery of, 4; Nipissing, 45; of the Hurons (early name of Georgian Bay); of the Stinkards (*see* Green Bay); of the Woods, 290, 293; Pontchartrain, 55; Sainte Claire, 32; Superior, Menard's visit to, 14; Radisson's description of, 16; called Lake Tracy, 22; Winnebago, 25; Winnipeg, 292.
Lalemant, Gabriel, 4.
Lancaster treaty of 1744, 90.
Langlade, Charles Michel de, 82; at Braddock's defeat, 96; attacks Piqua, 83; family of, 84, 129; early life of, 223, 224; in the Revolution, 223; in French and Indian War, 225; at massacre of Michilimackinac, 226.
Lansdowne Papers, 287.

INDEX

Lauderoute family, 59.
Laurens, Henry, peace commissioner, 284, 290.
Law, Judge John, 166.
Lead mines, 169.
Le Bœuf, 84, 129; capture of, 151.
Le Gras, 208.
Lee, Arthur, 299, 320.
Lee, Francis Lightfoot, 184.
Lee, Richard Henry, 184, 326.
Lee, Thomas, 73.
Lernoult, Major Richard Beringer, 211; builds Fort Lernoult at Detroit, 249.
Leslie, Lieutenant, 128.
Lewis, Captain, demands surrender of Northwest posts, 370.
Lewis, General Andrew, 190.
Liguest, Pierre Laclede, founds St. Louis, 169, 256.
Lincoln, General Benjamin, 361.
Lincoln, Mrs. Abraham, 324.
Linn, Colonel William, 220.
Little Turtle, 351.
Livingstone, Robert, plans English settlement on the Detroit, 43.
Lochry, Colonel Archibald, 267.
Loftus, Major, Expedition of, 172.
Logan, Iroquois Indian, 188, 212; revenges the murder of his relatives, 189; his message to Dunmore, 191; sketch of, 192, 212, 251.
Logstown, 76, 81, 85, 90, 156, 162.
Longfellow, Henry W., 343.
Longprie, Philip, 166.
Longueuil, De, 39.
Lorimer, 209.
Louden, John, Earl of, 245.
Louis XIII., 2.
Louis XIV., 25, 27, 44, 47, 53.
Louis XVI., 280, 284.
Louisiana, 33; named by La Salle, 37, 55; transferred by France to Spain, 141; transferred to France, 304.
Louisville, 29, 164, 220. (*See also* Falls of the Ohio.)
Lucas, La Salle's pilot, 32, 33.
Ludlow's Station, 353.
Lusson, Saint, at Sault Ste. Marie, 24.
Luzerne, French Minister, 284, 290.
Lyman, General, agent of Ohio Company, 176.

McAffee Brothers, 185.
McClure, Colonel A. K., 151.
McDougall, Lieutenant George, 112; detained by Pontiac, 123; escape of, 131.
McHenry, James, Secretary of War, 371.
McIlwraith, J. N., 102.
McIntosh, General Lachlin, 251, 252, 267.
McKee, Alexander, 211; early life of, 213, 260, 262, 275, 346, 348, 362, 364, 365, 366, 383.
McLaughlin, Andrew C., 305.
McLennan, William, 102.
McQuire, John, 85.
McTavishes, the fur-traders, 294.
Mackinac, 229. (*See also* Michilimackinac.)
Mahigan, an Ottawa Indian, discloses Pontiac's plot, 114.
Makemie, Rev. Francis, founds Presbyterian churches in America, 71.
Malden, British post at, 372, 383.
Manitoulin Islands, 11.
Mann, Captain Gother, his report on Northwest posts, 347.
Marest, Father, mentions Vincennes, 165, 166.
Margry, Pierre, his publications, 49.
Marietta, Settlement of, 334–336, 351.
Marin, French commander, 85.
Marquette, James, at Sault Ste. Marie, 22; hears of the Mississippi, 23; founds St. Ignace, 24; joined by Joliet, 25; they reach the Mississippi, 26; their return, 26; death of Marquette, 26; buried at St. Ignace, 26, 38, 168, 221.
Marshall, Chief-justice, decision of, 64.
Martin, Abraham, gives name to Plains of Abraham, 10.
Martin, Hélène, wife of Radisson, 10.
Martin, Jacob, on the Greenbrier, 148.
Martin, Major, Cherokee agent, 239.
Maryland proposes to divide the Northwest lands into several States, 315; refuses to enter Confederacy until Northwest lands shall be ceded, 316; instructs her delegates, 318; joins the Confederation, 319; effect of her action in regard to Western lands, 321.

INDEX

Mascoutins, 5, 56, 57, 58, 164, 165, 166.
Mason, Edward G., 258, 259.
Mason, George, 218.
Massachusetts, Boundaries of, 8, 66; confirms Cadillac grants, 50; cedes her Western lands, 320; her title indefensible, 321.
Massacres on Susquehanna and Mohawk, 248.
Matavit, Father, 222.
Matthews, Major, commandant at Detroit, 302.
May, Colonel John, his trip to Marietta, 340.
Meigs, Return Jonathan, 339, 342.
Menard, René, his voyage to Lake Superior, 14; death of, 15.
Menominees, 56, 57, 226.
Mer Douce (name of Lake Huron proper), 2.
Mercer, Lieutenant-colonel, 147.
Miami Indians, 78, 79, 80, 83, 346, 348, 364.
Miami River, 75.
Michigan, 66, 203, 320.
Michilimackinac, 23, 33; strategic point for fur-trade, 40; sale of brandy at, 47; massacre at, 128; during the revolution, 221–228; Patrick Sinclair at, 253; fort built on island of, 254, 346, 348; surrendered, 371; civil government established at, 378.
Miller, Christopher, 364.
Mingoes, 270.
Mirmet, Father, at Vincennes, 166.
Mississippi Company, The, 184.
Mississippi River, 5; Radisson near, 11; Allouez hears about the, 22; described to Marquette, 23; discovery of, 25; free navigation of, 281, 282, 285, 286, 322.
Missouris, 56.
Mobile, 261.
Mohawks, 210.
Molière's "Tartuffe," 41.
Moll, Herman, his map, 165.
Monckton, General, at Fort Pitt, 146, 149.
Money, kinds of, 165; scarcity of, 240.
Monongahela River, Virginia settlements on the, 148.
Monroe, James, 320; struggles with question for temporary government of the Northwest, 326.
Montcalm, General, 174, 245.
Montgomery, General, 205.
Montour, Andrew, 76.
Montreal, Capitulation of, 102, 246.
Moravian Indians, 262; at Detroit, 263; origin of, 264; established at Mt. Clemens, 265; massacre of, 266.
Morgan, George, Indian Commissioner, 168, 213, 229, 263.
Morgan, John, 369.
Mound-builders, 22, 335.
Mount Desert titles, based on Cadillac grant, 50.
Murray, Honorable John, 187.
Murray, General James, Governor at Quebec, 135.
Muskingum River, 76, 334.

NADONESERONONS. (*See* Sioux.)
Natchez, 55, 258, 261.
Navarre, Robert, 59.
Negro slavery, 67.
Neville, Captain John, 213, 267.
New Brighton, Pennsylvania, 157.
New Connecticut, 369.
New Haven colony, 8.
New Mexico, Mines of, 286.
New River, Settlements on, 148.
New York, Claims of, to Western country, 66; Indian trade in, 67; early settlements in, 178; cedes her Western lands to the United States, 318, 319; wins credit by giving up Western lands, 321.
Newark, Canada, Trade at, 381.
Newfoundland fisheries, 281, 285.
Newton, Mary, wife of Simon Girty the elder, 212.
Niagara, 310; surrendered, 371; trade at, 381.
Nicolet, Jean, protégé of Champlain, 3; voyage of, 4; death of, 6, 221, 294.
Niles, Michigan, 257.
Non-intercourse resolutions, 186.
North, Lord, defends Quebec Bill, 200, 203; succeeded by Rockingham, 283, 286, 290.
North Carolina, 65.
Northwest closed to settlers in 1763, 144; first charter of, 145; pledged

INDEX

to freedom, 193; included in Virginia, 195; civil government begins in, 205; independence announced in, 209; jurisdiction over lands in, ceded over by the States, 315–322.
Northwest Company, 292, 293, 381.
Northwest posts, United States demand surrender of, 296; British repair the, 347; surrender of, ordered by Dorchester, 370.
Northwest Territory, early laws of, 340. (*See also* Ordinance of 1787.)
Norvell, Senator John, 37.

O Post. (*See* Vincennes.)
Ohio, State of, planned in a Boston tavern, 334.
Ohio Company of Massachusetts, The, 332.
Ohio Company of Virginia, The, organized, 73; sends Gist to explore country, 75; company's post seized by French, 89; attempts to establish its rights, 145; financial affairs of, 147; coalesces with Walpole or Grand Company, 176, 182, 183.
Ohio country, included in government of Quebec, 200; influx of New-Englanders to, 308.
Ohio River, discovered by La Salle, 59; settlements on, 148; demanded as boundary, 302.
Ojibwas, 6, 82.
Old Britain, Indian chief, 83.
Old Point Comfort, 65.
Old Village Point, 15,
Onondaga, Mission at, 10.
Ontonagon copper bowlder, The, 22.
Ordinance of 1787, 324–329; principles of, 328; origin of, 329; authorship of, 330.
Osages, 56.
Oswald, Richard, negotiates treaty of 1783, 285, 288.
Oswego, 248, 310; surrendered, 371; trade at, 381.
Ottagamies, 56, 57, 58.
Ottawa River, 45.
Ottawas, 26, 34, 42, 56, 57, 79, 80, 82, 103, 111, 112, 114, 119, 120, 121, 122, 129, 158, 174, 211, 224, 226, 270.
Ouiatanon, 129.

Parent, Joseph, 52, 60, 129.
Parker, Gilbert, 14, 102.
Parkman, Francis, 2, 4, 8, 24, 112, 113, 155, 173.
Parkman Club of Milwaukee, 16.
Parsons, General Samuel H., 332, 333, 336, 339.
Paully, Ensign, 126.
Pease, Seth, 369.
Pellew, George, 286.
Penns, The, 102, 180.
Pennsylvania, Indian trade in, 67; immigration into, 71; appropriations for Indian gifts, 177; erects county west of the mountains, 182; claims Pittsburg, 185.
Pennsylvania Dutch in Shenandoah Valley, 80.
Pennsylvania Gazette, 209.
Pensacola, 261.
Pepys, Samuel, preserves Radisson papers, 13.
Perrot, 25.
Phips, Sir William, 38.
Piankeshas, 79.
Pickaway Plains, 190.
Pickering, Timothy, first proposes abolition of slavery in the Northwest, 325, 331, 361.
Pictured Rocks, 18.
Pinet, Yves, 52.
Pipe, Captain, Delaware chief, 213, 263, 273, 335.
Piqua, Croghan and Gist at, 78; French attack on, 83.
Pitt, William, comes into power, 99; his American policy, 100, 141, 143. (*See also* Lord Chatham.)
Pittman, Captain Philip, 171, 172.
Pittsburg, 76; Indians urge building fort at, 81, 89, 101, 209; centre of disturbances, 268, 340.
Plains of Abraham, 100, 337.
Plymouth colony, 8, 65.
Point Pleasant, Battle of, 186, 190, 214.
Pontchartrain, Count, 44, 46, 51, 53, 55.
Pontiac at surrender of Detroit, 103, 104; plots destruction of fort, 111; his character, 111; plot discovered, 117; summons Gladwin to surrender, 119; vain appeal to the French,

INDEX

135; sues for peace, 137; meets Croghan in Illinois country, 167; sends embassy to New Orleans, 172; his murder and burial, 173; his son friendly to the Americans, 114, 257.
Pontiac Diary, 114.
Poole, Dr. William F., 276, 330.
Port Huron, Michigan, 39.
Port Royal, 50.
Portage Lake, 19.
Porter, Augustus, 369.
Porter, Captain Moses, receives surrender of Detroit, 372.
Post, Frederick, 101.
Potier, Père, 229.
Pottawatomies, 34, 56, 57, 122, 127, 210, 257, 261, 270.
Pownall, Governor Thomas, 91, 183.
Prairie du Rocher, 170.
Presbyterians in America, 70.
Presque Isle (or Presq' Isle), 77, 84, 151.
Preston, Colonel, 189.
Prince Society, 9.
Prisoners surrendered to Bouquet, 161.
Proclamation of 1763, 144, 195, 196.
Purviance, Samuel, 341.
Putnam, General Rufus, 330; in the Old French War, 331; acts as Washington's chief of engineers at Boston, 331; petitions for the location and survey of Western lands, 332; plans the Ohio Company, 332, 336, 351.

Quakers, 81, 151.
Quebec, Boundaries of, in 1763, 144; capitulation of town, 102.
Quebec Act, The, 195–201, 198, 199, 306, 318.
Queret, Pierre, 96, 227.

Radisson, Peter Esprit, arrives in New France, 10.
Radisson and Grosseilliers, first voyage of, to Lake Michigan, 11; probably reach Lake Superior, 11; did not discover the Mississippi, 12; confusion in regard to their voyages, 13; return from Lake Michigan, 14; voyage to Lake Superior, 16; description of the Lake Superior coast, 20; return to Three Rivers, 21; they transfer allegiance to England, and found the Hudson Bay Company, 21, 294.
Raleigh, Sir Walter, 64, 65.
Rawlinson, Richard, 13.
Raymbault, Charles, 6, 8.
Ravvenal, 290.
Red Jacket, 299, 369.
Repentigny, Count, at Sault Ste. Marie, 60.
Revolution, The, 186, 193; ended in Northwest, 269; end of, announced at Detroit, 275.
Reynolds, John, 324.
Richardie, Father de la, 59, 115.
Roanoke colony, 65.
Rocheblave, Philip de, 96, 215, 219.
Rogers, Captain Robert, at Detroit, 102; his early life, 103; at siege of Detroit, 133, 134; plots to turn Michilimackinac over to Spain, 133; subsequent career of, 134, 320.
Rogers, Lieutenant John, 232.
Roman Catholic religion in Canada, 200.
Roosevelt, Theodore, 185.
Ross, Clinton, 102.
Royal American Regiment, 146, 155, 245, 246.
Russell, Alfred, 62.
Ryswick, Treaty of, 75.

Sacs, 56, 226, 256.
Sagard, 2.
Saginaw Bay, 33.
St. Ange de Bellerive, 164; at Fort Chartres, 167, 172; gives burial to Pontiac's body, 173; administers justice for Spain and America, 255; delivers St. Louis to Spain, 256; death of, 256.
St. Anne's church, Detroit, 46, 51, 54, 56.
St. Aubin, Charles, 60.
St. Aubin family, 59.
St. Clair, General Arthur, 212, 333; arrives at Marietta as Governor of the Northwest Territory, 336; early life of, 337, 338; disputes of, with the judges, 340; his expedition, 353; failure of his expedition, 357, 378.

INDEX

St. Clair River, 25.
St. Genevieve, 169, 171.
St. Ignace, 8, 24, 33, 47.
St. Joseph, 8, 36, 47; Spanish raid on, 257; population of, 258; occupied by the British, 381.
St. Leger, General Barry, 228, 259, 297.
St. Louis founded, 169; French flock to, 171; Sinclair's expedition against, 256–258; surrendered to Spain, 256.
St. Luc la Corne, 226, 245.
St. Philip, 170.
St. Pierre, Legardeur de, 88.
St. Theresa's Bay, 15.
Sandusky, Crawford expedition against, 269.
Sandwich, 60.
Sargent, Major Winthrop, 333, 336, 338; adjutant-general of St. Clair's expedition, 354, 358; erects the county of Wayne, 377.
Sargent, Winthrop, the younger, 312.
Sault Ste. Marie, first mission at, 6; permanent mission at, 22; imposing ceremony at, 24, 34, 37, 60, 61, 62, 294, 348.
Scalps, 153, 154; Washington advises paying for French, 154; received by Hamilton, 214, 262; collected at Detroit, 278.
Schaumburg, Captain, 370.
Schenectady, 178, 369.
Schlosser, Ensign, 127.
Schuyler, General, 289, 317.
Scioto Company, Troubles of the, 343.
Scioto Purchase, 333.
Scioto River, 78.
Scotch-Irish, 69, 70, 175.
Scott, Major-general, 365.
Scull, Gideon D., 9.
Senecas, 157, 159, 162, 177, 180, 211, 212.
Settlers, Character of, 150.
Seven Rangers, The, 334.
Sevier, John, 190.
Sewell, Stephen, 148.
Shawanese, 78, 156, 157, 162, 163, 180, 185, 188, 190, 209, 212; Clark not to make peace with, 241, 251, 270, 277, 348, 364, 367.
Shea, John Dawson Gilmary, 6, 15, 16, 26, 40.
Sheafe surrenders Fort Niagara, 375.
Sheganaba, son of Pontiac, 213.
Shelburne, Lord, approves Ohio project, 175; reluctant to grant independence, 283, 286; driven from power, 289.
Shelby, Isaac, 193.
Sheldon, Mrs. E. M., 45.
Sheridan, Richard Brinsley, 300.
Sherman, Colonel, plans invasion of Spanish territories, 308.
Shingiss, King of the Delawares, 85.
Shirley, Governor William, at Oswego, 99.
Sidney, Lord, 302, 314, 346.
Sillery, Battle of, 61.
Simcoe, John Graves, Lieutenant-governor of Canada, 362, 363.
Simple, Father Peter, 265.
Sinclair, Lieutenant-governor Patrick, 40; ordered to Michilimackinac, 253; builds fort on island, 254; expedition against St. Louis, 256, 257, 258; released from Newgate prison, 314.
Sioux, 20, 22, 24.
Six Nations, 78, 85; place their lands under English protection, 90, 108; complain of settlers, 149, 158; offer to part with title to Ohio country, 177, 181; loyal to the Crown, 243, 270, 299, 300, 362, 369. (*See also* Iroquois.)
Slavery in the Northwest Territory, 325, 330.
Sleeping Bear Point, 26.
Smith, Colonel James, his narrative, 95.
Sorbonne, The, decision as to sale of liquor at Michilimackinac, 47.
Soule, Anna May, 289.
Souligncy, 96.
Spain assists France in Seven Years' War, 141; aids Americans, 220; hostile to the English, 208; tamper with Indians, 180; Spain's raid on St. Joseph, 258; her claims to Western country, 260; designs of, on Northwest, 280, 289, 308, 310; aids the United States, 282; controversies with, 322.
Spottswood, Governor, leads a party to the Shanandoah Valley, 69.

INDEX

Sproat, Ebenezer, 342.
Stamp Act, 186.
Stanwix, General John, builds Fort Pitt, 102.
Sterling, Captain, at Fort Chartres, 255.
Sterling, James, 130, 173.
Steuben, Baron, 296.
Stewart, Henry, 85.
Stone, Frederick D., 330.
Stough, Captain, 356.
Straits of Mackinac, Discovery of, 4.
Sugar Island, 31.
Sulté, Benjamin, 3, 14.
Surveys, Government plan of, 326.
Swiss in the Northwest, 86.
Symmes, John Cleves, 334.

TALON, 24, 25.
Tassé, Joseph, 224.
Tazewell, Littleton W., 65.
Tennessee River, 181.
Thames, Battle of the, 194.
The Gladwin schooner, 121, 126.
Three Rivers, 5, 12, 246.
Thunder Bay, 33.
Thwaites, Reuben Gold, 6, 13, 33.
Ticonderoga, 226, 245.
Tobacco, 22; as medium of exchange, 240.
Tobacco Nation, 12, 23.
Todd, Colonel John, 220; establishes courts in Illinois country, 238; killed, 275; organizes courts at Kaskaskia and Vincennes, 323.
Todd and McGill, traders, 292.
Todd family, 324.
Tonnancour, Madeleine de, 132.
Tonty, Alphonse de, 45, 49, 51.
Tonty, Henry de, 30, 32, 39, 51, 55, 168.
Tories, Compensation for, 283, 286, 306, 312.
Townshend, Lord, 291.
Townshend, Thomas, 287, 291.
Tracy, Marquis de, 22.
Traders as cheats, 207; corner in Indian supplies, 249.
Transylvania, 216, 322.
Treachery with Indians legitimate, 125.
Treaty of 1763, 66, 279.
Treaty of 1783, 279-282, 307.
Trent, Captain William, 85, 89.
Trotter, Colonel, 350.
Tupper, General, 332.
Turner, George, 339.

UNITED STATES first mentioned in Northwest correspondence, 262; disastrous effects to, by British retention of Northwest posts, 304; announcement of, made to army and foreign courts, 319.
Upper Sandusky, 262.
Utrecht, Treaty of, 74, 75.

VAN CURLER, Arendt, 178.
Van Rensselaer, Patroon, 178.
Vanbraan, JACOB, 85.
Vandalia colony, 183.
Varnum, Judge James M., 333; welcomes St. Clair to Marietta, 336, 339.
Vaughan, Benjamin, 286.
Venango, 84, 101, 129, 151, 353.
Vergennes intrigues against including Northwest within the United States, 281, 283, 289; chagrined at success of peace treaty, 290.
Vermont project for reunion with England, 247.
Vessels, Private, on Great Lakes forbidden, 295; character of, 348.
Vierville, Gautier de, 96.
Vigo, Francis, captured by Hamilton, 231; assists Clark, 232.
Villeneuve, Daniel, 224.
Villieres, Neyon de, 171.
Vimont, Father, 5.
Vincennes, 82; beginnings of, 166, 208, 165, 218; surrenders to Americans, 219; surrenders to British, 230, 323; captured by George Rogers Clark, 332-338; judges at, make land grants, 324.
Vinsenne, François Morgan de, founds Vincennes, 166.
Virginia, early settlements in, 66; Indian trade, 67; Ohio grants, 89; boundaries of, 66, 153; settlements on the Ohio, 185; holds courts beyond the Alleghanies, 195; establishes county of Illinois, 238; lack of funds for war, 210; opens land office for sale of Northwestern lands, 317; remonstrance of, 318; offer of, to cede Northwestern lands refused by Congress, 319; reserves

INDEX

territory for Clark's soldiers, 320; her sacrifice, 321.

WABASH COMPANY, 187.
Wabash Indians, 346, 348.
Wabash River, 78.
Walker, Charles I., 276.
Walker, Dr., explores Kentucky, 185.
Walker, Joseph B., 103.
Walpole, Horace, makes sport of Washington, 94.
Walpole, Thomas, 175.
Walpole grant, 147, 174–176, 181, 183, 185, 320.
Walsingham opposes peace treaty, 291.
Walters, Major, 121.
War of 1812, 194, 348, 384.
Ward, Ensign, 89.
Washington, County of, organized, 342.
Washington, George, surveys Lord Fairfax's lands, 72; journey to the French on the Ohio, 85–88; at Fort Necessity, 92; with Braddock, 93; his bravery at Great Meadows, 97; in Forbes's expedition, 101; differences with Bouquet, 150; his connections with Lord Dunmore, 187; land claims, 184; offers non-intercourse resolutions, 184, 186; his opinion of the treaty of 1763, 195; at Cambridge, 205; unable to aid Detroit expedition, 243; Indian policy of, 298; his lands on the Ohio, 270; owner of Ohio lands, 309, 311; visit of, to Ohio country in 1784, 310; Gallatin's meeting with, 310; plans route for Western trade, 311, 320; plan for government of Northwest, 325, 343; plans to assert jurisdiction of the United States over the Northwest, 345; calls out militia, 349, 353; his anger over St. Clair's defeat, 359; congratulated on surrender of Northwest posts, 371.
Washington, John Augustine, 184.
Washington, Lawrence, 73; manager of Ohio Company, 80; favors religious toleration, 81.
Washington family, The, 68.
Watauga commonwealth, 190.
Wayne, General Anthony, 231; early life of, 359 - 361; expedition of, 360–367; concludes general peace with the Indians, 367; arrives at Detroit, 377; death of, 381.
Wayne county organized, 377.
Webster, Daniel, 327.
Weiser, Conrad, 90.
Weld, Isaac, Jr., 382.
Wert, George, 139.
West Virginia, Indian title to, 180.
Western Indian confederacy, 178.
Wheeling, 188.
White Eyes, Delaware chief, 209, 229, 263.
White Woman's Creek, 78.
Whitefish, 16, 34, 348.
Wild-hemp, 166.
Wilkinson, General, 353, 371.
William of Orange, 30, 71.
Williams, Colonel Ephraim, founds Williams College, 98.
Williamson, Colonel David, 266, 275.
Willing, Miss Anne, 155.
Willis, R. Storrs, 377.
Wills Creek, 89.
Winnebagoes, 226, 257.
Winsor, Justin, 8, 13, 14, 24, 321.
Winthrop, Fitz-John, 38.
Wisconsin, 66, 320.
Wisconsin River, 25.
Wolcott, Oliver, 299.
Wolfe, General James, 100, 337.
Woolson, Constance Fenimore, 382.
Worcester, General, 222.
Wyandottes, 122, 158, 174, 263, 270, 271, 272, 277, 364.
Wyllys, Major, 351.
Wymberley-Jones, George, 354.
Wythe, George, 213.

YADKIN RIVER, 135.
"Yankee Hall," prison at Detroit, 277.
Yellow Creek, 162, 189.
Yorke, Sir Joseph, 245, 254.
Yorktown, Surrender of, 279, 283.

ZANE, EBENEZER, 341.
Zeisberger, David, 263, 265.

THE END